Governance and Management of Technical Institutions

About Author

B.L. Gupta, is Professor in Education Management at National Institute of Technical Teachers Training and Research, Bhopal. He completed B.E. in Civil Engineering in the year 1982 from Shri Govindram Seksaria Institute of Technology and Science, Indore. He completed LL.B. from The College of Law and Legal Aid Shahdol in the year 1988. Then he completed Master of Technical Education in the year 1992 and Ph.D. in 2002 from Technical Teachers Training Institute Bhopal. Professor Gupta has 23 years of experience in the field of teaching and training. He is trained in Great Britain. He has received training from well-known personalities of the country. He has conducted more than 250 management development programmes for various clients such as teachers of technical institutions, trainers and managers of industries. He has guided more than 15 theses in the field of technical education and management of industries. He has published more than 30 papers in national and international journals. He has developed print and non-print instructional material for teachers of technical institutions. He has worked on various World Bank assisted projects. Earlier to this book he has written three books.

Governance and Management of Technical Institutions

Dr. B.L. Gupta
Professor, Education Management
National Institute of Technical
Teachers Training and Research, Bhopal

CONCEPT PUBLISHING COMPANY, NEW DELHI-110059

Cataloging in Publication Data—DK
Courtesy: D.K. Agencies (P) Ltd. <docinfo@dkagencies.com>

Gupta, B. L.
Governance and management of technical institutions / B.L. Gupta.
p. cm.
In Indian context.
Includes bibliographical references.
Includes index.
ISBN 8180693929

1. Technical institutes—India—Administration. 2. Technical education—India—Administration.
I. Title.

DDC 373.246 095 4 22

ISBN: 81-8069-392-9 (HB)
ISBN: 81-8069-393-7 (PB)

First Edition 2007

Published and Printed by
Ashok Kumar Mittal
Concept Publishing Company
A/15-16, Commercial Block, Mohan Garden
New Delhi-110059 (INDIA)

Phones : 25351460, 25351794
Fax : 091-11-25357103
Email : publishing@conceptpub.com

Preface

Over the past 60 years, the technical institutions have grown significantly. They have contributed for the technological, economic and social development of the country. They have earned a name at international forum as well. Technical education system in the country is emerging as a big system of education still it has an opportunity to have access to common man at one hand and international forum at another hand. The opportunity to serve local and global market has created a great challenge for the technical education system. It requires grabbing the opportunity for expansion and growth at the same time it has to focus on quality of products and services at a lower cost. To meet the challenges, competition, and uncertainty it has to work more scientifically on the principles of governance, management, educational psychology, educational technology, information technology, education research and so on.

Most of the technical institutions are governed and managed on the basis of the experiences of the governing body members and director of the institution. There is a wide variation in practices of governance and management of institutions. Apart from experiences of the people institutions are governed and managed on personal preferences and wishes of the promoters of the institution. Governors and managers are not aware about the principles of governance and management of the educational institutions. Most of the practices are personalized and not institutionalized. Reactive approach of governance and management of the institutions is observable which is not considered good for growth and development of the institutions. This approach can maintain the quality but does not permit to add value to it. Researches have proved that reactive approach of management is not a good approach to achieve excellence.

In technical institutions the behaviour of the students is shaped to become a professional. The faculty and staff members have to deal with human beings. The behaviour shaping process of management is different than production process. At the same time production processes teach us that process can be designed to achieve six-sigma level quality and it is essential also in today's context. A small human incompetence can create crisis and disaster for the society. The education imparting process can not be taken on casual and *adhoc* basis. The students and their parents are paying for the education so they should get value for it. Similarly the employers, government and other significant stakeholders are having variety of expectations from technical institutions. Their expectations need to be satisfied to win the confidence of the people in the technical education system.

In this book an attempt is made to explain application aspects of principles of management, educational psychology, androgogy, educational technology, educational research and other related disciplines. The focus of the book is to provide a tool kit of concepts, principles, strategies, approaches and processes to the governors, directors, head of the department, faculty members, senior officers in the technical institutions to select and use appropriate tool as per their needs for the growth and development of their institution at the same time delighting the students, employers, customers, clients and beneficiaries of their institution.

Bhopal **B.L. Gupta**

Acknowledgements

This book on governance and management of technical institutions is outcome of many precedent learning experiences and research studies conducted in past. I wish to record my sincere thanks to following persons.

Dr. Mahendra Singh Chauhan, Chairman, Governing body, National Institute of Technical Teachers Training and Research, Bhopal for approving sabbatical leave and encouragement.

Governing body members for continuous encouragement.

Prof. K.K. Shrivasta for extending guidance and support generously.

Ex Principals and Directors of National Institute of Technical Teachers Training and Research, Bhopal for providing opportunities to get international exposure.

Prof. R.K. Mani, Ex Director, National Institute of Technical Teachers Training and Research, Bhopal who formally taught, trained, encouraged and guided me to pursue the career in education management.

Dr. D.V. Chandrashekhara, Retired Professor, National Institute of Technical Teachers Training and Research, Bhopal for mentoring me on the job during conduction of training programmes.

Prof. (Mrs.) M. Saxena, Head of Education Management Center, National Institute of Technical Teachers Training and Research, Bhopal for nurturing, guiding and providing constructive feedback for thirteen years.

My colleagues at National Institute of Technical Teachers Training and Research, Bhopal for openly sharing the experiences.

Director Technical Education, Governing body members, Directors and Principals of Engineering Colleges and Polytechnics, faculty members of technical institutions, research scholars and administrators, who shared experiences openly.

Library staff of National Institute of Technical Teachers Training and Research, Bhopal.

Shri C.S. Varde, Principal Government Polytechnic, Jhabua for correcting grammatical mistakes.

Shri Ashok Kumar Mittal, Concept Publishing Company, New Delhi for publishing the book.

My wife Mrs. Suman Gupta, sons Kumar Gandharva and Kumar Gaurva for supporting me during the writing work.

Contents

PART III
MANAGERIAL SKILLS

PART IV
MANAGEMENT OF CHANGE AND INNOVATIONS

List of Exhibits

Summary

Today, technical institutions are facing unprecedented competition from sister institutions and other institutions of higher education. There is a great challenge for striving to quality of passouts, products and services. There are significant problems of placement of passouts, finance, obsolesce and disciplines. To meet the competition, challenges and problems there is a need for professional governance and management of technical institution. There was a long need to have a reference book that guides the governors and managers, significant institutional members, senior teachers and policy makers to professionally govern and manage the institution.

This practice-oriented book provides the reader with the concepts models, theory, strategy, tools and techniques to professionally govern and manage the institution for growth and development. This book incorporates the latest concepts of governance and management of technical institutions. This book can be used to train faculty members and staff members thoroughly and effectively so that they can make significant contributions to the growth and development of the institution. This book will guide all types of institutions to enhance effectiveness and efficiency in their core business that is academics.

This book is divided in four parts. First part covers the governance and management aspect of the institution. It spells out the role of significant functionaries to professionally govern and manage the institution. Second part covers the planning for development aspect along with planning tools and techniques. Third part is devoted to managerial skills that cover a wide range of managerial skills such as leadership, motivation, team building, problem solving, decision-making, communication, conflict management, crisis management, time management, stress management and record management. Fourth part is devoted to management of change and innovations that cover management of change, performance appraisal and development, learning organization, reengineering, total quality management, networking, marketing educational services and products, six sigma, ethics and project management.

PART I
GOVERNANCE AND MANGEMENT OF INSTITUTION

1

Governance of Institution

Objectives: The readers will be able to:

1. State the need for professional governance of the institution.
2. Describe concept of professional governance of the institution.
3. List various governance structures with their strengths and limitations.
4. Describe teams structure of governance.
5. Enlist composition of governing body and governing teams.
6. Describe functions of governing body and governing teams.
7. Enumerate methods of increasing effectiveness and efficiency of governing body and governing teams.
8. List circumstances under which governing body should be dissolved.
9. Describe role of head of the institution in the governance of the institution.
10. List the outcomes of good governance of the institution.

1. Introduction

Good governance of the technical institution plays an important role in the growth and development of the institution. The governance is exercised through a governing body. Governing body acts professionally and approves the ultimate goal of the institution. It also helps in exploring the alternative strategies to reach the destination. It helps to decide the path that is effective and efficient. In the present era all the technical institutions are facing competition in some way or other. There are many challenges ahead. Many institutions have started struggle for survival. This struggle started because of poor governance and management of the institution. Poor governance and management have caused variety of problems and crisis for the institutions. They are in turbulence and at the verge of close down.

Professional governing body promotes good governance and management in the institution. It provides sense of purpose for institutions those are sinking. It provides an ambitious vision for the growth and development for those who are performing well. Many autonomous and private institutions are having governing body that is phantom. The board acts as a rubber stamp. These boards are comprised of family members, relatives and old friends of promoters of the institutions. These boards are unable to provide professional guidance to the institutions. They can simply fulfil the legal requirements. They can do window dressing but cannot add value in the performance of the institutions.

The concept of governance and corporate governance has entered from the industrial world to technical education sector. In industrial sector this concept of governance did miracle in terms of growth and development of the business. It has helped the companies to compete and survive in the market. At the same time it has helped the companies to accelerate the growth in terms of profit, remove inefficiencies and expand market segment. It has increased the transparency in functioning, increased fairness in dealings and promoted accountability in performing the business.

The concept of professional governance promotes need-based learning in technical institution. It sets direction for learning to learn and promote importance for life-long learning. All the recent concepts of learning can be promoted without any delay. Then whole focus can be shifted from teaching to learning and overall personality development of the students. The professional governance promotes joyful learning in the institution. More emphasis is given on competency development at the same time students are prepared for the corporate world. The professional governing body approves the strategies for satisfying the needs and expectations of the stakeholders like government, statutory body, parents, industries, society, sister institutions etc. It protects the interest of all the significant stakeholders. It sees that laws are strictly complied with. Professional governance promotes equal opportunity for all potential clients, customers and beneficiaries. It defines the boundaries of the business of the institution. It encourages institution to practice and promote latest concepts of governance, management and learning in the institute. It helps institute to enhance its corporate reputation abruptly and significantly. It promotes innovations and changes in the institute with the capacity of risk taking. It protects pride of the employees through protecting their interest.

2. Concept of Professional Governance of Institution

Governance can be defined in many ways looking the stage of development of the institution. It is a process of setting direction for the growth and development of the institution and seeing that progress is being made accordingly. It is the process of policy making, perspective planning, major decision making, monitoring the progress on implementation and evaluating programmes and policies for institutional growth and development. In the process of governance all stakeholders are involved to express their interest and views. Involvement of stakeholders in governance of the institution ensures the reflection of their views in the form of policies and perspectives of the institution. The internal stakeholders are involved to lay the foundation of good governance. Their ideas interest, experience and expertise get reflected in the policies and plans. Professional governance takes the institutions at all heights of academics.

3. Governance Structures

The concept of professional governance is implemented in the institution through well-defined structure of governance. There are different types and numbers of structures available for use in technical institutions. Each type of structure has got advantages and limitations. The brief description of the commonly used structures is given below:

3.1 Hierarchical Structure

The secretary or director of the department governs most of the government institutions. The policies, rules and regulations are framed at centralised level for all the institutions under control irrespective of level, growth and development of the institution. It cannot be termed as governance because more emphasis is given on control and fewer efforts are made for growth and development of the institutions. The major limitation of this type of structure is that specific needs of the institutions are not addressed properly. The communication process takes long time and it may not be effective. The strengths of the institution are not tapped properly for the further growth and development. Hierarchy hinders the process of innovation and change. All the members of the institution are treated equally irrespective of their talent and capacity except low performers.

3.2 Matrix Structure

Many autonomous and private institutions have used matrix structure to design and implement change and innovation. They have designed and implemented academic and non-academic projects to bring desired change. In matrix approach resources are shared appropriately to complete the task. The communication is effective and challenges of the situation can be met. Informal way of working is common in matrix structure. The person is responsible for routine work as well as challenging work. Many innovations have been implemented in eighties to bring change using matrix structure. This structure overcomes the problems of hierarchical structures. Using matrix structure interdisciplinary projects have been completed successfully. Matrix structure facilitates change and innovation but it does not initiate innovations and change.

3.3 Teams' Structure

Teams structure is commonly observable in the autonomous institutions. Government and private institutions are using teams structure to implement innovations. Interdisciplinary work in teaching learning processes, research studies, projects, and problems has increased significantly in technical institutions. It has created the demand for teams' structures. Teams structure is very simple to create. Teams are constituted as per requirements of the institution. Number of teams and their composition depend on various factors like; number of diploma, under graduate, post-graduate programmes offered by the institute, development level of the institution, funding pattern, performance of the institution, vision of the institution etc. Teams structure is created through constituting Governing Body and Governing Teams, like Board of studies, Planning team, Evaluation team, Examination team, Appeal and Grievance team, Purchase team and Finance team. The governing body can also constitute governing teams for specific purpose. The governing body delegates the executive powers to governing teams. The governing body to make its work easy uses the expertise of these teams. Governing teams analyse the complete situation and work out the details with alternatives. The work of the governing teams can be reviewed and decisions can be taken in the governing body meeting. In governing teams detailed discussion is permitted and there are institutional members who participate in the discussion so it is a good forum to exchange views and know their comments on the decisions. The proposed governance structure is shown in exhibit 1.1. However, institution can create governance structure as per their needs.

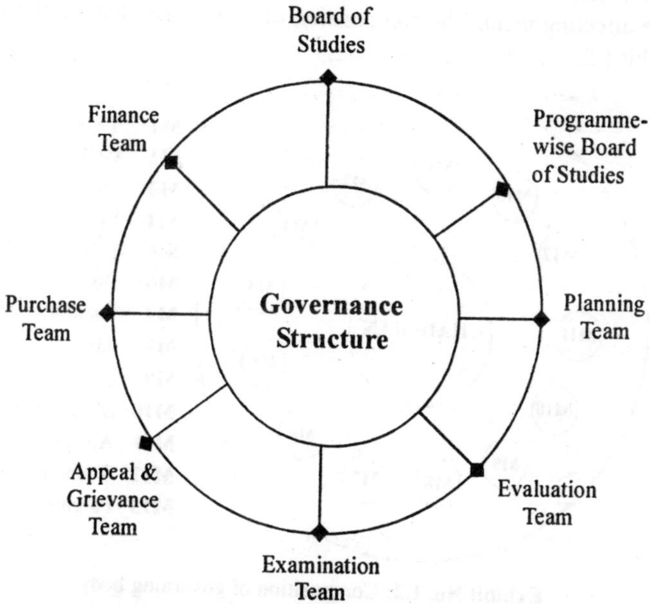

Exhibit No. 1.1: Model of professional governance

4. Composition of Governing Body

The Governing Body should be comprised representative members from significant stakeholders. There should be one representative each from Technical Examination Board (TEB)/Technological University, Government of India (GOI), Human Resources Development Organisations (HRD). There should be two representatives each from Directorate of Technical Education (DTE), Professional Bodies (PB), Faculty, and Supporting Staff and Managing Society (MS) in case of grant in aid institutions. There should be three representatives from

Industries (I) and three more representatives from the State Government (SG), All India Council for Technical Education (AICTE), Women and parents. The institutions can adopt other eminent persons to fulfil specific requirements. These members bring wealth of experiences to the academics and other related issues. There is a dichotomy whether students should be represented on governing body or not. It is observed that students are not permanently placed on governing body but their representatives can be called in the meeting while discussing the major issue affecting them. The composition of Governing Body is shown in exhibit 1.2:

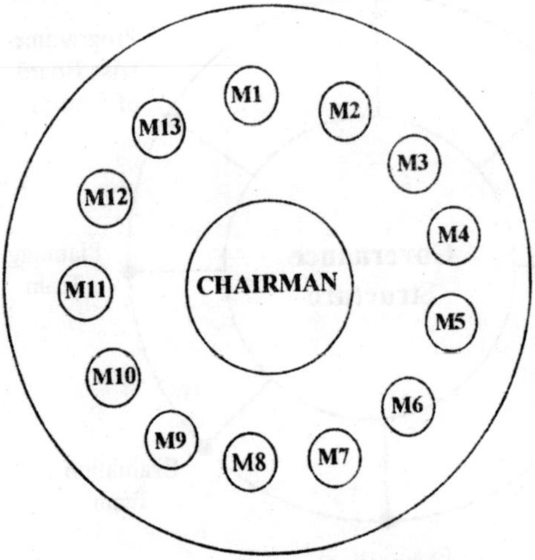

M1	TEB	1
M2	GOI	1
M3	HRD	1
M4	Staff	1
M5	DTE	2
M6	PB	2
M7	Faculty	1
M8	MS	2
M9	I	3
M10	State Govt.	1
M11	AICTE	1
M12	Women	1
M13	Parents	1

Exhibit No. 1.2: Composition of governing body

4.1 Size of the Governing Body

The size of the Governing Body should be between 15-20 members including secretary, chairman and other office bearers. Various criteria, like number of programmes offered, development level of the institution, number of projects in hand, number of students are used to decide the size of the governing body. The point is that variety of experiences and diversity should get reflected in the governing body meetings. It is not possible to handle larger board. There may be problems of interaction. Every member may not get an opportunity to put his/her view in detail because of time pressure at the same time the matter may not be relevant to other persons. So the size of the governing body should limit to 15-20 members.

4.2 Criteria for Selecting Governing Body Members and Chairman

All major stakeholders should get place on the governing body. Professionals should be attracted to become member of governing body so that they can provide vision and long-term perspective to the institution. People having similar experience and faced similar challenges can contribute more in the governance of the institution. They should have courage to ask questions and challenge the appropriateness of proposals submitted to them. They should have analytical ability and concern for students and employees of the institution. They should be able to develop the institution through their creativity and intelligence. Numbers of criteria are used for selecting governing body members and chairman. Some important criteria are mentioned in exhibit 1.3.

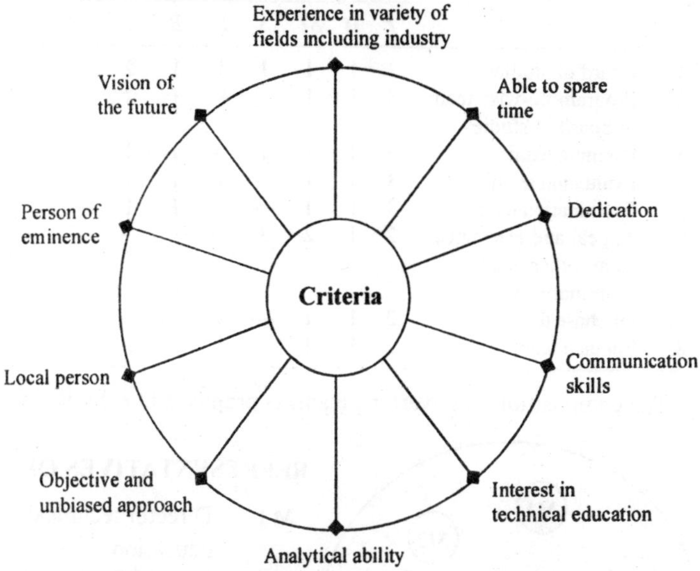

Exhibit No. 1.3: Criteria for selecting governing body members and chairman

Institutes' society, Government, and industry should jointly appoint the members to governing body. While selecting the members criteria mentioned in exhibit 1.3 should be kept in mind. They should feel that their experiences and skills are being used for social cause. They should be proud to be a member of the governing body. A token honorarium to governing body members can be paid for attending meetings. Outstation members should be paid travelling allowance and dearness allowance.

4.3 Composition of Governing Teams

The size of the governing team depends on the purpose of the team, area of functioning, importance of the work and urgency of the work. The size of each Governing team should be between 5-10 members. The composition of some governing team is given in exhibit 1.4.

Exhibit No. 1.4: Composition of governing teams

T—Teachers, M—Members of Governing Body, ST—Staff, S—Student, D—Director technical education, B–Board of technical education/Technological University, I—Industry, SO—Managing Society

Sl. No.	*Composition of teams*	*Average number*								*Total*
		T	*M*	*ST*	*S*	*D*	*B*	*I*	*SO*	
1.	Board of studies	3	1	1	1	1	1	2	—	10
2.	Programme-wise team of board of studies	3	1	1	—	—	1	2	—	8
3.	Planning team	3	1	1	1	—	1	1	—	8
4.	Evaluation team	3	1	1	—	1	1	1	—	8
5.	Examination team	3	1	1	—	—	1	1	—	7
6.	Appeal and grievance team (other than examination)	2	1	2	3	—	—	—	—	8
7.	Purchase team	2	1	1	—	1	—	—	2	7
8.	Finance team	2	1	1	—	1	—	—	2	7

The composition of governing teams is proposed in exhibit 1.5.

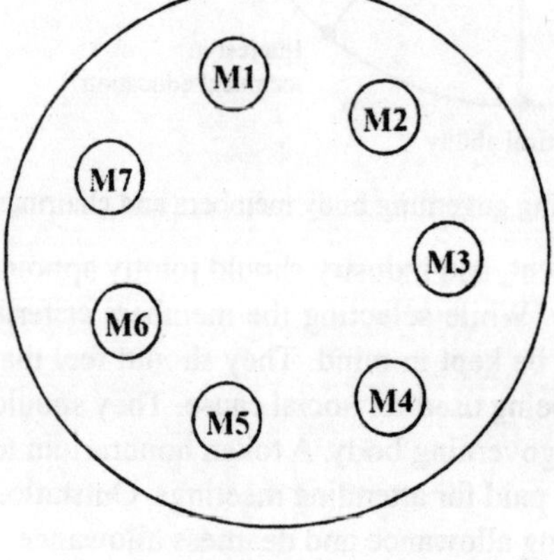

REPRESENTATIVES OF

M1	Director technical education
M2	Board of technical education
M3	Managing society
M4	Faculty
M5	Governing Body
M6	Supporting staff
M7	Students

Exhibit No. 1.5: Composition of governing teams

5. Functioning of Governing Body and Governing Teams

The governing body and governing teams of the institution should perform professionally. These teams should provide strategic direction, innovative and unique ideas to the institutions. They should be asset to the institution rather than burden and obstacle. The functioning of the governing body and governing teams is described briefly in subsequent paragraphs.

5.1 Term of Office of Governing Body and Governing Teams

The members of the governing body may take three to six months to understand the functioning of the institute. At the same time they bring fresh ideas from their respective areas of work that can be implemented for the governance of the institution. Their interest and expectations get reflected in the governing body meetings. After a period of time say three years they may lose interest in the functioning of the institute. They may see most of their ideas implemented. The creativity and uniqueness in their contribution may get reduced. Looking the performance of individual member in terms of their contribution in the governance of the institution term of members can be extended. The term of office of Governing Body and Governing Teams can be fixed between three to five years.

5.2 Frequency of Governing Body Meetings

The governing body should meet to address the significant policy and governance issues. The governing body may ask the governing teams to discuss and deliberate on governance issues and prepare the draft for approval. The preliminary work done by governing teams saves the time of the governing body. It should delegate most of the operational issues to the head of the institution. This will reduce the frequency of meetings of the governing body. The frequency of governing body meetings can be two to three times in a year. It is required to devote one full meeting in a year to review the performance of the institution and approve the plan for the next year.

5.3 Frequency of Governing Team Meetings

As suggested in the governance structure of the institution the governing body is supported by number of governing teams. These teams deal various issues in detail and suggest policy guidelines and solutions to problems.

The governing teams suggested in the structure are suggestive and institutions can adapt or adopt suggested structure as per their requirements. Some issues related to governance can be delegated to the respective governing teams. The Board of studies, Planning team, Evaluation team, Purchase team and Finance team should meet six monthly. The Programme-wise team of Board of Studies, Examination team, Appeal and Grievance team should meet quarterly. These teams should review the progress made in their respective area on yearly basis. The suggested frequency of meetings is not hard and fast. The institutions can call the meeting as per their needs. The only thing is that the meeting should be productive, effective, efficient and with a purpose.

5.4 Nature of Preparation to be Made before Governing Body Meeting

The governing body members are significant persons. They do not have time to waste. Every governing body meeting require a great deal of preparation on the part of the institution and governing teams. The Director/ Principal and support team should jointly make preparation to facilitate the Governing Body meeting. There should be a plan for meetings of all governing teams so that the matter can be discussed in the respective team before it goes for consideration to governing body. The nature of preparation to be made before governing body is listed in exhibit 1.6.

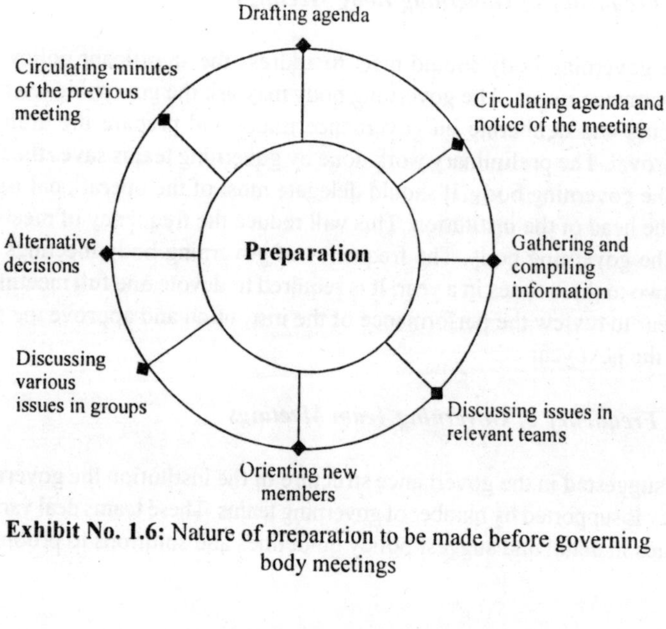

Exhibit No. 1.6: Nature of preparation to be made before governing body meetings

5.5 Governing Body Meetings

There should be 80 per cent attendance of members in governing body meetings. Quorum for decision-making should be 50 per cent of the total membership. Decisions should be made unanimously. Governing body should spend 60 per cent to 80 per cent time on major issues like vision of the institute, major courses to be started, collaboration with industries, networking with national and international educational institutions, approval of policies, perspective plans, rules, major developments, shift in direction if necessary, and major decisions. Governing body should make decisions, approve policies framed by governing teams, approve rules and approve perspective plans in all major areas of institution working. The proposed areas and sub-areas are mentioned below:

Academic: Starting new academic programmes, projects, continuing education programmes, learning resources development, staff development, curriculum development, industry institute interaction, enhancing quality of passouts, examination and placement of students.

Administrative: The sub-areas under administration are transfer, promotion, deployment and redeployment of faculty and staff members, and discipline.

Managerial: Approving vision and mission of the institute, new dimensions of the business to be entered, evaluation of the institutes programmes/projects, performance appraisal, incentives, problem solving, modernisation of existing academic and support facilities, recruitment, service conditions, student amenities, community development collaboration with other institutions and industries.

Financial: The sub-areas under finance are undertaking major purchase, doing financial planning, exercising financial management, conducting audit, financial evaluation and consultancy decisions.

Governing body should be responsible to all relevant stakeholders including government and society.

5.6 Functions of Governing Body

Governing body should perform all four types of functions, i.e. managerial, administrative, academic and financial. Governing body should perform following functions in each category:

Managerial

Provide vision: Governing body should initiate the process of crafting the vision statement and preparing vision document of the institution. The governing body should bring the environmental facts and issues for discussion. It should ask institution to consider the issues while crafting the vision statement of the institution. It should help institution to craft the vision statement. It should approve the vision statement and vision document of the institution. The approved vision statement is used for all official purposes. The vision document becomes the base for planning all major developments and changes. It explores the opportunities for the growth and development of the institution. The governing body takes major decisions keeping in mind the vision document of the institution. Its decisions are aligned to accomplish the vision of the institute. It should avoid *adhoc* and casual decision-making.

Decide the structure: Governing body decides the number of governing teams required to govern the business of the institute. Constitute governing teams in different areas of functioning of institution following suggested criteria. It approves guidelines and terms of reference for smooth functioning of various governing teams. It guides and solves the problems of governing teams. It evaluates the performance of various governing teams.

Approve policies: Governing body analyses all issues related to functioning of the institution and need for policy formulation. It delegates the work of policy formulation and rule making to governing teams and management teams and ask them to submit the policies and rules for approval. It discusses and approves the policies and rules to be followed in the functioning of the institute.

Approve strategic plans: Governing body approves the strategic, perspective and annual plans of the institute. It monitors the progress of the institute against the approved plans. It provides guidance to facilitate the implementation process. It solves policy related problems and facilitate the efforts of the institution in implementing the plans. It evaluates the performance of the institution against the approved plans. It undertakes the success analysis exercise from stakeholder's point of view. It suggests necessary remedy in subsequent year plans. It suggests innovations and approves innovations to be introduced in the functioning of institution. It particularly pushes innovations related to academic activities. It safeguards the interest of internal stakeholders like; faculty members, staff members, students and external stakeholders.

Inculcate values: Governing body encourages the establishment of value system to achieve vision, missions, and goals of the institution. The desired value system is created and promoted by the institution under the guidance of the governing body. Shift strategies are implemented to switch over from existing value system to desired value system. It ensures that there is no conflict in the value system of individuals and teams. It helps to speed up the strategy implementation. Value system should relate to academics and support activities of the institution and inconsonance to prevalent value system in society.

Act as a buffer: Governing body serves as a bridge and buffer between the institution and stakeholders. It should collaborate, network and mobilize the resources of external stakeholders to implement the plans of the institution. It should ensure that the needs of the stakeholders are considered and satisfied by the institution. Stakeholders should carry the good image with them. Especially the students and industry should carry moments of truth and high satisfaction with them. They should project the professional image of the institution in the society.

Support the head of the institution: Governing body should help the head of the institution to carryout the business of the institution. There should be good relationship between the head of the institution and governing body. It should keep him/her on right track that is enhancing the academic performance of the institution. It should ensure that the head of the institution is fully involved in academics and not in trivial activities. Since the head of the institution has to take and implement various administrative decisions in the interest of the institution that may be hard for a particular group of persons. Full executive autonomy should be granted to the head of the institution and teams for smooth functioning of the institution. This may require constant board support. It should solve policy related problems of the institution. It should promote open and effective communication among internal and external stakeholders. It should evaluate the performance of the head of the institution and encourage him/her to come with academic innovative plans.

Oversee the functioning of the institution: Governing body should monitor and evaluate the performance of the institution on regular basis against set goals. It should ensure that all processes are performed effectively and efficiently. It should not interfere in day-to-day functioning of the institute. If problems related to functioning of institution is observed it should review the plans, policies and rules. If these are all right then it should review the performance of the head of the institution.

Evaluate the performance of the self: Governing body should review the performance of the self every year and find out the ways and means to improve self-performance. It should implement the principles of corporate governance and function as professional board. It should openly discuss the achievements and drawbacks. It should organise seminars, conferences and meetings on governance of technical institutions.

Administrative

Delegation: Governing body should delegate administrative, financial and additional powers wherever necessary to the head of the institution and other functionaries of the institute for smooth functioning. Delegation is required to take quick decision and early action.

Approval: Governing body should approve annual reports of the institute. Annual report of the institution is an important document that tells about performance of the institution to the stakeholders and potential students. It is the document that is used for legal purposes as well.

Students benefit schemes: Governing body should approve the fees and other charges payable by the students. It should approve the scholarship, fellowship, facilities to needy students, and special schemes for the benefit of the students.

Discipline: Governing body should regulate and enforce discipline among members of teaching and non-teaching staff in accordance with the policies, rules, and procedures laid down for the functioning of the institution.

Approval of policies: Governing body should approve recruitment policy. It should approve and review procedures for selection, recruitment and transfer of faculty and staff members. It should approve service conditions, emoluments, and travelling allowances for teaching and non-teaching staff of the institute. It should approve the policy of appointing consultant, visiting faculty, experts, and other people based on need.

Evaluate the performance of head of the institution: Select, support and evaluate the performance of head of the institution. The governing body manages the institution and its performance through head of the institution. The head of the institution should posses abilities to manage the institution according to wish of the governing body. S/he should be a charismatic, transformational and transactional leader. S/he should be proactive and visionary.

Academic

Approval: Governing body should approve new programme of studies leading to diploma, post-diploma, undergraduate, postgraduate and Ph.D. It should approve modifications in present curriculum in order to accommodate the changing demands of the industry, society from time-to-time.

Continuing education programmes: Governing body should approve continuing education programmes or similar activities beneficial to the students/community/institute.

Academic consultancy: Governing body should approve policy to take academic consultancy projects.

Utilisation of academic resources: Governing body should ensure full use of academic potential of the institution in various academic activities.

Academic climate: Governing body should ensure academic climate in the institution.

Financial

Approval: Governing body should approve annual budget, expenditure, balance sheet and appropriation and re-appropriation of funds.

Accept: Governing body should provide permission to accept legal gifts, donations and resources.

Schemes: Governing body should institute scholarships, fellowships, studentships, cash prizes and certificates on the recommendations of the Board of Studies.

Audit: Governing body should appoint qualified auditor every year to conduct the audit. Consider the issues raised by the auditors for improvement in finance utilization.

Financial health: Governing body should ensure good financial position of the institution through proper planning and utilization of funds.

The head of the institution should ensure the implementation of decisions of governing body.

5.7 Functions of Governing Teams

The governing teams are constituted to support the governing body in discharging its functions. Governing teams should perform following functions:

Functions of Board of Studies

- To scrutinize and validate detailed proposals prepared by the programme-wise team for starting new programmes in the institute
- To examine curriculum developed/revised by programme-wise teams and approve it keeping in view the institutional objectives and the national requirements

- To suggest different innovations, reforms and changes those can improve academic effectiveness of the institutions
- To review the progress of various academic programmes offered in the institution
- To resolve academic problems brought to the notice of the team
- To guide and coordinate research, teaching, extension and other academic activities in the institution
- To create operational policies in academic areas
- To ensure high standards of achievement of students
- To recommend books for various courses of studies

Functions of Programme-wise Team

- To decide philosophy of curriculum design course-wise
- To analyse present needs
- To identify desirable changes, additions, deletions course-wise
- To identify training/development needs of teachers and technical supporting staff
- To formulate programme objectives
- To decide contents
- To design student evaluation scheme
- To decide resources required and development thereof
- To decide strategy of implementation
- To evolve mechanism for evaluation of programmes
- To provide feedback on the effectiveness of academic programmes
- To recommend equivalence for granting exemptions
- To design variety of appropriate continuing education programmes, through both formal and non-formal modes, to meet diverse target group requirements

Functions of Planning Team

- To formulate system of various activities in the institute
- To identify shortcomings in various areas of functioning like Industry liaison, Sports/Gymkhana, Extra curricular activities, Facilities to students, library, hostel, canteen, mess, problems of girl students and suggest measures to improve
- To approve academic calendar for the academic year of the institute
- To recommend structure of tuition fees and other fees

Functions of Evaluation Team

- To evaluate the performance of the institute as a whole
- To evaluate the progress of various schemes and project activities in the institute
- To obtain the feedback regarding implementation of various autonomous schemes and analyze the data so obtained
- To suggest the corrective measures for improvement
- To obtain feedback on performance of the students, supporting and teaching staff and analyze it to suggest corrective measures

Functions of Examination Team

- To finalize names for appointment of examiners, paper setters, moderators and other relevant expertise
- To call for manuscripts of question papers and do moderation of question papers
- To plan the timetable of examination
- To ensure the assessment of answer books, declaration of results, and arrange for re-verification cases
- To approve the award of diploma and degrees
- To take decisions regarding mal practices and other disputes
- To prepare policy related to examination

Functions of Appeal and Grievance Team

- To entertain complaints and grievance of the staff working in the institute
- To organize hearings of grievances
- To remove grievances
- To review the cases of appeal
- To suggest measures to reduce grievances
- To recommend serious matters of grievances to governing body as and when necessary

Functions of Purchase Team

- To scrutinize the proposals submitted by the institute and approve it
- To call for quotations/tenders and finalize the same for placing the orders
- To check the quality of material and pass the bills of the equipment

- To plan for write off the obsolete and worn-out equipments and suggest the replacement for the same
- To suggest measures to bring improvements in purchase procedures

Functions of Finance Team

- To scrutinize the budget prepared by the institute and approve it
- To appoint auditors
- To approve the expenditures made by the institution
- To scrutinize the financial policy prepared by the institution
- To suggest ways for properly using the funds

6. Strategies to Enhance Participation of Governing Body and Governing Team Members

The governing body may be ineffective and inefficient in its functioning. There may be various reasons, like long-term vacancy, poor attendance, conflict between members, lack of responsibility, less interest in academics, politics, lobbying, ego problem, poor preparation for the meeting, ineffective communication, procrastination, hidden agenda, insufficient time, unable members etc. There is no well-defined package that can be offered to enhance the participation of governing body members but some significant methods are listed in exhibit 1.6 that can be used as per need.

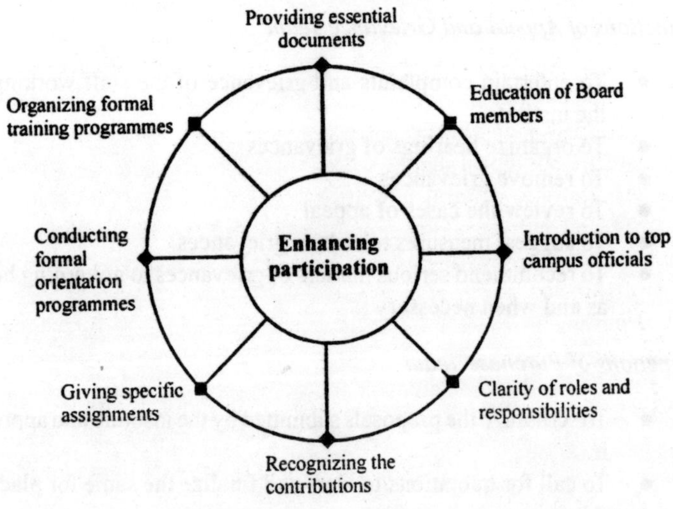

Exhibit No. 1.7: Strategies to enhance participation of governing body and governing team members

7. Effectiveness of Various Governing Teams

The effective and efficient functioning of various governing teams is essential for good governance and management of the institution. There are variety of strategies available and can be designed as per need. Using these strategies barriers to functioning of the teams can be removed. Some strategies are listed below with brief description.

7.1 Training

The members are briefed about the business of the institution, i.e. academics. All members are required to work in a team so they are trained in team building, leadership, planning, problem solving, policy formulation, reviewing the progress and evaluating the performance. They are appraised about their roles and responsibilities. They are given all necessary documents related to their area of functioning. They are briefed about the expectations of the stakeholders specially students. The members are invited to visit the campus and interact with students, staff and faculty members.

7.2 Recognition

The efforts made by various teams are sincerely recognised by the institution. Open recognition encourages other teams and team members to volunteer their services for the growth and development of the institution. Recognition can be given in variety of forms and ways. This can be decided at institution level. The members are encouraged to participate in institutional significant activities, like seminars, conferences, panel discussions, cultural activities and sports. They get sense of traditions and culture of the institution through participation. The benchmarking of performance is very popular to measure the accomplishments of various teams. Recognition promotes healthy competition among teams and team members. It encourages team members to continually perform better. The contributions of team members should be encouraged and appreciated openly by the institution.

7.3 Autonomy

All the teams should be granted autonomy to function within their terms of reference. The decision-making power and authority should be delegated to the lowest level. Autonomy should percolate down to avoid delay in any action. Teams should be empowered to prepare their own plans in consonance to institutional plans. The functioning of the teams should be independent without interference but it should be ensured that they should bring synergic effect.

7.4 Problem Solving

The teams may face variety of problems during functioning. Problems may relate to shortage of resources, incompetence of members, poor attendance of people, personal conflict, hidden agenda etc. There may be ego problems of the members also. The ego of members should be satisfied. The problems should be solved timely and effectively. The institute should create enough challenges for teams. Problems related to poor communication, delay in decision making and ineffective decision making are to be addressed through peer pressure.

7.5 Roles and Responsibilities

Roles and responsibilities of each team should be clearly defined and communicated to them. The expectations of the institutional members and stakeholders are clearly communicated to respective team. The accountability of the team as well its members is defined and commitment is obtained. The deadlines and performance standards are also made clear to them.

8. Circumstances Under which Governing Body should be Dissolved and New Governing Body should be Formed

There may be situations in which the governing body fails to discharge its functions effectively and efficiently. In such situations the causes should be removed to make it functional. Even if it fails to discharge duties it should be dissolved. Governing body should be dissolved in circumstances listed in exhibit 1.8.

9. Role of the Head of the Institution

The head of the institution is key person to enhance the participation of governing body and governing teams in the functioning of the institution. S/he plays very important role in involving governing teams in the business of the institution. The role of the head of the institution for enhancing the participation of governing body and governing teams is listed in exhibit 1.9.

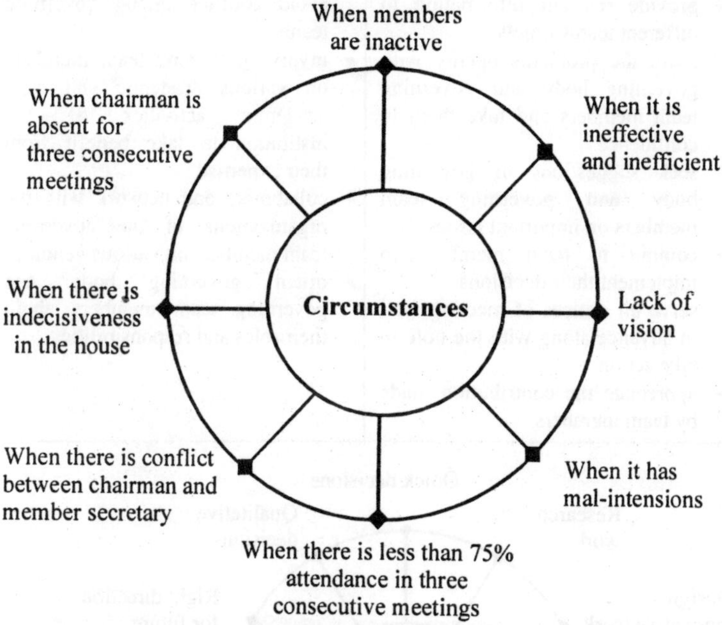

Exhibit No. 1.8: Circumstances under which governing body should be dissolved

10. Outcomes of Professional Governing Body

The governing team's structure should facilitate the functioning of the institution. It should mobilise the potential of experts and resources of the institution. It should help in designing and implementing cost effective strategies. It should promote synergic effect in the field of academics. The flow of information, experiences and achievements should become smooth. People should come forward on their own to initiate best practices and accept challenges. The excepted outcomes of professional governance are listed in exhibit 1.10.

Exhibit No. 1.9: Role of head of the institution to enhance the participation of governing body and governing team members

The head of the institution will:	
➢ pursue all significant issues personally ➢ provide relevant information to different teams timely ➢ share the problems openly with governing body and governing team members and take them in confidence ➢ seek suggestions of governing body and governing team members on important issues ➢ commit to team members to implement their decisions ➢ serve all notices of meeting well in advance along with the note to take action ➢ appreciate the contribution made by team members.	➢ ensure effective communication with team members ➢ ensure to set superordinate goals to avoid conflict among governing teams ➢ involve governing team members on various academic and non-academic activities of the institution to take benefit from their expertise ➢ collaborate and network with the organizations of the governing team members on various ventures ➢ orient governing body and governing team members about their roles and responsibilities

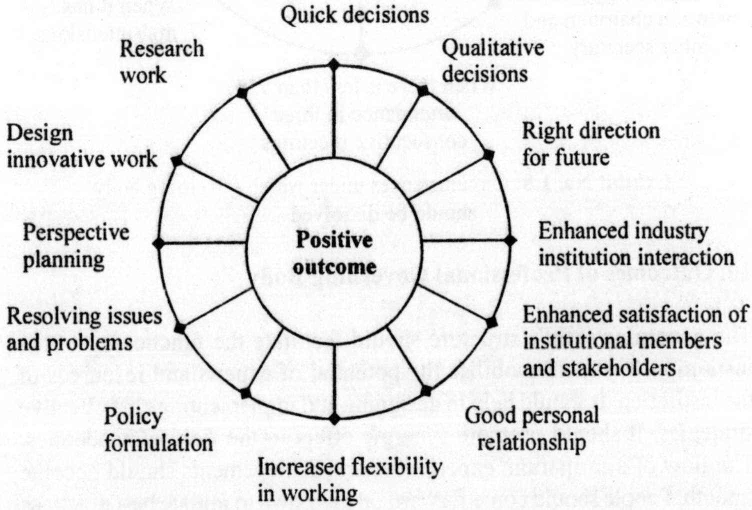

Exhibit No. 1.10: Positive outcomes of governing body

11. Summary

Corporate governance of the technical institution is necessary for growth and development of the institution. The vision, missions and goals are set for the institution through participation of internal and external stakeholders. Alternative strategies are explored to accomplish the vision. The institution prepares the strategic plan to accomplish the vision. The vision document is prepared by the institution and approved by governing body. New opportunities for the growth and development of the institution are explored and grabbed. Policy framework is developed to run the institution. This is carried out through corporate governance of the institution. The corporate governance is exercised through team's governance structure. A governing body is constituted drawing professionals from various fields. It is supported by governing teams to provide strategic support in different areas of functioning of the institution. The size of the governing body is kept 15-20 members and governing teams is 5–10 members. Important stakeholders get represented either on governing body or on governing teams. Members are selected on the basis of well-laid criteria like; experience, expertise, dedication, interest, communication and vision. They are oriented and trained to provide direction for the business of the institute. They work in respective teams and perform set of functions. Head of the institution plays a significant role to enhance the effectiveness and efficiency of governing teams. The corporate governance of the institution brings positive outcomes, like quick decisions, quality decisions, right direction for the future, enhanced interaction and collaboration with stakeholders, enhanced satisfaction of internal and external stakeholders, increased flexibility in working, planning for development, problem solving, innovations and researches. Professional governance enhances the corporate image of the institute that promote growth and development of the business of the institution.

12. Activity

Check Level of Corporate Governance of Your Institution

Please give your response briefly against the points given in response sheet. Provide current information for your institution. You can omit the points if the point is not relevant to your institution. Share your responses with significant members of the institution and identify the similarity and disagreement on responses. If discrepancies are more, then there is a need to develop consensus on the governance and implementation strategy of the institute.

Response Sheet for Corporate Governance

Sl. No.	*Points*	*Your response*
1.	Write the significant points of vision document of your institution	
2.	Write the main focus of governance of your institution	
3.	Write the three characteristics of governance structure of your institution	
4.	List the policies approved by the governing body	
5.	List the names of rules and regulations approved by your institution	
6.	List the three major innovations implemented in the governance of the institution in last three years	
7.	List the three challenges faced in the governance of the institution	
8.	List the three innovations implemented in the institution	
9.	List the three problems faced by the institution	
10.	List the major expansion took place in last three years in academics	
11.	List the consultancy projects institution has undertaken in last three years	
12.	List the three researches produced by the institution in last three years	
13.	List the three contributions made by the institution for the development of the society	
14.	List the national/state awards received by the institute	
15.	List the collaborations made between the industries and institution	
16.	List the three measures taken to improve the effectiveness and efficiency of the institution	
17.	List the three prevailing values in the field of academics of the institution	
18.	List major achievements in terms of placements of students in last three years	
19.	List patents received by the institution in last three years	
20.	List the major outcomes of evaluation of performance of the governing body	
21.	List decision of the governing body that were ineffective	
22.	List the percentage attendance of members in governing body and governing teams	
23.	List the major conflicts took place in the governing body meetings	
24.	List the major donations, grants, loans received by the institution in last three years	
25.	List the three major complaints of employees received in last three years	

REFERENCES

Abrahamsson, B. (1977). *Bureaucracy or Participation*, Beverly Hills, Sage.

All India Council of Technical Education (1996). A Scheme for Autonomous University Departments/Institutes/Centres/Schools of Technical Education.

Babai, K.S. (1996). A Case Study on Autonomy and Flexibility, Government Polytechnic For Women, Chennai.

Bastin Nigel, A. (1990). The Composition of Governing Bodies of Higher Education Corporations, *Higher Education Quarterly*, Vol. 44, No. 3.

Board of Technical Examination (1995). Guidelines on the Scheme of Autonomous Polytechnics, Maharashtra State, Mumbai.

Charles Margerism (1996). *Team Management Practical New Approaches*, Lawrey.

Chaudhari, E.M. (1996). Introduction and Implementation of Academic Autonomy and Programme Flexibility in Polytechnics of Maharashtra, M. Tech. Ed. Dissertation.

Corson John, J. (1975). *The Governance of Colleges and Universities*, McGraw Hill Book Company.

Cuckle Pat (1998). Governor Involvement in Development Planning: From Tea Parties to Working Parties, *School Leadership and Management* Vol. 18, No. 1, Carfax.

David Osborne and Tade Gaebler (1982). *Reinventing Government*, Prentice Hall of India Pvt. Ltd., New Delhi.

Golby, M. (1992). School Governors: Conceptual and Practical Problems, *Journal of Philosophy of Education* 26(2).

Government Resolution (1994). Higher and Technical Education and Employment Department of Maharashtra No. WUF-1093/(2640) (69)/VE-S, dated 31st May, 1994.

Graystone, John (1995). The New Governing Bodies for the 21st Century, Combe Lodge Report, The Staff College, London.

Graystone, John (1996). Governing Bodies and Boards of Management of Further Education and Sixth Form Colleges: Composition and Membership, Mendip papers, Bristol.

Graystone, John (1999). New Governing Bodies in Maintained Further Education: Size and Composition, Mendip paper 014, The College.

Green, F. (1991). Investing in Higher Education, American Council on Education.

Harper, C. (1994). *Managing Growth in Your Emerging Business*, McGraw Hill Inc.

James Lundy, L. (1996). *Teams*, Global Books & Subscription Services, New Delhi.

Jauhari Lal (1985). *Leadership Styles and Power Sharing to Business Enterprises*, Himalaya Publishing House, Bombay.

Katzenbach and Douglas K. Smith (1993). *The Wisdom of Teams*, Boston, Harward Business School Presses.

Kerr and Gade (1989). The Guardian: Board of Trustees of American Colleges and Universities, Association of Governing Bodies of University and Colleges.

Khan (1975). A Study on Governance and Administrations, M.A.A., Osmania University

Kshirsagar & Thete (1996). Case Study on Experimentation of Autonomy, G.P. Aurangabad.

Mehendiratha R.R. (1982). University Administration in India and the USA – A Comparative Study Ph.D. Management Kur. University

Rao M. Narayana (1996). The Vision of an Ideal Polytechnic, *Journal of Vocational Education* issue 13.

Thondy Angela (1998). From Political Servant to Community Democrat: An Impossible Future for English and Wales School Governors? University of Lincolnshire and Humberside, U.K.

Thondy Angela (1999). Developing School Governors, 1987-1997; Change or Inertia? *School Leadership and Management*, Vol. 19, No. 1, Carfax Publishing Ltd.

TTTI (1994). Project Proposal Introducing Institutional Autonomy and Programme Flexibility in Polytechnics of Maharashtra.

TTTI (1995). A study on implementing quality circles in polytechnics, Bhopal.

TTTI (1996). A Research Study to Determine Level of Rapport of Teachers, Assess Institutional Climate and Judge Present Status of Autonomy.

TTTI (1997). A Snap Study of the Dimensions of Institutional Autonomy for Maharashtra Polytechnics.

TTTI (1999). A Brief Report – Principals' Conference for Maharashtra Polytechnics, January, 1999, TTTI, Bhopal.

Zaheer Hamid & Gupta, B.L. (1999). A Study on the Informal Groups in Polytechnics and Formulating Strategies to Channelise Potential of Informal Groups for the Development of the Polytechnics, TTTI, Bhopal.

2

Management of Institution

Objectives: The readers will be able to:

1. State the need for management of institution.
2. Describe the concept of management of the institution.
3. Describe the management structure of the institution.
4. Enlist composition of management teams.
5. List the criteria for selecting members for various teams.
6. List various schemes of voluntary participation.
7. Describe functions of management teams.
8. Enumerate methods of increasing effectiveness and efficiency of management teams.
9. List the outcomes of management of institution.

1. Introduction

The governance structure of the institution approves the vision, missions and goals for the institution. In doing so it involves members of the institution. It also decides the alternative strategies to accomplish the vision of the institution. It is put in a vision document of the institution. The governing body also approves policies, rules, programmes and projects. These documents are available with the head of the institution and communicated to concerned teams and persons. It is the duty and responsibility of institutional members and teams to implement the strategies effectively and efficiently. Detailed planning is required on the part of the teams and individuals to run the day-to-day activities. Individuals and teams are responsible to satisfy the needs of the students and other stakeholders as per requirements of the institution. The institution is required to smoothly function doing the business of academics. The first customer or client or beneficiary, i.e. students should learn to become professional and exemplary citizen. Policies, rules and regulations guide the functioning of the institution but they need to be implemented in right spirit. This is possible through exhibiting and practicing behaviour that can be imitated by the students. Shaping the behaviour of the students is a difficult as well as challenging task. The institution needs to design its activities keeping in view the requirements of the curriculum and the students. The students desire a quick and adequate response. They want to learn from the teachers and instructors. They have dreams and aspirations. They want to undergo joyful learning experiences. They want respect and recognition for prior learning. They want to cooperate faculty and staff members for teaching learning process. Provided they get for which they are paying money and precious time of the life. All other processes of the institution should contribute towards improving effectiveness of the teaching learning process. There should not be delay, injustice, and wastage on the part of working. Management of institution is also expected to satisfy the needs of other stakeholder. The needs of the students, industry and stakeholders can be satisfied through scientific management practices. Faculty and staff members of the institution satisfy the needs of external stakeholders. They plan, organize, influence and control resources of the institution and carryout the activities as per demand of the situation. In turn the institution satisfies the need of the faculty and staff.

2. Concepts of Management of Technical Institution

It is a process of involving institutional members in planning, organising, implementing and evaluating the progress of work in the institution. People are empowered to have sense of ownership and accountability in institutional work. They are prepared to take the responsibility for the growth and development of the institution. It is possible through enhancing the self-image of the institution. The governing body sets the direction for the institution, and institutional members implement decisions of governing body to achieve goals of the institution. The structure of the institution is designed to facilitate the teaching learning process. The full potential of the institutional members and resources is utilised for the growth and development of the institution. The institutional members derive satisfaction from the noble profession of transferring knowledge and skills to students.

The institutional members are self-propelled and self-confident to take challenges and implement desired change. They monitor progress and take corrective actions. People are self-governed and self-disciplined. They set examples for others to follow. They are known for their expertise, experience and personality. They mobilise their own resources to achieve the objectives. They satisfy the work related needs on their own without conflict. They do not require instructions for each and every task. They remove operational problems communicating each other. Institution develops them to take and accept various academic and non-academic challenges. People not fitting in the system are compelled to leave the job.

Institutional processes are well designed and implemented in effective and efficient way. Every member of the institution is concerned about the quality of teaching learning process. Core processes are benchmarked and people continually improve the academic quality of programmes. Outdated processes and redundant elements of the processes are removed immediately when noticed. People believe in healthy relationship with students and other stakeholders.

3. Management Structure

Management structure is created constituting teams in different areas of functioning of the institution. This structure facilitates the day-to-day functioning of the institution. Teams structure is a best example of participatory management of the institution. People get an opportunity to use their talent for the benefit of the institution. They produce innovative and creative ideas in teams. They own the ideas and enjoy implementation. In addition to teams structure voluntarily participation is promoted through various schemes of voluntarily participation. The number of teams and their size depends on the purpose of the institution and development stage of the institution. The proposed management structure is mentioned in exhibit 2.1.

4. Composition of Management Teams

All the institutional members should be given an opportunity to participate in management of the institution. Faculty members, staff members, students and other relevant members should be involved in management teams. The composition of management teams is shown in exhibit 2.2. It should be considered in different areas of functioning of the institution. Size of management teams varies between five to ten members.

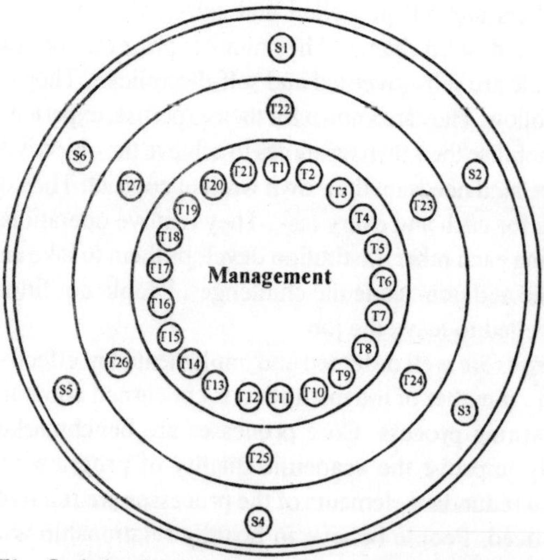

S1 Quality circles
S2 Suggestion box
S3 Co-operation & support
S4 Joint objective setting
S5 Organising creativity sessions
S6 Exchange of ideas

T1	Curriculum Development	**T2**	Admission of Student	**T3**	Learning Resource Development
T4	Library	**T5**	Staff Development	**T6**	Hostel Management
T7	Gymkhana	**T8**	Cooperative Store	**T9**	Examination
T10	Guidance & Counselling	**T11**	Administration & Discipline	**T12**	Industry Institute Interaction
T13	Continuing Education	**T14**	Research & Innovation	**T15**	Consultancy
T16	Community Development	**T17**	Building Construction & Maintenance	**T18**	Purchase
T19	Finance	**T20**	Internal monitoring	**T21**	Documentation & Publication
T22	Condemnation of Materials	**T23**	Campus Development	**T24**	Staff Appraisal
T25	Evaluation of Programmes and Projects	**T26**	Service Conditions	**T27**	Recruitments

Exhibit No. 2.1: Management structure

Teams are not formed for the sake of creating teams structure. Teams are formed in different areas of functioning so that they can make alternate solutions to problems. They design innovations and bring desired changes in functioning of the institution. They translate the decisions of the governing body in reality. They put greater focus on enhancing the quality of academics in the institution. They set the standards of performance in their area of functioning. They need to be carefully formed, developed and nurtured in the institution. Members for a particular team are selected using well-defined criteria. Teams are consciously formed and developed to produce desired results. Criteria mentioned in exhibit 2.3 are used for inclusion of members in management teams. These are general criteria besides this other criteria can be used for specific purpose. Management teams are constituted by head of the institution in consultation with head of the departments.

Exhibit No. 2.2: Composition of management teams

F–Faculty member, S – Staff member, St–Student, O–Others

Sl. No.	*Composition of teams*	*Average number*				*Total*
		F	*S*	*St*	*O*	
1.	Staff development	4	1	—	—	5
2.	Library	4	2	2	—	8
3.	Learning resources development	3	2	—	—	5
4.	Admission	5	3	—	—	8
5.	Examination	5	3	—	—	8
6.	Guidance and counselling	5	2	—	—	7
7.	Industry institute interaction	4	1	—	—	5
8.	Gymkhana	5	3	10	—	18
9.	Innovation	5	2	2	—	9
10.	Administration and discipline	4	1	5	—	10
11.	Finance	4	1	—	—	5
12.	Community development	4	5	—	2	11
13.	Building construction	2	1	—	1	4
14.	Curriculum development	3	1	2	—	6
15.	Purchase	2	2	—	1	5
16.	Continuing education	3	2	—	1	6
17.	Documentation and publication	2	3	—	—	5
18.	Time-table	5	2	—	—	7
19.	Student chapter	5	2	5	—	12
20.	Cooperative	1	3	5	—	9
21.	Consultancy	5	1	—	1	7
22.	Women empowerment	7	2	1	—	10

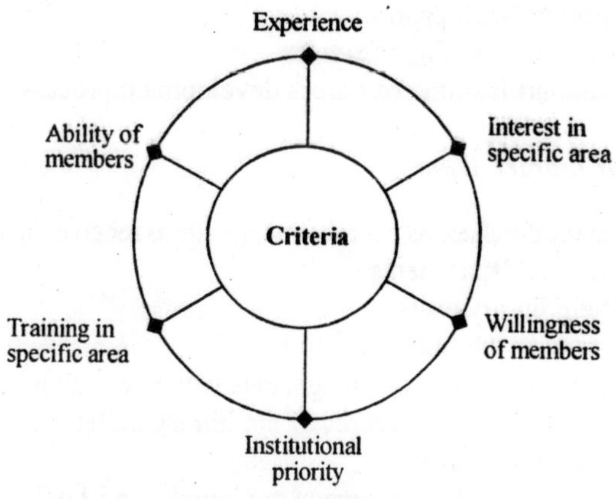

Exhibit No. 2.3: Criteria for inclusion of members in various management teams

5. Functioning of Teams

Functions of management teams are described in subsequent paragraphs. These functions should be considered as indicative functions and can be adopted by institutions depending upon their vision, missions and goals.

Term of Office of Management Teams

The term of office of management teams depends on purpose of the team and it can be from 1 to 3 years. These teams are relatively permanent in nature. They work proactively in their respective area of functioning. Temporary teams are also formed for a specific purpose. The functions of various management teams are listed below:

Functions of Staff Development Team

- To identify the training needs based on the performance appraisal of the employees
- To prepare training plans (in house and outstation)
- To sponsor the staff for outstation training programmes
- To receive feedback on training received by various employees
- To conduct in house training programmes with the help of experts
- To monitor and evaluate the effectiveness of such programmes
- To maintain the computerized information related to staff development
- To recommend books related to training and development
- To prepare staff profile
- To develop learning resources
- To support learning resources development process

Functions of Library Team

- To make purchase as per recommendations received from various teams and departments
- To help library users
- To up-keep the library facilities
- To condemn books and magazines which are not useful
- To computerize all records of the library including issuing and receiving of books
- To prepare budget statement for purchasing books and other magazines, journals etc.

- To create a book bank
- To exhibit the new arrivals
- To digitised library
- To network library with other institutions

Functions of Learning Resources Development Team

- To organise training for developing and using learning resources
- To guide teachers and technical supporting staff in developing learning resources
- To procure necessary material and equipment to develop learning resources
- To keep subject-wise computerized information of learning resources development centres and learning resource developed by them
- To prepare a list of experts who can guide and help learning resources development activities
- To prepare policy for the institute to develop and use learning resources
- To share the resources of other organizations

Functions of Admission Team

- To give admission to students
- To receive the filled up forms from students
- To scrutinize the forms as per rules and regulation
- To keep record of information
- To prepare and declare merit list
- To inform relevant agencies about admissions
- To advertise admission schedule
- To attend court cases
- To publicize the achievements of the institution
- To design strategies to increase admissions in various disciplines

Functions of Examination Team

- To make plans for conducting examination
- To make arrangements for question paper setting from resource persons
- To prepare seating arrangement plans

- To arrange resource as per needs
- To analyze the result and provide feedback to concerned teachers
- To arrange for valuation and revaluation of answer books
- To compile and declare results
- To distribute mark-sheets
- To keep computerized information of examination system
- To procure necessary material for conducting examination
- To process remuneration bills
- To bring the cases of unfair means in the notice of principal and relevant empowered team

Functions of Guidance and Counselling Team

- To guide students to select subject of their interest
- To guide students in further/continuing education
- To organize short training programmes with the help of experts in various areas like leadership, management, entrepreneurship etc.
- To diagnose the learning difficulties of students in different subjects
- To help students in their adjustment to curricular and co-curricular activities
- To provide career information
- To develop interpersonal adjustment attitudes
- To solve personal and academic problems
- To organize bridge courses

Functions of Industry-Institution Interaction Team

- To organize campus interview
- To establish and liaison with industries
- To involve industry experts in instructional processes
- To organize industrial training of teachers and technical support staff
- To conduct training programmes for industry personnel
- To improve training, placement and employment for students
- To conduct survey of industries and prepare a directory
- To offer consultancy and testing services
- To organize collaborative programmes with industry and stakeholders

Functions of Gymkhana Team

- To organize inter-class, local, district and inter-institution matches
- To organize cultural activities
- To organize competitions
- To encourage students and staff to regularly participate in Gymkhana activities
- To run health club
- To prepare proposals to purchase material for Gymkhana
- To organize different Gymkhana teams
- To host state level and national level sports

Functions of Innovation Team

- To gather information related to innovations in technical fields as well as in the field of institutional development
- To introduce the innovations to institutional members
- To design strategies to implement innovations in the institution
- To implement innovations with the help of institutional members
- To host and administer a full-fledged website on the network
- To train staff and students to use the internet
- To collaborate with higher level institutions and implement innovations

Functions of Administration/Discipline Team

- To organize get together sessions
- To diagnose discipline related problems and solve them
- To work as a platform for disseminating correct information
- To act as a buffer between management and students/employees
- To implement code of conduct in the institution
- To appoint class monitors
- To promote self-management
- To reward the best practices

Functions of Finance Team

- To maintain the accounts regularly
- To arrange for the audit of the accounts at the end of every

financial year and submit the report to the governing body and other agencies

- To prepare the budget of the institute at the beginning of financial year and get it approved from the finance committee and governing body
- To prepare policy for finance utilization
- To suggest ways for properly using the funds
- To conduct awareness programmes for institutional members for properly utilizing the funds
- To facilitate academic and non-academic processes of the institution

Functions of Community Development Team

- To undertake training need analysis of selective villages
- To do participatory rural appraisal and social assessment
- To organize non-formal training for village youth and capable persons in employable and productive trades
- To transfer technology developed by research organizations and laboratories
- To conduct socio-economic and technical survey to find out needs of the community
- To operate extension centres in cluster of villages
- To organize community support services in villages
- To develop a spirit and competence for entrepreneurial ventures
- To inculcate the attitude of self-dependence
- To maintain management information system on its activities
- To help villagers to start their own enterprise

Functions of Building Construction and Maintenance Team

- To prepare proposals for building construction as per requirement
- To make necessary correspondence with various agencies like Public Works Department, Electricity Board, Municipal Corporation, Architect, Directorate of Technical Education etc. for getting building construction work completed
- To prepare annual maintenance plans of the building
- To propose preventive maintenance plan
- To keep the building neat and clean

- To create adequate facilities for physically challenged people and women
- To develop gardens and other building facilities to promote academic culture
- To propose different agencies for building maintenance

Functions of Curriculum Development Team

- To develop, revise and modify curriculum as per needs
- To monitor the progress of the curriculum implementation
- To identify the needs of the society related to technical programmes
- To visit industry to know latest technology and techniques being used
- To review and revise the curriculum as per needs
- To develop new laboratory experiments
- To develop instructional material on new technology and new techniques
- To coordinate various activities related to curriculum development
- To impart training in curriculum development implementation and evaluation

Functions of Purchase Team

- To estimate the quantities of material to be purchased at the beginning of every year from various plans
- To prepare proposals for the purchase
- To get approval on the proposal
- To purchase the material as per rules
- To maintain inventory of items/material
- To verify the purchased material
- To pass the bill
- To evolve strategies to minimize the wastage

Functions of Continuing Education Team

- To undertake training needs analysis
- To negotiate with industries and other organizations for conducting short-term training programmes

- To identify experts from academic institutions, industries and professional areas for curriculum design and development for continuing education programmes
- To develop curriculum of short-term and long-term continuing education programmes
- To collaborate and coordinate with various continuing education providing organizations
- To implement the curriculum in right spirit
- To conduct need based training programmes for resource persons
- To undertake surveys to identify educational and training needs for technical people
- To identify most appropriate learning resources for proper implementation of curricula
- To establish mechanism for review and updating curriculum periodically and implement the same
- To evaluate the learning
- To award certificate of achievement

Functions of Documentation and Publication Team

- To prepare documents and disseminate them timely
- To liaison with various committees and principal regarding documentation
- To maintain record of various types of documents to be prepared and disseminated to various organizations
- To train employees on document preparation

Functions of Timetable Team

- To prepare the academic calendar of the institute
- To deploy the physical resources like space, furniture, equipment etc.
- To monitor and review the progress of academic activities
- To consolidate teaching load of all the years and branches
- To solve overlaps and clashes in timetable
- To make alternative arrangements for space, equipment and teachers
- To modify the timetable in case of transfer of teacher, change in curriculum etc.

Functions of Student Chapter

- To organize expert lectures on various topics of interest
- To organize field visits/industrial visits/excursion tours
- To organize student's seminar, workshops, conferences, symposium, exhibitions and other significant learning events by students for students on topics of interest
- To celebrate various occasions
- To publish magazine
- To organize competitions

Functions of Students' Cooperative

- To sale the articles at cheaper rates
- To maintain account of money
- To purchase things required by students
- To maintain inventory of the articles
- To run the canteen of the institute and mess of the hostel
- To prepare balance sheet and get the account audited
- To make new members

Functions of Consultancy Team

- To sale the expertise of the institute to industries and society
- To negotiate with industries and other organizations to bring business
- To keep the account of the revenue generated
- To prepare contract documents
- To complete the consultancy work with the coordination of different departments and sections of the institution
- Prepare a proposal to utilize the funds

Functions of Women Empowerment Team

- To organize awareness programmes on various topics of general interest with the help of experts
- To organize competitions in various areas relating culture, hobby and women right
- To organize entrepreneurial programmes
- To organize workshops for enhancing their participation in institutional activities

- To organize problem solving sessions
- To organize counselling sessions
- To prepare proposals to create facilities for women in the institution
- To make efforts for employment of women passouts

It is the responsibility of the head of the institution to provide resources and support to all management teams to implement the decisions of the governing body. The required resources are provided in adequate quantity and timely. S/he arranges resources from Government, Industries, Professional Bodies and Managing Society. The resources are generated undertaking consultancy programmes. Institutional resources are utilized fully to generate new resources. Written communication mode, i.e. minutes of the meeting and circulars are used to communicate the decisions of the governing body to different internal management teams. Verbal mode like face-to-face communication, meetings and telephonic modes are used to support the written mode.

6. Strategies to Enhance the Effectiveness of Management Teams

Varieties of strategies are used to enhance the effectiveness of management teams. These strategies are designed in the context of environment of the institution. After pilot testing strategies are refined and implemented. Well-designed strategies avoid problems and barriers that may occur because of teamwork. Some general strategies that can be implemented in institution are listed below:

6.1 Team Formation

Teams are constituted looking to the purpose. There are tasks that can be done by individuals for such tasks teamwork is wastage of time, effort and resources. It causes frustration among members. Teams are constituted for challenging, complex, difficult purposes that require multi skills and huge resources. Members of teams should be selected using criteria such as experience, institutional priority, ability, training in specific area, willingness etc. The purpose of team, expected outcome and performance standards are clearly communicated to teams. The roles and responsibilities of members are made clear to them. The functional conflicts are solved. Teams are developed to work collectively. If necessary, training is imparted to complete the task.

6.2 Interaction with Governing Body Members

Team members are given an opportunity to interact with governing body and governing team members to share experiences related to implementation of decisions. Team members get an opportunity to share their ideas and achievements. Governing body members clarify their expectation and provide constructive and open feedback to teams. Communication gaps are removed and grapevine communication is prevented through interactions. Interactions between governing body members and management teams generate new innovations and efficient ways of working

6.3 Solve Problems

Teams may face problems related to functioning, resources, ego, ineffective communication etc. Head of the institution solves the problems pointed by teams timely. One way to solve problems is that delegate decision-making powers and authority to teams and make them autonomous. Timely problem solving encourages team members to put their energy on the task honestly and sincerely. It indicates the seriousness of the head of the institution about the team task

6.4 Healthy Competition

Healthy competition within the team members and among the teams promotes sense of ownership. It motivates individuals and teams to accept the challenges. The performance-based rewards are introduced to create healthy competition. The best performance is recognised and rewarded. The process of giving rewards is kept open and transparent. The competition is also promoted with the targets and efficiency of other institutions. Competition may be promoted to improve the efficiency or minimize waste or implementing innovations in teaching learning process or generating revenue for the institution.

6.5 Training

Provide training to different teams to do the job effectively and efficiently. The training should be need based. Variety of training modes is used to impart the training. Even the competent team member of the same team provides the training to rest of the team members. Training in working in team is provided by the experts as well. Mostly on the job training approaches are used that are highly informal. Principles of androgogy are used to impart the training. The team leader plays an important role in maintaining the cohesiveness in the team and providing training as and when necessary. Constructive feedback provided by fellow team members' play a crucial role to improve the performance.

6.6 Self-evaluation

The culture of evaluating self-performance enhances the analytical abilities of the team members. They learn deeply about their strengths and weaknesses. Self-evaluation of the performance helps to recognise the achievements of the team. It also helps to correct the undesirable behaviour. It develops the confidence in team members that they can do something unique and different. It makes them aware about their talent, quality of performance and behaviour. They appreciate that committing a mistake is common phenomenon but learning from mistakes is important to prevent mistakes to recur.

6.7 Voluntary Participation

Teams' structure provides an opportunity to contribute for team goals assigned by governing body or formulated to achieve annual goals and objectives of the institution. This is a formal system of enhancing the participation of people. Besides this there are many tasks that can be performed effectively and efficiently individually. People have lot of potential that can be harnessed through voluntary participation. Assessing the talent, interest and creativity of the people they are invited to offer suggestions for various purposes. Their suggestions are received and acknowledged. Feasible suggestions are implemented individually or in teams. There are number of schemes like quality circles, suggestion box, creativity sessions, focus group discussion and specific meetings are available. The participation of people in the management of the institution can be enhanced using these schemes.

7. Outcomes of Teams' Structure

The outcomes of working in teams are varied, many and different. Teams overcome the limitations of other type of structure and create synergic effect. Implementing teams management practices in the institution bring outcomes listed in exhibit 2.4.

Exhibit No. 2.4: Outcomes of teams' structure

➢ Quick decisions	➢ Enhanced trust among members
➢ Enhanced quality of decisions	➢ Shared responsibility
➢ Increased responsibility and accountability	➢ Distributed work
➢ Enhanced commitment of members	➢ Risk factors lowered down
➢ Enhanced self-confidence	➢ Ready to face the challenges
➢ Increased transparency in working	➢ Sustained interest in working
➢ Enhanced co-ordination and co-operation among members	➢ Work does not suffer
➢ Improved quality of work	➢ Quick implementation of decisions
➢ Time saving	➢ Less conflict
➢ Increased flexibility in working	➢ Effective utilization of resources
➢ Training of members	➢ Effective communication
➢ Improved performance	➢ Good interpersonal relationship
	➢ Members satisfaction
	➢ Good self-discipline

8. Summary

Management of the institution is carried out in the light of vision, missions, goals and strategic plan of the institution. These elements are documented in vision document of the institution. The teams in the institution initiate the process of preparing vision document. All significant external and internal stakeholders participate in the process. Governing body approves the final vision document. It also approves policies, rules and regulations that are followed to implement vision reach strategies. To implement the annual and perspective plan of the institution the head of the institution with specific terms of reference constitutes numbers of management teams. These teams prepare annual plan of implementation. They function according to their plans following policies, rules and regulations. If there is any implementation problem they suggest necessary changes to appropriate authority for approval and then they implement the change. The size of the management teams is kept five to ten members according to needs and task of the team. Teams are formed and developed to bring synergistic effect in the functioning of the institution. Apart from teams structure voluntary participation is also promoted to harness the potential of individuals and informal groups of the institution. Well-designed strategies are used to make the teams effective on the task. Management teams are expected to produce variety of improvements and innovations in the functioning of the institution.

9. Activity

Prepare the list of teams of permanent nature and voluntary teams functioning in your institution. List their composition and function and compare their functions with the functions listed in this chapter. Also list the significant outcomes of different teams.

REFERENCES

Abrahamsson, B. (1977). *Bureaucracy or Participation*, Beverly Hills Sage.

All India Council for Technical Education (1996). A Scheme for Autonomous University Departments/Institutes/Centres/Schools of Technical Education.

Board of Technical Examination (1995). Guidelines on the Scheme of Autonomous Polytechnics, Maharashtra State, Mumbai.

Charles Margerism (1996). *Team Management Practical New Approaches*, Lawrey.

David Osborne and Tade Gaebler (1982) *Reinventing Government,* Prentice Hall of India Pvt. Ltd., New Delhi.

Green, F. (1991). Investing in Higher Education, American Council on Education.

James Lundy, L. (1996). *Teams*, Global Books & Subscription Services, New Delhi.

Katzenbach and Douglas, K. Smith (1993). *The Wisdom of Teams*, Boston, Harward Business School Presses.

TTTI (1995). A Study on Implementing Quality Circles in Polytechnics, Bhopal.

TTTI (1996). A Research Study to Determine Level of Rapport of Teachers, Assess Institutional Climate and Judge Present Status of Autonomy.

TTTI (1997). A Snap Study of the Dimensions of Institutional Autonomy for Maharashtra Polytechnics.

TTTI (1999). A Brief Report – Principals Conference for Maharashtra Polytechnics, TTTI, Bhopal.

Zaheer Hamid and Gupta, B.L. (1999). A study on the Informal Groups in Polytechnics and Formulating Strategies to Channelise Potential of Informal Groups for the Development of the Polytechnics-TTTI, Bhopal.

3

Roles of Significant Functionaries

Objectives: The readers will be able to:

1. State the importance of the role description.
2. Explain the role derivation process.
3. Describe the role of significant position holders.
4. Explain the concept of role efficacy.
5. Describe the methods of role enrichment.

1. Introduction

The governing body and governing teams approve the strategic, perspective and annual plan of the institute. The plans contain number of innovative strategies. These strategies are to be translated into actions. Different individuals and teams perform these actions. The role of governing body, governing teams and management teams is described in previous chapters. The role of various functionaries like head of the institution, head of the departments, faculty members and staff members should be clear to them. Even the students should know their role in the functioning of the institution. The sum of role of individuals and teams should contribute to accomplish annual objectives and goals of the institute. In the chapter on motivation role related motivational aspects are described in detail. The role of a person and a team should be clear, challenging, significant and enriched to keep them motivated through out the day and all days.

2. Use of Role Description

The well-designed role of individuals and teams is very useful to achieve short-term as well as long-term objectives of the institution. Some of the important uses of role description are listed in exhibit 3.1 and described briefly in subsequent paragraphs.

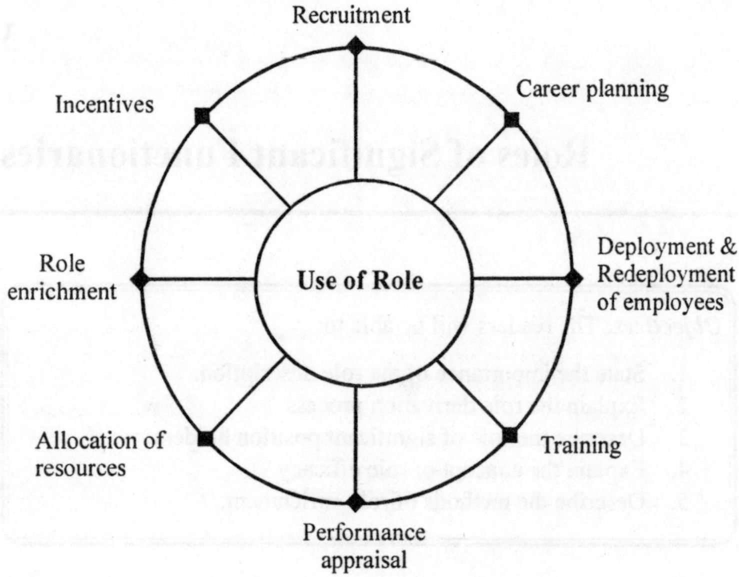

Exhibit No. 3.1: Use of role description

2.1 Recruitment

Role for permanent posts and temporary posts should be well defined. Well-defined roles are helpful in selecting right person for right work. The right person with right role will work professionally for the growth and development of the institution. The profile of a person on various areas of functioning of the institute can be prepared that helps to make the selection process effective. A wrong person on a permanent post may be a waste and nuisance for the institute. The person becomes the liability on the institution for the whole life.

2.2 Career Planning

Role description is useful in career planning of employees of the institution. They can be prepared for performing dynamic role and to take up future challenges and innovative roles. The previous performance record of employees is useful to select the employees for specific assignments. Continuous path of progression can be provided to employees to keep them motivated. For example a lecturer having research attitude may be assigned the project work of undergraduate, research work of postgraduate and Ph.D. work of Ph.D. pursuing candidates. A continuous career opportunity for a person can be planned for 5–15 years and s/he can be developed accordingly. Similarly other paths related to teaching learning, instructional material development, evaluation of students achievement, consultancy, community development, technology development, etc. can be evolved. Strategic and perspective plan of the institute also guides to decide the paths for career advancement.

2.3 Deployment and Redeployment of Employees

The individuals and teams can be appropriately deployed for various tasks of the institute. Clear role helps the management and the employees to negotiate on the roles and responsibilities. Right person can easily be found out to take up the role. Employees who are temporarily free or have less work can be redeployed for purposeful work. The drivers, sweepers, gardeners, clerks, lecturer who do not have full time work can be trained and redeployed for other appropriate tasks. Clerks who do not have sufficient work in one section can be redeployed in another section with training to take up new role. For example, in one institution gardeners did not have sufficient work to do in a day were deployed for set making and binding purpose with additional incentives. Sweepers were deployed in the library to lift the books. Drivers were redeployed to help the directors' office when they are in office. Teachers were redeployed to produce multimedia on recent technology; head of the departments were redeployed to do negotiations with national and multinational companies on various dimensions of collaborations.

2.4 Training

Well-defined roles help to identify the training needs for individuals and teams. Need based training programmes can be designed and organized to develop the competencies in individuals and teams. It helps to design the training material and resources as well. The impact of the training can be assessed scientifically on the basis of performance on role. The trainer can be specific in selecting role related examples during the training. The trainee can also remove his/her doubts related to role. S/he can think new and innovative methods of performing the role.

2.5 Performance Appraisal

Objective performance appraisal can be carried out using well-defined roles. Each role holder sets objectives for a year or a semester. The performance can be assessed against set objectives. It is also helpful for providing constructive feedback for improvement. The role related individual counselling could also be organized in problem area. The role performer can assess his/her performance on the basis of role and set targets. Self-assessment of performance provides sense of accomplishment and feedback for improvement.

2.6 Allocation of Resources

Clearly defined roles help to allocate resources to perform the role. Resources are allocated on the basis of roles and not on the basis of designation or status. Role related delegation of authority could be planned easily. Allocation of resources as per roles and responsibilities enhances resources utilization factor in the institution because necessary resources are allotted to role holders.

2.7 Role Enrichment

Role description of individuals and teams is helpful in identifying the match between the talent of the role performer and scope of challenge in the role. The scope of role enrichment can be improved if roles are properly described and personal profile is known. The performance of the individuals, teams and whole institution can be enhanced through proper role planning. Prioritization among roles can be done if role description is available. People for innovative and mundane work can be identified easily. Role description is helpful in expansion of academic as well as non-academic activities. For example, one Senior Lecturer is excellent in organizing cultural programmes, and has interest to work in cultural activities. S/he can be assigned the role of organizing inter college cultural programmes. This new role will definitely enrich his/her role.

2.8 Incentives

Role descriptions are helpful in deciding the incentives for excellent performance at the same time remedial actions like counselling, help, guidance, encouragement can be planned for poor performers. Incentives for roles leading to development of the institution can be fixed and declared well in advance. People having capabilities will come forward to assume the roles. Incentives for challenging roles create some sort of competition among institutional members.

3. Role Derivation

Role is a dynamic concept. It changes with respect to time and situation. In a growing and developing institution changes and innovations are very common. It demands for changing role. It invites creativity of people to perform better and different. It compels people to carryout experiments because traditional options are no more effective and efficient. In flexible teams structure people work to satisfy the needs of the fellow members and all employees work for the better academic image of the institution. The institution has to satisfy the needs of the students, their parents, employers, government, statutory body, professional body, networked partners and so on. The needs of the stakeholders can be satisfied when stakeholders satisfy the needs of the institution. In fact it is a mutual process because all are dependent on each other. Well-performed academic roles lead to enriched teaching learning process and satisfaction of students, their parents and employers. Well performed academic roles would naturally prevent the negative behaviours of the students and teachers such as conflict, strikes, mass bunking from classes, involvement in unlawful activities, creating nuisance for the nearby society etc. It would also reduce complaints about learning and poor performance. Teachers will devote more time in performing their duties rather than playing unwanted politics in the institution. It would also reduce conflict on resources and other trivial issues. There would be integrated performance among different roles there by the impact of performance would be visible. Similarly well-performed financial roles satisfy the needs of employees and other stakeholders. The role of significant positions is briefly described in subsequent paragraphs.

3.1 Role of Head of the Institution

The head of the institution is a key link between governing body and employees of the institute. S/he is expected to perform variety of roles to make balance between the expectations of the governing body and employees. At the same time s/he has to satisfy the expectations of stakeholders and perform vivid roles to collaborate, network, negotiate and influence external stakeholders. Role description of head of the institution is given briefly in subsequent paragraphs.

Academic

The head of the institution should ensure good academic governance of the institution. S/he should feed relevant information to the strategic, perspective and annual plans of the institution. S/he should introduce demand driven courses at certificate, diploma, undergraduate, postgraduate and Ph.D. level. S/he should see that academic programmes are offered at right time as per needs of the employers and potential students. S/he should introduce flexibility in programme offering as per requirements of the students. Flexibility can be introduced in duration of completion of the programmes, selecting path of specialization, entry level, exit level etc. S/he should introduce the use of recent concepts of curriculum development, course design, course offerings, measurement and evaluation of learning, use of information technology in teaching learning, use of multimedia, web sites, industry shop floor, managerial skills development etc. S/he should lead the faculty and staff members through vision of the institute. All academic programmes should focus on professional development of the students. S/he should encourage the faculty and technical staff members of the institute to set examples for others and act as a role model for students. To promote academic professionalism in the institute all the persons involved in teaching learning process should be continuously trained to excel their best. S/he should develop the infrastructure, laboratories, workshops, class rooms, seminar halls, self learning centres, learning resources development and utilization centres, library etc. to facilitate the teaching learning process. S/he should study the best academic practices being used nationally and internationally for bench marking purpose. The bench marking should be done for academic inputs, processes, products and services. S/he should enhance the academic corporate image of the institution in society. S/he should encourage academic experimentation for innovation purpose. S/he should increase confidence and risk taking capacity of the teachers to translate innovative ideas into action. S/he should involve internal and external stakeholders to actively take part in academic activities.

Administrative

All academic ventures require administrative support. Administrative processes and decisions should be supported by policies. S/he should ensure that policies, rules and regulations make the work easy to satisfy the expectations of employees and external stakeholders. There should not be delay, waste, poor quality of product and services because of administrative rules and regulations. It should supplement and complement the academic processes. All the records should be computerized to facilitate the decision making process. S/he should encourage employees to observe self-discipline. Well-defined problem solving and complaint handling mechanism should be functional in the institute. All the administrative matters should be amicably solved. S/he should use positive techniques such as counselling, coaching, constructive feedback etc. even in adverse situations. S/he should ensure to decentralize the administrative decision-making process under the broad framework of the institution. S/he should ensure not to indulge in resolving administrative matters. Rather s/he should define, refine and revise policies to support the decision-making and problem solving system.

Management

The head of the institution should constitute and develop management teams. S/he should create necessary support facilities to facilitate academic and non-academic functions of the institute. S/he should approve all academic and non-academic developmental plans. S/he should continuously monitor the progress of various programmes, projects and schemes to enhance and sustain academic climate. S/he should empower various teams and individuals to excel better. S/he should convene meetings of teams and individuals to pass on correct information and receive feedback. S/he should encourage proactive management in the institution. To encourage proactive management, s/he should organize number of planning and objective-setting workshops. As a head of the institute s/he should ensure proper coordination and cooperation amongst teams and individuals. S/he should ensure that all the teams and individuals work systematically and not in a casual way. S/he should ensure that all the problems, grievances and complaints are solved at lowest level. All the systems, procedures and policies are in place. It is his/her role to lead the teams and individual by vision of the institution. As a figurehead s/he should record his/her presence in all the institutional functions. S/he should sign all official documents related to collaborations, networking, and memorandum of understanding, loans, consultancy, negotiations, and legal papers. S/he should encourage experimentation to bring innovations in the functioning of the institutions. S/he should ensure that minimum basic facilities are available to employees and students. S/he should encourage use of appreciations, recognition and reward techniques in the institution at all levels. S/he should encourage optimum utilization of all types of resources including academic facilities like library, learning resource centre, self-learning centre, laboratories, workshops, computer centre and seminar halls. At the same time steps should be taken to minimize the wastage of resources. S/he should act as a change agent for all new and innovative initiatives. S/he should act as mentor, guide, coach, facilitator, and role model for institutional members and other heads of the institutions. S/he should implement in-house and outstation training programmes for faculty and staff members. S/he should ensure that institution fulfil its responsibility of social development. S/he should ensure that institutional members do aggressive marketing of institutional products and services. The placement of passouts is very important aspect so far marketing of institutional programmes is concerned. S/he should ensure that all statutory rules are followed in functioning of the institution. S/he should ensure that institution finds proper representation at state, national and international level. S/he should inculcate and ensure that employees of the institution observe shared values, norms, ethics, and performance standards.

Financial

Financial health of the institution is necessary to sustain academic and non-academic activities of the institution. The head of the institution should do financial planning to implement annual plan, perspective plan and strategic plan. S/he should grab the opportunities contributing to good financial health of the institution. S/he should explore alternative ways to do the academic as well as non-academic business of the institution. S/he should explore which activities require huge resources and what are the alternative strategies available to perform the activities. One alternative way could be networking with sister institutions. Other alternative could be sharing resources such as auditorium, library, learning resource center, faculty, and laboratories with sister institutions on mutual basis. This requires development of planned networks among the institutions. Sharing is possible because in big cities numbers of institutions are coming up. Networked partners can develop facilities of high standards in specific discipline and share it on mutual basis. Networking is an alternative way to save high investment and maintenance cost. Collaboration with industries, field agencies and government departments is another alternative to cut down expenditure on infrastructure. Collaborative venture creates win-win situation for collaborating partners on financial and academic aspects. Institute can use industry as extended laboratory at the same time can help the industry to maintain and update the machinery and equipment. It can solve human resources related problems of the industry. The third alternative is generating revenue from various sources and activities. Fourth alternative is saving money, minimizing wastage of man, material, machine, time, instructional resources, space, energy, water etc. The head of the institution should explore alternative ways of performing activities and generating resources to ensure good financial health of the institution.

3.2 Role of the Faculty Members

Faculty members are considered to be the backbone of the technical institution. They can make or break the academic image of the institution. Their role is required to be defined and appropriately allocated to them. Their main role is related to academic activities of the institution. They should be professionally developed to assume the multiple roles in academic area. The broad role dimensions of faculty members are shown in exhibit 3.2.

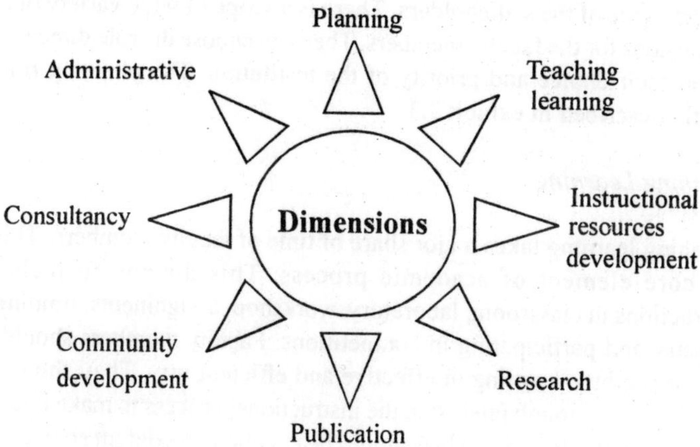

Exhibit No. 3.2: Role dimensions for a faculty member

Individuals and teams are assigned various role dimensions according to their strengths, ability, experiences, networking and willingness. The role assignment is carried out through their consensus. The extent of involvement of individuals and teams may vary on various role dimensions. The roles should be assigned in such a way so that it fulfils the total role requirements of the institution. While allocating the role dimensions, prioritization on the basis of the interest of the individuals can be done. It should be ensured that all individuals get some significant, challenging and core role dimensions. Every faculty should assume roles related to growth and development of the institution. Mundane, routine and boring roles should also be distributed equally. Role gapes, role overlaps, role conflicts, role over loads should be avoided. The role should match to the personality and interest of the person. To increase the role efficacy the role of the individuals can be rotated, shifted, changed and enriched over a period of time. Same person should not be permitted to do the same work again and again. The brief description of the role dimensions of faculty members is given in subsequent paragraphs.

Planning

Faculty members participate in planning function of the institution. They contribute to strategic, perspective and annual planning of the institution. They also prepare departmental, team and individual plans for a year. The role of the faculty members emanates from the annual plan and expectations of the stakeholders. There is a scope of wide variety of role dimensions for the faculty members. They can choose the role dimensions as per their choice and priority of the institution. The planning role is briefly described in exhibit 3.3.

Teaching Learning

Teaching learning takes major share of time of faculty members. This is the core element of academic process. This dimension includes instructions in classroom, laboratory, workshop, assignments, training in industry and participating in competitions. Faculty members should be able to produce learning in effective and efficient way. They should be able to create enough interest in the instructional process to make it joyful and unforgettable event. They should be excellent in content so that they can plan and deliver the goods in simpler, logical, and sequential way. They should be able to teach the student's new concepts, principles, theories, and models to produce right learning. They should be able to make the complex things simple and interesting. They should be able to

Exhibit No. 3.3: Planning role of faculty members

Planning curricular activities

- Design curriculum using recent concepts, principles and models of curriculum.
- Revise, modify and refine the existing curriculum as per needs.
- Establish the linkages among subjects and topics within the subject.
- Identify prerequisites to opt for a subject.
- Evaluate the impact of the curriculum on the performance of the passouts.
- Maintain own data base to give input to curriculum design.

Planning cocurricular activities

- Plan industrial visits, industrial training, project work, seminars, experience sharing, industrial projects, industrial problems, assignments etc.
- Plan to participate in competition, seminar, conference, quiz etc.

Planning extracurricular activities

- Plan and organize cultural activities, sports, personality development programmes, services to community and social activities in the institution.

Planning development

- Plan developmental activities of the department such as laboratory development, learning resources development, library development, procurement of learning resources.
- Plan staff and students amenities.

create interest in the topic using concrete examples, multimedia and case studies. They should be able to select appropriate teaching, learning method to achieve stated objectives. They should have hold on the topic. Their voice should be clear to understand and loud to hear. They should be able to take feedback during teaching learning process. They should be proficient in use of media and learning resources. They should have a list of books in which the topic is covered. They should also have the addresses of websites from where more learning material on the topic can be downloaded. They should be skilful to use multiple channels of communication. They should be able to develop challenging assignments on the topic and subject. They should continuously assess the progress of learning of students and provide them constructive feedback for improvement. They should be able to provide informational source of literature for further reading. They should be able to develop important notes for ready reference.

Guide

They should be able to guide the students to complete assignments, seminars, projects, practical and research work. They should be able to provide them tips, innovative ideas, and guidelines to achieve the competence level. At the same time they should be able to guide the students to select the career of their choice. They should act as role model for the students. They should have formulas of success to be shared with students.

Problem Solver

Students come from varied background in technical institution. They have variety of problems including learning problems. Their problems need to be identified and addressed appropriately. Teachers can assist the students in problem solving because they remain in constant touch with the students. It is their duty to find out individual and group problems and solve them. Learning problems of students require solution at right time otherwise numbers of problems may get accumulated and it can create disinterest in a subject. It has consequent effect on other subjects also. Students are in the age of turbulence they need friendly and parental treatment to channelize their energy for productive work. Only teachers can extend this help to students.

Facilitator

Faculty members should facilitate the learning process. They can use variety of modes to facilitate thc learning process. Some sort of healthy competition among the students can be created to speed up the learning process. It would also increase the responsibility of students for learning. There are good teachers who do not teach they simply facilitate the learning process using variety of learner-based techniques. Well-designed individual and group assignments can produce purposeful learning. Faculty members should be able to design assignment, case studies, problems, projects, field studies and interactions with experts to facilitate the learning. Initially the role of the faculty members would be more demanding for designing the assignments but later on they will be relaxed. They can produce effective learning using learning resources. Students possessing advance knowledge and skills in a particular topic may be used as resource students to facilitate the learning process. Teachers should:

- Prepare lesson plans to conduct theory classes.
- Organize resources to carry out teaching learning processes.
- Relate the topic with practice and other topics to establish its importance.
- Use variety of teaching learning methods such as improved lecture, group discussion, simulation, case method, game, demonstration, discovery learning, quiz, action learning, tutorials, seminars, competition and multi media to change the stimulus and sustain the interest of the students.
- Organize industrial visits and training to relate theory with practice and to know latest industrial practices.
- Assess the progress of learning taking tests and giving variety of assignments such as industrial problems, seminar papers, project, laboratory work, library assignment, survey work, research work etc.
- Provide constructive feedback for improvement.
- Impart remedial instructions for weak students.
- Maintain and use the records of students learning for counselling, coaching and guidance purpose.
- Distribute the important notes to students.

Instructional Resources Development

The fast development of the technology and rapid change in industrial practices require latest literature on the topic. Faculty members are required to impart latest knowledge to students. Apart from this, students demand for complete, simple and easy to understand literature. Faculty members are expected to develop learning resources that can be used by students and faculty of other institutions also. This may give revenue to the institute. They should:

- Review the literature and visit the industries to know latest developments in their discipline.
- Develop learning resources such as text books, work books, practice books, assignments, case studies, games, simulations, models, power point presentations, video films, multi media packages, self learning packages etc.
- Procure leaning resources developed by resource institutions.

Research

Researches are the base for development of the technology. Technical institutions can earn high level academic image developing new technology to solve existing problems, or create something new that add to the quality of product or services or both. Industries and society will regard the institution when it has proven ability and credibility to give something new and different to it. Industries and society renew themselves to meet the changing demands. Right kind of renewal can be designed through researches. Institutions are also required to renew and change their way of working to meet the changing needs. Faculty members should:

- Define the technological problems of the industries and society to find practical solutions. They can conduct research studies to know the accurate needs of the industries and society. They can conduct researches related to efficiency, effectiveness, wastage reduction, saving energy, update technology, value addition to product and services, environment protection, marketing, reduce hazards on shop floor, increase safety in the industry, manage inventory, improve logistics, work place ethics, human resources development, impact of the product or services etc.
- Design new products and services to satisfy customers needs.
- Develop appropriate technology to improve quality of life in urban and rural areas.
- Carry out researches to enhance the effectiveness of teaching learning process in the institution.
- Carry out the researches for developing systems and processes for the growth and development of the institution.
- Conduct tracers study, action researches, and impact analysis.
- Develop and install quality assurance system in the institution.
- Carry out researches on human resources development.
- Do experimental researches to improve teaching learning process.

Publication

Publication of researches, innovations, positive changes, experiences, and achievements at national and international level enhances the corporate image of the institution. Apart from this faculty members should publish the learning resources developed by them for wider use. This would reduce the duplication of the work and bring revenue to the institution. The institution would earn name and fame in the technical education system. The institution can start its own publication in a specific area of its specialization. Faculty members should:

- Participate in publication.
- Encourage cofaculty members and students to publish their contributions.
- Help passouts to publish their innovative and unique contributions.
- Start publication of the institution.
- Receive patents for their work.

Community Development

Institution has obligation for the development of the society. It should extend the use of resources to the society for improving the quality of work life. Faculty members should:

- Design and offer flexible programmes on skill upgradation, capacity building, planning, awareness, crisis management, empowerment, use of technology, energy saving, environment protection, sanitation, drinking water, health related subjects, water harvesting etc.
- Transfer technology to increase effectiveness and efficiency to minimize drudgery.
- Help community members to establish micro enterprises.
- Form and build self-help groups to undertake community development activities.
- Provide technical support services to improve productivity and add value to quality of life.
- Develop awareness related to use of technology for development.

Consultancy

It is the real area of challenge for the faculty members. The consultancy assignments indicate the capability and capacity of the faculty members to earn revenue for the institute. It projects the corporate image of the institution. Consultancy assignments are very helpful in maintaining financial health of the institution. Consultancy creates scope for learning and experimentation. The faculty members should:

- Offer continuing education programmes for industry personnel.
- Undertake assignments such as problem solving, product development, business process reengineering, quality improvement of product and services, design of marketing strategy, preparation of vision document, preparation of strategic plans, customer awareness, learning resources development projects, social audit, customer survey, marketing researches, organizational development, etc.
- Offer testing and calibration services.
- Do valuation of the property of the industry.
- Prepare maintenance manuals, work manuals, customer guide, presentations for marketing the product, services, and project design.
- Organize seminars, conferences, symposiums and joint programmes.
- Deliver expert lectures.

Administrative

The academics of the institution require support from managerial, administrative and financial processes. Faculty members better understand their requirements from the supporting processes. They should:

- Maintain and computerize records of the students progress to take academic decisions.
- Maintain and sustain linkages with industries, field agencies, professional bodies, statutory bodies, research organization and alumni.
- Guide the process of introducing autonomy, flexibility, deployment of the resources, generating revenue, marketing institutional services, quality improvement programmes, training of faculty and staff, welfare of employees and student etc.
- Guide schemes of governments such as direct central assistance, national service schemes, community polytechnic, admission of students, examination, training for physically challenged persons etc.
- Ensure academic discipline in the institution.
- Build capacity of faculty and staff members to accept challenges.
- Promote high standards of performance in functioning of the institution.

4. Role Efficacy

The concept of role efficacy is very important for the growth and development of the institution. Udai Pareek has done pioneer work on this concept. He has stated that the performance of the person depends on his potential effectiveness and the design of the role he performs in the organization. He has described that role efficacy has many aspects such as self role integration, proactivity, creativity, confrontation, centrality, influence, personal growth inter role linkages, helping relationship and super ordination. He has suggested many strategies to enhance the role efficacy in the organization. A.K. Jamuar conducted a study in technical institution and suggested strategies such as role integration, role enrichment, role defining, role delegation, effective communication, role linkage, participative decision-making, flexibility, training, role transition, time management, resources generation, team building, interpersonal relationship, physical exercise, yoga and meditation to enhance role efficacy in technical institutions. He has stated that resolved role conflict and increased role efficacy has increased job satisfaction, commitment towards work, interpersonal relationship, motivation, adjustment, personal effectiveness, confidence, performance, morale, interest and creativity of faculty members. He stated that it has reduced tension, anxiety, frustration and exhaustion. He has described that use of these strategies has increased organizational culture, commitment, climate, discipline morale, attendance, effectiveness, satisfaction, interpersonal relation and communication. It has reduced turn over of employees, unrest and complaints.

5. Research Findings

P.D. Dale (1998) conducted a research study on factors affecting job satisfaction of teachers in technical education and studied the social, personal, morale, professional and financial factors. He concluded that factors listed in exhibit 3.4 have high rank for contributing for teachers' satisfaction.

6. Summary

The role of various functionaries is derived on the basis of expectations of the external and internal stakeholders. The strategic, perspective and annual plan of the institution also provide guidelines about the type of

Exhibit No. 3.4: Factors contributing for job satisfaction of teachers in technical institutions

Sl. No.	*Factor*	*Category*
1.	Attainment of high position in society by students	Morale
2.	Enjoying not only teaching but also developing personality of students	Morale
3.	Enhancement of knowledge	Professional
4.	Teacher student relation	Social
5.	Enhancement of professional qualities and capabilities	Personal
6.	Teaching as challenging job	Personal
7.	Solving academic problems and providing guidance	Personal
8.	Sufficient opportunities for development	Personal
9.	Least chance of corrupt practices and unfair means	Morale
10.	Disliking of discussions and delivering lectures	Personal

the roles to be performed to implement the plans. The role description of individuals and teams provide clarity in functioning of the institution. It removes conflicts and confusion. The training and non-training interventions can be planned properly to perform the role effectively and efficiently. The role of individuals and teams should be balanced. Meaning thereby there should not be role gaps, role overlaps, role encroachments, role deficiency, and role conflict in the institution. The role of individuals and teams should be enriched. The role of individuals and teams should be changed according to the needs of the institution, as role is a dynamic concept. Role rotation should be exercised periodically to maintain the interest of the role performer. There should be enough scope for career development of individual in the role. The role of the head of the institution, faculty members and other significant persons is described. The role description of various functionaries mentioned in this chapter should be considered as guideline. It is not necessary that every faculty member perform equally on all role dimensions. Looking to the competence, interest, experience and priority of the institution the role can be assigned to individuals. The institution can also decide minimum involvement on each role dimension for all faculty members. The amount of involvement may be decided on time, objectives, quantity and quality etc. It all depends on the development plans of the institution. The institution should ensure that roles are reviewed and modified every year as per needs of the institution. The institution should also ensure that roles of individuals are enriched and there is enough challenge for them to excel better.

7. Activity

List the various functionaries working in your institution and describe the role performed by each position holder. Compare the role being performed and expected role performance and find out the role gap for the whole institution. Identify the causes of role gap and design strategies to refix the gap. Design the role enrichment strategies for individuals and teams.

REFERENCES

AICTE Circular On Qualifications and Experience for Teaching Posts.

Dale, P.D. (1998). Factors Affecting Job Satisfaction of Teachers in Technical Education, TTTI, Bhopal.

Jamuar, A.K. and Gupta, B.L. (1997). *A Study on Role Conflict in Polytechnic Teachers and Designing Strategies to Minimize it*, Technical Teachers Training Institute, Bhopal.

Udai Pareek (1993). *Making Organizational Roles Effective*, Tata McGraw-Hills Publishing Company Limited, New Delhi.

PART II
PLANNING FOR DEVELOPMENT

4

Planning for Development

Objectives: The readers will be able to:

1. State the importance of planning for the growth and development of the institution.
2. Describe various planning approaches.
3. Describe the planning process for technical institution.
4. Describe types of plans prepared in technical institution.
5. Explain the process of crafting vision statement.
6. Describe the process of deriving mission statements.
7. State the relationship between goals and objectives.
8. Describe planning model for technical institutions.
9. Explain preparation to be made to implement the strategy.
10. State factors affecting the implementation of plans.
11. Describe strategies to be used to achieve vision of the institution.
12. List the tools used in the planning process.
13. Describe the criteria for evaluating the effectiveness of the plan.
14. Describe the format of annual plan.

Introduction

lanning is one of the management functions. It is a process used by romoters, governors, and leaders to prepare the institution for future. he promoters, governors and leaders decide the point of ultimate estination of the institution in the future. They explore alternative paths reach the destination and decide the strategies. The ultimate destination decided on the basis of analysis of external environment and future forecasting. It is also based on aspirations of the promoters, governors and leaders of the institution. The promoters, governors and leaders get educated through the process of planning. They educate themselves about the future and environmental forces. They gain experiences and it develops confidence in them to take the risk and decide the long-term and short-term goals. It helps the promoters to meet the challenges, diagnose the potential problems, mobilize the resources and control the academic as well as supporting processes.

The process of planning helps people to introduce and manage change effectively. It helps in improving performance of the institution in present and future as well. To ensure effectiveness and efficiency in the functioning of the institute alternatives are generated and decisions are taken. Planning helps the promoters, governors and leaders to see the core business, i.e. academics holistically. It helps the performers to organize themselves and their resources to achieve the institutional goals. It helps to remove the perception, biases and subjectivity in the functioning of the institution. The process of planning helps to minimize wastage of efforts, time and money. It guides to focus on academic processes. Participative methods of planning help leaders to obtain commitment of individuals and teams for action. Everyone in the institute understands the complete business and his/her share of work.

Planning is essential to assure healthy rate of growth of the institution. It is one of the professional management techniques. It helps promoters of the institution to progress in right direction and progress with supersonic speed. It helps to harness the full potential of individuals and teams. It tells about what type of abilities needs to be developed in individuals and teams to execute the plans and achieve the goals. What type of resources needs to be arranged and when it needs to be arranged. It guides the promoters to run business of academics. It helps in time of turbulence and crisis to remove the hurdles and move ahead.

Participative decisions-making is a key in the process of planning. Any unthoughtful decision may derail the business of the institution. It helps to continuously monitor the progress of the institution. It provides competitive advantage to move ahead with success. It is a proactive approach of management of the business. It helps to avoid use of crisis management and problem management approaches. People do thing with joy and fun because there is no urgency and no surprises. The ambitions of institution are clearly defined and put on the time line. This time line prevents people to procrastinate and postpone things. Institute plans help the promoters to impress students, their parents, government departments, employers and other stakeholders to trust, help and cooperate to implement the plans. Institutional members also get inspired to implement the plans. Alternative ways are generated to achieve the goals. This builds up the confidence of the people that they are working on effective and efficient plans.

2. Approaches to Planning

There have been various approaches of planning in practice. Each approach has got strengths and limitations.

2.1 Blue Print and Process Approach

Earlier blue print approach was common for development of educational institution. The plan of the institution to start the educational programmes was developed by the promoters of the institution. The institution was established according to plan of promoters. This plan was considered to be fixed and generally no major changes were implemented. Minor changes according to the dire need of the time were implemented. There were no much technological developments taken place in past. It was application of same technology for years. In the past the competition in technical education business was almost negligible. Established institutions were expected to repeat the programmes for years together. Now unprecedented growth has seen in technology especially in information technology. The demands for passouts have increased nationally and internationally. At the same time technical institutions have increased manifold. Now they are in tough competition and require to perform variety of roles. The expectations of the stakeholders have increased significantly. Today the technical institutions cannot be static and their development is not possible using blueprint approach only. Therefore prosperous institutions have started the use of process approach as well. They are learning through experiences and modifying, refining, and even changing the way of working. They are preparing on-going plans to fulfil the dynamic needs of the stakeholders. They are involving all significant stakeholders in the process of planning and inviting them to tell their needs and demands clearly so that they can fulfil them. They are planning frequently to meet the changing demands of the students and stakeholders.

2.2 Reactive and Proactive Approach

Earlier people used reactive approach to planning. Meaning thereby whenever government spelled out demands, they used to plan to offer new programmes or bring changes in the existing curricula. The problem-based approach of planning was popular in earlier days because there was monopoly and no competition. Whenever system faced significant problems people wakeup to solve the problems. The government funding was adequate to run the institution. There was not much pressure for major innovations and change. Now the situation has changed significantly. Institutions cannot enjoy the luxury of using reactive approaches and wasting time, money and resources. They cannot dare to dissatisfy the customers. Planners have to be proactive, adoptive and responsive to the stakeholders. They have to predict the future requirements and plan for development accordingly. This approach of planning is called proactive approach.

2.3 Top Down and Bottom Up Approach

Earlier, Central or State government owned most of the technical institutions. To maintain the uniformity in functioning of institutions planning and policy formulation was carried out centrally. Same plan was implemented in all the institutions irrespective of individual difference. Everything was governed and controlled centrally. There was less scope for specific changes and innovations. The communication was one way and delayed. It delayed the performance of processes and dissatisfied the customers and internal members of the institutions. It was not effective and competitive way of working. It could not fulfil the dynamic needs of the system. Now it is realized that top down approach has numerous limitation and irrelevant in today's context. So most of the institutions have been granted autonomy to function independently under certain broad guidelines. Private institutions are also functioning independently. The planning and implementation is being done at institutional level. Institutions have also realized that the process of planning should start from bottom. Most of the institutions are involving and empowering people and teams to do planning at their level to satisfy the needs of the students and stakeholders.

3. Planning Process for Technical Institutions

As described earlier planning is a process and plan is the product of planning process. The planning is carried out in the present for the future. Naturally the future should be ambitious, broad and big. The process of planning in present for the future is shown in exhibit 4.1.

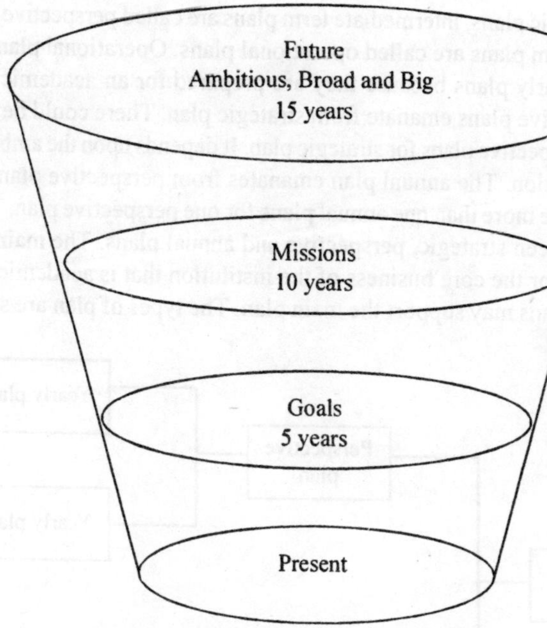

Exhibit No. 4.1: Process of planning

The broader, larger and attractive future is described in vision and mission statements of the institution. Alternative strategies are explored to achieve the vision and missions of the institution. Strategies to build up quality culture and corporate environment are also explored. Resources are estimated to accomplish the vision and mission of the institution. The process of planning requires creativity. All institutions are required to undergo planning process whether they are new, grown, developed or excellent. Planning is a continuous, flexible and participative process so every institution has to prepare plans, implement the plans, review the progress and evaluate the achievements. The learning from evaluation of annual plan goes for subsequent year planning process as planning is a continuous process. It ensures the effectiveness and efficiency for the development of the institution.

4. Types of Plans

Every institution has to put lot of efforts in planning process to prepare long-term, intermediate term and short-term plan. Long-term plans are called strategic plans, intermediate term plans are called perspective plans and short-term plans are called operational plans. Operational plans can be called yearly plans because they are prepared for an academic year. The perspective plans emanate from strategic plan. There could be more than one perspective plans for strategic plan. It depends upon the ambitions of the institution. The annual plan emanates from perspective plans and there could be more than one annual plans for one perspective plan. There is logic between strategic, perspective and annual plans. The main plan is prepared for the core business of the institution that is academics and rest of the plans may support the main plan. The types of plan are shown in exhibit 4.2.

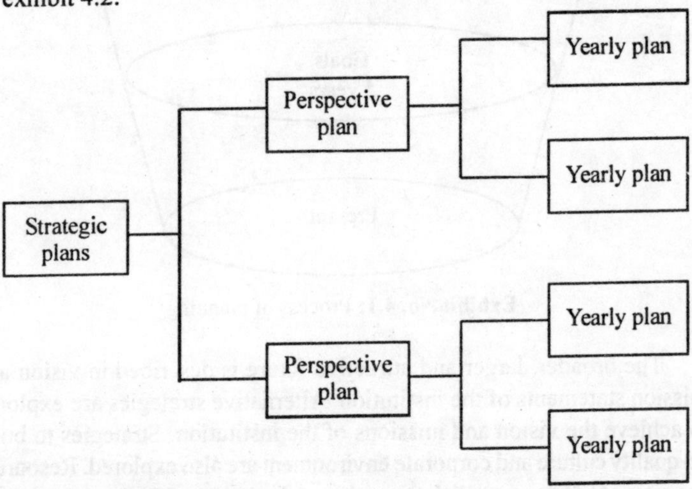

Exhibit No. 4.2: Types of plans

4.1 Strategic Plan

Strategic plan is prepared for 10-20 years. The strategic plan is very broad in nature. It contains vision, missions, goals and alternative strategies to accomplish vision of the institution. Strategic plan provides base for perspective and annual plans. It acts as a foundation for further planning process. The soundness of the strategic plan decides the future of the institution. Some institutions devote adequate time, effort and money to prepare strategic plan. These institutions steadily grow and develop to heights of excellence. They remain stable in times of turbulence when other institutions struggle, fail and close down. They grow exponential and in innovative way when opportunities exist. Properly worked out strategic plan of the institution fit into the larger purpose of technical education system.

4.2 Perspective Plans

Perspective plans emanate from strategic plan of the institution. These plans grab immediate future opportunities, which are visible. These plans are worked out in more detail than strategic plan. These plans are flexible in nature and leave ample scope for creativity and innovations. Latest trends, technologies, resources and practices are used to implement the perspective plans. All perspective plans of the institution should be integrated to provide continuity in growth and development of the institution. Promoters, governors, leaders and stakeholders of the institution participate in preparation of perspective plans. The effectiveness of previous perspective plan also provides inputs for successive plans. Fresh scanning of the environment is also carried out to give inputs to perspective plans. These plans are prepared for three to five years. Perspective plans are also broad but indicate specific strategies and approaches to accomplish the missions.

4.3 Annual Plans

Annual plans are derived from perspective plans and are also based on priorities of the current year. Annual plans are prepared every year and are detail in nature. Yearly objectives, major actions, resources, responsibilities, time period for actions are clearly mentioned in these plans. The plan of the institution is then translated in departmental, team and individual plans. Apart form this programmes, projects are also planned to achieve new non-repetitive objectives. All concern individuals and teams participate in preparing annual plans. The head of the institution and governing teams validates these plans. Resources are committed to the plans by the management of the institution. These plans are prepared in detail to make implementation and monitoring easy. The performance of the institute is evaluated against these plans. These plans motivate people to put efforts to achieve the annual objectives and goals. People get rewards and recognition on the basis of achievements of annual objectives. Experiences gained during implementation of annual plans go as input for subsequent year plans.

5. Planning Model for Technical Institutions

The planning of technical institutions is carried out analyzing the external and internal environment. The planning is carried out participatively using various tools and techniques of educational management such as meetings, discussions, creativity sessions, panel discussions, force field analysis etc. Individuals, teams and stakeholders participate in the planning process of the institution. They express their views and ideas openly. The external and internal environment is analyzed on present parameters and future parameters. The output of external and internal environment analysis is expressed on parameters shown in exhibit 4.3.

Exhibit No. 4.3: Parameters for expressing output of external and internal environment analysis

➢ Future challenges in technical education system	➢ Aspirations of promoters and employees of the institution
➢ Competition with sister institutions	➢ Present and future opportunities for the institution
➢ Likely problems the institution is going to face	➢ Government policies related to industrialization, employment and technical education
➢ Emerging needs of the society and economy for technical manpower	➢ Major changes in functioning of the institution
➢ Shift or diversification required	

The outputs of the analysis of external and internal environment go as input to the process of crafting vision and mission statements of the institution. The process of crafting the vision and mission statements is shown in exhibit 4.4.

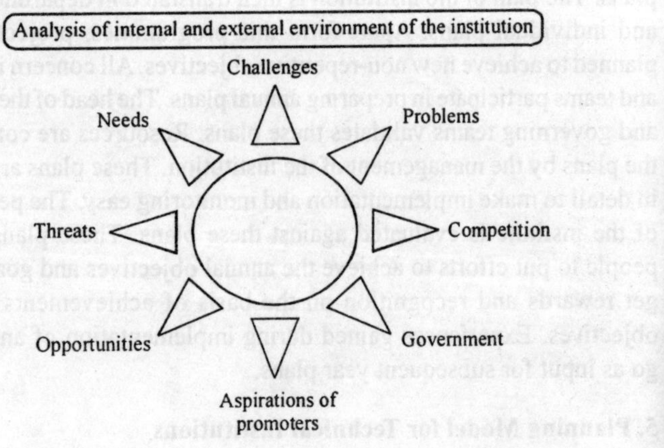

Exhibit No. 4.4: Planning model for technical institutions

All types of institutions irrespective of their size, age, and growth can use this model. The elements of the model are described in subsequent paragraphs.

5.1 Analysis of External Environment

Each institution is required to analyze the external environment in which it is functioning. The external environment is analyzed on various elements like social, economical, political, technological, educational, industrial etc. The present and near future environment can be easily forecasted and analyzed. Intention of government gets reflected in various policies like education policy, industrial policy, economic development trends in the country, and development thrusts. The political stability can also be analyzed on the basis of majority in the government and main issues before the nation. Inclination of the students towards technical education and specific disciplines can be identified through present expansion and employment in the market. The trends in expansion of industries and service sectors hint about expansion of education in specific area. The use of technology by society to make the life comfortable provides information for continuing education programmes and transfer of technology.

A stakeholders survey helps the institution to know the trends in various dimensions of development in external environment. Entrepreneurial opportunities are also expanding both in production as well as in service sector. The data collected through survey are analyzed and interpreted to know the challenges ahead, major issues in technical education, problems, opportunities, needs of the society, future trends, participation of women, needs of physically challenged students, paying capacity of the parents, availability of educational loans, technologies available for educational use, different government, semi-government and private grants and schemes available for the institution and students, training and employment opportunities available, favourable condition for starting own enterprise for passouts, developments in the field of educational technology, educational management, statutory provisions related to educational programmes, preferences and interest of students, opportunities for continuing education programmes, demands of the students for the new courses, competition from local and international institutions, opportunities to develop collaborative ventures for the growth of the institution, statutory requirements for technical institutions, other associated ventures like human resources development, continuing education programmes, coaching for competitive examination, hobby courses, instructional material development projects, organizing seminars. The analysis would exactly tell about the density of the technical institutions, potential competition and threat to them.

Number of tools and techniques are used for scanning the external environment. The commonly used techniques are SWOT analysis, competition analysis, 7S analysis, force field analysis, Pareto analysis, issue analysis, focus group discussions, creativity sessions, interviews, etc. These tools and techniques are briefly described in next chapter.

5.2 Analysis of Internal Environment

It is also necessary to analyze the internal environment of the institution. The analysis can be done on various parameters of input, processes and output of the institution. The analysis focuses on students-competence level of students seeking admission, level of understanding, quality and employability of passouts, their status and salary. Similarly it focuses on competence of faculty and staff, their experience, motivation level, capability and capacity to work in changing environment, effectiveness of leadership at all levels. Academic and supporting process – quality and relevance of curriculum, quality of academic activities, quality of supporting activities, financial status of the institution, adequacy of resources, effectiveness and efficiency of internal processes, values, norms and ethics prevalent in the institute, corporate reputation of the institution, net working of the institution with other institutions of repute and industries, quality of governance, faculty student ratio, management information system, institutional structure, style of decision-making etc. Analysis of institutional internal environment on such parameters would help to know the preferences of employees for various institutional programmes and potential programmes, their strengths and weaknesses.

Number of tools and techniques can be used for scanning the internal environment. The commonly used techniques are SWOT analysis, attitude survey, 7S analysis, force field analysis, Pareto analysis, problem analysis, alternative analysis, leadership style analysis, culture analysis, profile analysis, job satisfaction survey, training need analysis, efficiency analysis, stress analysis, etc. These tools and techniques are briefly described in next chapter.

The external and internal analysis of environment is a research work. It has to be carried out sincerely. Different types of research instruments are designed and used for scanning the environment. The research is conducted using instruments such as structured and semi-structured questionnaires, interview schedule, opinionnaire, observation schedule, attitude inventory, and points for focus group discussion. The standard instruments can be used or they can be adopted for the institution or new instruments can be designed. The instruments are designed for different stakeholders, which are based on the present and future stake between the institution and stakeholder. Suitable techniques are used to collect data from respondents. These instruments and techniques are used to collect significant, valid and reliable information. Instruments are designed in such a way so that they are easy to respond, consume less time and seek precious data.

Data are collected using variety of methods like mailing, personal contact, interview, observation and focus group discussion. If environmental scanning is being done for the first time observation of the functioning of the institution is also carried out on well-laid criteria. Data collected from various sources are combined, classified and interpreted to identify the strengths, weaknesses, opportunities, threats, problems, issues, crisis, values, ambitions of promoters and employees, competition, challenges and emerging needs of the institution. The commonly used techniques for data analysis are problem analysis, attitude analysis, force field analysis, Pareto analysis, alternative analysis, pie diagram, fish bone diagram, problem tree analysis diagram etc. These tools and techniques are briefly described in next chapter.

5.3 Visioning Process

On the basis of analysis of internal and external environment the vision of the institute is crafted. The analysis of environment would inspire promoters and leaders to craft an ambitious vision for the institute. It represents the broad future of the institution as shown in exhibit 4.1. It is the ultimate destination of the institution decided in the present. It acts as a guiding philosophy for the institution. Besides this the promoters and leaders of the institution initiate the process of visioning and it is carried out throughout the institution. Each and every member of the institution participates in the process of visioning. Creativity sessions are organized to craft the vision statement of the institution in small teams by resource persons. The process of visioning and ideas generated during various creativity sessions are listed. The list of ideas is given to a team of resource persons. The process of arriving at vision statement is shown in exhibit 4.5.

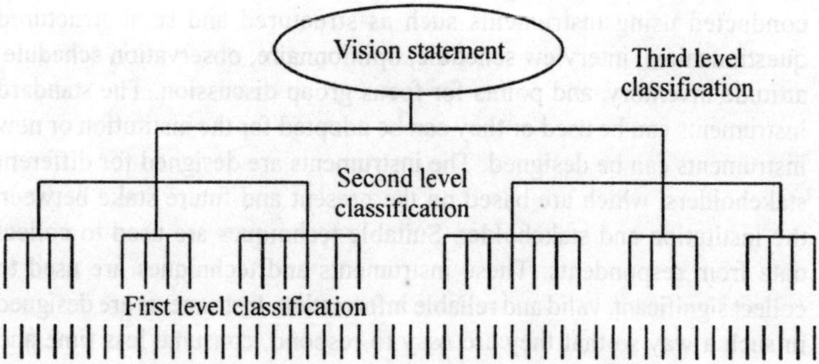

Exhibit No. 4.5: Process of crafting a vision statement from creative ideas

The resource person's team analyzes the ideas removing repetition of ideas and clubbing ideas of similar meaning together. They also segregate the ideas that represent strategy, problems, description of present situation, weaknesses, strengths, opportunities etc. The resource persons prepare a final list of ideas related to ultimate destination of the institution. Once the list is ready ideas are classified, given a broader term and put under a broader, deeper and comprehensive term. The hundreds of ideas generated during creativity sessions get reduce to less than twenty-five through first screening. Then second classification is carried out to put the terms again under further broader terms to reduce the number of terms. The third classification is carried out to put the terms under a broader term and there may be two to three terms. Finally, these ideas are put under single word or phrase, or sentence. This final statement is thought over and refined by the resource person's team and written in the form of vision statement. Then it is matched with the result of internal and external environment analysis. The vision statement is further fine turned in the light of results of external and internal analysis of the environment. It is discussed in the larger population of the institution. Ccmments of the institutional members and teams are received on it. Again based on the comments it is refined if necessary. Once the institution finalizes the vision statement it is taken to stakeholders for their comments and suggestions. Again the vision statement is reviewed in the light of comments received from the stakeholders. Finally, it is used as vision statement of the institution. The vision crafted for the institution is not permanent one enunciated for once. As the time passes say five or ten years and major changes takes place the vision is reviewed and refined if necessary.

For another set of institutions that is fairly grown and developed strengths, weaknesses, opportunities and threat analysis is carried out. On the basis of SWOT analysis the vision statement is derived. Some institutions are already having vision statement but it is not relevant in today's context, they review the vision in the light of the past performance and future ambitions. Then do issue analysis and value analysis to modify, refine or fine-tune the existing vision statement. The relationship between vision, missions, goals and different plans of the institution is shown in exhibit 4.6.

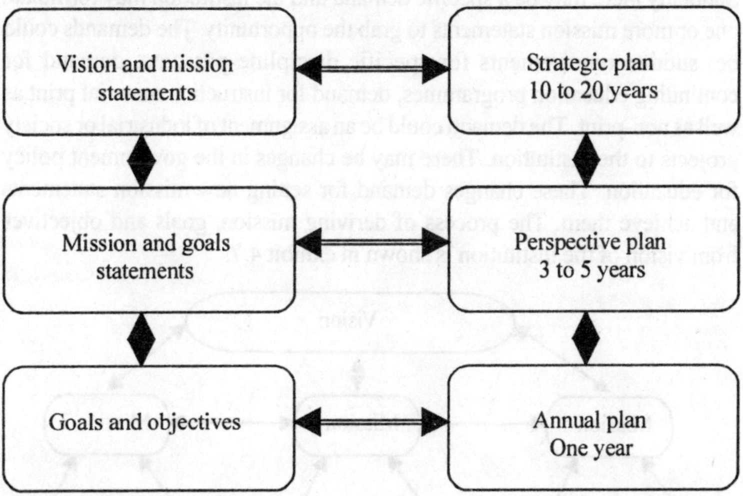

Exhibit No. 4.6: Relationship between vision, missions, goals and different types of plans

5.4 Mission Statements

Mission statements are derived from vision statements. Mission statements clearly define the long-term milestones. These are generic, broad and challenging. Mission statements starts with strong action oriented verbs. The mission statements are written in broad and comprehensive terms. Mission statements are written for three to five years. Mission statements are used to communicate the intermediate destinations in the journey to reach the vision of the institution. These statements are used to communicate the challenges ahead to inspire people to contribute. There could be more than one mission statement for a vision. The number of mission statements depends on the type of vision statement and time period to achieve it. It also depends on the current status of the institution. For newly established institution mission statements are more and logically derived from the vision statement. Old institution already having vision statement and mission statements are reviewed in the light of previously derived mission statements. If necessary they are fine-tuned, modified and new statements are added. The process of revision of mission statement is essentially adopted because major changes take place in internal and external environment. In some institutions internal changes take place considerably like a big lot of faculty and experienced staff members get retired, there is a change in the ownership of the institution. Suddenly there may be a specific demand and the institution may formulate one or more mission statements to grab the opportunity. The demands could be; sudden requirements for specific discipline passouts, demand for continuing education programmes, demand for instruction material print as well as non-print. The demand could be an assignment of industrial or society projects to the institution. There may be changes in the government policy for education. These changes demand for setting new mission statements and achieve them. The process of deriving mission, goals and objectives from vision of the institution is shown in exhibit 4.7.

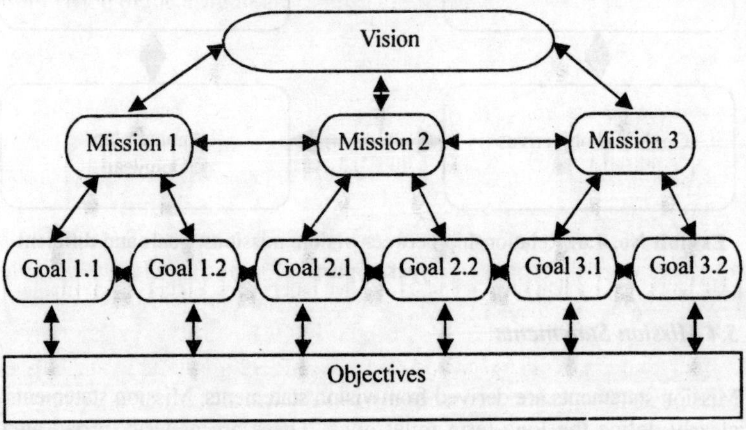

Exhibit No. 4.7: Process of deriving missions, goals and objectives from vision

5.5 Goals

Each mission statement is further described in specific, measurable, attainable, realistic and time bound goals. These goals can be written in academic, administrative, managerial and financial areas. One goal can contribute to achieve many missions or one mission may require more than one goals. Similarly one goal is accomplished achieving many objectives.

Goals can also be written in an integrated way it all depends on how the mission statement is written. Alternative methods to achieve the goal are identified and documented along with resources required. This document is called perspective plan. The perspective plan provides continuity in the process of planning. The team constituted by the governing body and head of the institution carries out the process of preparing perspective plan. This plan becomes the basis for annual planning. The process of deriving objectives from goal is described in exhibit 4.8.

Exhibit No. 4.8: Deriving objectives from annual goals

5.6 Objectives

Institution level annual plans are prepared in detail. The objectives for yearly plan emanate from the missions and goals of the institution. Previous years performance evaluation helps the process of objective setting for the current year. The objectives can be formulated in four major areas of functioning of the institution as shown in exhibit 4.8. The objectives for annual plan should have characteristics shown in exhibit 4.9.

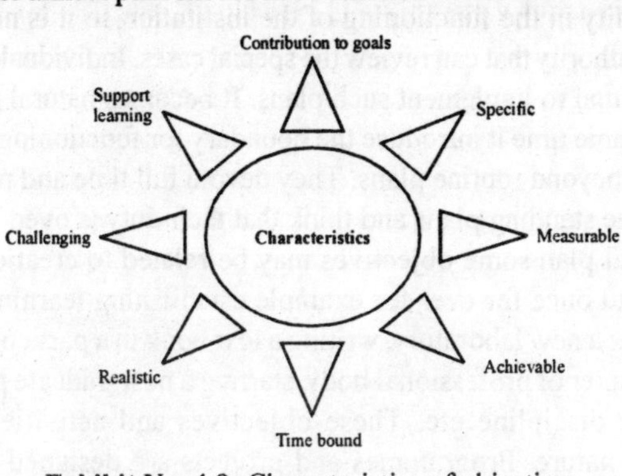

Exhibit No. 4.9: Characteristics of objectives

The annual plans are prepared in detail indicating major objectives to be achieved, activities to be carried out, resources required, responsibility for carrying out activities, time period required to carry out the activities, nature of collaboration required to carry out the activity etc. Activities are implemented to achieve the objectives. Alternatives are generated for objectives and major activities to achieve the goals and missions. The process of generating alternatives requires lot of valid and reliable information. Annual plans are prepared participatively so it requires effective communication in the institution. Head of the institution obtain commitment of individuals and teams to implement the plan. S/he discusses the potential problems with the institutional members. Head of the institution clarify the doubts, remove the apprehensions and answer the questions of institutional members. Leaders solve the conflict related to implementation of the plan. They periodically monitor the progress and solve problems. Leaders provide the resources in adequate quantity at right time. There are many objectives that are achieved every year to accomplish the goals and missions of the institution. These objectives and major activities are repetitive in nature, for example implementation of curriculum, assessment of students, record keeping, use of laboratories, library, workshop, learning resource center, hostel mess, giving rewards, training of faculty and staff members, purchasing, recruitment, hiring consultant, faculty members and staff members, placement of students in industry etc. To achieve repetitive type of objectives and implement major activities policies, processes and rules are framed and made public. These are called standing plans. These plans are refined and revised over a period of time. These standing plans are helpful in enhancing the effectiveness and efficiency to achieve the objectives. Standing plans enforce rigidity in the functioning of the institution so it is necessary to have some authority that can review the special cases. Individuals and teams become habitual to implement such plans. It becomes natural process for them at the same time it introduce the boundary for functioning also. They do not think beyond routine plans. They devote full time and resources to implement the standing plans and think that their duty is over.

In annual plan some objectives may be related to creation of some thing new and once for ever for example establishing learning resource center, setting a new laboratory, writing a text book in a particular subject, starting a chapter of professional body, starting a postgraduate programme in particular discipline etc. These objectives and activities are non-repetitive in nature. Programmes and projects are designed to achieve such objectives.

6. Strategies to Accomplish Vision and Missions of the Institution

It is very easy to craft the ambitious vision of the institution but without well-designed strategies it is futile exercise. Strategies are designed to accomplish the missions derived from the vision of the institution. They are designed to enable the institution with competitive advantage to achieve the vision. These strategies are designed on the basis of analysis of external and internal environment analysis. Strengths of the institution are grabbed in the strategies so that it can be easily implemented to accomplish the vision. Provisions to remove weaknesses of the institution are made in another set of strategies. The strategies should be distinctive than rest of the institutions. It should use all latest technology, techniques and resources to accomplish the mission. Strategies should focus on future developments. The vision, mission, and goals of the institution guide the formulation of strategies. Strategies are expressed in general terms. The leaders should be fast, innovative and creative thinkers to generate strategies. They should possess ability to quickly scan the environment and design appropriate strategies. The strategy should incorporate the requirements of students, provision to meet competition from other institution, and competencies of faculty and staff members. The focus of work should be clear in the mission and goals of the institution and strategies should address the same. The strategies should focus on major areas of functioning of institution. The major area is academics but what is major focus in academics that has to be addressed. The strategies should be new, different, unique, better than institution is using currently. Whether the institution will focus on formal programmes, continuing education programmes, distance learning programmes, online programmes, research studies or combination of these. Whether the institution wants to develop in particular disciplines of engineering and offer range of programmes right from certificate level to Ph.D. Degree programmes including consultancy and research in the chosen area. Whether it wants to focus on undergraduate programmes. Whether institution wants to work traditionally or wants to use high technology in all areas of functioning. Whether the institution will permanently employ faculty and staff members on the basis of tasks in hand or wants to use mix strategies i.e. permanent, temporary and outsourcing. Whether the institution will develop complete infrastructure or network and collaborate with sister institutions, industries and research organisations. Such issues are appropriately addressed in strategies. Faculty and staff members should be trained to implement the strategies. Their commitment should be obtained to implement the strategies. Well-designed strategies may be waste if not implemented in right spirit and integrated way.

Institutions can no longer afford to be static. The changing demands of employers and society demands for regular change in programmes of the institution. It also demands for major shift in functioning of the institution. The institution requires to be vigil to changes taking place in the employer market, society and technology. It should develop mechanism to diagnose such changes at early stage so that appropriate strategies are designed and implemented timely.

Once the nature of the stake and its intensity is clear the institution should design strategies to seek cooperation and favour of the stakeholder. If the stake is negative institution should design strategies to reduce the influence of the stakeholder. If the stake is competitive the institution should design strategies to meet the competition. The strategy design is based on the preferences of the stakeholders and their strategy also. The effective communication, negotiation, collaborations, networking, diversification, sharing the market, developing core competence, improving the quality of academics, value addition in the offering, marketing, publicity etc are the commonly used strategies to seek the cooperation of the stakeholders or reduce their negative influence.

7. Implementation of Strategy

Well-designed strategy may fail if it is not implemented effectively and efficiently. It is easy to design the strategy to satisfy the needs of the stakeholders. But it is very difficult to implement the strategy because people do not have competence, adequate resources, commitment, information, task, and role clarity, work overload, supportive policy, proper control points, and favourable atmosphere to implement it. Sometimes due to change in the internal or external environment, changes are required in the strategy, resources, time and competence of the implementers. People don't implement the strategies because of fear of failure or apprehension about adverse consequences. In some situations rewards associated to the achievement are not clear to them. The expectations of the stakeholders also vary frequently that is difficult to fulfil. One has to be in constant touch with the stakeholder to know their expectations and satisfy them legally.

8. Implementation of Plans

The procedure for formulating strategic, perspective and annual plan is discussed in preceding sections of this chapter. Formulating different types of plan is not enough. The head of the institution, different teams and individuals working as leader at different positions must ensure that the strategies are implemented effectively and efficiently. Implementation is related to doing things in right way. There is no use of well thought plans if they are not implemented properly. The detailed annual plan, Gantt chart, network diagram and budget are prepared for major activities. They are helpful to understand the implementation process. Well-designed processes are also used for implementation of plans. The implementation of plans depends on many factors as listed in the exhibit 4.10.

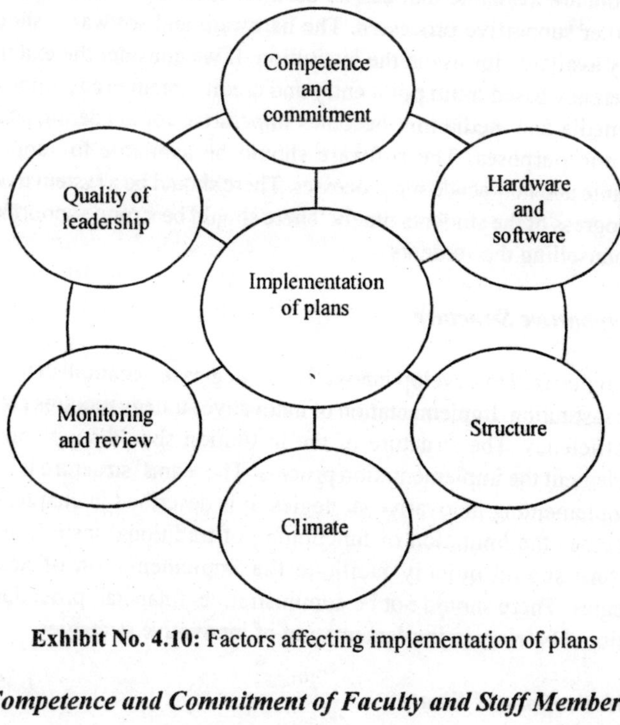

Exhibit No. 4.10: Factors affecting implementation of plans

8.1 Competence and Commitment of Faculty and Staff Members

The institution should have adequate, competent and committed employees to implement the plans. The competence of employees should be updated through continuous training and retraining. The institution should invest heavily on training of employees. There may be competent employees but they may not be committed to implement the changed plan. Their commitment to new plans may be low because of certain reasons. The incentive and reward policies should also match the effort of the people. For example the institution has decided to introduce competency-based curriculum that is based on multi point entry and credit system. Faculty and staff members are not trained to implement competency-based curriculum. They will perform traditionally and nothing better will come out rather it would be mess. Even if they are trained they should get some incentives for implementing it.

8.2 Availability of Hardware and Software

With the explosion of information technology and computers, numbers of media are available that can be used for teaching learning processes and other supportive processes. The hardware and softwares should be readily available for use in the institution. If we consider the example of competency based multi point entry and credit system programme use of multimedia and media mix becomes imperative for academic and non-academic purposes. The software should be available to support the academic and non-academic processes. There should be a system to inform the progress of the students timely. There should be strong support system for counselling the students.

8.3 Supportive Structure

It is emphasized to develop innovative strategies to accomplish the vision of the institution. Implementation of innovative strategy requires creativity and efficiency. The structure of the institution should supplement and complement the implementation process. The teams' structure is suitable for implementing innovative strategies. It is described in chapter one. It overcomes the limitation of functioning of traditional institutions. The structure should quickly facilitate the implementation of academic strategies. There should not be administrative, financial, procedural and functional barriers in implementation of innovative strategies.

8.4 Motivational Climate

The climate of the institution should be motivational to support the implementation of strategies. There should not be unnecessary leg pulling, conflict, criticism and doubts. Unhealthy practices and loose talk should be discouraged at every forum. The policies, norms, ethics, values and beliefs of the changed strategies should be made clear to all the employees of the institution.

8.5 Continuous Monitoring and Review

The annual plan is detailed plan. The plan indicates the checkpoints at the completion of significant activity. The implementers should develop monitoring indicators for check points and do continuous monitoring. If any deviation is noticed it should be corrected without wasting time. At the same time implementation problems should be solved. Continuous improvement tools and techniques should be used to enhance the effectiveness of the teaching learning processes.

8.6 Quality of Leadership

The leadership plays significant role in the implementation of the plans. People need some stimulus to initiate, carry out and monitor the progress. They need guidance, support and help. They expect some good words of encouragement, appreciation and recognition. They look forward to leaders for such charging behaviour. The leaders behaviour towards implementation of the plan makes the difference. S/he should act as catalyst.

9. Criteria for Evaluating the Effectiveness of a Plan

Plan is a foundation for effective implementation. If the plan is not effective its implementation may result in huge wastage of money, efforts and time. On finalization of plan its effectiveness should be evaluated then it should be put for implementation. The effectiveness of the plan is evaluated on numbers of criteria. The criteria for evaluating the plan are shown in exhibit 4.11. Each criterion is explained briefly in subsequent paragraphs.

9.1 Contribute to Vision of the Institute

Each plan should contribute to accomplishment of vision and mission of the institute. It should be comprehensive to cover the academic business of the institution rather than financial planning. The whole plan should focus on academics and other plans if any should supplement and complement it. The effectiveness of other plans such as building, laboratory, maintenance etc. should be measured on the basis of its direct contribution to academics of the institution.

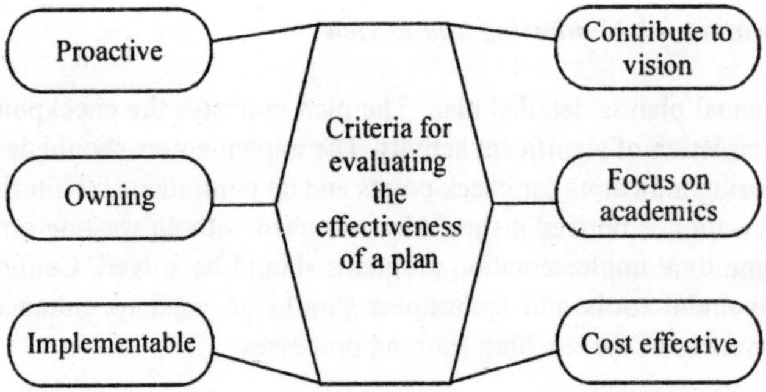

Exhibit No. 4.11: Criteria for evaluating the effectiveness of a plan

9.2 Focus of Academics

The plan should focus on core academic business of the institution. Institutions offering undergraduate programmes should have focus on enhancing teaching learning focus and other related academic activities. Institutions offering postgraduate programmes should have focus on research, innovation and development. They should concentrate on solving industrial problems and undertaking joint projects.

9.3 Cost Effective

The academic business of the institution should be cost effective. The institution should explore alternative means for carrying out the activities. There is no need to create all the facilities in the institution and have permanent staff for temporary work. The institutions should explore opportunities such as contracting, hiring, temporary appointment, redeployment, outsourcing, joint ventures and so on. The institution should also compare benefits and decide between long-term investment and short-term investment.

9.4 Implementable

The plan should be implementable. It should not be an unrealistic plan. People should have abilities and capabilities to implement the plan. It should be flexible enough to make necessary changes during implementation. People should know what is to be achieved and how it is to be achieved. The plan should provide continuity to future plans and there should not be dead ends in the plan.

9.5 Owning

All the plans are important so they need to be implemented at right time and in right way to produce expected results. People should own these plans for effective implementation. There should be individual and collective responsibility for planning and implementation of plans in the institution. People must know the consequences of implementation and non-implementation of plans. They should be empowered to design and implement the plan.

9.6 Proactive Planning

There is a need for proactive planning for growth and development of the institution. The plans should be prepared to grab the opportunity rather than waiting for the problem and solving it. The institution should use forecasting techniques to predict the technological developments, changes in economy, manpower requirements etc. and prepare plans accordingly.

You can use a detailed rating scale to evaluate the effectiveness of a plan of your institution. A rating scale for your ready reference is provided in exhibit 4.12. This rating scale can be modified or adopted as per specific requirements of the institution.

10. Summary

The planning process is carried out to decide the ultimate destination of the institution that is expressed in vision of the institution. To craft the vision of the institution external and internal environment is analyzed. The analysis of the environment is carried out using scientific technique and creativity methods. The missions, long-term and short-term goals are derived from the vision of the institution. To reach the vision alternative strategies are designed. It is ensured to design effective, efficient and productive strategies. Strategic, perspective, and annual plans are prepared in a participative way. Different resources are arranged and mobilized at right time to implement the activities to achieve objectives and goals. These objectives and goals directly contribute to enhance effectiveness and efficiency of teaching learning process. Strategic plan is broad, comprehensive and brief to accomplish vision and missions. Perspective plans address the missions and goals of the institution. These plans are more elaborative than strategic plan. Annual plans are prepared to accomplish short-term goals and objectives. These plans are shared with

Exhibit No. 4.12: Rating scale for evaluating the effectiveness of a plan

Sl. No.	*Criteria*	*Extent of fulfilment*			
		4	*3*	*2*	*1*
1.	Objectives and goals contribute to accomplish missions and vision				
2.	Focus on major issues of academics				
3.	Objectives and goals are measurable				
4.	Objectives and goals are challenging				
5.	Assumptions are clear and manageable				
6.	Alternatives explored and decisions are taken				
7.	Management tools and techniques are used in planning process				
8.	Views of people considered in the plans				
9.	Previous year plan implementation experiences used in planning				
10.	Plans focus on future development				
11.	Plans focus on continuous improvement				
12.	Plans are developed participatively				
13.	Plans are based on valid and reliable data				
14.	Plans are flexible				
15.	Plans are simple				
16.	Plans are cost effective				
17.	Plans are prepared timely				
18.	Contingency plan prepared				
19.	The effectiveness of the plan checked				
20.	Authority, responsibility and accountability decided				
21.	Implementation schedules prepared				
22.	Monitoring schedule prepared				
23.	Resources have been allocated to plans				
24.	Problem solving mechanism set up				
25.	Training imparted for new activities				

all the employees of the institution. These plans are flexible and integrated with each other. All the plans are reviewed on yearly and five yearly bases to make necessary modifications. Performance of the institution is evaluated against set of objectives and goals stated in the plan. Annual plan works as a base plan for individual and team planning.

11. Activity

Activity on Vision Document

Prepare the vision document of your institute following the model given in this chapter. The vision document should contain brief history, vision statement, mission statements, goals, values, vision reach strategies and SWOT analysis. You are already aware that to prepare the vision document number of techniques and methods are used. Looking to the growth level of your institution use appropriate methods and techniques.

Activity on Perspective Plan

Prepare the perspective plan of your institution. You are aware that perspective plans are prepared on the basis of strategic plans. These plans are prepared to accomplish the missions and goals of the institution. Perspective plans are prepared for a period of 3 to 5 years. Major goals and goal reach alternative strategies are identified and listed in the perspective plans. Major resources are allocated to implement the strategy. Time frame for achieving major goals is indicated clearly in the perspective plans. Strategies to build capacity and capability to implement the plan are also described briefly. Major changes in the structure and policy of the institution are addressed properly.

Activity on Annual Plan

Prepare an annual plan of your Institute on the basis of vision document, strategic plan, perspective plan and current priorities. You can use following format or any other suitable format.

Activity on Programme or Project Formulation

Identify the non-repetitive objectives in your annual plan and list them. Design a programme or project to achieve them. Similarly identify the areas of functioning of your institute that require formulation of standing plans, i.e. policy, possesses and rules. Formulate policies, design processes and frame set of rules for different areas of functioning of your institution.

Sl. No.	Area of functioning	Objectives	Activities	Duration		Resources	Responsibility	Funds
				From	To			
1.	**Academic programmes** New disciplines ➢ Diploma certificate ➢ Post-diploma ➢ Undergraduate ➢ Post-graduate ➢ Ph.D.							
	Revision of curriculum for programmes ➢ Diploma certificate ➢ Post-diploma ➢ Undergraduate ➢ Post-Graduate ➢ Ph.D.							
	Research studies and publications in the area of ➢ Technology ➢ Education ➢ Social development ➢ Human resources development ➢ Patents							

(Contd.)

Sl. No.	*Area of functioning*	*Objectives*	*Activities*	*Duration*		*Resources*	*Responsibility*	*Funds*
				From	*To*			
	Development of print and non-print material ➢ Multimedia learning packages ➢ Video programmes ➢ Power point presentations ➢ Photographic album ➢ Slides ➢ Transparencies ➢ Models ➢ Books ➢ Work books ➢ Teacher guide ➢ Journals ➢ Project guide ➢ Games ➢ Simulations ➢ Case studies							

(Contd.)

Sl. No.	*Area of functioning*	*Objectives*	*Activities*	*Duration*		*Resources*	*Responsibility*	*Funds*
				From	*To*			
	Organizing ➤ Seminars ➤ Conferences ➤ Symposiums ➤ Workshops ➤ Competitions ➤ Activities of professional body							
	Awareness programmes in schools							
	Training programmes for faculty							
	Training programmes for staff							
	Counselling sessions for students on ➤ Career ➤ Subject problem solving ➤ Personal problem solving							

(*Contd.*)

Sl. No.	*Area of functioning*	*Objectives*	*Activities*	*Duration*		*Resources*	*Responsibility*	*Funds*
				From	*To*			
2.	**Industry institution interaction**							
	Training of students							
	Training of teachers							
	Training of technical staff							
	Industrial visits							
	Industrial projects and problems							
	Research and innovation work for industry							
	Training programmes for industry personnel							
	Documentation of industrial processes, techniques working etc.							
	Testing							

(Contd.)

Sl. No.	*Area of functioning*	*Objectives*	*Activities*	*Duration*		*Resources*	*Responsibility*	*Funds*
				From	*To*			
	Calibration							
	Training material							
	Ancillary for industry							
	Engaging industry personnel in academic activities like: ➢ curriculum development, ➢ curriculum revision ➢ teaching learning, ➢ evaluation ➢ instructional material development ➢ seminar ➢ conferences ➢ developmental activities ➢ modernization of laboratories ➢ campus interview ➢ research studies etc.							

(*Contd.*)

Sl. No.	Area of functioning	Objectives	Activities	Duration		Resources	Responsibility	Funds
				From	To			
3.	**Collaboration with sister institutions and research organisations**							
	Faculty exchange							
	Invitation to expert faculty							
	Instructional material development							
	Seminars							
	Conferences							
	Symposium							
	Workshops							
	Interaction of students							
	Extending use of ➢ library ➢ learning resource centre workshops ➢ laboratories ➢ other facilities ➢ industrial projects ➢ placement							

(Contd.)

Sl. No.	*Area of functioning*	*Objectives*	*Activities*	*Duration*		*Resources*	*Responsibility*	*Funds*
				From	*To*			
4.	**Continuing education programmes**							
	Organizing training programmes for faculty and staff members							
5.	**Infrastructure development**							
	Classroom							
	Laboratories							
	Library							
	Learning resource centre							
	Amenities for staff							
	Amenities for students							
	Amenities for guests							
	Auditorium							
	Renovation							

(Contd.)

Sl. No.	*Area of functioning*	*Objectives*	*Activities*	*Duration*		*Resources*	*Responsibility*	*Funds*
				From	*To*			
6.	**Social development**							
	Participatory rural appraisal for villages							
	Socio-economic project development							
	Awareness programmes on ➢ environment ➢ health ➢ sanitation ➢ water conservation ➢ social evils							
	Transfer of technology							
	Assistance to use technology							
	Skill development training programmes							

(*Contd.*)

Sl. No.	*Area of functioning*	*Objectives*	*Activities*	*Duration*		*Resources*	*Responsibility*	*Funds*
				From	*To*			
	Assistance in establishing micro enterprises							
	Assistance to sick rural industries							
	Training and help to women							
	Training and help to physically challenged people							
	Value addition projects							
	Market research							
	Finance							
	Revenue generation							
	Loans							
	Donations							

(Contd.)

Sl. No.	*Area of functioning*	*Objectives*	*Activities*	*Duration*		*Resources*	*Responsibility*	*Funds*
				From	*To*			
	Functioning of the institution							
	Policies							
	Rules and regulations							
	Management information system							
	Institution profile							
	Faculty profile							
	Involvement of stakeholders in the governance and management of the institution							

REFERENCES

Geof Cox (1995). *Solve that Problem*, Pitman Publishing, London.

Geoffrey Petty (1998). *Creativity*, Kogan Page India Private Limited, New Delhi.

Gerald F. Smith (1998). *Quality Problem Solving*, Prentice Hall of India Pvt., Ltd., New Delhi.

H.B. Karp (1996). *The Change Leader*, Jossey-Bass, Pfeiffer, San Francisco.

Leon C. Megginson Donald C. Mosley Paul H. Pietri, Jr. (1989). *Management, Concepts and Applications*, Harper & Row Publishers, New York.

Paul M. Elkin (2003). *Mastering Business Planning and Strategies*, Viva Books Private Limited, New Delhi.

Steve Smith (1999). *Solve that Problem*, Kogan Page India Private Limited, New Delhi.

Stephen C. Harper (1994). *Managing Growth in Your Emerging Business*, McGraw Hills Inc., New Delhi.

5

Management Tools and Techniques

Objectives: The readers will be able to:

1. State the importance of use of management tools and techniques.
2. List the tools and techniques used for management of the institution.
3. List the purpose and use of tools and techniques in management of the institution.
4. Describe the use of various management tools and techniques in performing various management functions.
5. Compare the strengths and limitations of various management tools and techniques.

1. Introduction

Governance and management of technical institutions is a science and art also. Numbers of concepts, theories, models, principles and propositions are used in governance and management of the institution. There are numerous management functions and activities performed by an institution to satisfy the needs of the students and society. At the same time it has to grow and develop to achieve excellence in the technical education system. A wide range of tools and techniques is available to make the management of institution simple, purposeful and effective. These tools and techniques are versatile and can be used innovatively for specific purpose. Each tool can be used for more than one functions of management. At the same time more than one tool can be used for one management function. Each tool and technique has strengths and limitations. The user should have ability to select appropriate tool or technique for a specific purpose.

2. Purpose of Management Tools and Techniques

Use of appropriate tools and techniques enhance the effectiveness and efficiency of management processes tremendously. They save time in understanding the complex things because of graphical representation or projection of data in a meaningful manner. They help in understanding whole picture at the same time inter-relation between parts. They serve as a tool for effective communication. They are used to reduce confusion, conflict, ambiguity, resistance, problems, crisis, wastage and so on. At the same time they enhance the effectiveness of planning, decision-making, problem solving, monitoring, analysis, communication, influencing, participation and innovations. They serve the purposes listed in exhibit 5.1.

Exhibit No. 5.1: Purposes of management tools and techniques

Planning ➢ Need analysis ➢ Prioritization ➢ Deciding the data to be collected ➢ Idea generation ➢ Data collection process ➢ Data classification ➢ Data presentation ➢ Forecasting ➢ Analysis ➢ Projecting picture ➢ Benchmarking **Decision-making and Problem Solving** ➢ Defining the problem ➢ Problem analysis ➢ Prioritization	➢ Risk assessment ➢ Exploring alternatives ➢ Action planning **Monitoring** ➢ Generating monitoring indicators ➢ Monitoring and review ➢ Controlling ➢ Problem solving **Evaluation** ➢ Evaluation of plan ➢ Success analysis **Participation** ➢ Seeking consensus ➢ Seeking commitment ➢ Analysis of resistance to change

3. Management Tools and Techniques

Various tools and techniques are used to discharge management functions. A brief description of these tools and techniques is given in subsequent paragraphs. Use of these tools and techniques help the people involved in the process of governance and management of the institution to better understand the present, future and bridge the gap.

3.1 SWOT Analysis

SWOT is an acronym used for strengths, weaknesses, opportunities and threats. It is scientific method used for analyzing the internal and external environment of the institution. Strengths and weaknesses are identified scanning the internal environment of the institute. Strengths and weakness are identified on various parameters of institutional functioning. The strengths and weakness can be identified on inputs, processes and outputs. It can be identified on major areas of functioning of the institution, like academic, administrative, managerial and financial. It can be identified on availability and utilization of all types of resources. Resource persons decide the approach to be used for SWOT analysis considering the purpose of SWOT analysis. Information is collected from faculty members, staff members, students and stakeholders to identify the strengths and weaknesses. Similarly scanning of the external environment of the institution is carried out to identify the opportunities and threats. Opportunities and threats are identified on various areas of functioning of the institution as it is done in internal scanning of the environment. The information is collected from major stakeholders, like government representatives, industries, employers, potential students, parents, professional bodies, statutory body, passouts, alumni etc.

The information collected is classified, analyzed and interpreted to know the major strengths, weaknesses, opportunities and threats. Based on the SWOT of the institution strategies are designed to accomplish the long-term and short-term goals of the institution. SWOT analysis of the institution should be carried out every year to provide inputs to planning process. It helps in making the choices and taking the decisions. The management can keep close watch on changes taking place in the environment. The understanding of environment changes helps in making safe adjustments in the plans of the institution. It is a tool that equips the management to successfully deal with future challenges, problems and competitions. Variety of tools are designed and used to collect the valid and reliable information. Commonly used tools are structured questionnaire, semi-structured questionnaire, interview schedule, points for focus group discussion, themes for creativity sessions etc. Commonly used techniques are creativity techniques, discussions, observation, interview, mailing the questionnaire, telephonic interviews, e-mail, on-line response, document analysis etc. The SWOT analysis of one institution is given in exhibit 5.2.

Exhibit No. 5.2: SWOT analysis of one technical institution

Areas of functioning	*Strengths*	*Weaknesses*
1	2	3
Academics	Highly qualified and experienced faculty 30 per cent more than required academic as well as non-academic facilities Undergraduate passouts are well placed	Faculty and staff not trained to perform academic and non-academic activities professionally Rigid curriculum Work to rule Research, continuing education programmes, community development activities, innovations and networking totally absent No support scheme for needy students
Managerial	All the posts are filled up	No vision and strategic direction Bureaucratic way of working Weak leadership at all levels
Administrative	Routine work is carried out satisfactorily	80 per cent surplus non-academic staff Faculty and staff work in their own way and live very comfortable life (50 percent underutilized) *Adhoc* and causal way of working
Financial	More than required grant is available from Central and State Government	Poor utilization (Infrastructure 80 per cent, Equipment 90 per cent, Finance 40 per cent) of all types of resources No revenue generation activities No incentive scheme for excellent performance

(*Contd.*)

Areas of functioning	*Opportunities*	*Threats*
1	3	4
Academics	Ample opportunity for Post-graduate and Ph.D. programmes (in six disciplines) Continuing education programmes (50 programmes of one week duration) Undertaking research work (5 in each discipline every year) Community development activities-(20 days in a year) Instructional material development (multimedia packages 10 every year) Industrial project (10 every year) Multinational companies are looking for competent passouts Greater autonomy Flexible programmes	Private institutions are coming up very fast Need of passouts in new disciplines changing very fast Statutory provisions are changing very fast International institutions are entering in the competition
Managerial	Strategic planning Rigorous training and development at all levels System design and processes reengineering If necessary employ new leaders	Professional faculty may be employed by the private institutions
Administrative	Professional people need to be employed Effective and efficient processes to support academics	Political interferences
Financial	Increase in students fee Development of corpus fund Internal revenue generation (Rs. 20 million per year) Collaboration with other institution	Gradual withdrawal of Government support Less admission due to competition

3.2 Issue analysis

Issue analysis is a technique used to define the core and major area of growth and development of the institution. The issues are defined in present context and near future demand of the environment. Issue analysis is a useful technique to craft the vision, decide the mission, formulate alternative goals, objectives and strategies. Some of the issues related to technical institutions are listed in exhibit 5.3. Individual institutions find out issues related to their institution and analyze it. Tree analysis, flow chart and cause and effect diagrams are commonly used for issue analysis. Creativity techniques and document analysis support the issue analysis process.

Exhibit No. 5.3: Significant issues for technical institution

Market ➢ To fulfil the needs of multi-national companies or national companies ➢ To develop entrepreneurs or employable people ➢ To focus on conventional disciplines or shift in emerging and new disciplines ➢ To go for new markets with slide change in existing business	**Finance** ➢ To depend on the government funding or generate its own source of income ➢ To go for revenue generation or depend on fees ➢ To invest in the faculty and staff or hire the expertise ➢ To go for major quality improvement programmes or move ahead with maintaining the quality
Core Business ➢ To offer educational programmes or enter in technological research and development area ➢ To offer regular campus programmes or reach out through distance and on-line mode ➢ To cater the needs of same target group or explore different target groups	**Functioning** ➢ To collaborate with the sister institutions, research institutions, foreign institution or function independently ➢ To modify curriculum or make it competency based and flexible ➢ To conduct programmes for unorganized sector or formal sector

3.3 Competition Mapping

Competition mapping is a technique used to analyze the competition. The original technique was developed by Michael Porter to understand the competition and design cope up strategies. At the same time competitive strategies are designed to harness the potential of the institution. One can design different, unique and better strategies to gain competitive advantage. This difference can be introduced in terms of quality of passouts, teaching learning processes, more amenities to students, better incentives to teachers, comparatively less fees etc. The institution can also develop core competence in one or two areas of functioning. The institution can also collaborate with competitors. The institution prepares strong base and academic image to minimize the threat from new institutions. There are many new programmes designed and introduced by non-engineering institutions such as Master in Computer Application, Bachelor of Science, Master of Science and Integrated Programmes. These programmes may be a threat for the engineering institutions. Engineering institutions should continuously diagnose the need of such programmes and build capacity to start the parallel programmes that are in demand. Institution should design strategies to move out and approach the schools and parents to market its services and products. Institution should design strategies to build relationship and market their passouts to major employers. The intensity and focus of the institution should be greater, deeper and unique than their competitors.

3.4 Creativity Process

Creativity and innovation have become need of the day. As mentioned earlier institutions need to be unique, different and innovative in its products, services and functioning. Creativity is required at every moment of time in the institution. It is useful in issue analysis, problem solving, quality improvement, process design, teaching learning, curriculum design, marketing the services and product of the institution. Use of creativity for crafting the vision of the institution, mission statements, goals, strategies, plans, procedures, problem solving, decision-making is very common in a professional institution. It provides competitive edge to the institution in its functioning. Innovations and changes cannot be designed without creativity. There are number of creativity techniques that can be used by institutions for various purposes. In each creativity technique two steps are predominantly used. First is idea generation and second is idea analysis. Idea generation is important and significant step in creativity. The uniqueness of the idea lies in effectiveness of this step. Psychologists, sociologists, technologists and management experts have developed individual and group creativity methods for wide applicability. All the methods focus on generating creative ideas.

Right from childhood, people work under family norms, social norms, rules, regulations, laws and religion. They are taught not to be creative. At the same time for the growth and development of the individuals and institutions creativity is necessary to differentiate them from others. This uniqueness can only be achieved by implementing creative ideas. All creativity techniques focus on creating conducive environment to generate creative ideas. Once the creative ideas are generated they are analyzed with a purpose for implementation. The second step to creativity is analysis. The analysis of ideas is based on some criteria that are limitations of the institution under which it will implement the ideas. The limitations are expressed in terms of criteria and each idea is evaluated against the listed criteria. The process of creativity is shown in exhibit 5.4.

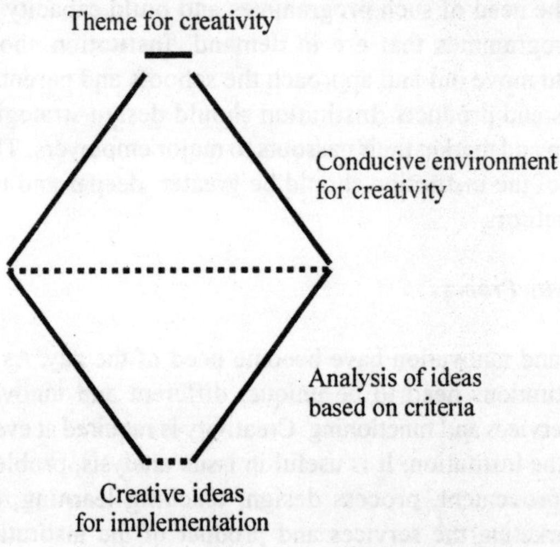

Exhibit No. 5.4: Creativity process

To generate favourable environment for creativity following creativity brain storming, nominal group technique and mind mapping methods are used in technical institutions.

3.5 Brainstorming

It is a group creativity method often used to unleash the creative side of the work. It helps to explain the situation or problem in more imaginative and untraditional way. It is a commonly used creativity method in a group. It helps to create conducive environment to generate as many ideas as possible. In conducive environment people forget to apply their logic to ideas being generated. The brain storming session is organized in five steps. The team leader brings in the notice of the team that:

- a problem is to be worked out
- a decision is to be made
- a change is to be designed
- a commitment is to be obtained
- a theme is to be elaborated
- an innovation is to be designed
- a consensus is to be made

The leader invites team members and explains clearly the theme of the brainstorming. The theme can be written in question form or statement form. The theme should be clear, easy to understand and require creative solutions. Then s/he explains the rules for brainstorming to team members. The rules are; only idea generation, no criticism or evaluation of idea, no discussion or cross communication, diverse ideas are welcomed, listing and projection of ideas, other's ideas can be used to generate new ideas.

The brain storming session starts with welcome statement of the leader. Team members freely generate ideas and they are recorded as stated. The session continues till last idea is recorded. The leader picks up each idea and clarifies it. S/he combines similar ideas. S/he also rephrases the ideas to give better meaning. A list of ideas is finalized. Then in a small team criteria are decided to evaluate the idea for acceptance and implementation. Each idea is evaluated against decided criteria and decisions are taken to accept or discard the idea. Finally, a list of workable ideas is prepared and communicated for implementation to team members. The major steps of brainstorming are summarized in exhibit 5.5.

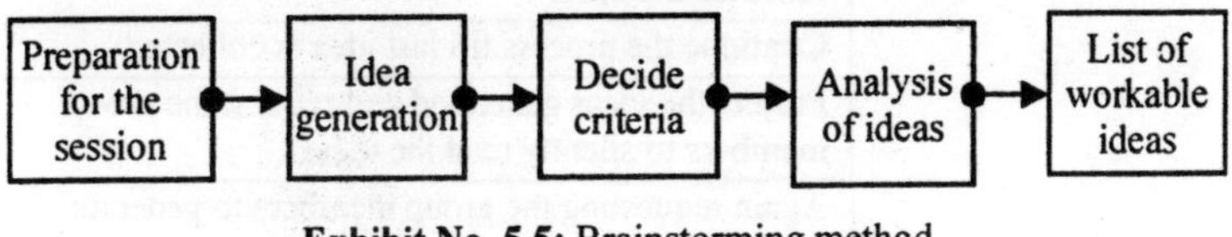

Exhibit No. 5.5: Brainstorming method

3.6 Nominal Group Technique

Nominal group technique (NGT) is a group creativity technique to generate creative ideas with a purpose. These ideas are generated to solve the problem, design the innovations, prepare plan, take the decision, involve people in the functioning of the institution. In the process of NGT 5 to 10 members are invited to generate ideas on a theme. These people are chosen from various areas of functioning of the institution. A trained resource person carries out the NGT session. The scriber assists the resource person to record the ideas. The steps of NGT process are described in exhibit 5.6.

Exhibit No. 5.6: Steps of nominal group technique

Major steps for conducting NGT	Activities and resources
Preparation for NGT session	Comfortable sitting arrangement in U shape for 5 to 10 persons
	White Board, Drawing sheet, Flip Chart, Overhead Projection facility, or Power point presentation facility
	Writing pad and pen for participants
	Welcome of the participants
	Purpose and topic of NGT session
	Explain rules of NGT–Silent generation and noting of ideas individually, writing ideas in words or phrase or small sentences, no cross communication, no criticism, no evaluation of idea in the mind
Idea generation	Present the well defined theme
	Promote idea generation environment
	Silent generation of ideas
	Listing of ideas without evaluation
Recording of ideas	Collecting one idea from each member serially
	Recording the ideas serially with modification to give it broader meaning on white board or on other resource available
	Continue the process till last idea is collected
	Project the ideas generated and request the group members to silently read the ideas
	Again requesting the group members to generate new ideas
	Collecting and recording the ideas serially
	Repeat the process again

(Contd.)

(*Contd.*)

	After three or four rounds of NGT club and combine the similar ideas
	Prepare a final list of ideas
Discussion on ideas	Clarify the idea
	Modify it to give it a meaning
	Combine similar ideas
Generate criteria and apply criteria	Generate criteria to evaluate ideas or prioritize ideas. These criteria may be relevance, time, money, resources, acceptability etc.
	Evaluate each idea on criteria to accept or reject or prioritize
	Finalize the list of accepted ideas and have a discussion on it to further clarify
	Seek consensus of members
	Implement ideas

There are number of benefits of NGT method. The benefits are opportunity for equal participation, avoidance of interruption, adequate time, depersonalization of idea, no conflict, synergy, clarity on ideas, argument and finalization of idea.

3.7 Mind Mapping

Mind mapping is a creativity method that can be used individually or in a group. The mind mapping is used to solve complex problem, design new innovations, design curriculum, design training plan of faculty and staff, marketing strategy etc. Mind map helps to generate ideas on all connected dimensions of a situation. It helps to complete the logic. The relationship among different significant elements can be shown. The importance of the dimensions of the situation can be shown using the colours in the mind map. The holistic version of the situation can easily be communicated to many people to comment, commit and implement. The mind mapping work can be done on a big drawing sheet using pencil and eraser. The mind mapping should be done without interruption and in one sitting only. The mind mapping for training is shown in exhibit 5.7.

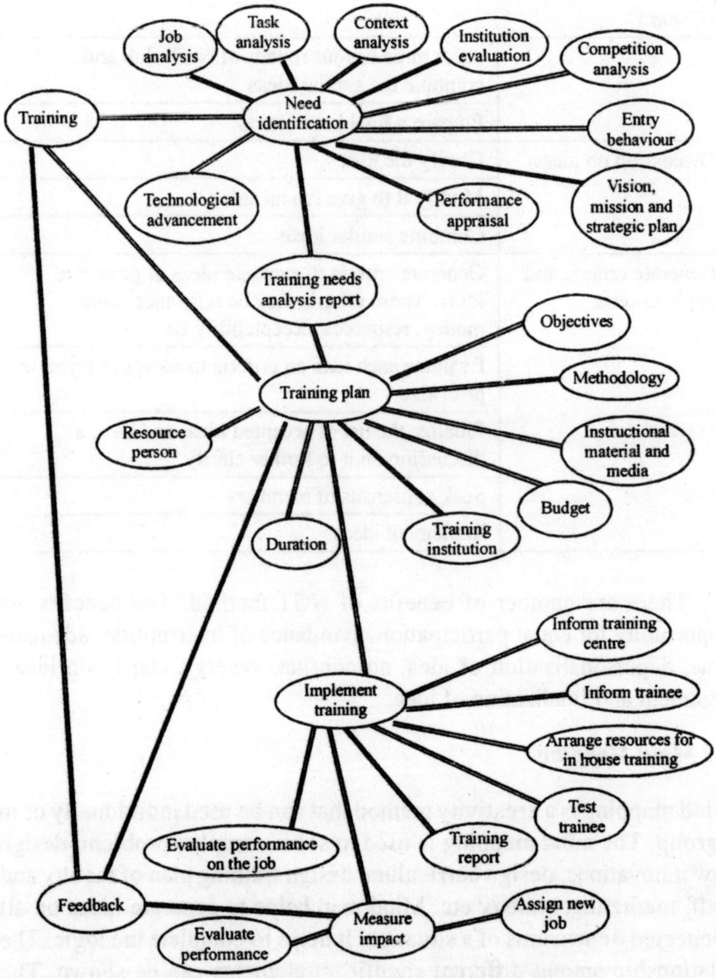

Exhibit No. 5.7: Mind mapping for training

3.8 Focus Group Discussion

It is a method to collect and validate data from representative respondents and significant persons. This technique is used to investigate the complex problem or to design something new. In identifying opportunities and threat focus group discussion of significant stakeholders can be organized to collect valid and reliable information. This method is also useful for policy formulation, strategic planning, training need identification, curriculum design, process design, reducing wastage, quality improvement, employment of passouts, identification of needs of industries and client. The steps of focus group discussion are shown in exhibit 5.8.

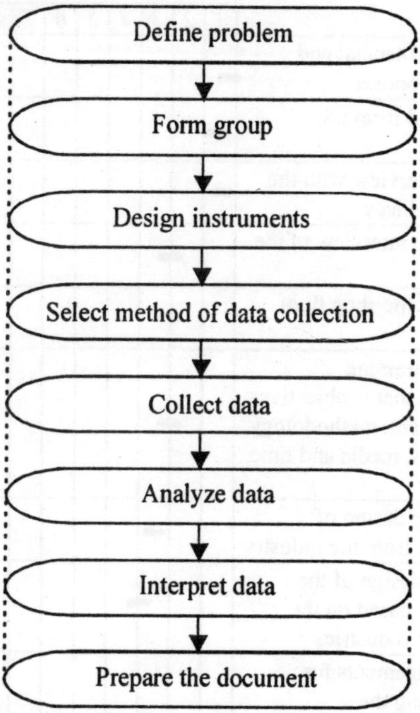

Exhibit No. 5.8: Steps of focus group discussions

3.9 Gantt Chart

The strategies to achieve objectives are detailed out in annual plans of the institution. Apart from routine activities of the institution there are non-routine objectives or activities. These objectives are achieved through a project. The project activities are detailed out and put on a time frame. The Gantt chart is used for implementation, monitoring and completion of activities. It helps in deploying the resources at right time thereby saving the wastage of resources. The progress of work can be monitored and reviewed on time scale. A Gantt chart for conducting one-week continuing education programme for industry personnel is shown in exhibit 5.9. The industry has requested the institution to conduct 20 programmes in a year for one-week duration in the evening.

Exhibit No. 5.9: Gantt chart for conducting one-week training programme for industry personnel

Sl. No.	*Activities*	*Months*											
		1	*2*	*3*	*4*	*5*	*6*	*7*	*8*	*9*	*10*	*11*	*12*
1.	Design the financial and technical proposal	—											
2.	Get approval from the industry	—											
3.	Conduct interview with the potential trainees	—											
4.	Conduct the interview of the manager			—									
5.	Understand the shop floor problem			—									
6.	Design the training programme that is objectives, course content, methodology, assignments, media and time frame			—									
7.	Validate the design of programme from the industry			—									
8.	Refine the design of the programme based on the feedback of industries				—								
9.	Make arrangements for implementing the programmes that are, classroom, projector, discussion room, etc.				—								
10.	Intimate the schedule of the programme to industry and potential trainees				—								
11.	Conduct programmes				—	—	—	—	—	—	—	—	
12.	Take intermediate feedback and refine the programme conduction					—	—	—	—	—	—	—	—
13.	Prepare the completion report												—

3.10 Cause and Effect Diagram

Cause and effect diagram or Ishikawa diagram is used to present the analysis of complex problems. It helps to break the problem into main categories of causes. Cause and effect diagram is used to analyze the situation, complex problem, challenges, crisis and competition. To analyze a problem likely causes are generated using creativity techniques. Information on causes is also collected using data collection techniques. The likely causes are classified under main categories like man, material, machine, minute, maintenance, and money. Causes of academic problems can be classified on students, teachers, curriculum, instructional material, time and money. The nature of the problem or situation and generated likely causes also give hint about classification of causes. The classified causes are listed on the diagram as shown in exhibit 5.10. Similarly solution diagram can be prepared on the basis of cause and effect diagram under same classification of analysis. The cause and effect diagram is also called fish bone diagram. It is a participative process of analyzing the situation or problem and generating solutions. The output of the process is analysis of the problem and its solution. This diagram is used to communicate effectively the solution of the problem and the action to be taken. This technique can be used individually as well as in the group. The fish bone diagram for absenteeism problem is shown in exhibit 5.10.

3.11 Problem Tree Analysis

It is a technique used to analyze the causes of a problem. The likely causes of the problem are listed using creativity technique. The relevant information is also collected and written on post it slips. After listing all the likely causes the focal problem is listed in the center and slips of causes are pasted below it. The causes identified may not be a cause but it may be the effect and the cause of it may be different. So the related slips are pasted beneath one another using the logic. If the root cause is not identified during the process of creativity it can be generated using the logic. All the slips are arranged in a logical order under different categories till the root cause in each category is identified. It is said that if root cause of the problem is treated it requires minimum efforts, resources, time and money. Remaining slips may be related to effect. The slips related to effect of the problem are pasted above the problem. Using the logic the order of effect is completed to know the ultimate effect of the problem. This problem analysis tree helps in setting the objectives to solve the problem. It is helpful in generating the alternatives and taking the effective decisions. This technique can be used individually as well as in groups. The problem tree analysis for poor results of students is shown in exhibit 5.11.

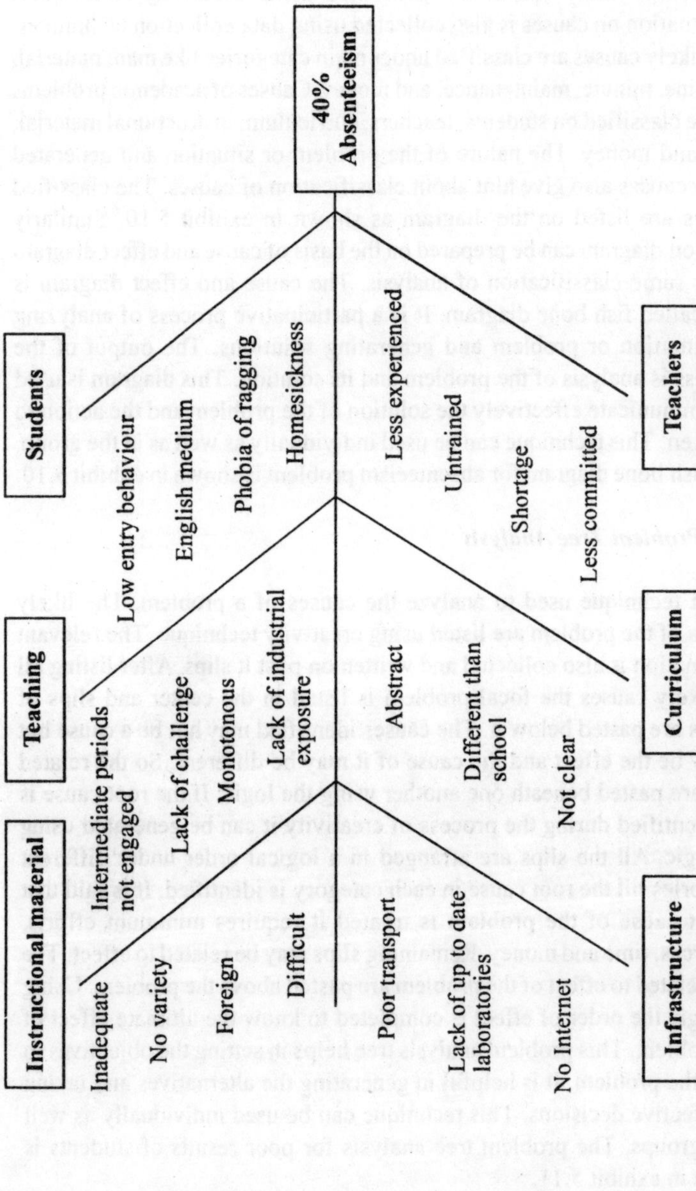

Exhibit No. 5.10: Cause and effect diagram on absenteeism of students in the institution

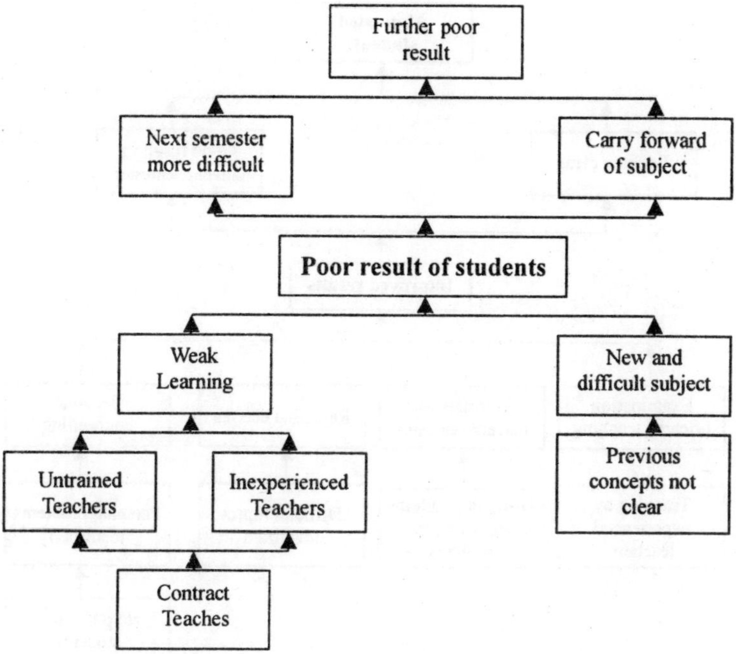

Exhibit No. 5.11: Problem tree analysis for poor results

3.12 Alternative Analysis

Alternative analysis technique is used to find the alternative solutions to a problem. It is also used to explore alternatives for achieving goals in a given situation. If the solutions are generated for a problem, the problem tree analysis is used to generate the alternative solution for the root cause of the problem. Alternatives are generated in two types of situations. In first situation a problem persist and alternatives are generated to minimize the effect of the problem that has already made some damage. In second type of situation no problem persists but alternatives are generated so that problem does not occur. The alternative tree analysis to 'poor result' problem is given in exhibit 5.12.

3.13 Pareto Analysis

It is a technique propagated by Count Vilfedo Pareto. Pareto principle states that most of the effect is accounted for by a few of the causes, is

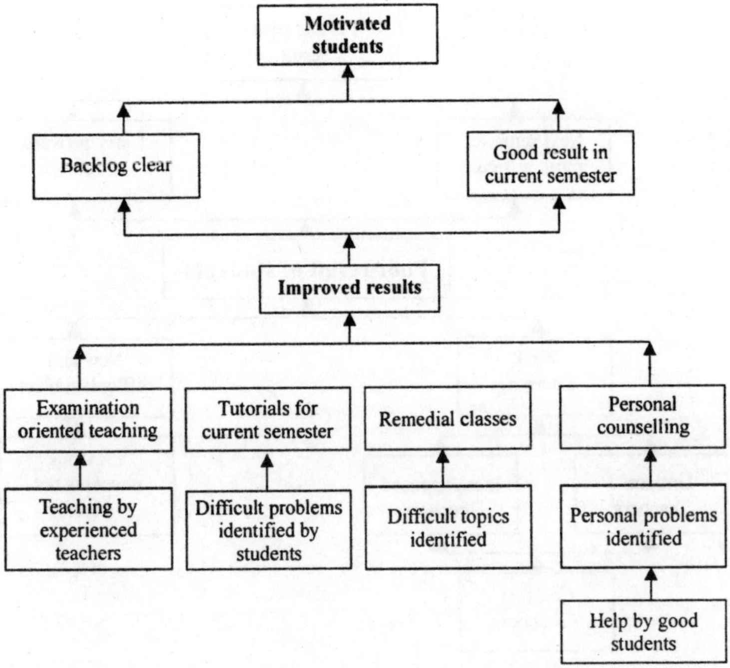

Exhibit No. 5.12: Alternative analysis tree for 'poor result problem'

found to be true in all situations. It is also known as 80/20 rule. Pareto analysis helps us to segregate important few from trivial many. There could be many objectives to be achieved in a year. But amongst these all may not have equal importance on academic performance of the institution. Pareto analysis helps us to segregate the important objectives. Then, importance of the objectives can easily be emphasized and communicated to the persons responsible to achieve it. People who contribute or support the process of achieving the objectives are well aware about the importance of the objectives. Pareto analysis is a versatile technique to isolate important things from trivial. This principle is applicable in situations where prioritization is required such as factors affecting the situation, separating the most contributing causes to a problem from least contributing, deciding the priority among objectives. One can work on significant factors, causes, objectives and achieve more impact in spite of working equally on all. The graphical representation of Pareto analysis on causes of absenteeism is shown in exhibit 5.13.

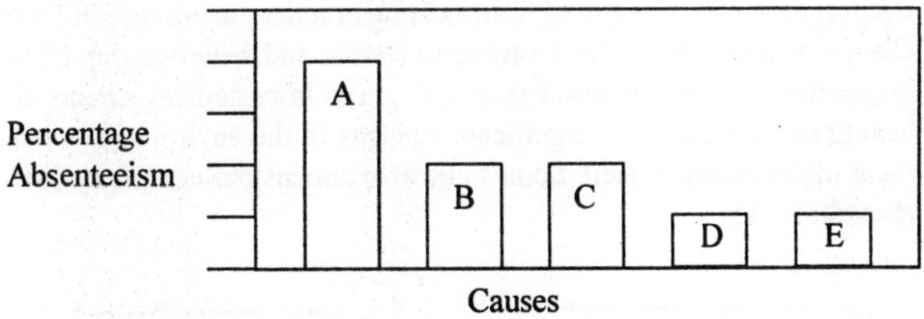

Exhibit No. 5.13: Pareto analysis on causes of absenteeism

3.14 Analysis on 7S

McKinsey '7S' model is used for assessing the readiness of the institution for growth and development. In McKinsey 7S model strategy and shared values indicate that both should be aligned to accomplish the vision, missions and goals of the institution. Institution should mobilize the full potential to inculcate the values in institutional members and implement the strategies. The current values and strategies can be assessed and the desired shift can be found out. The gap between the current and desired will decide the level of efforts required. Rest of the 5S that is style, staff, structure, system and skills should support the shared values and strategies. The analysis of the institution on 7S helps to understand the current weaknesses and shift required. It helps in strategy design to implement the shift. The 7S model is shown in exhibit 5.14.

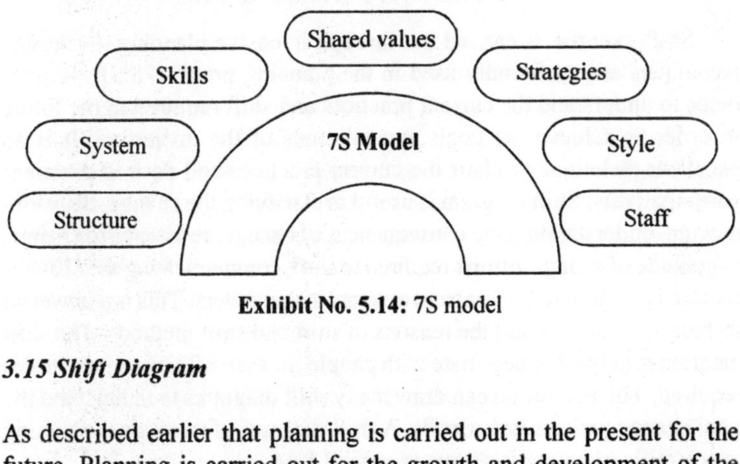

Exhibit No. 5.14: 7S model

3.15 Shift Diagram

As described earlier that planning is carried out in the present for the future. Planning is carried out for the growth and development of the institution. A shift is required from existing practices in order to fulfil the changing demands of the customers, clients and beneficiaries of the institution. In some situation shift is required in customers, clients and beneficiaries because of significant changes in the environment or the focus of the business itself. Some indicative dimensions of shift are listed in exhibit 5.15.

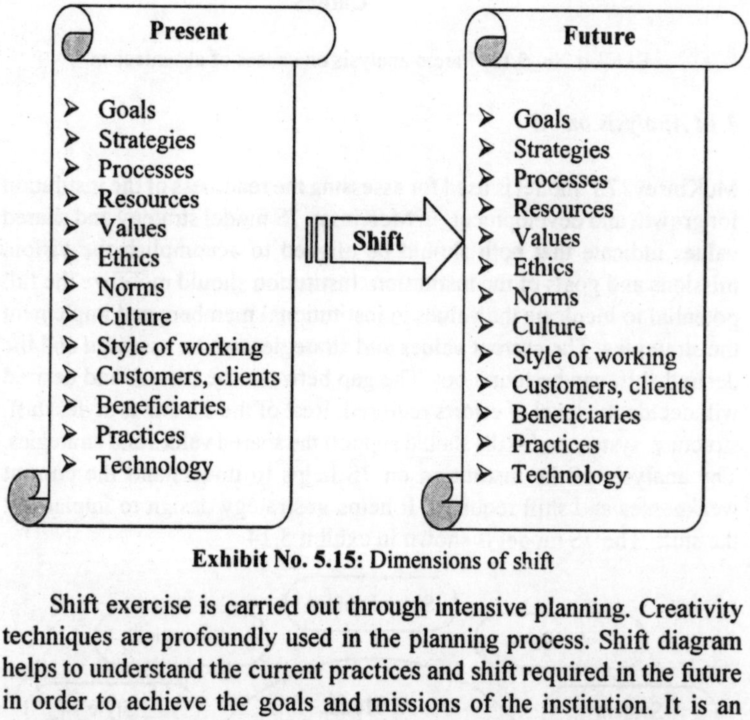

Exhibit No. 5.15: Dimensions of shift

Shift exercise is carried out through intensive planning. Creativity techniques are profoundly used in the planning process. Shift diagram helps to understand the current practices and shift required in the future in order to achieve the goals and missions of the institution. It is an excellent technique to chart the current practices and desired practices participatively. Shift diagram is useful in clarifying the change, decision-making, understanding the consequences of change, resistance to change, magnitude of change, efforts required to shift, communicating the changes required in future to internal and external stakeholders. This is a powerful technique to understand the reasons of shift and shift methods. The shift diagram is helpful to negotiate with people for their efforts and resources required. The institution can draw many shift diagrams to understand the total change process holistically. A shift diagram of traditional planning to scientific planning is shown in exhibit 5.16.

Exhibit No. 5.16: Shift from traditional planning to scientific planning

Criteria	*Traditional planning*	*Scientific planning*
Focus	Maintain the performance	Growth and development
Philosophy	Reactive	Proactive
Responsibility for planning	Head of the institution	Distributed at all levels
Participation	Selected people	Almost all stakeholders and employees of the institution
Authority	Head of the institution	Shared
Methods	Traditional	Scientific
Emphasis	Incremental planning	Planning for growth, development and excellence
Creativity and innovation	Less scope	Based on creativity and innovation
Information	Based on experience	Data, fact and forecasting
Types of plan	Mostly budget and Routine activity annual plans	Strategic, perspective as well as annual plans

3.16 Force Field Analysis

Kurt Lewin has proposed this technique. It is a technique of identifying the intensity of facilitating factors and hindering factors responsible for change. Force field analysis is a technique to enhance the participation of institutional members to understand the change process collectively. This technique is used to know the views and feelings of the institutional members about desired change. Using this technique situation can be analyzed for understanding the effectiveness of variables. This technique is used in planning for development. The analysis helps to design the strategies to harness the potential of facilitating factors or driving forces and minimize the intensity of hindering forces. In one set of situations the strategies are designed to minimize the intensity of hindering forces if there is no scope for increasing the intensity of facilitating forces. In other set of situations the strategies are designed to maximize the intensity of driving forces if there is no scope for minimizing the intensity of hindering forces. In third set of situations strategies are design to take advantages of facilitating forces and minimizing the effect of hindering forces. It is ensured through well-designed strategies that driving forces outweigh the hindering forces. The example of force field analysis for participation of people in institutional activities is shown in exhibit 5.17.

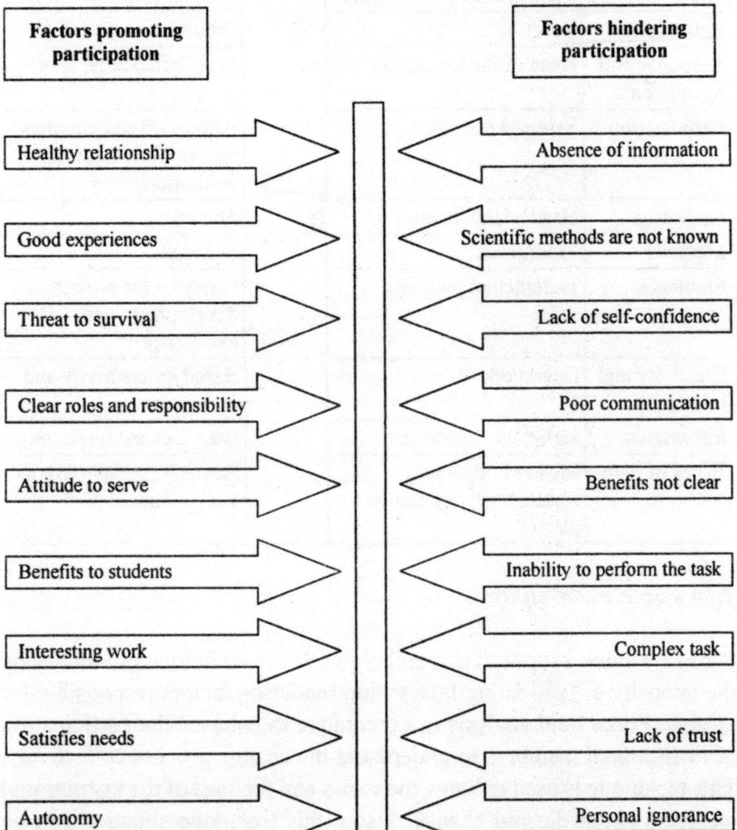

Exhibit No. 5.17: Force field analysis

3.17 Pie Diagram

The data collected can be classified and a pie diagrams can be prepared to communicate the distribution of the whole in percentage. It is a commonly used method to communicate the distribution and extent of different causes for a problem, factors in a situation, results achieved etc. It is presentation technique used very often to communicate effectively and precisely. The distribution of employment of passouts is shown on pie diagram in exhibit 5.18.

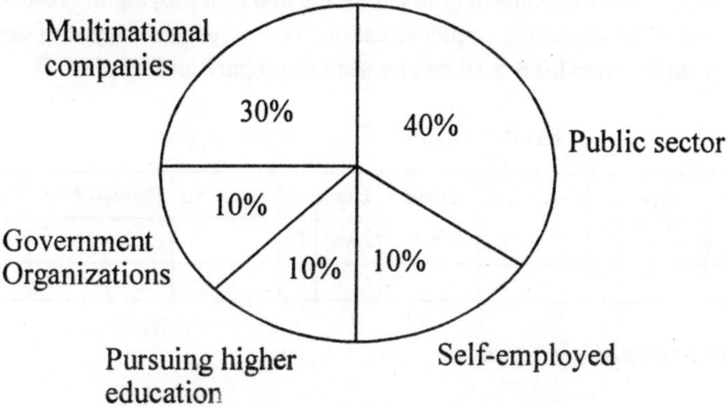

Exhibit No. 5.18: Employment status

3.18 Action Plan

The goals and objectives are derived from the perspective plans of the institution. Once the goals and objectives and their priority is finalized action plans are prepared. Action plans are detailed plans indicating what to do, how to do, when to do, who has to do, where to do, what resources are required, how much need to be done to achieve the goals and objectives. It details out significant activities to be performed. It helps to conceptually connect present with future. It is a detailed programme of implementation prepared by the people to be involved in implementation. Action plan helps to explore the alternative ways to achieve the objectives. The process of action planning helps to identify the feasibility of activities, potential problems, amount of resources required, competence required to implement, responsibility etc. Apart from annual planning action planning is used for improving the quality of teaching learning process, minimizing the waste, utilizing the resources, involving the people in planning process, communicating the plans to affected parties etc. Action plan is prepared in variety of formats it depends on the purpose of the planning. Generally points like objective, major activities, time frame, resources required, responsibility, support required, monitoring indicators are mentioned in the format of the plan. Action plan is supported by other techniques like Gantt chart, Pareto analysis, Network diagram, Bar diagram, Pie diagram etc. to bring clarity in complete planning process.

Action plans enhance effectiveness of implementation. It helps in deploying right resources at right time thereby minimizing wastage of resources. Action plans help in deploying and redeploying the resources in case of crisis during implementation. The suggested format of action plan shown in exhibit 5.19 can be used to prepare annual plan.

Exhibit No. 5.19: Format of annual plan

Sl. No.	*Area of functioning*	*Objectives*	*Activities*	*Duration*		*Resources*	*Responsibility*	*Funds*
				From	*To*			

3.19 Stakeholders' Analysis

Stakeholder analysis is a significant element in the design of the strategic plan, perspective plan and annual plan of the institution. Stakeholders can make or break the business of the institution. Stakeholders are those individuals, groups and organizations that can affect the business of the institution significantly in a positive or negative way. The survival, growth and development of the institution depend on the influence of the external and internal stakeholders of the institution. It is necessary to obtain the cooperation, support, and help of the stakeholders to run the institution successfully. The stakeholders decide the fate of the institution. Stakeholders' management is of prime importance for the management of the institution. The stockholders' analysis can be done using steps described below:

Identify the Stakeholders

First step is to identify the stakeholders and prepare a list of them. These stakeholders may be potential students, parents, All India Council for Technical Education, Government, employers, professional bodies, Alumni, sister institutions, research organizations, politicians, opinion leaders, local and district administration, suppliers, teachers, supporting staff, schools, media etc.

Analyze the Stake

Identify the nature and intensity of potential influence of each stakeholder. Their influence on the performance of the institution could be positive or negative. The analysis of stakeholders is carried out to find out their strengths, weaknesses, problems and interest in the institution. The analysis can be done using interview, focus group discussion or survey technique. The data collected are interpreted in the light of the nature of the stake and its intensity. On the basis of the analysis of the stake the institution can position itself. For example, the AICTE may or may not approve the new programmes so the stake is significant and important also. Institution should consider the statutory provisions for preparing the proposal for obtaining the approval for new programme. On the other hand if the stake of the professional body is low and if not abide to it may not make much harm to the business of the institution.

3.20 Process Design

There are many academic and non-academic functions performed in the institution. These functions are of routine type. Processes to perform these functions can be designed to improve the efficiency and effectiveness of performance. If institutional processes are designed, documented and used they can be refined based on experiences and technology inputs. People will follow the same practice to perform the functions. The value addition to improve the efficiency of the process becomes easy. It eliminates the casual way of doing the work. A process is a series of activities designed to produce specific output. To complete activities various types of resources are used including knowledge, skills and attitude. The processes of technical institution can be broadly classified in four major areas of functioning of the institution as shown in exhibit 5.20.

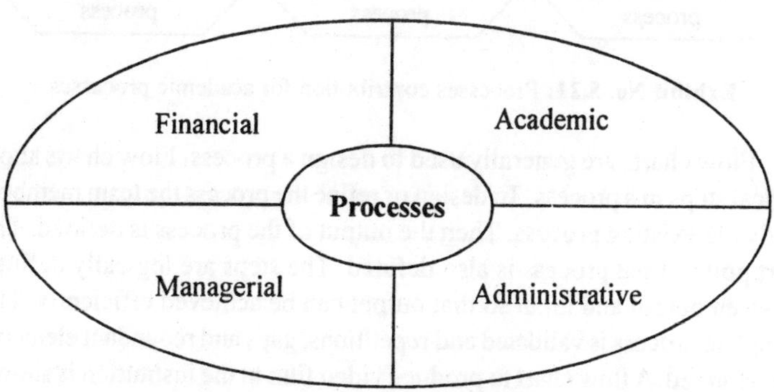

Exhibit No. 5.20: Major areas of functioning of institution in which processes are designed

The process could be design for major functions that are routinely performed such as curriculum design, curriculum revision, organizing continuing education programmes, organizing training for faculty and staff, preparing annual plan of the institution, examination of the students, conducting practical in the laboratory, purchasing material, developing instructional material, organizing industrial training for students, hiring a consultant, recruitment of faculty and staff etc. In each area of functioning there could be many processes. The output of one process may go as input to another process or it may be an independent product or service of the institution. The summation of output of all processes in major areas of functioning of the institution produces total output in terms of product and services. If this output is compared with the annual goals and objectives of the institute the performance of the institution can be judged. All process should support the academic processes. All processes should function in integrated way to support the academic processes as shown in exhibit 5.21.

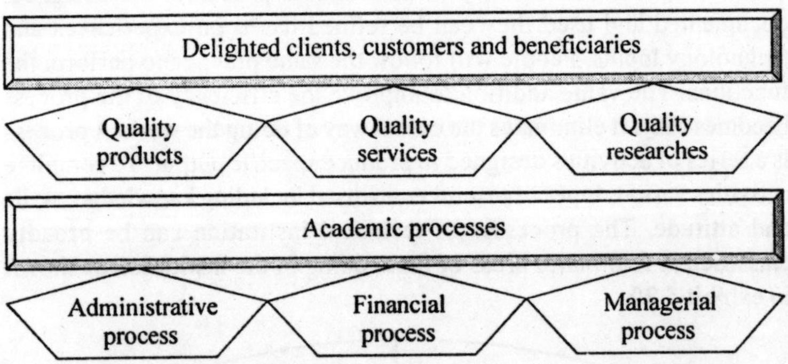

Exhibit No. 5.21: Processes contribution for academic processes

Flow charts are generally used to design a process. Flow charts show logical steps in a process. To design or refine the process the team members study the existing process. Then the output of the process is defined. The start point of the process is also defined. The steps are logically defined between output and input so that output can be achieved efficiently. The complete process is validated and repetitions, gaps and redundant elements are removed. A flow chart to produce video film in the institution is shown in exhibit 5.22.

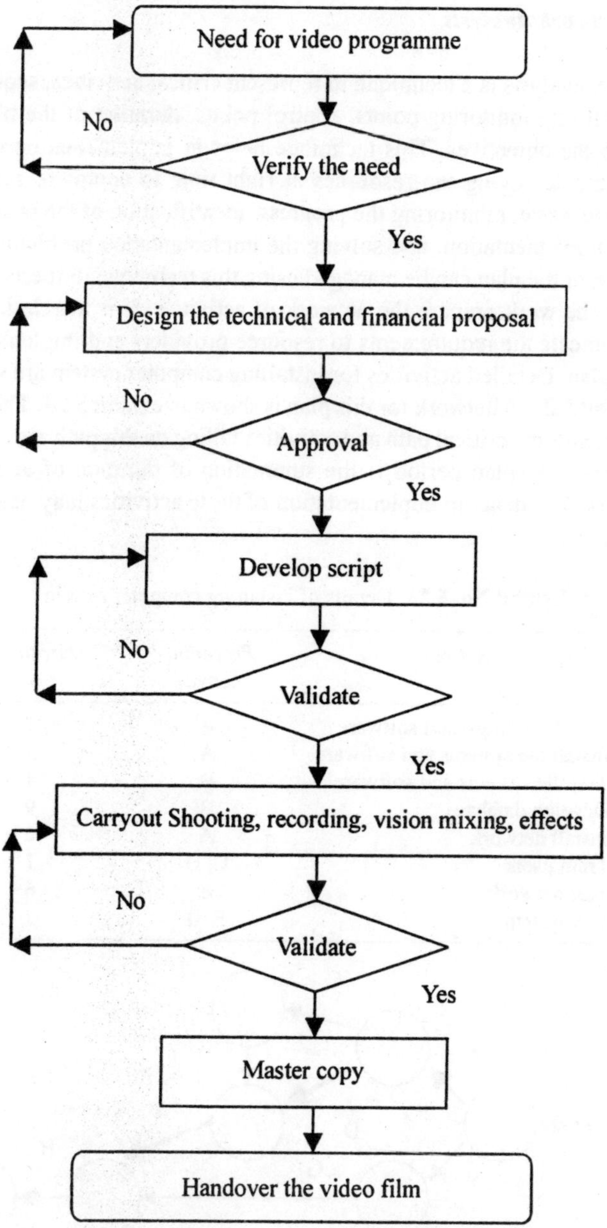

Exhibit No. 5.22: Process of producing video film

3.21 Network Analysis

Network analysis is a technique to represent critical activities, sequence of activities, monitoring points, control points, duration of the plan to achieve the objectives. This technique helps in implementation of the activities, deploying the resources at right time to complete activity, minimize waste, monitoring the progress, identification of the problems during implementation, and solving the implementation problems. The duration of the plan can be managed using this technique. Experts in the area of the work prepare the network of activities. It is a technique to communicate the requirements to resource providers and implementers of the plan. Detailed activities for installing computer system are shown in exhibit 5.23. A network for this plan is shown in exhibit 5.24. The dark arrows show the critical path and activities falling on this path are critical activities. The plan period is the summation of duration of activities ABDFH. Any delay in implementation of these activities may delay the plan period.

Exhibit No. 5.23: Details of installing computer system

	Activity	*Preceding activity*	*Duration of activity in weeks*
A	Select hardware and software	—	2
B	Install the systems and software	A	3
C	Test the systems and software	B	4
D	Develop database	B	9
E	Install network	A	2
F	Train users	C, D	1
G	Test network	E	6
H	Use system	F, G	2

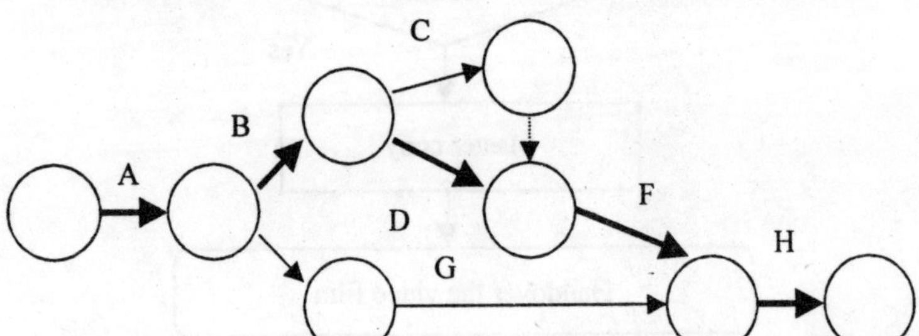

Exhibit No. 5.24: Network diagram for installing computer system

3.22 Affinity Diagram

It is developed by Jiro Kawakita and known as KJ method. It is a group creativity method used to collect and classify ideas, data, information, views and responses on a specific complex situation. The situation may be related to problem solving, decision-making, planning, crisis analysis, strategy design, innovation etc. The output of the creativity session on a particular theme can be grouped and put in the affinity diagram for better understanding, analysis and evaluation. It is also used for obtaining participation of people their commitment and consensus on specific problem or issue. An affinity diagram on analysis of heavy retraining cost in industry is shown in exhibit 5.25.

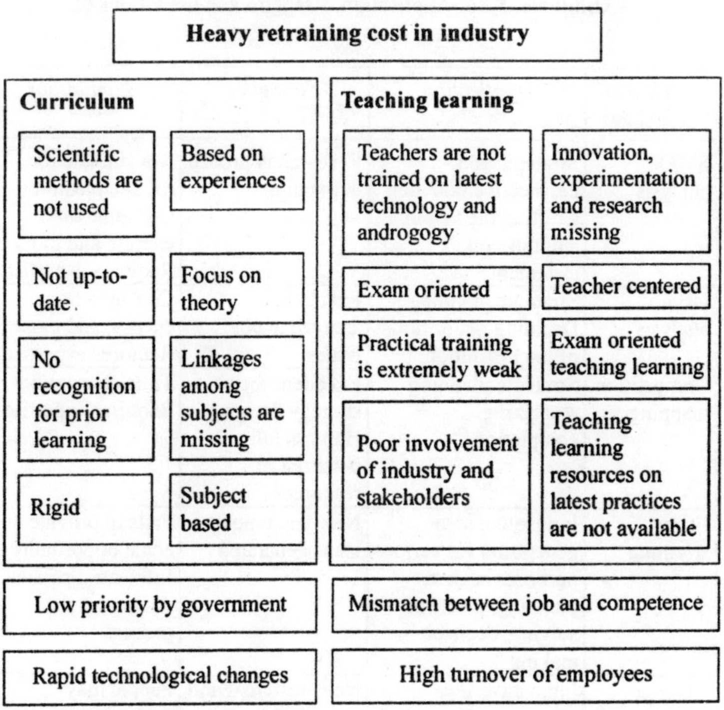

Exhibit No. 5.25: Analysis of heavy retraining cost in industry

4. Summary

Management tools and techniques are useful to decide data to be collected, data collection, data classification, data presentation and analysis. These tools and techniques improve the effectivencss and efficiency of managing the data for a purpose. These tools and techniques enhance the relevance and quality of various management functions and processes. They add value to planning, decision-making, problem solving, forecasting, innovating, leadership, influencing, and motivational activities of the management. They directly contribute to enhance the functioning of the institution quality of services and product of the institution. They are used as means to obtain commitment, consensus and involvement of the people. The talent of the internal and external stakeholders can be harnessed using these tools and techniques. Application, strengths and limitations of various tools and techniques is stated in exhibit 5.26.

Exhibit No. 5.26: Application, strengths and limitations of various tools and techniques

Tools and techniques	*Application*	*Strengths*	*Limitations*
SWOT analysis	Strategic and perspective planning Crafting the vision and mission statement	Research approach to planning	Not suitable for routine planning, Consume time, energy, and money Requires expertise
Issue analysis	Strategic planning Deciding major thrust of the institution	Excellent to analyze major issues	Consume time, energy, and money Requires expertise
Competition mapping	Strategic planning Analyzing completion	Excellent for strategy design Harness full potential of resources	Time consuming Requires expertise
Brain-storming	Innovative idea generation for various purposes such as planning, problem solving, decision-making	New and unique ideas generated	Fails to provide equal opportunity Influential person dominates the process
Nominal group technique	Innovative idea generation for various purposes such as planning, problem solving, decision-making	New, different and unique ideas generated	People may evaluate the ideas generated

(*Contd.*)

(*Contd.*)

Tools and techniques	*Application*	*Strengths*	*Limitations*
Mind mapping	Innovative ideas Inter-relationship Holistic picture	Excellent for research, curriculum design and lesson planning	Requires time
Focus group discussion	Knowing views, ideas and feelings of stakeholders	Total coverage in short time	Requires expertise
Gantt chart	Planning, monitoring and evaluation	Easy to use	Cannot be used for quality aspects
Cause and effect diagram	Problem solving, planning and conflict management Consensus seeking	Excellent in quantitative problem solving	Cannot be used for quality aspects
Problem tree analysis	Problem solving, planning and conflict management Consensus seeking	Excellent in quantitative as well qualitative planning, problem solving and decision making	Requires thinking skills and creativity
Alternative analysis	Problem solving, planning and conflict management Consensus seeking	Excellent in quantitative as well qualitative planning, problem solving and decision-making	Requires thinking skills and creativity
Pareto analysis	Prioritization of objectives, problems, issues, causes etc.	Segregates significant few from trivial many	Cannot be used for quality aspects
Analysis on 7S	Diagnosis of institutional climate	Clear inter-relationship among dimensions	Requires research approach
Shift diagram	Designing and implementing change Consensus seeking	Present and projected picture of future	May be away from reality
Force field analysis	Designing and implementing change Consensus seeking	Intensity of forces can be measured	May be away from reality
Pie diagram	Data presentation	Distribution of population	Fail to show quality

(*Contd.*)

(*Contd.*)

Tools and techniques	*Application*	*Strengths*	*Limitations*
Action plan	Planning, implementation, monitoring and evaluation	Deployment of resources	Rigidity may take place
Stakeholders analysis	Collaborating, networking and cooperating Minimizing conflict and competition	Good tool for effective communication and negotiation	Reveals trade secret
Process design	Standardizing routine activities	Improves effectiveness and efficiency	No scope for creativity
Network analysis	Planning, monitoring, controlling, and evaluation	Time based planning	Cannot be used for quality planning
Affinity diagram	Data collection and classification	Improves understanding of situation	Weak in logic and relation

REFERENCES

Geof Cox (1995). *Solve That Problem*, Pitman Publishing, London.

Geoffrey Petty (1998). *Creativity*, Kogan Page India Private Limited, New Delhi.

Gerald, F. Smith (1998). *Quality Problem Solving*, Prentice Hall of India Private Limited, New Delhi.

Karp, H.B. (1996). *The Change Leader*, Jossey-Bass, Pfeiffer, San Francisco.

Paul, M. Elkin (2003). *Mastering Business Planning and Strategies*, Viva Books Private Limited New Delhi.

Stephen, C. Harper (1994). *Managing growth in your emerging business*, McGraw Hills Inc., New Delhi.

Steve Smith (1999). *Solve That Problem*, Kogan Page India Private Limited, New Delhi.

PART III
MANAGERIAL SKILLS

6

Leadership

Objectives: The readers will be able to:

1. State the importance of leadership for the growth and development of the institution.
2. Describe the concept of leadership.
3. Describe the importance of situational leadership, institutional leadership and visionary leadership.
4. Review the leadership theories, models and their applicability in technical institutions.
5. Describe abilities of visionary leader.
6. List challenges faced by a leader.
7. State methods to develop leadership skills.

1. Introduction

Many institutions have shown excellent performance in the past. Others have grown and developed rapidly. Rests of the institutions are declining in performance. One of the factors responsible for excellent performance or poor performance is leadership. In the fast changing scenario of the employers market effective leadership is required to meet most challenges ahead. Effective leadership is required at every level of functioning of institution to sustain and improve the quality of passouts, services to industries and society and develop new technology. At the same time the leaders have to ensure the cost effectiveness in the functioning of the institution.

Now-a-days, institutions cannot remain static. They have to change as per demands of the time. They have to expand their business of education. They have to be competitive in the market of education. They have to willingly accept the challenges posed by industries and society. The visionary, transformational and transactional leaders can fulfil these demands. The expansion, growth and development needs of the institutions require leadership at all levels of institutional functioning. Leadership at institution level, department level, team level and individual level is required. A teacher as a leader influences the teaching learning process. S/he can do miracle so far learning achievements of students are concerned. Head of the department can take the department at all heights leading the academic, administrative, managerial and financial processes. Head of the institution as a leader can capitalize all opportunities for the growth and development of the institution.

2. Concept of Leadership

In educational context leadership can be viewed from two levels. First level is related to influencing the behaviour of the institutional members to set long-term and short-term goals for functioning. Leader can encourage institutional members to release their energy voluntarily to achieve set objectives effectively and efficiently. In the process of influencing leaders at all levels establish close interpersonal relationship with the followers. Leaders effectively communicate with followers and encourage them to put efforts for goal accomplishment. Leaders create motivational climate in which the energy of the followers is naturally released for goal accomplishment. Leaders and followers enter in an agreement of mutual accountability for achieving shared goals. They also enter in an agreement for fulfilling the expectations of each other. In the process of influencing they have trust on each other and provide mutual support.

Second level of leadership is related to influencing the behaviour of the students for competency achievement. They encourage professional development of students through process of teaching learning. Teacher as an effective leader creates joyful and healthy environment for learning. They influence the process of curriculum design, curriculum implementation and curriculum evaluation. They set and achieve academic goals using interpersonal relationship. They plan and introduce necessary change and innovations in academic processes. They implement the change and innovations encouraging the students to pursue entrepreneurial career.

3. Levels of Leadership

In technical institutions leadership can be seen at situational level, institutional level and visionary level. Situational leadership deals with present and immediate future of the institution. It deals with the situation, which affects day-to-day performance of the institution. Numbers of scholars have studied situational leadership and proposed theories. Theories of situational leadership are listed and briefly described in subsequent paragraphs.

3.1 Hersey Blanchard Situational Leadership Model

This model describe the behaviour of the leader on two variables, i.e. relationship behaviour and task behaviour. Relationship behaviour is called supportive behaviour. In supporting the followers' leader communicate, help, solve problems, counsel and guide the followers to complete the task. Task behaviour is the extent to which the leader spells out the task. S/he clarifies the task in terms of defining the task, explaining the method of completing the task, resource to be used to complete the task, time limits for completing the task, level of responsibility etc. The behaviour of the followers is defined in terms of their readiness to complete the task. Readiness is defined as the ability and willingness of the followers to complete the task. Ability is the knowledge, experience and skills followers bring to the task in a specific situation. Willingness is the extent to which the followers have confidence, commitment and motivation to complete the task in that situation.

The style of leader in a particular situation depends on readiness level of the followers. If the followers are unable and unwilling and the concern for task is high the telling style is a suitable style. In other situation the followers are unable but they are willing to contribute and concern for task is high selling style is suitable. In third situation followers are able but they are not willing to contribute and the concern for task is low participating style is suitable. In fourth situation followers are able and willing to contribute and concern for task is low delegating style is suitable.

This model of situational leadership guides leaders to analyze the behaviour of leader, behaviour of followers and then use the appropriate style of leadership. It suggests that leaders should shift in style as per requirement of the situation. Use of appropriate style of leadership helps the leader to achieve the goals and satisfy the needs of the followers. This model of situational leadership can be used in day-to-day situations and goals can be achieved effectively and efficiently.

3.2 Path Goal Theory

Robert house propagated the path goal theory. This theory is based on expectancy theory of motivation. He suggests that leaders should remove the barriers, obstacles and problems so that the followers achieve the goals. The leaders action to remove the barriers from the path to goal enhances morale and job satisfaction of the followers. This theory takes into account the characteristics of followers such as locus of control, likeness for authoritarianism and ability to perform the task. If the locus of control is external and ability to perform the task is low, and likeness of authoritarianism is high the directive style is considered to be appropriate. Similarly the style of leadership also depends on requirement of the task or situation. If the situation were not structured followers would prefer directive style of leadership. Robert House suggested four styles of leadership, i.e. directive, supportive, participative, and achievement oriented. He suggested diagnosing the situation, requirement of environment, and characteristics of followers to use appropriate style. Use of appropriate style improve the productivity and enhances the morale of the followers. Theory of path goal can be used following the steps mentioned in exhibit 6.1.

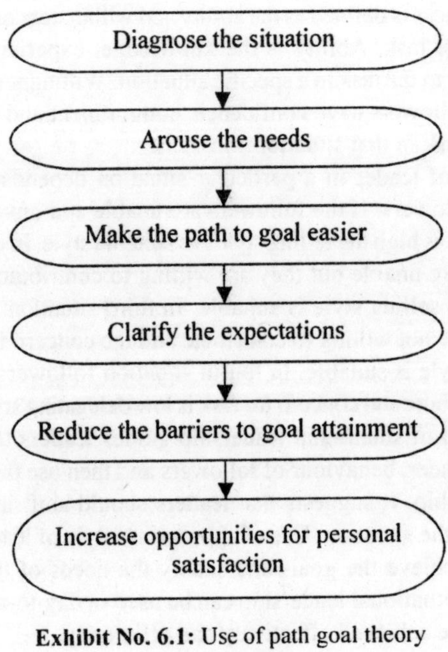

Exhibit No. 6.1: Use of path goal theory

3.3 The Managerial Grid

Blake and Mouton proposed managerial grid. They have considered two variables concern for production and concern for people. They have proposed 81 different leadership styles on 9 by 9 grid. The situation has to be analyzed and matched with the grid to know the leadership style. One can analyze the style of leadership using grid. The grid suggests the style of leadership and not the results. The grid helps leaders to understand their style of leadership in a better way. It helps them to improve their style of leadership. Blake and Mouton suggested that in situation like high concern for production and people team management should be used. This style is suitable for growth, development and innovation of the institutional business. Similarly, low concerns for people and production indicates that the business will remain continue. This style requires minimum efforts on the part of the leader as well as followers. High concern for production indicates that greater degree of authority is used to produce more. In this style leader is not concerned about relationship with the people. This style matches with telling style in Heresy and Blanchard model of leadership. High concern for people indicates maintaining friendly relationship with people to create comfortable atmosphere and work tempo.

3.4 Application of Situational Leadership Theories for Teaching Learning Processes

The situational leadership theories suggest activities described in exhibit 6.2 for teachers to increase the morale, motivation and satisfaction of the followers.

Exhibit No. 6.2: Activities to be carried out by a teacher to increase the morale, motivation and satisfaction of students

Identify the needs and activate them: Teachers as a leader can inform the importance of the subject and topic to students from examination point of view. They can establish horizontal and vertical linkages of the subject with other subjects. Clearly established linkages will justify the significance of the subject. They can relate the subject with practice and elicit the interest of the students in the topic. They can stress upon significance of the subject to pursue a particular career. In this way learning needs can be activated. **Recognize and reward high performance:** Teachers as a leader can promote continuous assessment of the learning through monthly tests. They should

(Contd.)

(Contd.)

recognize and reward high achievers in the test. They should provide constructive feedback to low achievers and create healthy competition among students. They can point out distinctive strengths of individuals and motivate them to harness the strengths.

Coach and guide to choose challenging goals and make the path easier: Teachers as a leader should create challenging goals for the students. These goals may be related to live problems, projects and innovations. They participatively set the goal to solve the problems, complete the projects and design innovations. They should remove the barriers and provide resources to make the learning process easy.

Establish link between expectation, performance and reward: Teachers as a leader enhance the expectations of the students for learning. They should link the high expectations for learning with better learning outcomes and better learning outcomes with high grades. Teachers as a leader should be available to guide, counsel and support students. They should provide reference material to read and complete the assignment. They should inform about sources to get information.

Increase satisfaction: Teachers as a leader should increase opportunities for personal satisfaction of students. A group of students may be interested to work on a specific project or obtain training in a particular industry. If such opportunities are provided to interested students they will enjoy the work and get more satisfaction.

Bring variety in teaching learning process: Teachers as a leader can reduce use of one-way communication and open other methods of learning which are students friendly like; self-learning, learning through problem solving, learning through projects, learning through simulation, learning through actions, learning through experimentation, learning through observation, learning through mistakes etc. These methods provide opportunity for flexible learning. The flexible learning is rewarding in itself. Teacher as a leader should provide the broader framework for self-learning and inform the students in advance. Teacher as a leader delegate the responsibility of learning to students. They promote students centered methods of learning. They should initiate the process of learning in a particular subject or topic and then give full control of learning to students. They should promote collective and collaborative learning. They act as a facilitator to the process of learning.

4. Institutional Level Leadership

Institutional leaders deal with the growth and development of the institution. They deal with challenges in near future. As described in the chapter on planning, the leaders forecast the near future, set the goals and prepare the plans to meet the challenges. The role of leaders is broader and varied. They influence the behaviour of the people on large scale to achieve the goals in the near future. They encourage people to come out of their roles to contribute for broader perspectives. The leaders focus on the future of the institution and external environment. They explore to see the opportunities available in the environment. They design strategies to grab these opportunities. Leaders smell the nature of competition the institution is likely to face. They prepare the people to compete successfully. At institutional level leaders organize resources to achieve the goals. They analyze potential problems and prepare the contingent plans to face the likely problems. In this way they clear the path to success and lead to people. They encourage people to achieve the goals. They encourage people through norms, ethics, values, rewards and beliefs. They use participatory methods in functioning of the institute. The teams' structure proposed in this book helps to promote motivational climate in the institution. In motivational climate people release their energy naturally for a greater cause. They achieve super ordinate goals without much of problems and resistance.

5. Application of Institutional Level Leadership

The leaders should come out from day-to-day situations and think and apply their leadership skills for the growth and development of the institution as a whole. They should use the situational and behavioural theories of leadership for the growth and development of the institution. The application of institutional leadership is stated in exhibit 6.3.

Exhibit No. 6.3: Application of institutional leadership

- Scan the external environment in which the institution is functioning
- Design and conduct manpower forecasting studies. These studies should focus on manpower requirement, their type, competencies required, salary package offered by industries and prioritizing the demand
- Design the new programmes and their detailed curriculum based on the results of the study
- Offer the programmes to grab the opportunity at the earliest
- Undertake technological forecasting studies with industries, field agencies, sister institutions and research organizations to update the curriculum with regular interval of time
- Market the services of the institution to expand the programmes of the institution to cover larger population and different groups of client
- Undertake and solve major problems of the industries and society to demonstrate the capacity and capability of the institution

- Take advantages of various government programmes and schemes designed for the benefit of the institutions involving faculty, staff and students
- Collaborate with industries, professional bodies and foreign institutions to work on projects of mutual benefits
- Undertake research studies to improve the effectiveness and efficiency of the institutes functioning. These studies should focus on minimizing wastage of time, money, resources, efforts and machines. They should focus on increasing utilization of expertise, time and efforts of the faculty, staff and students for purposeful learning
- Setting performance standards in different areas of functioning of the institution
- Benchmark the outputs and results with the best institutions implementing the best practices to satisfy the learning needs of the students and needs of other stakeholders
- Continually improve the performance of the institution based on the feedback received from various sources
- Organize and reorganizing the processes and resources to excel better

6. Visionary Leadership

Visionary leadership is related to crafting the purposeful, shared and desirable vision for the institution. The vision of the institution is crafted using participatory processes. The members of governing body, governing teams and internal management teams participate in visioning workshops and craft the vision statement. The vision statement of the institution is then widely circulated among internal and external stakeholders to offer comments. The vision statement is refined and finalized based on the comments. The head of the institution leads the process of visioning. The leaders play important role in designing the vision reach strategies and influencing people to implement vision reaches strategies. They encourage institutional members and external stakeholder to contribute generously for achieving the vision of the institution. They constantly scan the external environment and make necessary adjustments in vision reach strategies. They periodically review the vision statement and strategic plan of the institution.

7. Application of Visionary Leadership

The leaders should come out from day-to-day functioning of the institution and apply their leadership skills for the growth and development of the institution. They should use latest theories of visionary leadership to achieve the excellence. They should focus their efforts on innovations. They should challenge old rules and regulations to enhance efficiency in functioning of the institution. The application of visionary leadership is stated in exhibit 6.4.

Exhibit No. 6.4: Application of visionary leadership

Vision document: Head of the institution initiate the process of visioning in the institute. S/he conducts series of workshops to generate ideas on vision statement of the institution. S/he creates the atmosphere of free flow of ideas related to vision statement. S/he opens multi channels of communication among internal and external stakeholders. The complete experience of visioning exercise is documented and widely circulated. S/he finalizes the vision statement under the guidance of governing body and widely shares it. Visionary leader develops the vision document using the experiences of governing body, governing teams and management teams. The vision document is widely shared among institutional members and their commitment is obtained to implement it. Visionary leader encourages the teams to prepare strategic, perspective and operation plans.
Infuse values: The visionary leader exercises and encourages institution-building processes. S/he motivates management teams to create building blocks for innovation and change. S/he designs strategies to shift from prevalent values, beliefs, norms, ethics and culture to new systems. The visionary leader creates and shares values, beliefs, norms, ethics and culture aligned to the vision of the institution. S/he leads people by values to implement vision reach strategies.
Satisfaction of people: The visionary leader employs and deploys wholehearted followers on challenging tasks. S/he satisfies the aspirations of the people assigning them appropriate role and authority. S/he focuses on modifying, aligning and fine-tuning the culture of the institution. S/he creates culture driven institution. The culture that promotes learning organization principles in the institution.
Empowerment: The visionary leader empowers him/her through empowering faculty and staff members in the institution. S/he promotes the culture of empowerment, which is based on trust and confidence. Even students are empowered to take charge of learning. S/he promotes flexible atmosphere for smooth functioning of the institution.
Innovations: The visionary leader designs new and unique innovations and also encourages others to design innovations. These innovations may be related to educational programmes, teaching learning processes, co-curricular activities, consultancy etc. S/he encourages faculty and staff members to implement these innovations.

Opportunity: The visionary leader explores new opportunities that can be taped for the growth and development of the institution. New opportunities may be related to consultancy, project work, collaborations, exchange of all types of resources, financial soundness etc. The visionary leader is stable and confident in times of crisis. S/he channelizes energy of people in a positive direction.

Self-development: The visionary leader thinks big and motivates people to do so. S/he promotes self-development and self-control concept in the institution. S/he sets a model and standards for institutional members to practice.

Creating visionary leaders: The visionary leader creates many visionary leaders in the institutions. S/he involves all significant people in thinking and visioning process. Even the students are given opportunities to assume leadership role on various occasions.

8. Abilities in a Visionary Leader

The visionary leader possesses variety of abilities. Some of the significant abilities are stated in exhibit 6.5 and described briefly in subsequent paragraphs.

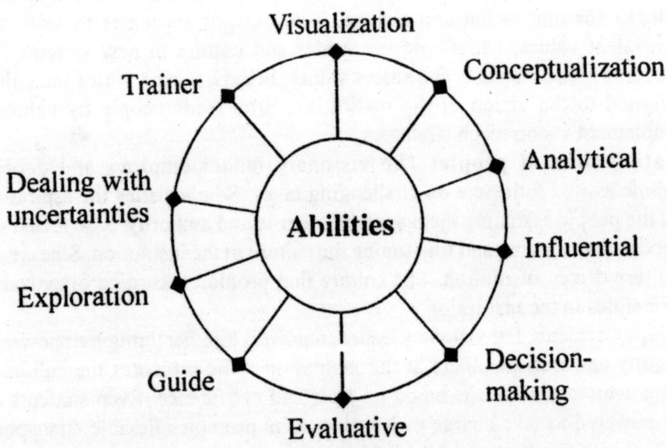

Exhibit No. 6.5: Abilities of a visionary leader

8.1 Visualization

The visionary leaders should be able to analyze the environment in which the institute would function. They should be able to forecast the future and provide the alternative vision of the institution in concrete terms. They should be able to communicate the vision and missions of the institute to the institutional members and rest of the world.

8.2 Conceptualization

The visionary leader should be able to conceptualize the missions, goals and objectives of the institute. The missions, goals and objectives are based on strong logic. They should be able to design alternative strategies to accomplish the vision of the institute. At any moment of time they should be able to decide the academic business of the institution rapidly, clearly and ambitiously.

8.3 Analytical

Visionary leader should have ability to scan data based on criteria and use relevant and authentic data for decision-making. They should be able to make out sense from the incomplete and inadequate information. They should be able to evaluate the alternative strategies to attain the goals, missions and vision of the institute. These strategies should be based on strengths and opportunities at the same time overcome the weakness and threats. They should be able to evaluate the strategies of the competitors and design new strategies to meet the requirements. Visionary leaders should be able to identify the major weaknesses of the institution rapidly. They should be able to design alternative strategies to cover up the weaknesses. They should be able to design strategies to win the competition based on the weaknesses of the institution in competition. They should be able to explore the opportunities before competitors. They should be able to design strategies to grab opportunities at the face of it. They should be able to visualize the opportunities of farther future. They should be able to design strategies without sufficient data.

8.4 Influential

Visionary leaders should be able to influence the institutional members to voluntarily release their full potential to achieve the goals. They should be able identify their personal power, authority, expertise and use it for larger purpose. They should be able to change the preferences of the institutional member and take out salt from the sea.

8.5 Decision-making

Visionary leaders should be able to take decisions in different situations. They should be able to visualize the future scenario on the basis of present changes in the environment. They should be able to make out the situation, as does the police on the basis of hunches and segregated evidences. Police makes out situation on the basis of past but visionary leaders visualize situations in future. They are stable in times of turbulence. They make effective decisions. They involve people in decision-making. Their decisions are acceptable to those who are going to be affected.

8.6 Evaluative

Visionary leaders are evaluative and critique. They evaluate the plans, decisions, strategies and performances. The evaluation process goes on continuously. They make fast adjustments on the basis of results of evaluation. They should be able to appraise the impact of the designed strategies before it is implemented. They should be good in evaluating the business of the competitors.

8.7 Guide

Visionary leaders should be able to guide the institutional members to implement the vision reach strategies. They should be able to develop capabilities and capacities in people to dedicate themselves to the vision of the institute. They should be available for guidance at all times. They guide through their expertise and experience.

8.8 Exploration

Visionary leaders should be able to explore the strengths of the people for their deployment and redeployment. They should know the personal profile of individuals and teams in the institution. On the basis of this profile the structure of the institution needs to be organized and reorganized to develop competitive edge. At the same time they mobilize the physical, financial and informational resources for the growth and development of the institution.

8.9 Dealing with Uncertainties

Visionary leaders should be able to deal with uncertainties. They should analyze the data available and design strategies to deal with uncertainty.

They should not hesitate to take opinion of others. They should think creatively and innovatively to deal with ambiguous situations. They should take steps to prevent similar ambiguity and uncertainty in the future. They should be able to take calculated risk to do something new.

8.10 Trainer

Visionary leaders should be good trainers. Continuous training is necessary to design and implement innovations. It is also necessary to make desired changes in the functioning of the institution. They should be able to identify the training needs and design training programmes to develop desired competencies in the faculty and staff members. They should be able to impart training in joyful and informal environment using principles of androgogy.

9. Challenges Ahead

Visionary leaders have to face many challenges related to external environment as well as internal environment of the institution. They have to cope with the challenges stretching the capacity and capability of the institutional resources. Some of the common challenges are shown in exhibit 6.5 and briefly described in subsequent paragraphs.

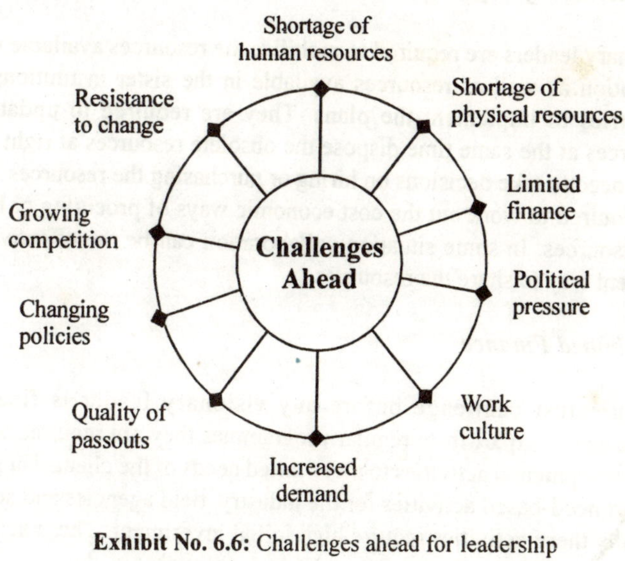

Exhibit No. 6.6: Challenges ahead for leadership

9.1 Shortage of Human Resources

Visionary leaders are required to manage the functions of the institution with minimum number of faculty and staff members. This requires them to select and develop multi skilled people who can fulfil changing requirements of the institution. Development of human resources is a big challenge before the leaders because the trained and professional people are not available for technical education unlike other sectors. The vision cannot be translated into actions without competent and dedicated persons. No technical institution in the country is offering exclusive engineering programmes to develop teachers to take up jobs in technical institutions. Most of the persons are developed as teachers in their service span through gaining experience. They are trained through on-the-job and off-the-job training. They do what they have learnt from their seniors but this is not enough in today's context. One has to be professional teacher than only s/he will be able to meet the challenges. Continuous refinement and up gradation in skills is required to take up the academic, administrative, managerial and financial challenges. Leaders are required to encourage the faculty and staff members to quit the job if they are not fit to changing requirements of the institutions.

9.2 Shortage of Physical Resources

Visionary leaders are required to mobilize the resources available in the institution as well as resources available in the sister institutions and industries to implement the plans. They are required to update the resources at the same time dispose the obsolete resources at right time. They need to take decisions on hiring or purchasing the resources. They are required to work out the cost economic ways of procuring or hiring the resources. In some situation collaboration can be the effective and efficient way to share the resources.

9.3 Limited Finance

The greatest challenge before any visionary leader is financial management. Apart from regular programmes they are required to take up developmental activities to meet varied needs of the client. They have to start need-based activities for the industry, field agencies and society. Initially these activities require high initial investment. These activities should be self-sustained and continuous through out the year. These activities will definitely connect many stakeholders and beneficiaries with the institution. These activities will help the institution to increase the resource utilization factors. On one hand leaders have to expand the academic business and on the other hand there is shortage of resources.

9.4 Political Pressure

Political pressure and out side intervention are increasing day-by-day in the functioning of the institutions. Political intervention and political activities in the institution may hamper the teaching learning process at the same time spoil the corporate image of the institution, if it is unhealthy. Visionary leaders are required to assess the impact of political activities and control it. They should be able to make the political intervention in their favour. At the same time internal politicization of the institution should be stopped.

9.5 Work Culture

Work culture is a great concern in functioning of the institutions. Faculty and staff members are interested in more incentives. There is a pressure to fulfil growing demands of faculty, staff and students. At the same time there is a challenge of keeping them motivated, encouraged, committed and energized for achieving institutional vision. Encouraging them to readily accept the challenges is a complex task for the leaders. There is a need to prepare faculty and staff members to work in different teams and assume different roles in the institution. Visionary leaders need to build work culture through values, beliefs, norms, ethics and acceptable behavioural standards.

9.6 Increasing Demands of Stakeholders

Industries and fields agencies look for solution of their technical and managerial problems in technical institutions. They want to upgrade the technology and techniques. They want to enhance the quality of product and services. Many industries and field agencies are interested to re-engineer the complete business. They look for the guidance and consultancy to bring innovations and change. Technical institutions are required to develop the required level of expertise and it should be available on demand. There is a need to develop institutions in planned way in different locations and different areas to provide world-class expertise to industries and field agencies. This is possible only when technical institutions work shoulder to shoulder with industries and field agencies. Society has many expectations from technical institutions. It expects that technical institutions develop appropriate and cheap technology that matches to the culture and habits in the society. Society expects engineers who can solve its problems and make the life comfortable. Society expects that technical institutions create technical awareness related to different aspects of its life. It expects that the technical institutions become nucleus to develop vocational and technical competencies in the people to obtain gainful employment. Visionary leaders are supposed to develop the institutions in a way to satisfy the changing expectations of the stakeholders.

9.7 Quality of Passouts

Quality of passouts is a great concern for the government, employers and parents. Parents are paying beyond their capacity to make their sons and daughters engineers. They are highly serious and concerned about the quality of instructions. They want return of their investment. Employers are equally concerned about the quality of passouts. They want competent employable passouts. They are also in tough competition. They cannot afford to employ less competent people. Industries want to pay more and offer best perks but they are not interested to compromise with the quality of potential employees. Students are also brilliant now-a-days they are trained by professional organizations and get admission in the institution through rigorous process of selection. They expect that their talent should be appropriately utilized in the teaching learning process. They cannot tolerate incompetent teachers. Government is also concerned about the quality of passouts because it has very high investment in technical education system. It has to answer many questions related to quality of passouts. Whenever any accident takes place or some thing bad happens public question the quality, capability and capacity of the person responsible for that. Poor quality of passouts leads to unemployment and underemployment. This furthers the problem for the family, society and government. Underemployed and unemployed engineers may become the nuisance for all because they are very intelligent people. The visionary leader is expected to set the standards of quality of inputs, processes, products and services of the institution through regular researches. S/he should be able to ensure the quality at every stage of educational process and in all processes. S/he should achieve excellence in the core business of the institution, i.e. academics.

9.8 Changing Policies of the Government

Government often changes policies related to admission of students, fee structure, recruitment rules, space requirement, resource requirements, functioning of the institution, reporting patterns etc. These changes require visionary leader to make appropriate changes in the functioning and comply the changed policies, rules and regulations of the government. Government asks technical institutions to do some social and technological development work to improve the quality of life of the people. The visionary leaders need to fulfil the social obligations with the expected effectiveness and efficiency.

9.9 Competition from Sister Institutions

Technical education is no more monopoly in the country. Numbers of government aided and private institution have been set up and many more are coming up. Technical institutions are increasing in number and creating competition for each other. Their density has already been increased and saturation has come in many states so far undergraduate programmes are concerned. This competition will decide the fat of many institutions. Opening up of the economy and globalization policy of the government international institutions are establishing their centers in the country. These foreign institutions are creating different type of competitions than sister institutions. Technical institutions in country are not prepared to face external competition with international institutions. They have not thought to expand, grow and develop internationally. Their curriculum is not designed to meet international requirements. Visionary leaders are required to put lot of efforts to internationally market the services of the institutions.

9.10 Resistance to Change

All conventional and old institutions are having great resistance to change. They have become comfortable with the practices they have followed although they have gained significant experience also. Traditional disciplines and practices are not much relevant in today's context. Their renewal, reengineering and rejuvenation are a great challenge to their leaders. Even leadership is questionable in these institutions. Faculty, staff, resources, processes, and structure everything needs to be assessed in today's context. The habit of reactive management need to be changed in the habit of proactive management and this is a big challenge to leadership.

10. Charismatic Leadership

Technical institutions require persons as a leader at all levels that can set unique and challenging goals to achieve. They inspire people through their personal power to pursue the goals. They set examples for followers to imitate and practice. They set new and variety of examples. They dedicate themselves to the set goals with strong determination. They compel people to align themselves towards goals and release energy for goal accomplishment. They shape the attitude of people and obtain their commitment for unique goals. Leaders dealing with academic matter should set example, which can be modelled by other teachers. The rest of the teachers inspire, imitate and follow modelled behaviour. They get emotionally involved in the persuasion of set goals. They trust in the ability, expertise, experience and behaviour of the leader. They want to associate themselves with the leader. Charismatic leaders use their referent power and expert power to influence the people in the institution. Teachers should be known for their expertise in their respective discipline.

11. Shift from Present to Future Leadership

The educational leaders need to move out from their comfort zone of working traditionally and shift on various dimensions of leadership. They have to use the knowledge, skills and attitude to transform the educational institutions to serve the larger purpose of the society. A shift required on various leadership dimensions is shown in exhibit 6.7 for ready reference.

Exhibit No. 6.7: Shift from present to future leadership

Criteria	*Present leadership*		*Future leadership*
Focus	Present		Future
	Task		Vision
Philosophy	Principle based leadership	⇒	Value based leadership
Number of Leader	Single		Multiple, Shared
Role	Monitor and supervise people		Guide, support, and help people

Criteria	*Present leadership*	*Future leadership*
Motivation	Influence the behaviour of the people	Promote self-motivation
Power	Enjoy authority	Delegate authority Empower people
Emphasis	Task completion	Team and relationship building
Thinking	People need to be controlled	People enjoy autonomy
Recognition	Take credit for the success	Share success
Rewards	Individuals	Individuals and teams
Information	Control information	Free flow of information
Task allocation	Assign task to people	Align people to accomplish vision
Base of decision making	Effectiveness and efficiency	Vision of the institution
Tough decisions	Procrastinate	Immediate decision-making
People development	Develop followers	Develop leaders
Problems	Leader own the problem	Followers own the problem
Marketing	Market the services and product	Market the image of the institution
Communication	Often one way	Multi channel
Creativity and innovation	Welcomes	Foster
Criticism and opposition	People approach to leader	Invite people to criticize and oppose and challenge existing practices
	Transactional	Transformational
Training of people	Dependent on training institutions	Create learning institution
Perspective	Limited to macro level	Meta level
Approach	Proactive	Visionary, Holistic, Entrepreneurial, Collaborative, Diversified, Multidisciplinary
Uncertainty	Risk taker	Clear uncertainty and find path to vision
Build	Teams	Winning culture
Effect	Growth and development	Synergetic, excellence and enhanced corporate image
Strategy	Push	Pull

12. Strategies to Improve Leadership Effectiveness

Every person working in leadership role wants to improve leadership skills and develop new leadership skills, thereby enhancing leadership effectiveness. There are many strategies that can be used by leaders independently or mix of them. All these strategies suggested here might not be suitable for all leaders working in different institutions. One can pick up the strategies as per need to improve the leadership skills. These strategies guide the interested leaders to sharpen the existing leadership skills and learn new leadership skills. Strategies to improve leadership effectiveness are stated in exhibit 6.8 and described briefly in subsequent paragraphs.

Exhibit No. 6.8: Strategies to improve leadership effectiveness

12.1 Self-analysis of the Leadership Skills

One can become conscious and self aware of the one's leadership skills. They can chart the leadership skills and assess the leadership effectiveness on each skill. The assessment can be done periodically say monthly. The assessment results can be analyzed and positive feedback can be taken for self-improvement. The assessment results can be shown to other leaders and their feedback can also be obtained. Self feedback as well as feedback from others on use of leadership skills and its effectiveness help the leader to improve the leadership skills significantly and intensively. Sincere efforts of the leader in self-analysis bring continuous improvement and refinement in skills. Leader may encounter new situations in which different set of leadership skills are required. Such skills can be listed and developed.

12.2 Attend Training Programmes

Leadership development programmes are offered by many professional organizations. The duration of these programmes varies from 3 days to 30 days. These programmes are well designed comprehensive and rigorous. The leadership skills of individuals are diagnosed in these programmes through standard tests and test results are validated from the concerned individuals. The trainer draws the skills profile of the person and offers constructive feedback on the leadership profile. The trainer suggests constructive remedies for improvement in the leadership skills. These leadership programmes are generic and formal offered by the training organizations. Apart from these leadership development programmes leadership development workshops can be organized in the institution to develop and refine leadership skills. This approach is better than formal training programmes because leadership skills are developed in work setting. In leadership skills development workshop small teams are formed and leadership role is assigned to different persons. The team has to accomplish the set goals under the leadership of a particular person. The following and similar tasks are assigned to different teams:

- Craft vision statement of the institution looking to the present scenario of the country
- Design mission statements to achieve the crafted vision of the institution
- Carry out strengths, weaknesses, opportunities and threat analysis of the institution or department or section
- Value analysis of prevailing values and design new values aligned to the vision of the institution
- Prepare strategic plans to achieve vision, missions and goals of the institution in different areas of functioning of institution
- Write a book on a particular topic which is latest and books are not available or if books are available they do not cover the curriculum

- Design innovative experiments related to teaching learning processes, co-curricular activities and other processes of the institution
- Draft policies like staff development policy, admission policy, examination policy, discipline policy, resources distribution policy, incentive policy, procurement policy, consultancy services policy, collaborating policy, industrial training of students policy, faculty and staff exchange policy etc.
- Design specific projects related to problem solving of institution, industry and society
- Live problem-solving assignments of institution or industry
- Prepare guidelines to organize seminars, conferences, symposiums, quiz, competitions etc. and organize the same
- Strategies to reduce waste of time, money and resources

Experts observe effectiveness of use of leadership skills by leaders. They observe the behaviour of the leader continuously and on the completion of the task experts provide constructive feedback. Experts offer feedback to the leaders about the leadership skills on which they are excellent and also leadership skills on which they need improvement. They suggest the methods for improving leadership effectiveness. The outcome of the assignment also becomes the source of immense satisfaction and provides feedback on performance. The role of trainer in conducting such workshop is demanding. S/he has to design the real problems, challenges, projects, issues, etc. cautiously and clearly. Future challenges as well as present problems are addressed in the assignments and deliberations.

12.3 Leadership Seminars

Leadership seminars, conferences and symposiums can be organized at state level, regional level and national level. Leaders are invited to such seminars to share their experiences of leadership effectiveness. They are provided opportunities to share their problems, achievements and future prospects. All these problems, achievements and future prospects are documented and a summary of the experiences is prepared and made available to rest of the leaders working in educational institutions for their development.

12.4 Mentoring

Head of the institution or head of the department possessing leadership skills can become the mentor. One to three persons can be attached with them for mentoring. These mentors are professionally trained. They guide, coach, train and share leadership skills with the potential leaders. They transfer the leadership skills effectively and efficiently. Mentors have intimate relationship with the potential leaders. They openly communicate with each other. The potential leaders do not hide any thing with mentor. They enter in a social contract to develop leadership skills and behave according to it. Mentors minutely observe the behaviour of the potential leaders and appreciate the effective use of leadership skills at the same time offer constructive feedback for improvement. This feedback may be related to; knowledge related to task, communication, interpersonal relationship, problem solving skills, decision-making skills, organization of resources, motivating the followers, selecting the method to complete the task, distribution of responsibility among followers etc. Mentors have formal and informal relationship with potential leaders and listen each other effectively to understand the point of view of each other.

12.5 Reading

Lot of and variety of literature is available on leadership. Articles on leadership appear in journals and newspapers. Research papers are published in professional journals. One can have a habit of reading literature on leadership regularly. Leaders can take membership of library where management literature is easily available. One can assess depth of leadership knowledge reading the literature on leadership. S/he can think how to apply the knowledge gained through reading in real life situation and work situation. Institution can devote a separate section of books and journals on leadership and management in their libraries.

12.6 Trial and Error

One can design strategies to use leadership skills in a specific situation. The effectiveness and efficiency of the use of leadership skills can be assessed analyzing the achievement of goals. The reasons of success or failure can be analyzed and actions for improvements can be planned for future situation. One can document the points learned during trial and error process of leadership and share it with other leaders. The process of trial and error is a comparatively slow process of learning. There is a risk of wrong learning, ineffective and inefficient learning.

12.7 Quality Circle

A quality circle can be formed in the institution to share and solve leadership problems. New leadership skills and innovative methods of leadership can be generated. Quality circles provide an opportunity to apply the leadership skills learned through other methods of learning. New methods of leadership can be generated exclusively applicable in educational institutions. Specially leadership skills applicable in teaching learning situation can be developed, refined and applied through quality circles.

12.8 Competition on Leadership

Leaders should get an opportunity to test their knowledge and share experiences of developing leadership. Competitions can be organized on leadership and best leader can be chosen at the end of every semester or year. Similar competitions can be organized for staff members and students. The experiences of the competition can be documented for learning purpose.

13. Summary

Each and every person in the institution should acquire leadership skills. They have to lead the teams of employees and students for achieving specific goals. Leadership can be seen at three levels. At situational level situational objectives are achieved influencing the behaviour of team members. Teachers as a leader have great deal of leadership leading the group of students for joyful, productive and effective learning. They initiate the process of learning through teaching. They mobilize, encourage and influence the behaviour of the students for learning. To be effective and efficient leaders teachers need to be expert in their subjects at the same time they need to use effective and efficient methods for producing learning. They make the learning experiences joyful event maintaining good relationships with students. Students carry learning experiences to their whole life. Teachers make and shape the behaviour of their students. Good teachers enhance the corporate image of the institution.

The second level of leadership is related to expansion and growth of the institution. It is related to design and implementation of change for continual improvement in the performance of the institution. At institutional level the role of the leader is broader and expanded. The focus of leadership shifts from day-to-day situation to performance in near future. Leaders initiate the process of planning for next year involving individuals and teams. They set ambitious goals and obtain commitment of people. They take major decisions to start new programmes, initiate changes and implement innovations. Leaders use full potential of followers and their creativity to enhance the academic climate of the institution. They built up teams to take up the challenges.

The third level of leadership is visionary level. At this level leaders visualize the long future of the institution. They decide the ultimate destination of the institution in present. They develop alternative strategies to achieve vision of the institution. Visionary leaders lead people by vision and values. They build up culture in which people naturally achieve the vision. They remove the barriers, hurdles and obstacles from the way to vision. Visionary leaders clear the uncertainties and make out the future of the institution. They communicate the future of the institution and lead people to achieve it.

There are many challenges ahead like shortage of staff, resources and money. Political intervention is increasing day by day that has to be controlled. Work culture requires significant shift for survival, growth and development of the institution. The expectations of stakeholders are increasing day by day. They want professional services at every front. There is a concern for quality of passouts. The government policies are changing frequently to meet the needs of the technical institutions. Competition from sister institution is increasing on many dimensions of business of technical institution.

Psychologist, sociologists and management experts have done significant work on the topic of leadership. They have propagated theories and models that can be used to improve the leadership effectiveness. Leadership skills can be learnt, refined and used. Various methods are used to learn the leadership skills, namely self-analysis, attending training programmes, workshops, seminar on leadership, reading literature on leadership, trial and error, quality circles and organizing competitions. To be a leader one has to use the leadership skills to influence the behaviour of the people and business of the institution. The effectiveness of leadership can be measured on academic achievements of the institution. The leaders build and break the records of academic achievements of the institution.

14. Activity

Checklist for Visionary Leaders

Check level of your visionary leadership responding the questions stated in the check sheet.

Sl. No.	*Check points for Visionary leader*	*Yes*	*No*
1.	Have you crafted shared vision for your institution?		
2.	Have you prepared vision document?		
3.	Have you communicated the vision statement to internal and external stakeholders and got it validated?		
4.	Have you evolved participative values, beliefs, norms, and ethics for the institution? Are these aligned to vision of the institution?		
5.	Have you developed faculty members, staff members and students to contribute their full strengths to accomplish the missions and vision of the institution?		
6.	Have you emotionally charged faculty members, staff members and students to attach themselves with the institution?		
7.	Have you prepared people to experiment, innovate and adopt change?		
8.	Have you encouraged people to go out of fear and take risk?		
9.	Have you created climate of self-initiation, self-control, self-development, self-concept, self-projection, self-confidence, self-persuasion, self-inspiration, self-assessment and self-evaluation?		
10.	Have you designed flexible institutional structure to suit to needs of the functioning of the institution/department/section?		
11.	Have you satisfied the needs of the faculty, staff and students?		
12.	Have you collaborated and networked with centre of excellences i.e. industries, universities, sister institutions, research organizations etc.?		
13.	Have you inspired people frequently using variety of approaches like participation with them, demonstrating trust in them, organizing creativity sessions, creating urgency for work etc.?		
14.	Have you promoted strategic thinking at all levels in the institutions?		
15.	Have you performed the role of change agent in the institution?		
16.	Have you designed flexible processes, systems, and resource base to meet the changing requirement?		
17.	Have you created learning organisation?		
18.	Have you installed inspiring reward and incentive system?		
19.	Have you promoted the use of evaluation techniques for improvement?		
20.	Have you organized competitions on leadership in your institution?		

REFERENCES

Alan Mumford, *Encyclopedia of Management,* Jaico Publishing House, Bombay.

Angela Vint Carlena Recaldin & Des Gould, *Learning to Fly*, Kogan Page.

Burt Nanus, *Visionary Leadership,* Jossey Bass Publishers Sons, Francisco.

Keith Davis & John, W. News, *Strom Organizational Behaviour*, Tata McGraw Hills Publishing Company Ltd., New Delhi.

Organizational Behaviour, Fifth edition, Moorhed.

Ricky, W. Griffin, *Fundamentals of Management,* Houghton Mifflin Company, Boston.

Roy Choudhary, Namita, *Motivation Management in Education,* APH Publishing Corporation, New Delhi.

Stephen, P. Robbins, *Organizational behaviour*, Eighth edition. Prentice Hall of India, New Delhi.

Stephen, S. and Herper, G *Managing Growth in Your Emerging Business*, McGraw Hills Inc.

Vin Clemmer & Art Mccil, *Leadership Skills for Every Manager,* July, Piatkur Ltd., London.

Walter, J. Wadsworth, *Encyclopedia of Practical Management Leadership*, Gemini Books, New Delhi.

William, R. Trancey, *Leadership Skills*, Amacom.

7

Motivation

Objectives: The readers will be able to

1. State the importance of motivation.
2. Describe the concept of motivation.
3. List the theories of motivation.
4. Explain Maslow's theory of motivation.
5. Describe McClelland theory of motivation.
6. Explain Hergberg's two factor theory of motivation.
7. Describe goal setting theory of motivation.
8. Explain theory of reinforcement.
9. Explain equity theory of motivation.
10. Describe behaviour modification model.
11. Describe the application of above theories in educational institutions.
12. Define the concept of intrinsic and extrinsic motivation.
13. Explain the concept of self motivation.

1. Introduction

In the governance and management of technical institutions people play very important and significant role. The functioning of the technical institutions cannot be computerized like high technology industries. The governing body members, governing team members, management team members, faculty members, staff members and students thereby need to be motivated to accomplish the goals of the institution. The real challenge before technical institutions is shaping the behaviour of students in such a way so that they remain motivated through out their life to pursue their career. The focus of the leaders in education is to enhance motivation of all the teams and individuals to create motivational climate for teaching learning process. All supporting processes in the institution are required to contribute to facilitate the academic processes. The focus of motivation is very concentric in technical institutions. There are many concepts, theories, models and principles propagated by psychologists and management experts in different contexts. These are equally applicable for technical institutions as well. A brief account of the same is described in subsequent paragraphs.

2. Concept of Motivation

Different authors define the motivation in different ways, but there are three things, which are universally applicable to motivation. One variable is the situation or context in which motivation of people is required. The other element is the person responsible to perform the task. Both are dynamic variables and affect the motivation of the person. The behaviour of the person is not static. The third variable in the situation is behaviour of leader who is trying to motivate the person to put efforts to complete the task. Looking to all variables the person gets motivated to perform the task or withdraw from the task. Motivation can be defined as internal urge to do the task. This internal urge may depend on many factors. It all depends on the situation. In education setting students are highly motivated to learn a particular subject from a teacher but the other batch of students may not be interested to learn same subject even from the same teacher. It means the motivation depends on the needs of the students.

It is the case with teachers also. One teacher takes interest in a particular batch of students and s/he teaches them every semester till they passout. S/he does not give attention to other batches. Why s/he is motivated to teach one batch of students and not to other? There are number of questions we ask ourselves dealing with motivational cases. Let us examine the different theories of motivation to have better understanding of motivation and to answer such questions.

3. Theories of Motivation

Psychologists, sociologists and management experts have studied motivation with different purposes and propagated theories of motivations. A brief account of significant theories is given in subsequent paragraphs.

3.1 Maslow's Need Hierarchy Theory

Abraham Maslow proposed five major types of human needs. He proposed these needs in hierarchical order. Maslow's hierarchy of needs model is shown in exhibit 7.1.

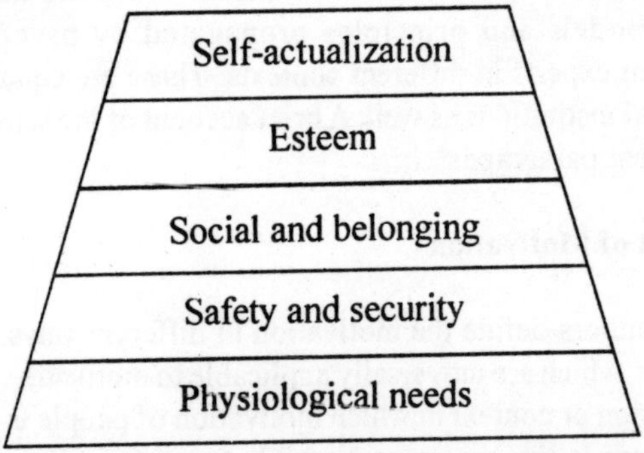

Exhibit No. 7.1: Maslow's hierarchy of needs

He believes that people satisfy their needs in an order proposed by him. The needs start from lowest order and moves up to highest order. The hierarchy of needs proposed by Maslow are physiological needs, security needs, social needs, esteem needs and self-actualization. The hierarchy of needs proposed by Maslow has relevance in motivating the faculty and staff members in technical institutions. People who are searching job will immediately join the institution if they are offered a particular job. Even if it is below their qualification and experience or it may not be related to their interest. They join the post because they have to fulfil the physiological needs. But they will keep searching the job of their choice and status. As soon as they get better opportunity they will quit the job. The Maslow's theory has relevance to selection of the people and satisfies their physiological needs. If the position offered in the technical institution is of person's choice and interest but it is temporary like employment for a fixed period, contract employment, temporary employment etc. S/he will try to search for the opportunity where permanent job is available in technical institution only. According to Maslow's theory of motivation s/he will do so because s/he wants to be secured, and protected against threat to physiological needs. Once the person gets permanent job s/he looks for the friendship to share ideas, feelings, emotions, sorrows, joys, experiences, achievements, problems etc. S/he fulfils social needs joining groups and making friends.

Then come the esteem level needs. The person wants advancement, achievement, freedom, status etc. in his/her career. S/he wants to enjoy autonomy and satisfy her ego. Needs at esteem level are very important in technical institutions. Faculty members, staff members, and students have different kinds of esteem needs. It is the duty of the leader functioning at different levels to identify needs of the people provides opportunities to fulfil the same. There has to be a match between needs and opportunity to increase motivation level of the persons at self-esteem level.

Then next need is the highest order need in the hierarchy of needs. This is self-actualization need. Everyone is interested to harness full potential of the self. This is possible in the situation where opportunity is provided to individuals to excel their best in the area of their ability and interest. The self-actualization step is the highest stage of realization of one's aspirations. Self-actualization needs of the individuals need to be identified appropriately and opportunities should be provided to them. It is said that the extent of match between the needs and opportunities motivate people to the level of match. If there is full match between the two one can do miracles. It is the duty of the leaders to identify the self-actualization needs of the individuals and provide them opportunities to excel their best. Each one in the institution has got different self-actualization needs. One may be interested to become prestigious project leader, second one may be interested to create new technology through research, third may be interested to do community development activities, fourth may be interested to do the liaising work, fifth may be interested to write books and so on. The potential of people has to be identified by the leaders. Sometimes people working in the institution may not know their potential, in that case it is the duty of the leaders to inform about their potential and provide them opportunity to harness the same.

In Maslow's hierarchy of needs theory lower order needs get satisfied when people are working for satisfying higher order needs. There may be fluctuation in needs with respect to time one may go up to self-actualization stage in a particular situation or time span and after that s/he may come down to social needs. Maslow's theory of motivation provides a base for designing motivational programmes at institutional, team, and individual level.

Maslow's theory is relevant for teaching learning process. This theory advocates the fulfilment of social, esteem and self-actualization needs of students. The teachers should diagnose above needs of the students and use learner-centred methods of instruction. Teachers can satisfy the social needs of the students using group discussion, group creativity, action learning, working in a team, role play, multiple role play, group problem solving, methods of instruction. Teachers can satisfy the esteem and self-actualization needs using above methods and some other methods, like problem solving, project, seminar, case method, research, simulation, presentation methods of instruction.

3.2 David McClelland Needs Theory

McClelland identified three basic needs that motivate people to put efforts on a particular task. He propagated that three types of needs are normally prevalent in all human being. These needs are shown in exhibit 7.2.

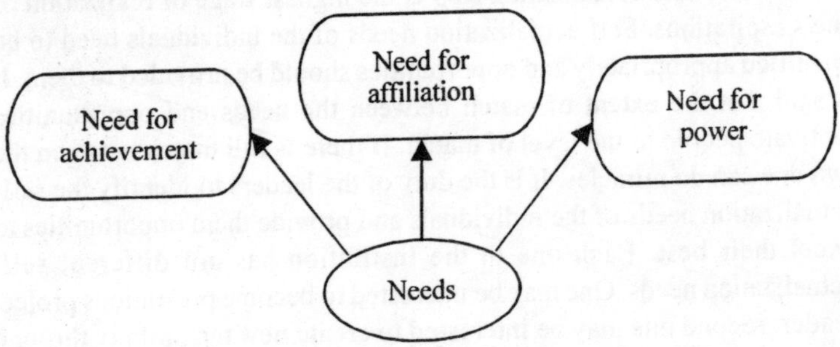

Exhibit No. 7.2: Three types of needs

He clarified that one need is generally found predominant out of three in all the human beings. There may be some people who may have predominant two or all the three needs. It is the duty of the leader to diagnose the needs of the people and assign them works accordingly. If a person is having achievement as predominant need, s/he can be assigned the goal-oriented task of his/her interest and ability. S/he will complete the task without the demand of much of resources and complaint. People having need for achievement are silent workers. They do not publicize their achievements rather they take up or search for new challenging goals. They are not bothered about rewards and incentives. It is the duty of the leader to find out such people and assign them challenging goals. While assigning the work they should keep in mind that the work should match to their ability and interest. Research work, time bond work, task that can be performed by individuals, task that is complex and demanding can be assigned to such type of persons.

If a person is having affiliation as predominant need, s/he can be assigned the work, which requires cooperation from many people. S/he can network with people and organizations to complete the assignment. The job of the training and placement officers, purchase officer, hostel warden, in charge co-curricular activities, physical training officer, state officer, librarian, resembles to this kind of needs.

If students are having strong need for affiliation instruction methods such as group discussion, seminar, games, excursion tours, industrial visits, industrial training etc. can be organized to make them learn effectively. These methods of instructions can be used after continuous theory classes for a week. Students will get an opportunity to interact with each other and resource persons. They can clarify their questions and doubts with each other and resource persons. Variation in methods of instruction will also change their mood and create interest in learning. They will be able to establish relevance of the subject to the practice.

If a person is having power needs predominant, s/he can be assigned the role of a leader or manager. Assignments which require team work in the institution such as curriculum development, preparation of plans, organizing co-curricular activities, organizing seminars, examination, developing instructional material, preparing proposal, etc. can be assigned to such person. They will take responsibility and get the work done. People having need for power have very good influencing and communication skills. They know how to get the work done. Task requiring teamwork and networking can be assigned to such people with leadership role. In-group methods of learning there is a need of a leader to coordinate the different activities of the groups. At the same time there is a need of maintaining discipline. Students having strong need for power, can be assigned leadership role for seminars, group discussions, action learning, problem solving, projects etc.

If a person is having two or more than two predominant needs, there is choice to assign any type of or combination of work to him/her. If a person is having need for affiliation and need for achievement as predominant needs s/he can be assigned work demanding high level of efforts and networking. If a person is having need for achievement and need for power s/he can be assigned new and unique task that has never been performed in the institution. If a person is having all the three needs equally strong s/he can do miracle on any front in any situation. The full potential of the person should be appropriately utilized for the benefit of the institution. People at higher positions should be selected who are having all the three needs as predominant needs.

Diagnosis of these needs is also helpful in selecting the career. One can opt for the career, which fulfils his/her predominant needs. Generally people having need for; affiliation join marketing job. People having need for achievement join research jobs. People having need for power join leadership and managerial position. People having need for achievement and affiliation join teaching and social service job. People having need for power, affiliation, and accomplishment join politics.

3.3 Fredrick Herzberg Two Factor Theory

Herzberg has developed two types of sets of factors through his research work. He defined these factors as hygiene factors and motivating factors. Both the types of factors are listed in exhibit 7.3.

Fredrick Herzberg two factor theory

Hygiene factors	Motivating factors
Policy and administration	Achievement
Quality of supervision	Recognition
Interpersonal relationship	Creative and challenging work
Salary	Responsibility
Job security	Advancement
Working conditions	Growth
Job status	
Personal life	

Exhibit No. 7.3: Fredrick Herzberg two factor theory

One set of factors responsible for dissatisfaction is called hygiene factors. He proposed another set of factors responsible for motivation called motivating factors. If these factors are present in job situation they may cause no dissatisfaction or dissatisfaction. He puts pay and security, company policy and administration, interpersonal relationship, working conditions, supervision under hygiene factors. If these factors are favourable to individuals there will be no dissatisfaction. No dissatisfaction does not indicate that people are motivated. He proposed another set of factors called motivating factors which includes; career advancement, responsibility, the work itself, recognition and achievement. If these factors are favourable in job situation people will be motivated to work and get satisfaction in absence of which there will be no satisfaction. Motivating factors are related to work content and hygiene factors are related to work environment.

As discussed in Maslow's theory of motivation the practices related to contract appointment, *adhoc* appointment, low pay, less facilities to employees are related to hygiene factors. The issue of ladies toilets, safe drinking water, common rooms for faculty and staff members, non-availability of recreation facilities, no facility for crèche, inefficient transport facility, fear of retrenchment, teaching the subjects on which there is no command of the teachers and quality of supporting staff all are the examples of hygiene factors. If we look from students' point of view apart from the above factors poor library and learning resources facilities, use of traditional learning methods, less use of media during the process of teaching learning process, less interaction from industry personnel are examples related to hygiene factors. These factors need to be considered while opening up a new institution and during the process of accreditation and certification.

Hygiene conditions need to be developed and sustained for no dissatisfaction. Absence of hygiene factors is the biggest reason for non-availability of excellent faculty and staff in such institution. If you don't get excellent faculty and staff members how can you get good students? How can you ensure the quality of education?

As discussed in Maslow's theory esteem and self-actualization level needs are very important needs for people in educational institutions. Herzberg has also suggested motivating factors. Apart from hygiene factors there is a need to promote many motivating factors like: career advancement based on performance and experience of the people, enhancing the responsibility level with status, assigning the work of choice and interest, providing recognition and appreciation for extra ordinary contributions and achievement, providing opportunities for research, development and achievement, deputing for training in the area of interest, assigning co-curricular activities of choice, assigning the projects and problems of big industrial houses etc.

If we look at motivating factors from students point of view there are many motivating factors which can be considered, like library facility, shifting the responsibility of learning to them, giving well designed students centered assignments, challenging industrial assignments, involving students in consultancy projects and sharing consultancy amount, offering variety of co-curricular activities according to the choice of students, arranging interaction with well known expert in the field, providing recognition for unique contribution, creating all favourable condition for joyful learning as per demand of the situation. There is a lot of scope for promoting motivating factors in teaching learning process.

3.4. Expectancy Theory of Motivation

Victor Vroom proposed the expectancy theory of motivation. Vroom proposed that level of motivation depends on three factors, i.e. expectancy, valence and instrumentality as stated in exhibit 7.4. It is a process-oriented theory. This theory accounts for individual and situational differences. Victor Vroom described the behaviour of individuals in terms of their goals, preference for the goals and expectations of achieving the goals.

Motivation	**Expectancy** Increased efforts will lead to increased rewards	**Instrumentality** Perceived likelihood that performance will be followed by a reward	**Valence** A person's preference for particular outcome

Exhibit No. 7.4: Expectancy theory of motivation

Expectancy refers to person's perception of the likelihood that efforts will lead to performance. Valence refers to a persons' perception of the value of the projected outcomes in other words the extent to which the person has preferences for outcome. Valence can be positive or negative. Situations in which perception and valence is high motivation is also likely to be high. Instrumentality refers to a persons' perception of the probability that outcomes will be attached to the performance. If the person perceives that there is more likelihood for performance her motivation level will be high.

It is the duty of the leader to identify the potential of followers and assign them suitable job. S/he should increase expectancies about their performance. S/he should provide all necessary resources in time. S/he should promote healthy climate of mutual trust, respect and support. In a healthy climate people will perform better. People must know the performance objectives and performance standards when the task is assigned to them. Leader can provide opportunities to followers to develop potential for growth. S/he can attach the rewards and incentives to the performance outcome. There has to be link between goal accomplishment and rewards. S/he should set examples of rewarding the performance. S/he should inspire followers to increase their perception about their potential, expectancy, valence and instrumentality.

The expectancies of the students can be increased informing them about the career opportunities available in different market segment related to particular subject. During the course of instruction, the teacher can design different learning assignments and their expectancies can be increased. The teacher can give simple assignment in the beginning of the subject. Later on difficult assignments can be given to them with some hints to keep their perception high for performance. The performance can be linked to their continuous assessment grades. Teachers can follow the scheme of assigning grades and demonstrate that they are honest in awarding performance. Other rewards could be many like; best boy or girls in a particular subject, monetary benefit on consultancy projects, certificate of achievement etc. Teachers can raise the motivation level of the students through appropriate recognition and rewards for performance.

3.5. Goal-setting Theory of Motivation

This is a cognitive theory of motivation. Latham and Locke developed it. It stresses on process of setting the goals. Well-set goals can help people to find out alternative ways to achieve them and thereby satisfying their needs. Goals that are challenging, attractive, clear, specific and acceptable motivate people to put efforts. People mobilize their resources to achieve the goals because they want to see the outcomes of their efforts. The achievement of the goals is rewarding in itself. It enhances the motivation level to pursue another goal. Goal setting process of motivation leads to pursue another goal. Goal setting process of motivation is widely used in the process of planning. Management by objective philosophy of planning is based on the theory of goal setting. Participative method of goal setting enhances acceptance and commitment of the people for goal accomplishment. This theory of motivation has been in practice for a long time. Specific feedback can be given to people for improving the performance on the basis of goal attainment. Persons performing the task can also take self-feedback on performance. The positive, constructive and specific feedback enhances the performance of the people. If people in the very beginning know the goals or they are set participatively they cannot deny achieving them.

Leaders can involve individuals and groups in the goal setting process in different areas of functioning of the institution and can set achievable and challenging goals. This is generally done during the processes of planning. It helps leaders to allocate the resources to perform the task. They can monitor the progress of the work and help followers to solve the problems. At the end of the semester the goal accomplishment can be assessed and actions can be taken to improve the performance. This analysis would help to offer feedback and rewards to the people.

The theory of goal setting is relevant for teaching learning process as well. The teachers and students can jointly set the goals for learning. The goals can be set subject wise according to curriculum. Routine goals and objectives are given in the curriculum document apart from this some challenging goals can be set. These goals may be related to time management, seminars, projects, technology development, research paper writing etc. The examples on goal setting are explained in a chapter on planning. Some examples of goal statements are given here for ready reference to

- ensure 80 per cent students get more than 65 per cent marks in a subject
- generate solution for two industrial problems
- organize three students' seminars on emerging topics.
- conduct two industrial visits a week duration in a semester
- organize six continuing education programmes in a semester

3.6 Reinforcement Theory of Motivation

B.F. Skinner has proposed the theory based on the experiments conducted by him. He emphasized the importance of feedback and reward in motivating a particular kind of behaviour. He explained that the previous behaviour if reinforced there is likelihood that the behaviour will get repeated. Using reinforcement techniques behaviour of the people can be controlled and shaped in a desired manner. This theory is significant so far teaching learning is concerned. It is directly related to behaviour modification of the persons working in the institution and students. Skinner suggested that the desired behaviour should be paired with positive reinforcements, feedback or reward. He has suggested that punishment techniques should not be used to shape the behaviour of the person. The punishment techniques may have long-term adverse effect on the behaviour of the person. The punishment technique should be used as last resort.

The reinforcement techniques have been used with theories of learning in programmed instruction successfully. Self-learning lessons and supervisor assisted learning instructions are designed using theory of reinforcement. The lessons are designed in a very simple way. The text is presented to the students for comprehension and then they are asked to respond set of questions. If their answer is correct they take further course of learning this is a reward for them. If they fail to answer the question remedial instruction is presented to them till they achieve the minimum desired level of learning. Teachers should learn reinforcement techniques and design computer aided instructions for self-learning. Reinforcement techniques are very much relevant and required in developing distance learning resources, self-learning resources and individualized learning resources. Teachers should learn reinforcement techniques and use in their own situations to produce desired learning.

3.7 Behaviour Modification Model

This model is based on theory of reinforcement. It is based on the principle that behaviour depends on its consequences. If the behaviour is reinforced positively there are chances that people will repeat it. If the behaviour is not reinforced or reinforced with negative reinforcement (not desired by the person) there are no chances of its repetition. The leaders should create healthy atmosphere to learn and demonstrate desired behaviour. The behaviour modification is required to enrich the academic processes for effective and efficient learning of students. One can use computers and enhance the efficiency to a greater extent whether it is academic or supporting processes. Any major change in processes definitely requires change in behaviour of the people. In behaviour modification model five steps are followed. These steps are shown in exhibit 7.5.

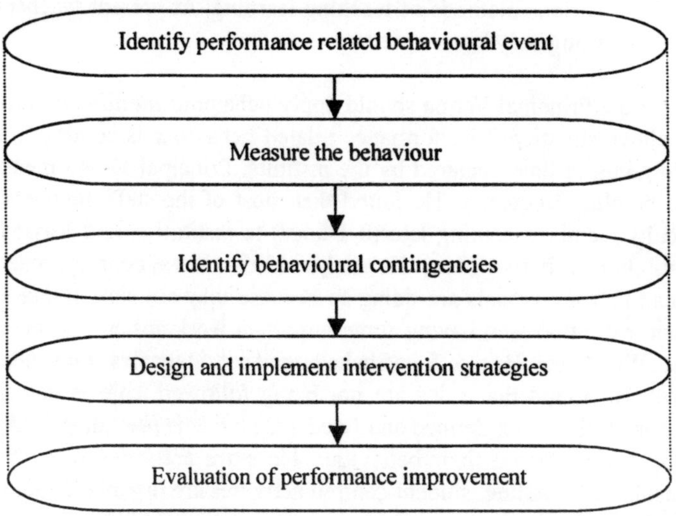

Exhibit No. 7.5: Behaviour modification model

This model has got wide applicability in technical institutions because varieties of behavioural changes are enforced on faculty and staff members. For example, use of variety of teaching learning methods, use of media mix and preparing students for the job. One behaviour modification example related to staff coming late and going early is explained in the situation given below:

Behaviour Modification Situation

Government polytechnic, which runs 7 diploma and two advance diploma programmes is having 30 per cent shortage of faculty members and 15 per cent shortage of supporting staff. Because of late admission and supplementary examination schedule working days get reduced to 70 per cent (of 180 days) out of these 70 per cent (126 days) 30 per cent days (37 days) are left unutilized because of some reasons or another. Most of the faculty and staff members are habituated to come late (0-1 hour) and they also leave the institution early (0-1 hour). Because of these two reasons curriculum cannot be covered fully. So the results of this polytechnic are not encouraging. Principal Verma has taken over the charge recently. He wants that:

- Each member of the institution should come in time.
- Curriculum should be covered in actual available days using various methods of teaching learning. At present teachers are using only lecture method.

How Principal Verma should apply behaviour modification model in above situations? Performance related behaviour is coming in time and going in time declared by the institute. Principal Verma measured the baseline frequency. He found that most of the staff members and faculty members coming late (0-1 hour) to institution and leaving the institution early (0-1 hour). He analyzed behavioural contingencies and found that individuals are doing so because they are sick, living away from institution, and having some important work at home in first and last official hour. He also found behavioural contingencies at institutional level. He found that rules are not being followed, role is not clear, responsibility is not defined and fixed and no one is providing feedback to such persons on their behaviour. No extra activities like official consultancy, training, student-centred activities are organized. Students also leave the institution early because of non-availability of teachers. There is a social acceptance for coming late and escaping from work.

Principal Verma also analyzed contingencies that emit the behaviour on the basis of the persons who are coming in time and leaving in time. He found that individuals are healthy, stay in campus, and do not have important work at home. He also found behavioural contingencies at institutional level. He found that people are assigned interesting and balanced work, are personally responsible for the task, are involved in extra activities and have been provided good title and resources.

Principal Verma designed intervention strategies for individual and institution level on the basis of analysis of contingencies. He designed strategies for individuals like; provide quick response to their health related matters such as providing medical advance, clearing up medical bills in time, providing help to consult specialist, provide transport facility or sanction vehicle advance at priority basis and provide them flexibility in time with targeted work. He designed strategies for institution level such as adhere to rules, make the role clear, provide specific responsibility during first hour and last hour, provide continuous feedback, promote extracurricular or curricular activities in last hour, keep difficult subject period as last period, force students to stay in the institution during scheduled time, enhance punctuality your self and of heads of departments, curb the habit of escaping from work through job rotation, redesign job, practice job involvement and make people personally responsible.

He made above strategies explicit to each latecomer and early leaver before implementation. He asked them to tell frankly about their views on the strategy. He had declared rewards attached to each type of behaviour and declared the date of implementation. He had made clear both types of reinforcement positive as well negative for desired behaviour. He implemented the strategies with continuous monitoring, feedback and reinforcement. He monitored the implementation of above strategies each week and reviewed the progress. He modified the strategies and corresponding reinforcement. He implemented the strategies till desired behaviour became permanent. He monitored the progress through resource persons. Principal Verma punished few people who have not adhered to desired behaviour in spite of request and counselling.

3.8 Job Enrichment

Hackman and Oldham propagated the model called job enrichment model. Using this model the new jobs can be designed and existing jobs can be enriched. Existing jobs can be enriched in a way to provide greater opportunity for recognition, advancement, growth and responsibility. People get satisfaction performing the job itself. According to this model the job of a person should be designed in such a way that five job characters or dimensions are present in the job. These characteristics are shown in exhibit 7.6.

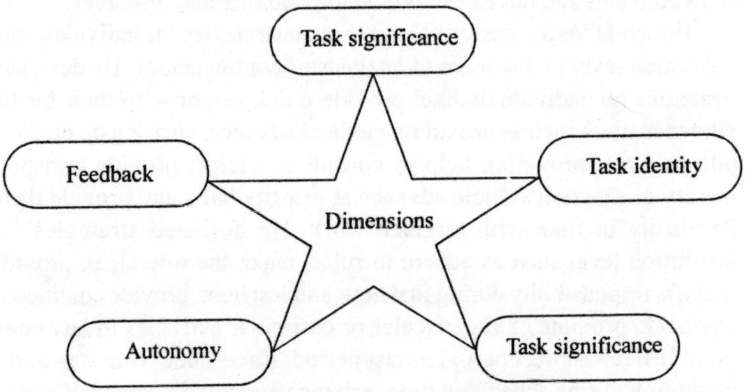

Exhibit No. 7.6: Characteristics of job

The job should be designed in such a way so that it requires variety of skills to perform. The job will create challenge for the performer to use the ability and experiences to complete it. The job should be complete in itself. The person plans it, perform it and evaluate the achievements. People should be involved in job design process right from beginning to its finalization. The job should be whole and the responsibility should be given to a person or a group. The job should be significant. If the job is not performed it should have adverse effect on many people. If it is performed effectively and efficiently it should satisfy the needs of people. People should be granted autonomy to plan, take decisions and mobilize resources on their own. There should be provision of internal as well as external feedback on the progress of the jobs and outcomes of the job. To make the job enriched the extent of presence of these characteristics in the job should be is more.

The presence of these characteristics in a job makes it meaningful and increases internal motivation of a performer to do it. S/he feels that the job is challenging and inviting her/him to perform. S/he also feels that the job is important and it should be performed. S/he feels more responsible for the job and put her/his best talent to the job. S/he produces high quality of services and products. S/he derives satisfaction out of it.

S/he enjoys the autonomy and receives feedback on the progress of the work and results. S/he gets intrinsic satisfaction performing such enriched jobs. S/he is more motivated to perform subsequent jobs in next cycle. Many jobs can be easily enriched through horizontal and vertical loading meaning thereby combining the similar tasks which are being performed by colleagues, superiors and subordinates and making it one complete natural work unit. The complete unit of work is linked to the customer services.

Open environment for receiving and giving feedback can be created in the institution to provide constructive and positive feedback for improvement. The job performer also gets feedback from the progress of the work and quality of the work. For example a teacher may be assigned linked subjects to make the job complete and meaningful for her. S/he can be assigned linked subjects such as applied mechanics, strength of material, structural design and structural analysis subjects. S/he should guide and get involved in the curriculum design process. S/he can be assigned conduction of the practical classes of all above subjects. S/he guides the students' assignments, seminar, professional body chapter activities, research work, field projects and problems related to above subjects. S/he gets involved in instructional material development, formative and term end assessment of students learning. S/he is given responsibility of organizing continuing education programme for industry people. Many other activities can be added looking to the interest of the person in above subjects. S/he can be given autonomy to take decisions related to her/his responsibility in above subjects. S/he gets involved right from curriculum design to assessment of learning and placement of students. S/he is given opportunities to attend training programmes, seminars, conferences and symposium on above subjects. S/he contacts employers for placement of students so s/he gets internal as well as external feedback on the extent of learning of students and her/his achievements. This gives her immense satisfaction.

Similarly a teacher can enrich the learning process for students. An indicative example of enriching learning process is shown in exhibit 7.7. S/he can create challenge and interest in learning process using variety of methods of teaching, media and methods of assessment. S/he can use combination of various teaching learning methods such as industrial projects, problem solving, failure analysis, seminars, industrial visits, self-learning, action learning, group discussion, case analysis, action research, project analysis to enrich the learning of students.

Exhibit No. 7.7: Method of enriching learning process for students

Curriculum	Teaching learning methods	Examination
➢ Explain the complete curriculum ➢ Linkages of curriculum with other subjects- previously learnt, learning in preset and future ➢ Importance of subject for the job ➢ Expectations of teacher from students ➢ Assessment criteria ➢ Timetable	Use of variety of methods such as: ➢ Lecture-practical-field visit-feedback ➢ Industrial training- presentation of learning and theory ➢ Group discussion-action learning, ➢ Lecturer-seminar feedback ➢ Lecture – competition- feedback ➢ Self-learning-tutorial– self-learning	➢ Test ➢ Observation ➢ Assignments output ➢ Group output ➢ Seminar ➢ Competition ➢ Self-assessment ➢ Report ➢ Case study ➢ Project work ➢ Job ➢ Research work

3.9 Job Rotation

Persons get boredom performing same job year after year or continuously for a year. Initially s/he may get interest in the job but over a period of time but later on s/he may feel no challenge in the job. To break the monotony and to create challenge and interest new jobs should be assigned to a person. New jobs should be assigned looking to her/his ability and interest. After a certain period a teacher can choose another stream of connected subjects or s/he may choose some subjects of old stream and some other related subjects of new stream. It all depends on the branch of engineering and teachers working in that engineering department. The job rotation design can be discussed among teachers and on their acceptance it can be implemented to serve the specific purpose. There may be some jobs, which are boring type, but because of requirement of the law or management it needs to be carried out. These types of jobs can be rotated among the people in the institution. They assign repetitive nature of jobs to individuals along with liked jobs. Similarly, job rotation can be designed for other positions with a purpose. Teachers have to perform variety of job dimensions. The distribution of these job dimensions can be planned during role design. One teacher may be assigned one significant job dimension predominantly say teaching learning and other dimensions such as research, continuing education and placement on nominal basis looking to her/his interest and ability. Next year s/he may be assigned another significant role dimension say consultancy predominantly and other dimensions such as training and placement, research and teaching learning on nominal basis. In this way the jobs can be designed and rotated among institutional members. This process will ensure job enrichment. The options for job rotation for a teacher is shown in exhibit 7.8

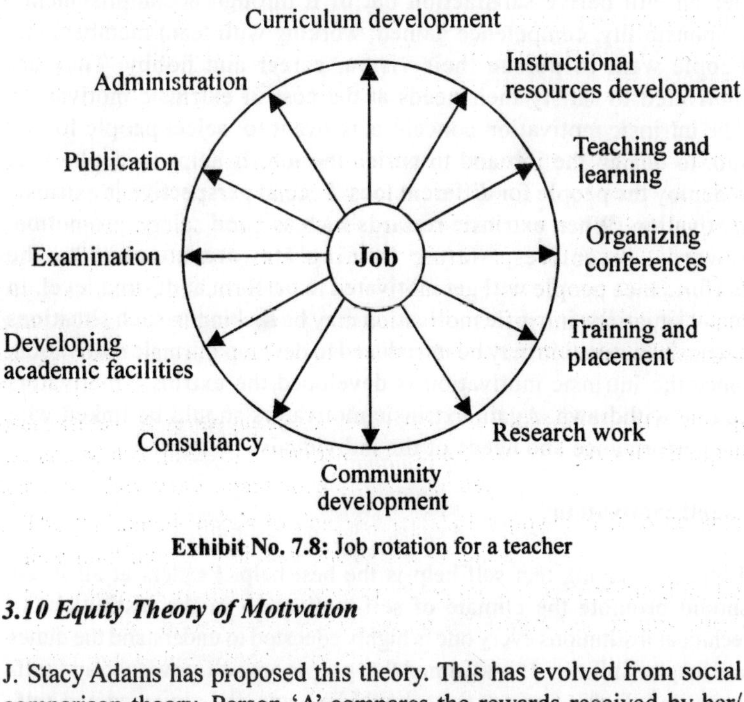

Exhibit No. 7.8: Job rotation for a teacher

3.10 Equity Theory of Motivation

J. Stacy Adams has proposed this theory. This has evolved from social comparison theory. Person 'A' compares the rewards received by her/him with her/his comparison person 'B'. S/he thinks that s/he is comparing with the right person. It may be wrong also. S/he compares the ratio of output to input of self with the output to input of other. If the ratio is equal it makes no change in motivation level. If it is less than her/his comparison s/he will try to reduce the inputs and make the ratio equal. Outcomes may be salary, incentives, status etc. The inputs include effort, expertise, experience, attitude etc. The adjustment in input and output depends on the job situation and type of institution in which the person is working. If some one is complaining about equity the situation require to be analyzed from institutional functioning point of view and decisions should be taken.

4. Intrinsic and Extrinsic Motivation

Motivation can be seen from two perspectives. First focuses on intrinsic motivation, which comes from within. It comes from within because of interest, ability and likeliness for a particular job. The person will derive satisfaction out of it through accomplishments, responsibility, competence gained, working with team members etc. People want to pursue their vision, career and hobby. They are motivated to satisfy their needs at the cost of extrinsic motivation. The intrinsic motivation concept is relevant to; select people for the job, to design the job and to enrich the job. It helps to deploy and redeploy the people for different jobs. Second perspective is extrinsic motivation. When extrinsic rewards such as good salary, promotion, rewards, incentives, status, training etc. are attached to the performance people will get motivated to perform at desired level. In many situations intrinsic motivation may be lacking in such situations extrinsic motivation may be introduced to develop intrinsic motivation. Once the intrinsic motivation is developed the extrinsic motivators can be withdrawn. Again extrinsic motivators should be linked with the performance and needs of the individuals.

5. Self-motivation

There is a saying that self-help is the best help. Leaders at all levels should promote the climate of self-motivation in the institution. In technical institutions every one is highly educated to understand the duties and responsibilities. It is assumed that people are self-governed and self-motivated. If they are not they should be made self-governed and self-motivated. They should control their behaviour and reactions in situations, which they do not like. They should posses great tolerance attitude in the situations of dislike. They should listen the criticism and take it positively for self-improvement. People should appreciate that for the larger benefit they are supposed to change their behaviour. They should align their behaviour to achieve the goals of the institution and not to merely practicing something because they like it. The leaders should develop climate of self-motivation using variety of methods. Every method used for promoting self-motivation should focus on 'self'.

Institutional members should be encouraged to take initiatives to identify, own, plan and complete the job. People in work setting can mutually encourage attitude of self-initiation. Self-initiation will prevent many likely problems to occur. This will also solve many problem related to functioning, delay, ego, conflict, crisis, communication etc. The second method is developing confidence among the people that they can do whatever they want to do. Self-confidence overcomes the fear of failure. When they are out of fear they feel free to do any thing they like. The third method is developing the habit of conscious and continuous learning from the environment. Self-learning should be promoted in the field of one's own area of interest. It can be related to present job and future career growth.

Each person can shape her/his behaviour aligned to the values, beliefs, ethics, norms and expectations of the institution. S/he can impose self-discipline and prove herself/himself that s/he is sincere, faithful, trustworthy and honest to the institution and its activities. S/he would have proud to be called self-disciplined person. The continuous appraisal of performance is necessary to ensure the progress towards goal, mission and vision accomplishment. Self-appraisal at regular interval of time may help to identify the performance problems and take corrective actions. One can be self-governed through proper planning of the work. Institution can help the people providing autonomy to take decision. Self-introspection helps people to know what I am. People should be provided an opportunity and forum through which they can interact with themselves and find out their inner strengths and weaknesses. They can be facilitated and supported by the leaders to bank upon their strengths for further development of self-confidence. In this forum opportunities are provided to individuals to share their strengths, achievements and feelings with colleagues and trained mentor. A trained mentor can help people to improve self-concept. Human beings are selfish. They see their benefit in the work. Their selfishness can be identified and they can be awarded works fulfilling selfishness at the same time it is a selfless work. Doing so their internal needs get satisfied. People want to use their self-style to do the work. This requires flexible approaches of working in the institution. Some people may be self-centered, there is nothing wrong being self-centred but they should not forget that they are elements of social system. They should join the formal and informal teams and open up to people. Formal and informal teams provide an opportunity to learn from others and receive feedback about self.

6. Self Motivation Strategies

Variety of methods can be used to motivate self. Some of the important approaches are listed in the exhibit 7.9 and briefly described in subsequent paragraphs. One can pick up one or more methods looking to her/his requirements. One can use standard instruments to assess the self-motivation level and design appropriate strategies to enhance the same. One can ask others to observe and provide feedback on self-motivation level on significant parameters. Based on the feedback received one can improve upon self-motivation.

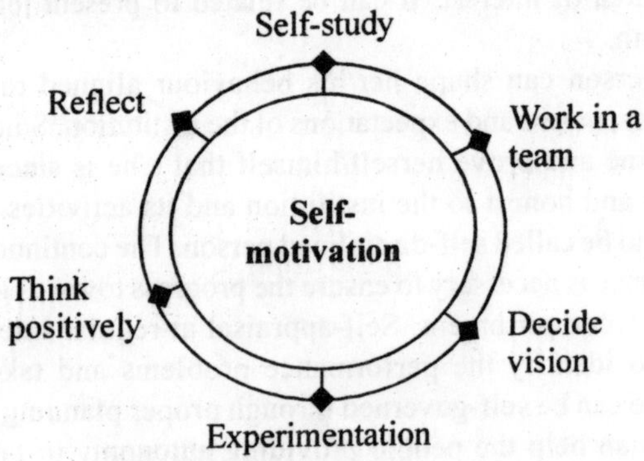

Exhibit No. 7.9: Self-motivation strategies

6.1 Self-study

Do self-study asking set of questions such as: Who am I? Where I have come from? Where am I going? What is stopping me? How will I get there? What will I need to get there? What will it be like when I get there? The answers of these questions tell you about your inner self. Understanding your inner self you can improve upon your self-motivation level using appropriate methods.

6.2 Work in a Team

Always try to work in successful teams. Experience of working with others would help you to know yourself and others. You can discuss and share everything related to your work with team members. You get praise, appreciation, recognition and respect from fellow team members. Recognition from fellow members helps you to get further motivation.

Team members support each other and criticize each other. This event of receiving feedback and providing feedback to fellow members during working in team is helpful to modify the behaviour naturally.

6.3 Decide Vision

You can craft your own vision and fix up the milestones with reference to time. Your vision keeps you motivated, encouraged and energized. It guides you to take relevant decisions in uncertainty. Make your vision known to everyone who can help you. People will definitely help you to pursue it. Resemble the high calibre, high profile and great people to your vision. Study more about them and try to adopt their lifestyle in your life. You can fix their photographs at workplace.

6.4 Experimentation

Do experiments and record your self-motivation. Implement new and innovative ideas. The results on innovation are self-rewarding and self-motivating. Think different and think big about you and your work. Assume responsibility for your innovative ideas. When you assume responsibility, accept challenge, face competition you feel self-motivated to fulfil the requirements.

6.5 Think Positively

List your strengths, weaknesses, capabilities, capacities, achievements, relationships, habits, resources, experiences, expertise, hobbies, etc. Think positively to improve on above parameters so that you can grab the opportunities to pursue your vision. Think positively to find more effective and efficient ways of working to continuously improve your performance.

6.6 Note Down Learning

Every moment of time you learn from the environment. Whatever significant ideas you learn during the process of performing the task note it down in your diary or make a quotation of it and paste it on fennel board. Keep it there till you remember it by heart and follow it naturally. You learn many things through reading. Take notes of important points related to behaviour modification. Use your notes for enhancing self-motivation. Share the learning with your colleagues, superiors and subordinates.

7. Guidelines for Motivating Faculty and Staff Members

The teachers and staff members are the main resources of the institution. They should be motivated and self-motivated to set challenging goals and achieve them. Some indicative guidelines for motivating the faculty and staff members are noted in exhibit 7.10 for your reference.

Exhibit No. 7.10: Guidelines for motivating faculty and staff members

- Diagnose the situation in which level of motivation is low or likely to be low. Analyze the problem and find out the causes of demotivation. Find appropriate motivation techniques to remove the causes.
- Identify the type of persons required to do the task and assign the task to the right person. This can very well be done using need identification techniques. In some situations you have to elicit the needs of the people to make them accept the task. Do not assign the task to a person because s/he is sincere.
- Balance distribution of work among people. People should not be overloaded or under loaded. The distribution of work should be done according to the ability, interest and availability of time to people. In some situations you have to develop the ability and interest or both.
- Maintain the profile of the faculty and staff members. This will help you quickly identify the person for a particular task. This profile can be compared with the vision, mission, strategic plan and task requirements. If the profile does not match develop the people to cover up gap. Remove your biases about people. Go by facts, data and results.
- Inform the performer about your expectation in terms of performance and performance standards. Ensure that you have effectively communicated your expectation and performer knows what s/he has to do. Declare the rewards associated to performance at the time of awarding the task. Reward the people accordingly and immediately on the basis of performance.
- Create challenges in the work of individuals and teams. Challenges can easily be created knowing the strengths and weakness of individuals and team. Create higher standards of performance than their strengths and weaknesses. People should stretch themselves to meet the challenges.
- Motivate yourself to accomplish the task. Look motivated and committed to the task even if you are exhausted. Then only you will be able to motivate the people to work hard. Your motivation level decides the motivation level of the people performing the task. Create the environment for self-motivation.

(Contd.)

(*Contd.*)

- Continuously improve hygienic conditions in the institution. If you cannot increase the pay of the people do not worry. Try to increase the hygienic conditions like: good toilet facilities, drinking water, maintenance fund for laboratories, workshops, library, learning resources centre, classroom, relationships among people etc. Improve cleanliness and aesthetic appearance in the campus but not at the cost of teaching learning process.
- Decentralize power to the lowest level of employee. Empower individuals and teams to take decisions and implement without any delays. Decisions should be taken in consonance with institutional policies. Empower people who are in direct touch with stakeholders and students to manage the things at their level.
- Tell people that they have potential to complete the task. Tell them that earlier also they have completed the task successfully although they had been hesitant. Develop 'can do' attitude in the people. You can make it clear in the beginning of assigning the challenging assignment that no harm will be there even it they fail to perform. Encourage people to take calculated risk on their own.
- Design the job of the people involving them. Review the job of people and try to refine, modify or even change it with their consensus. Introduce job enrichment factors like task variety, task identify, task significance, autonomy and feedback in the job. After certain interval of time you can rotate the person on various job dimensions.
- Use participatory approaches of management like working in a team, creativity sessions, consensus seeking sessions, problem solving sessions, participative planning, quality circles, meetings etc. to fulfil the social and institutional needs of the people.
- Motivate people by vision, values, beliefs, ethics, norms and emotions. Establish value loaded shared vision, values, beliefs, ethics and norms that are observed by every faculty member, staff member and students. They should put pressure on each other to follow the set values. There should not be any conflict among values, ethics, norms, beliefs and behaviour of the people required to implement vision reach strategies.
- Training, re-training and continuous training is essential to deploy and re-deploy people for variety of changing jobs. Like industries, there is a growing demand of developing multi-skilled faculty and staff members who can assume changing roles, enriched roles and new roles effectively and efficiently. This requires flexible, autonomous and empowered systems of functioning in the institution.
- Remunerative and non-remunerative jobs should be distributed equally and as per interest of the individuals or groups. Jobs which are non-productive but must be performed because of legal requirement and other requirements should be shared jointly on rotational basis by all the persons competent to perform the jobs.

(*Contd.*)

(Contd.)

> ➢ Establish well-defined communication channels and create an atmosphere to convey the expectations to each other. The leaders and followers should be open in communicating the expectations. The messages should be taken in the spirit they are communicated. If there is any gap in communication that should be rectified immediately. Effective communication keeps people informed on different aspects of their performance. They know the answers of questions like: what to do, how to do, when to do, where to do, what quality of performance, what level of performance, what are the rewards associated to performance etc. This motivates them to put efforts to the task.

8. Rewards and Incentives

Each institution should have the rewards and incentive policy. The policy should clearly spell out the type of incentives (extrinsic as well as intrinsic) offered by the institution. The policy should be clear on the criteria for awarding the rewards and incentives. The process of awarding the incentive should be transparent, objective and participative. All India Council for Technical Education has recommended the salary structure and other incentives for faculty and staff members of technical education. These recommendations are general in nature. When institutions are pursuing their own vision they need suitable faculty and staff members. To employ suitable faculty and staff members unique but different incentive policy is required. The institutions are required to prepare the incentive policy to attract the best people as per their requirement. The AICTE recommendation can be considered as a basis for crafting the policy. Many new dimensions are added as per needs of the institution. Different people have different needs so variety of incentives need to be introduced in the policy to satisfy the extrinsic as well as intrinsic needs of the people.

Incentives should be linked to performance. Performance of the individuals should be assessed through performance appraisal and development system and rewards should be attached to performance. Merit system is used for yearly pay increase or promotion. It is decided on performance of individuals. Apart from this incentive system is used to pay for their contribution on a specific task. There are many versions available to incentive system like; incentive per lecture or per practical or per module or evaluation of students' performance in practical per students, valuation of answer sheet per answer sheet can be fixed. The second version is profit sharing. In this version the team members share profit. Norms are fixed for this in the policy. This is very common in consultancy projects. Third one is gain sharing. A particular team that exhibits outstanding performance is given incentives. Fourth one is lump sum incentive. This can be declared in the policy for innovations, outstanding performance etc.

9. Summary

The faculty members, staff members and students should be motivated to achieve the academic and non-academic goals of the institution. The motivation level of individuals and teams decides the future of the institution. A highly motivated teacher can take students to all heights of learning. The needs theories of motivation educate to identify needs of the people and provide them opportunity to satisfy the needs. Maslow propagated that there are hierarchy of needs and they occur in order. Hierarchical needs proposed by Maslow are physiological needs, safety needs, social needs, esteem and self-actualization. People get more motivated to fulfil lower order needs than higher order needs. The job can be designed to fulfil the specific needs of the people. David McClelland proposed three types of needs that is need for achievement, need for affiliation and need for power. People have all three types of needs: but they have one or two needs as predominant needs. The allocation of job should match with the needs of the person. The perfect match between the need and job ensures high motivation of people. Fedric Herzberg proposed two-factor theory of motivation. He proposed that hygienic factors should always be present to prevent dissatisfaction. He also proposed that scope for career advancement, responsibility, recognition, and achievement are motivating factors in work setting. These factors should be promoted in work setting to motivate people. Expectancy theory of motivation emphasizes the importance of increasing expectancy, instrumentality and valence in work setting. If the perception of people about expectancy, instrumentality and valence is high they will be highly motivated. Goal setting theory proposed that challenging, attractive, clear, specific and realistic goals motivate people to release energy. These goals should be participatively decided. Reinforcement theory of motivation propagated that if desired behaviour is reinforced appropriately, there is likelihood that behaviour will get repeated. This theory has relevance to behaviour modification. Job enrichment theory proposes to incorporate five factors in the job, i.e. task identity, skill variety, task significance, autonomy and feedback. Presence of these factors creates challenge in the job. People feel responsible and receive constructive feedback on the progress of work. Job rotation is used to share the monotonous jobs.

Equity theory of motivation propagated that people compare their input with the inputs of fellow members. They also compare the incentives and rewards received. They try to make the ratio of output to input equal. Theory of self-motivation highlights the importance of self-motivation in institutional setting.

Theories of motivation have largest application in technical education system. First of all these theories should be used to increase the motivation level of faculty and staff members. Institution should have incentive and reward policy to motivate people to perform better. Incentive and rewards should be performance based. The incentives and reward giving process should be open, transparent and objective. It should motivate people to excel better. Motivated faculty members and staff members can use theories of motivation to motivate students for learning.

10. Activity

Activity – One

Identify factors facilitating and hindering motivation in your institution. Prepare a complete list of the factors then prioritize them according to their strength. You can consider all types of factors affecting motivation. These factors may have positive impact on motivation of the people or negative effect. These factors will differ from institution to institution.

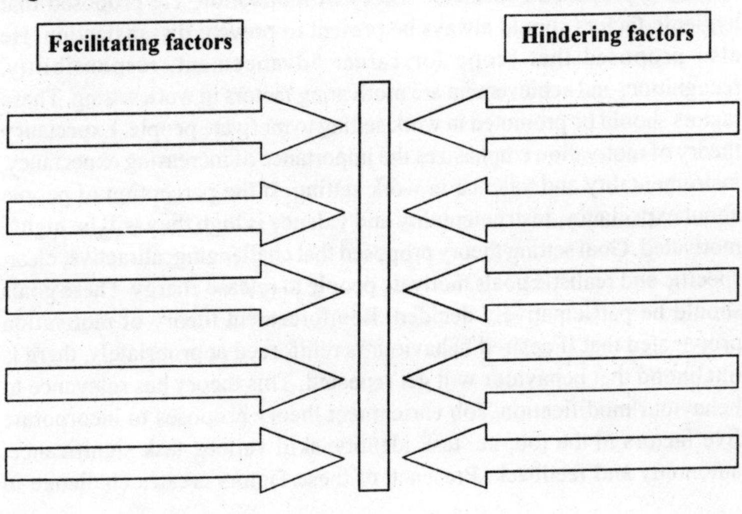

Activity – Two

You know the long-term and short-term goals of your institution. You are equally aware about the motivation level of the faculty member, staff member and students. You are familiar with the incentive policy or practices prevalent in your institution. The incentive policy and practices may not be well documented and strictly followed. You are also aware about the heart burning took place in the institution in absence of or lack of relevant and acceptable incentive policy. You also know that opportunistic people have misused it and taken undue benefits out of it. That has caused adverse effect on the motivation level of the deserving people and consequently performance of the institution. You must have noticed similar cases with students also.

You have gone through various theories of motivation and their applicability in technical institutions and teaching-learning process. You are also aware about the strengths and limitations of the motivational theories. You appreciate the importance of the rewards and incentives. At the same time you know the importance of intrinsic motivation. You have also identified the factors promoting and hindering motivation in your institution. You have prioritized the factors according to their impact on the motivation level of the people. Considering the present scenario and future goals of your institution design a reward and incentive policy for your institution, which is transparent, objective and data based. This policy should be applicable to faculty members, staff members and students. The policy should address the individual motivational requirements as well as team motivational requirement. Have a discussion on the policy to refine it and get it approved from the governing body of your institute.

Activity – Three

A Case on Expectancy Approach

Mr. C.L. Gupta belongs to poor family. His father is a teacher in primary school. Mr. Gupta completed school education from a town school. His teachers have been very honest sincere and value driven. His family culture and teachers inspired him to become a teacher. Mr. Gupta joined Civil Engineering course after completing the school education. He completed engineering course in the year 1982. Mr. Gupta joined the post of site engineer with a consultant. He was completing the construction work of Military Engineering services and few other private projects. Mr. Gupta worked in the project for 3 months. His experience of working in field was not good. It was not suiting to him because of lot of adjustments and corrupt practices. Cheating with customer was routine practice. The objective of completing the projects was to earn more and more money. The earning was at the cost of engineering and quality of work. Mr. Gupta did not like it. He decided to quit the job. He applied for the post of lecturer in polytechnic and got selected.

He joined Government Polytechnic Usha Nagar in 1982. When he joined the polytechnic many senior faculty members told Mr. Gupta that you have a bright future in polytechnic education. They told Mr. Gupta that most of the existing faculty members are diploma holders. They cannot become head of department. Then told Mr. Gupta that you are B.E., if you stay in polytechnic education for six years you will become head of department. That time the entitlement for the post of head of department was B.E. plus five years experience. They also told Mr. Gupta that two channels are open to become head of department in polytechnic. One is through departmental promotional quota (50%) and another is through Public Service Commission (PSC).

Mr. Gupta thought that if I serve technical education for 5 years I would become head of department. He thought that he might get chance in engineering college also. So he made a plan to continue his service in polytechnic. He experienced that the job of the lecturer is easy going and without much of responsibility as compared to field. In 1983 PSC advertised about 600 posts of Assistant Engineer for state irrigation department looking to huge number of posts, Mr. Gupta applied for the post and appeared in the written test conducted by the PSC in June 1984. He qualified the test and faced the interview but finally he could not get success. So he continued to remain in the polytechnic. Again in 1984, State Electricity Board advertised the post of Assistant Engineer Civil. Mr. Gupta applied for the post and qualified the written test. This was the second chance when he qualified the written test but could not get success. He cursed his fate for these two failures.

In 1987, State Government revised the recruitment norms and pay scale of polytechnic teachers and declared it implemented with effect from January 1986. Mr. Gupta was surprised to see the revised eligibility condition for the post of head of department was Master of Engineering/ Master of Technology/Master of Technical Education + 5 years experience + 100 per cent recruitment through PSC.

By this time Mr. Gupta made his mind to leave the job but he could not get any opportunity so in 1987 he applied for study leave to undergo

Master of Engineering (M.E.) course but could not get it sanctioned. Again in 1988, he applied for study leave and it was approved. He put very hard efforts to complete M.E. He ranked first position in the M.E. Now he was pleased enough because he possesses requisite qualification for the post of head of department. He started waiting for advertisement to appear for the post of head of department. He also had an impression that being a senior in the polytechnic and having a good academic record he will be selected for the post. He also started putting more efforts in the institutional activities so that he can show his work to the PSC. After obtaining M.E. he did following significant works in the institution.

- He became incharge of National Service Scheme (N.S.S.) and conducted many social and environmental protection activities in the campus and nearby villages. He organized awareness campus for community in the area of education, health, sanitation and drinking water.
- He became Assistant Project Officer in community wing and expanded the work. Eight extension centres were opened in tribal villages. Extension centres organized training programmes for women in different vocations. Apart from this youth clubs have been opened to take up variety of village development activities. Youth clubs have undertaken many village development activities. They helped schools, health centres and *Aganwadies.*
- He became member of Project implementation unit under World Bank Assisted Project of Civil Works that time the project was just at implementation stage and persuaded Public Works Department to complete the construction work in time.
- He undertook design of overhead water tanks under consultancy work. Testing of cement, bricks, and soil has been a regular activity in the institute. Some continuing education programmes have been organized for sub-engineers of Water Resource Department.
- He developed self-learning packages in irrigation engineering subject. Prepared number of transparencies of complex diagrams and used in the classroom. Negotiated with Municipal Corporation to undertake projects for the students. Three major projects completed successfully and earned money for the institution. A survey project was undertaken from Western Coal Field India Limited.

In April 1991, PSC advertised 4 posts of head of department in which 2 posts were reserved for the SC/ST/OBC candidates. He applied for the post. In March 1992 PSC conducted interview, which lasts for three days. In the interview he was surprised to see a large number of candidates. He was expecting a few candidates. This crowd has discouraged him. Many candidates were two to five years junior to him in experience. They were from engineering colleges. Some candidates were from field they were not satisfied with their job because of some reasons or other. PSC declared the result on last day of interview for which Mr. Gupta was eagerly waiting. When he saw result he was awaked, his name was in waiting list.

Brief

Analyze the case study from expectancy theory of motivation point of view.

Activity – Four

A Case on Motivation

Ms. Asha Jain had joined the Government. Polytechnic, Dun Dun situated in Bhilpradesh in 1990 as Lecturer Civil Engineering (*ad hoc*) after receiving her B.E. from a prestigious Engineering College of the State. Right from her engineering education, she was enthusiastic to join teaching. This was her first job. In her department there are four lecturers and a Head of Department. All other persons in the department including supporting staff are 10-20 years older than her. The previous years result of the department was average when it is compared with state result.

Since her appointment was *ad hoc*, so she had not been given much of responsibility except teaching in the beginning. But she showed lot of interest in teaching and other activities like maintaining the records of students, examination work and arranging library of the Institute. She also developed good relations with staff members as well as students. Within six months of tenure, she made it clear that she is a hard worker, quick learner and strong performer. Recognizing her potential Head of Department and Principal provided her an opportunity to work in difficult and complex areas of working. In March 1991, one lecturer was transferred to other institution who was teaching material technology. His work was assigned to Ms. Jain including the charge of testing laboratory. She prepared a proposal for modernization of testing laboratory and submitted it to Principal through Head of Department. The proposal was convincing so Principal made some modification and submitted it to Central Government to allot funds under D.C.A. scheme. The proposal got materialized and institution received Rs.6 lacs to modernize testing laboratory. Principal gave full autonomy to Ms. Jain to set the laboratory. She prepared details of each activity and implemented to plan. In this endeavour each concerned person helped her to full extent. This tremendous encouragement from all the concerns made her more responsible to complete the task. She set the laboratory and wrote laboratory manual for testing laboratory. She prepared charts and diagrams of new equipment and machinery with the help of students. She put tireless effort. In December 1991 she was confirmed through Public Service Commission so she was placed for induction training programme at Technical Teachers' Training Institute. During the training she conceived many innovative ideas in following areas:

- Classroom instruction
- Laboratory instruction
- Assessment of students performance
- Use of media
- Developing and using learning resources

So going back to her institution she started implementing the ideas. She refined the material, which she prepared for the material-testing lab. Now she is a popular teacher in the institution whose name is tagged to challenging work. She has taken the full subject, innovative and field related projects and developing instructional material in the related field. In three years of time she implemented many innovative ideas in the institution and derived self-satisfaction out of her work. She set an example for other people to work.

In March 1993, the Principal called her and praised her work. Then he gave her the responsibility of revising the detailed Project report of World Bank Assisted Project. She hesitated and told Principal that this project is on in the institution since last three years but she has no idea about it. So she would require guidance and training in this area then only she would extend full cooperation. She accepted the challenge and worked hard to complete the detailed project report (D.P.R.). She contacted all the persons concerned in the institution, at Directorate of Technical Education (D.T.E.) and received training at Technical Teachers Training Institute (T.T.T.I.). Within two months she revised the D.P.R., which was accepted by D.T.E. with some minor modification. Now her institution would get Rs. 3 million more amount than incorporated in original D.P.R.

Principal called a big gathering and he openly recognized the work done by Ms. Jain. Principal also declared that now and onwards Ms. Jain would look after the work of Polytechnic Project Implementation Unit (PPIU). When the revised D.P.R. was at implementation stage she was transferred to Government Polytechnic, Jim Jim. The environment of this institution is not good and it is a worse polytechnic in the state. The Principal is very much interested in personal work. Faculty members are having their own business or coaching centre. Classes were irregular and nobody bothers about institutional activities. She tried to improve the situation but Head of Department and senior faculty members discouraged her. She applied for transfer but she could not get it so she resigned the post and joined with an Architect as Design Engineer.

Brief

- Analyze the personality of Ms. Jain with reference to her teaching job.
- Design the strategies to motivate good faculty to stay in technical institutions.

Activity – Five

Employee Motivation

Sampur Polytechnic was established in the year 1953. It offers diploma in 4 disciplines that is Civil, Mechanical, Electrical and Textile Engineering. Six months ago Mr. Vasi was appointed as Head of Department (HOD) Mechanical Engineering through Public Service Commission. He took charge from Mr. Ragade who was transferred to Charoli Polytechnic. Mr. Vasi is a young and energetic man having good academic record. He has 8 years of industrial experience earlier to polytechnic service. This was Mr. Vasi's first academic position and he was eager to perform well.

From the beginning, however, Vasi felt that a barrier existed between him and his faculty members, many of whom are older than him. Most of them had diploma while he is post-graduate. Some of them had been promoted from Assistant Lecturer to Lecturer 2 year back. He perceived that the problem is because of his age and education. The resentment is because some lecturers might feel ill being headed by a young person.

One day during a meeting with other Head of departments Mr. Das, head of department electrical remarked saying, "Mr. Vasi you seems to be very liberal to your subordinates, whereas Mr. Ragade was very strict. He was a believer to authority. He used to supervise the work of subordinates very closely and direct them in each and every activity. People were always afraid of him". Vasi replied Mr. Das I don't believe in strict supervision and giving direction at each stage. People like work, it is natural human activity, and we must give them freedom in their work. Only thing is that we must fulfil personal needs, then he will be committed to work. Everybody has abilities and interest to work. These are under-utilized in the organization because of some reasons.

At the end Das made a remark. Oh I forgot you are from industry, and these things are taught there. In due time, however, Vasi came to conclusion that the working style of Mr. Ragade was the problem for behaviour of his lectures. During Ragade's tenure the departmental climate was not open and congenial for work. The results of students and other departmental work was at acceptable level, but not outstanding. The World Bank Assisted Project was implemented at a moderate level. But there were no extra activities taken up in the department. Innovative ideas were neither encouraged nor implemented in teaching-learning process. Whatever work Ragade assigned to subordinates somehow they had completed it.

Thus Vasi believed that the solution of problem is to improve relationship with the lecturers and remove their dissatisfaction at work reversing Ragade's previous approach to work. But unsure of how to make change he let things continue as they had under Ragade's tenure with the exception of trying to be friendlier and open with the lecturers than his predecessor.

Recently, however, Vasi felt he had found a solution to his and the departmental problems. He attended a workshop on "Enhancing faculty contribution" at Technical Teachers Training Institute (TTTI). Among the topics discussed were theory X and theory Y and job enrichment. During the workshop example were given related to improved faculty satisfaction and contribution, resulting from using theories of motivation. Vasi impressed with the ideas of motivational approaches and appreciated the potential of motivational approaches. Vasi resolved to implement these theories of motivation immediately in his department wasting no time. He developed a plan to motivate the employees. He organized a meeting with faculty members and discussed their problems. He assigned new subject to teachers, which they were teaching since long. Asked each faculty to submit the annual teaching plan and the list of learning resources required. Moreover he redistributed the World Bank Assisted Project sub-component work and changed the in charges. In addition he asked each faculty member to set annual goals and prepare action plan to achieve them.

Then the changes were first announced, in the meeting nobody opposed it. The reaction was limited. Little was said about the changes and faculty members showed no enthusiasm. Vasi was somewhat surprised, but thought that faculty members would become exited about the change, as they understood them better and implement them.

In three months, however, Vasi admitted to himself that his plan was a failure with expectation. The faculty members appeared to resent the changes. Many complained that they did not understand why the changes were made and what they were supposed to do while others seemed to resent to their increased responsibility. There is a decline in the teaching activity. Everybody seemed frustrated. They are over burden. The work of preparing learning resources was seemed as tedious and time consuming. One of the faculty had angrily told Vasi that if you want to improve the working put them back like they were and first settle the pay fixation which has been pending since 2 years. Disillusioned and somewhat better Vasi told to his colleague Mr. Das that most of the members are security seekers who want to do as little as they can for as much money as they can squeeze out of from the institute. Das smiled and replied: that's why Ragade used to behave with them rudely I told you earlier.

Brief

- Evaluate Vasi's initial conclusion that lecturers' misbehaviour was because of Ragade's approach to get the work done. Do you agree or disagree with his conclusion? Explain.
- Do you feel that Vasi's plan to implement theory Y and job enrichment was a sound one? Why or why not?
- Is Vasi's final conclusion concerning most of the faculty members correct in your opinion? Explain your viewpoint.
- What does this case tell us about effective employee motivation?

REFERENCES

Keith Davis & John W. News Strom, *Organizational Behaviour*, Tata McGraw Hills Publishing Company Ltd., New Delhi.

Namita Roy Choudhary, *Motivation Management in Education*, APH Publishing Corporation, New Delhi.

Organizational Behaviour, Fifth edition, Moorhed.

Ricky W. Griffin. *Fundamentals of Management,* Houghton Mifflin Company, Boston.

Stephen P. Robbins. *Organizational Behaviour*, Eighth edition. Prentice Hall of India, New Delhi.

William R. Trancey. *Leadership Skills*, Amacom.

8

Team Building

Objectives: The readers will be able to:

1. State need and importance of a team.
2. Define a team.
3. State common elements of a team.
4. Explain advantages of working in a team .
5. List the criteria for forming a team.
6. State the criteria for deciding the size of a team.
7. Describe characteristics of an effective team.
8. State the barriers to effective functioning of a team.
9. List the areas of institutional working in which team can be formed.
10. Describe team building model.

1. Introduction

There are several tasks that are complex and cannot be performed by individuals. These complex and challenging tasks require variety of skills that can be provided by a team of persons. The team can easily perform complex tasks because teams produce synergetic effect. Team members bring their competence and resources to the task. With increasing complexity of demands on institution teams are required to be formed and developed. Teams stimulate members to put greater and better efforts to the task and derive job satisfaction.

Teams confer sense of importance and high morale in the members, which in turn increase productivity. Teamwork generates a creative problem-solving approach through cross-fertilization of ideas, stimulating discussion, pooling of knowledge and exposure to different viewpoints. Creativity is more predictable in a team effort than in an individualistic approach. Teamwork satisfies the task requirements as well as human needs.

2. Importance of Teams

Management experts have expressed their opinion on importance of teamwork. Some of the significant opinions are stated in exhibit 8.1.

Exhibit No. 8.1: Opinions of management experts about importance of teams

- 'Team work' is key to modern management. Successful managers will work through the team and their success will depend upon the team succeeding. Charles, 1996
- Teams will become even more important in the future. In fact, most models of the organisations of the future that we have heard about 'networked', 'clustered', 'non-hierarchical', 'horizontal', and so forth are premised on teams surpassing individuals as the primary performance unit in the company. Katzenbach, 1993
- Teams and work groups are considered to be the fundamental units of organisations and also key leverage points for improving the functioning of the organisation. French, 1996
- Teamwork needs to extend across all functions and should include both administrator and employees. Sallis, 1993
- Teams are a most powerful tool for solving problems and meeting continuous improvement objectives. Joseph & Susan Berk, 1995
- There will continue to be an emphasis on teamwork as opposed to individual contribution. Hierarchy and authoritarian structures don't involve as many people, so employees don't buy in. Therefore key trend to be less successful. Anthony R. Montebellow, 1996
- Participatory organisations find that they must eliminate layers and flatten their hierarchies. Wherever we have found participatory organisation, we have teamwork. Small groups are, quite simply, the basic organisational building blocks of excellent companies. David & Tade, 1982

3. Definition of Teamwork

Numbers of management experts have proposed definition of teamwork in various contexts. Some of the significant definitions are stated in exhibit 8.2.

Exhibit No. 8.2: Definitions of teamwork

- ➢ A group of individuals becomes a team when, and only when, they commit to achieving high performance goals. A key characteristic of high performance team is discipline. Groups become team through disciplined action. They shape a common purpose, agree on performance goals, define a common working approach, develop high levels of complementary skills, and holds themselves mutually accountable for results. A team is a small number of people with complementary skills who are committed to a common purpose, performance goals and approach for which they hold themselves mutually accountable. Katzenbach and Smith
- ➢ A team is a group of people who understand each other, who know individual strengths and weaknesses, and who cooperates with one another. Charles Margerison
- ➢ It is a group, which shares, and says that it shares, a common purpose and recognizes that it needs the efforts of everyone of its members to achieve this. A team is a team when it sees itself as a team, is going in the team direction, and has worked out its own team ways.
- ➢ A team is an organized group of professionals from different disciplines who have unique skills and a common goal of common cooperative problem solving. Pfeiffer
- ➢ A team is any work group that shares common agenda. Green
- ➢ Teams are made up of individuals with different personalities, ideas, strengths, weaknesses, levels of enthusiasm, and demand from their jobs. Sallis Edward

We have examined the various views of experts on team and working in a team. If we analyze the above definitions we observe common points in a team. These points are stated in exhibit 8.3.

Exhibit No. 8.3: Common points in a team

4. Benefits of Teamwork

Working in a team brings variety of benefits to individuals, team and institution. Some of the significant benefits are listed in exhibit 8.4 and described in subsequent paragraphs.

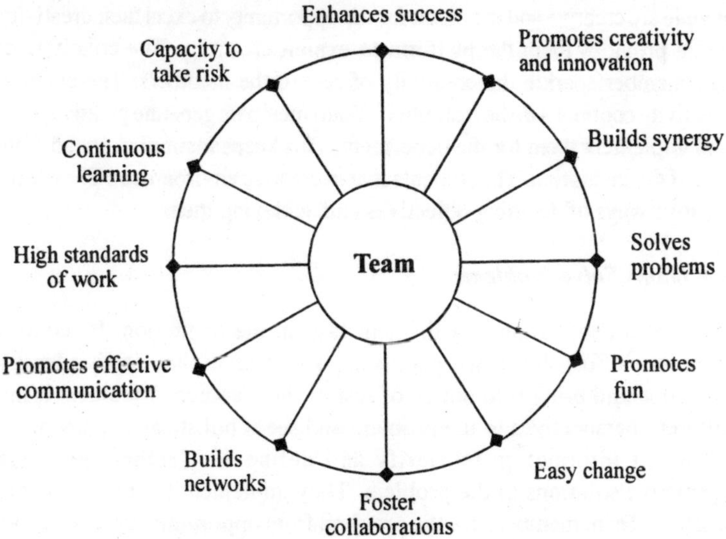

Exhibit No. 8.4: Benefits of working in teams

4.1 Teamwork Enhances Success

Teams prepare detailed plans to perform the task that build confidence for success in team members. Team members share the strengths and cover up the weaknesses of each other that assures the success. There are fewer chances for shirking from the work because the team leader or active member of the team would always remind the team about its commitments.

4.2 Teamwork Promotes Creativity and Innovation

In a team members come from different disciplines and backgrounds. They bring different perspectives to the situation. They have different ideas on the problem. When opportunity is given to team members they collectively generate ideas that are unique, different, new and innovative. They present different dimensions of the problem and solve it forever.

Team members see every problem from opportunity point of view and ensure that the problem never recurs. Team members generate creative ideas that can bring easy change in the way of performing the task.

4.3 Teamwork Builds Synergy

People are creative and they look for the opportunity to excel their creativity. Team provides them the platform to exhibit creativity. The creativity of one member sparkle the creativity of rest of the members. The cycle of creativity continues in the institution. Team members generate creative ideas and implement them for the betterment. This keeps institution ahead from rest of the institution. The students live in creative environment. They learn creative ways of deciding objectives and achieving them.

4.4 Teams Solve Problems

Problem identification is a difficult task in the institution. It requires conscious efforts but when people work in a team they easily identify problems and bring it to notice of rest of the members. Members bring different perspectives to the problem and see it holistically. They bring sufficient information to clarify and define it. Members generate alternative solutions to the problem. They implement the most feasible solution. Team members see the problem from opportunity point of view. They try to convert every problem as an opportunity. Problem solving skills are developed in each and every individual.

4.5 Teamwork is a Fun

Team members have individual and group needs. These needs are different and require different types of treatment. All the needs cannot be addressed and satisfied by the institution. Team members meet with each other, they share task related ideas and also share their personal needs. Team setting and rest of the team members on work setting satisfy the needs of members. Members have intensive interaction and they find out ways and means to reduce tension on work setting. They use social skills and enjoy performing work.

4.6 Teamwork Responds to the Challenge to Change

The process of change is difficult and challenging. It is dame difficult to bring change working individually. Teams have capacity and capability to diagnose the need for change, design change and implement change strategy. Teams can analyze the situation requiring the change in a better way. It can reduce the resistance to change involving people in the process of change. Change becomes the way of life of people working in teams.

4.7 Teams Foster Collaboration

Teams work on the principle of interdependency. The effectiveness of the teamwork can be improved through increasing interdependency. Situations demanding more competence and resources forces members to collaborate. It forces to bring their full potential to resolve the situation. Collaborative ways of working are considered to be best to utilize the full collective capacity of the institution.

4.8 Teams Build Lasting Networks

Teams are not permanently formed in the institutions. They are formed to achieve specific objectives. Once the objectives are achieved teams adjourn. But team members have close contacts and relations. They interact with each other and share ideas and feeling as friends. Institutional members develop long lasting relationship with seniors and juniors, experienced and inexperienced people, working in different departments of the institution. The intimate relationships among institutional members naturally solve problems related to cooperation, coordination, sharing resources and experiences. Members help each other informally to complete the task.

4.9 Teams Promote Effective Communication

Members work closely with each other. They understand each other and their work. The flow of the information and ideas become smooth among the members. They openly share the information related to their task. The openness promotes transparency in the functioning of the team. Openness in sharing of information promotes decision-making process and enhances commitment for implementing the decisions.

4.10 High Standards of Work

Team members set work standards and behaviour standards for smooth functioning of the team. They create pressure on each other to stick to standards of the work and adhere to team norms. They have their own mechanism to compel team members to follow the team norms and ethics. They promote culture in which members are accountable to each other.

4.11 Teams Provide an Opportunity for Continuous Learning of the Members

Team members work closely on different tasks with different people. They exchange ideas and views on the task. They share the problems and achievements. Members provide constructive feedback for improvement to each other on their performance. They observe the behaviour of each other on the task. Expert and experienced members impart training to new members. They jointly monitor the progress of the work and learn problem solving and decision-making skills. In team setting there is a great scope for continuous learning and learning new and different skills. Teams provide an opportunity to develop multi skills.

4.12 Teams Develop Capacity to Take Risk

In team working team members predict their strength and capacity to meet the uncertainty. They also work out the efforts required to come out from uncertainties and take calculated risk to grab the opportunity. If the magnitude of the risk is high they pool and mobilize their resources to win over the situation. In risk situation they work comfortably and stably with full competence and capacity. They motivate and encourage each other to achieve the objectives. Their success in uncertain situation boosts their confidence to take another risk.

5. Composition of a Team

A team is not a group of people but group of people that posses complementary skills. They cover the weaknesses of each other through their strengths for a particular task or activity. It does not mean that the people working in the same section should form a team. A team can also be formed of the people who belong to different sections. One thing should be made clear at this point that team is formed to accomplish specific objectives or goals. Keeping these objectives in mind team members are identified. There are other criteria that also decide the inclusion or exclusion of a person in a team. These criteria are listed in exhibit 8.5.

Exhibit No. 8.5: Criteria are selecting the member for a team

Criteria to be used to form a team	**Criteria not to be used to form a team**
➢ Goal or purpose complexity ➢ Requirements of the task ➢ Ability of the person ➢ Interest and willingness of the person ➢ Creativity of the person ➢ Attitude of the person ➢ Leadership ➢ Followership requirements ➢ Availability of a person ➢ Experience of a person ➢ Expertise of the person	➢ Availability of a person ➢ Some work has to be shown in the name of that person ➢ Person having no time ➢ The person is to be obliged ➢ Because some one wants her/him in a team ➢ Nobody wants to work with her/him ➢ S/he is influential person ➢ S/he has nuisance value

6. Size of the Team

The number of members in any team is generally kept five to fifteen. If less than five members are kept in a team there would not be enough ideas generated for the task or problem. If more than fifteen members are kept in a team there will be repetition of ideas. This would waste the time of other members. As mentioned earlier, the size of the team also depends on the purpose for which it is formed. If it is formed to perform the task, which is clear to the members, then it requires only technical and working in a team skills. On the other hand when a team has to solve complex problem more number of members having diverse background are required. No member of a team should be a redundant member in any case otherwise the teamwork may result costly.

7. Characteristics of an Effective Team

A team is effective when it adds more value than the value to the task and results. Characteristics that make teams effective are complex and varied. Teams bring together competence; experience, attitude and values in integrated way suitable for the purpose. Describing characteristics of an effective team is a difficult task and carries all the risks of conveying only a partial picture. A team of brilliant individuals can often be less effective than a brilliant team of individuals. A flavour of characteristics of an effective team is listed in exhibit 8.6.

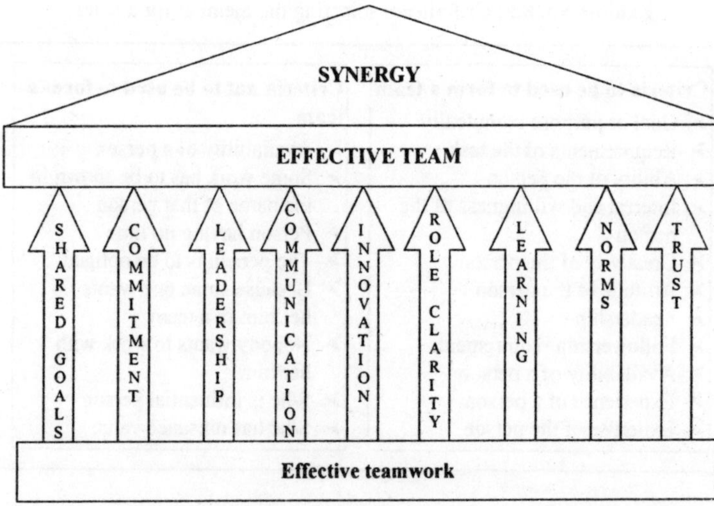

Exhibit No. 8.6: Characteristics of an effective team

7.1 Shared Goals

The goals are crystal clear to team members and they are persistent in pursuit of it. Team members jointly set the goals to be achieved. The team should agree to achieve the goals if management communicates goals. The goals of the team should be clear to all the team members collectively and individually. The goals of the team should be specific, measurable, achievable, realistic, and time bound. The goals should be challenging to invite the efforts of the team members. For example, the goal for an interdisciplinary team could be "to write a book on environment engineering" for students of all disciplines in six months covering the curriculum of the university" or to prepare a multimedia package to impart training to one thousand engineers or to design a curriculum for an emerging discipline.

7.2 Committed Members

The members are committed to design and implement the strategies to achieve the goals. They have sufficient time for implementation of the strategy. They are committed to quality of performance and other aspects of the working in a team to complete the particular task. They use creative and flexible strategies to achieve the goal. Team members remove all the hurdles from the path of goal accomplishment. Team members actively build formal and informal networks, which includes people who matter to them and who can help them. Team members make themselves visible and accessible to others. They welcome advice and comments from outside. Team members are action oriented. They respond quickly and positively to problems and opportunities. Team members are committed to the success of the team and their department. They work in an open culture where responsibility and authority is delegated to them to produce agreed results.

7.3 Transformational Leadership

Team members value leader who maintains the team direction, energy and commitment. They expect the leader to be supportive not dominating. All the members are ready to take leadership position in any situation. They do not fight for leadership but respect leadership. Leaders are transformational and they carry out all activities in a healthy way. Leaders develop good followers as well as good leaders. The decisions of the team are respected and carried out by its members.

7.4 Effective Communication

Team members effectively communicate with each other. They put the critical issues in a positive way. Ego problems are solved through interpersonal relationship. Team members maintain effective communication among themselves. They build common language to be used in work situation. Grapevine communication is prevented and wrong messages are corrected immediately. Conflicts are resolved amicably through dialogues. Corridor talks are not permitted in teams. All the formal as well as in formal channels of communication are used in a team. Team members work best with principles and guidelines as procedure rather than rules.

7.5 Innovation

Team members are creative and innovative. They are prepared to take risk in order to achieve significant gains. An opportunity to work innovatively is given to all members. Team members continuously try to improve on every aspect of task and way of working. Team members value people for their knowledge, competence and contributions rather than for position. Team members always try to work with others rather than working for or against others. In some situations calculated conflict is created in a team to foster creativity.

7.6 Role Clarity

The role of the team in the institution and the role of a member in a team are clear to each and every member of a team. There is no role conflict, role erosion, role encroachment and role gap. The members know what to do, how to do, when to do, what resources are to be used, where to get resources, what are the expectations of fellow members, what are the standards of the work and what behavioural norms to be observed. Team task is understood and accepted by team members. Members develop themselves to perform the role effectively and efficiently. Fellow team members help, support, and guide the role holder to perform the role as per team norms. There is a proper balance between planning and action.

7.7 Continuous Improvement

Team members continuously strive for improvement. They explore and innovate ways and means to improve their performance on the task. They diagnose the problem and analyse it for solution. The problem is solved forever. Team members learn from experiences and mistakes. They use scientific tools and techniques to bring improvements and enhance efficiency. They ensure that there is no wastage of time, money, material and machines in performing the task. Team is comfortable with disagreement and does not avoid conflict simply to keep everything in agreement. Criticism is frequent, frank, and relatively comfortable. There are no personal attacks. Team members are free to express their feelings and ideas on the team's problems.

7.8 Norms

Team members develop norms for functioning. These norms are set jointly and govern the functioning of the team. Each and every team member is bound to follow these norms. Team members work in motivational environment. They motivate each other. Members are available for consultation and guidance. Cooperation, coordination, commitment and communication found to be perfect in team functioning. The atmosphere in team is mutually supportive, informal and relaxed but not too comfortable. Teams have standards of excellence.

7.9 Continuous Learning

Team members share experiences and create an opportunity for learning. They also provide constructive feedback to fellow members for improvement. They learn from mistakes and do not repeat the mistakes. After an interval of time they analyse the progress of the work and take corrective actions if problem is found. They learn task related skills and social skills. They do experimentation to innovate new and different methods of performing. They reflect upon the experiences and note down the learning points for the future. Collective learning is very common in teams. This learning helps to build desired culture in the institution.

7.10 Team Members Trust Each Other

Trust is the essential foundation for effective teamwork. Trust allows the team members to function as an integrated unit to achieve common goals. Team members periodically assess the progress on work and celebrate on achievement of goals. Team members manage their culture, processes, systems and relationship to become effective. Trust begets trust. Team members promote trust and faith in functioning of the team. Leader is always approachable and within reach of team members. Leader encourages open communication and creates an atmosphere that encourage for expression of criticism and disagreements. Leader has personal rapport and interest in team members.

8. Barriers to Effective Teamwork

The functioning of a team is not easy because the team members have different background and behaviour. Teams face variety of barriers and obstacles in its functioning. These barriers make them ineffective and inefficient and prevent them to achieve the team goals. The indicative list of barriers to effective team-working are sated in exhibit 8.7.

Exhibit No. 8.7: Barriers to team working

➢ Inadequate time and finance	➢ Uncertain nature of work
➢ Lack of motivation	➢ Lack of training
➢ Lack of rewards and recognition	➢ Complex government rules
➢ Irregular meetings	➢ Ineffective leader
➢ Lack of interest of members	➢ No agreement on goals
➢ Lack of administrative and financial autonomy	➢ No agreement on approach ➢ Lack of challenge in the task
➢ Ineffective communication	➢ Strict rules and regulation
➢ Inappropriate team formation	➢ No scope for creativity
➢ Personal conflict	➢ Misuse of members

9. Areas of Working in a Team

Teams can be formed and developed in all the areas of functioning of the institution. As mentioned in chapter two that each institution should have teams structure for smooth functioning. Some teams may be constituted for a longer duration say three years to maintain consistency in action. The areas of such teams are mentioned in chapter two. Rest of the teams may be constituted looking to the needs of the objectives and tasks. Teams can be constituted to develop instructional material such as book writing, case bank preparation, item bank preparation, question bank preparation, assignments preparation, work book preparation, video film preparation, software development, curriculum design, developing norms, undertaking consultancy projects, designing continuing education programmes, implementing specific innovation, document preparation for specific purpose like accreditation, obtaining ISO certification, organizing specific functions of professional body, specific problem solving of students or staff etc. Teams of students can be formed to produce effective learning in the classroom, laboratory and in industry. Teachers should use teaching learning methods listed in exhibit 8.8 to promote teamwork in learning process.

Exhibit No. 8.8: Teaching-learning methods based on teamwork

➢ Action learning ➢ Group discussion ➢ Project ➢ Problem solving ➢ Role play ➢ Case method ➢ Brain storming ➢ Nominal group technique ➢ Focus group discussion ➢ Buzz group	➢ Seminar ➢ Conference ➢ Symposium ➢ Survey ➢ Research ➢ Simulation ➢ Game ➢ Competition ➢ Debate ➢ Experimentation

10. Team Building Model

The benefits and characteristics of an effective team have already been emphasized. Teams to be effective they need to be build otherwise they will not produce expected results. Team building exercises can be taken up for existing teams to improve their performance. As a leader you are under external and internal pressure to improve the performance of the team. You are also concerned about the low morale of the team members. Situation demands for teamwork and individuals are working independently. A new team is formed to meet out the challenges and competition needs to be developed. There are teams in place but there may be lot of misunderstanding, confusion and conflict. The sense of cooperation, trust and team spirit in general may be missing. There may be many such reasons, which forces you to take up team building exercise. Team building means promoting the characteristics of effective team in existing or new team. Developing confidence in each other to agree mutually acceptable objectives and ensure the best possible use of team members. Team building exercise can be taken up under the guidance of external expert or trained person within the department.

It can be a routine activity or special event in the department. It is an art, a science and a skill. The art of team building is to understand about people individually and in a group. The knowledge about the working of the department helps a lot to a team developer. The art of team building is concerned with talking through needs, differences and individual contributions. The team builder's art is the ability to see the team as a whole, and to release the energies of the members towards the solution of joint problems.

The science of team building is the collection of the facts about the behaviour of the people. It is the complete analysis of facts on the behaviour of the people. There are number of instruments which can measure personality, ability and performance of team members. These instruments provide both valuable diagnostic information and wealth of discussion material. Team builder can use these instruments during the process of team building.

The skill of a team builder is that of a juggler. The juggler knows what the act is, knows the price of failure and against that balances the excitement of the risk and the likelihood of success. Practice and confidence in assessing situations and making interventions are the real skills for juggling and team building. The team builder's crucial skill is to open new doors, to unfreeze attitudes, and shape the attitudes as per need of the situation.

The team-building model developed by B.W. Tuckman is a very popular model commonly used in all types of organisations. Tuckman has proposed team-building process in four stages. First step is forming that describes the actions of team members after team formation. In this step team members try to explore the purpose of team formation, task to be performed, their role in the team, urgency of the task, quality of leadership, level of commitment required, rewards associated to performance, views of other members, probability of success of achieving objectives etc. Team members cautiously interact with each other on team related issues. They try to gather information on the team task from other sources. Team members experience confusion, uncertainty and isolation. They are uncomfortable in a new and unfamiliar situation with a different group of people. They are very cautious in interacting with others. They do not share their feelings and views.

Second stage is storming that describes the clarification of doubts, questions, apprehensions and similar issues with each other. They try to define the task and issues related to task in their own way. They start opening up on issues and their feelings. They put forth their views on the task and functioning of the team. They oppose the views of other members and enter in confrontation. They try to demonstrate their expertise and power on the task. Some members withdraw themselves after initial discussion because other members do not hear their views. They also interact on issues related to task and working in team. They try to settle issues and prepare plan for performance and norms for functioning.

Third stage is norming, that is most of the issues resolved in previous stage are approved collectively. Team members commit to perform the task. They develop close relationship and have respect for each other. They collaborate and cooperate to develop strategy. The leadership is shared and every member gets involved in thinking to do better perform the task. The process of trust building gets stronger and deeper. Team members open up and share feelings and expertise.

Fourth stage is performing that is team members perform as per plan and follow the team norms. They have trust in each other and respect leadership. They interact openly and share the experiences gained during the performance. Continuous guidance, learning, problem solving and interaction take place among members. They continuously monitor the progress and cooperate with each other. They share the resources to complete the task. They use full potential to complete the task. They use flexible approaches to meet out the needs of the task. They observe the team norms and respect the views and feelings of each other. They collectively take the risk to grab the new opportunity. They work with harmony and rhythm. They encourage criticism, conflict and confrontation, disagreement, competition and opposition to enhance the quality of performance. At the same time they use collaborative and cooperative approaches to share the work. At the end members evaluate the achievements and celebrate the success.

In institutions teams need to be formed and developed so that they posses characteristics to design processes, modify and redesign processes as per needs. The model given in exhibit 8.9 is used for team building.

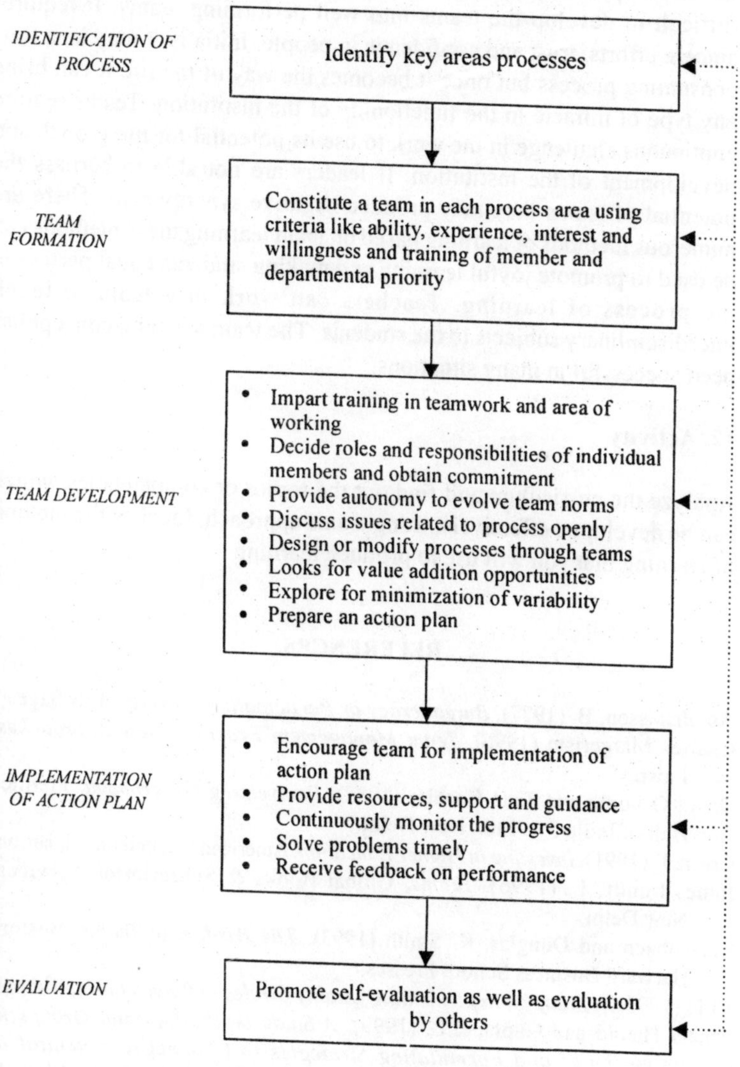

Exhibit No. 8.9: Team building model

11. Summary

Working in a team is the need of the day. Through teamwork participation of the people can be obtained at highest level. It is very easy to form teams for specific purpose in the institution. At the same time it is very difficult to develop the teams into well performing teams. It requires sincere efforts, trust and confidence in people. Initially it may be a time consuming process but once it becomes the way of the life it can bring any type of miracle in the functioning of the institution. Teams require continuous challenge in the work to use its potential for the growth and development of the institution. If leaders are not able to harness the potential of teams they may produce negative synergy also. There are numerous methods of learning based on team learning these methods can be used to promote joyful learning and making students equal partner in the process of learning. Teachers can work in a team to teach interdisciplinary subjects to the students. The team teaching concept has been successful in many situations.

12. Activity

Analyze the curriculum and find out the topics or competencies, which can be developed effectively, using teams approach. Identify the method of learning that you will use to produce learning.

REFERENCES

Abrahamsson, B. (1977). *Bureaucracy or Participation*, Beverly Hills Sage.

Charles Margerism (1996). *Team Management Practical New Approaches*, Lawrey.

David Osborne and Tade Gaebler (1982). *Reinventing Government*, Prentice Hall of India Pvt. Ltd., New Delhi.

Green, F. (1991). *Investing in Higher Education*, American Council on Education.

James Lundy, L. (1996). *Teams*, Global Books & Subscription Services, New Delhi.

Katzenbach and Douglas, K. Smith (1993). *The Wisdom of Teams*, Boston, Harward Business School Presses.

TTTI (1995). *A Study on Implementing Quality Circles in Polytechnics*, Bhopal.

Zaheer Hamid and Gupta, B.L. (1999). *A Study on the Informal Groups in Polytechnics and Formulating Strategies to Channelise Potential of Informal Groups for the Development of the Polytechnics*, TTTI, Bhopal.

9

Problem Solving

Objectives: The readers will be able to:

1. State the need of solving the problems.
2. Describe the concept of problem in technical institutions.
3. Explain the importance of prioritisation of problems.
4. Explain the qualities of a problem solver.
5. Explain the models of problem solving.
6. List the tools and techniques used at various stages of problem solving.
7. List benefits of problem solving in a team.
8. Assess creativity level of the self.

1. Introduction

Problems are considered sign of life in many traditional institutions. People are busy in solving problems only. The whole day is spent in solving the problems. They feel lonely and bored if they don't have problems to solve. This may be an extreme example but this is a reality also. If the institution is having many problems and being managed by problem solving approach it means it is following reactive approach of managing the institution. It should review its plans and decisions. There must be something wrong with it. It should focus more on proactive approaches discussed in chapter on planning. If there are few small problems emerged out of situation then it is not a serious concern because man proposes and god disposes. There would be problems in any institution whatever management approaches it is practicing. In fact problems are situation based. As a leader every one should possess skills to solve problems.

2. Concept of a Problem

The problem cannot be identified and defined unless there is some plan or standards or indicators. It means there should be a plan or norms for comparison. In absence of a plan, people express problems in terms of concerns and worries. But their concern or worry may be personal perception of the situation and there may not be problem at all. The perception of problem also varies from person to person. Some people perceive every situation as a problem and try to solve it others do not perceive the problem even though it exists. Some people consider the problem situation as an opportunity and solve it forever. So the problem cannot be defined unless there are some standards or planned activities. If standards are available the actual situation can be compared with standards and problem can be identified in terms of deviations or gap. In many situations it is very difficult to diagnose the problem itself. One should be very clear on problem otherwise it may become disaster if unnoticed or not diagnosed. It may consume huge resources to fix. The problem can be diagnosed using monitoring techniques against planned activities. One thing is clear that problem arises because of past. Something is not done appropriately or done wrongly or not done at all leading to a problem. This problem is detected through monitoring process that means data, and facts are required to be collected on the current situation. The analysis and comparison of data with desired results tells about the problem and its seriousness. The problem solver should be motivated to solve the problem and s/he should be of firm belief that s/he can solve the problem.

3. Weight of a Problem

The institution may have numbers of problems at a given time. All problems may not have equal urgency and importance. The management of the institution does not solve all the problems but it provides resources to implement the solutions. It is necessary to prioritize the problems based on the criteria. Before considering a problem for solution one can ask question listed in exhibit 9.1.

Exhibit No. 9.1: Questions to be asked before considering a problem for solution

➢ How important is the problem to the institution? ➢ How important is the problem to the problem solver? ➢ How important is the problem to the students or employers point of view? ➢ How much of a priority does this problem have over other problems? ➢ When would be the best time to solve the problem? ➢ How much resources are required to solve the problem?	➢ Does the institution have the resources to solve the problem? If the problem is solved does it affect other? ➢ Is it a problem or opportunity to do re-planning? ➢ How much damage this problem is causing? ➢ Who is responsible for this problem? ➢ Who is affected by this problem? ➢ Is it a problem or suggestion or opinion? ➢ Are you right person to solve the problem?

4. Qualities of a Problem Solver

A problem solver should possess variety of qualities to diagnose and solve the problems. Some of the indicative qualities are listed in exhibit 9.2.

Exhibit No. 9.2: Qualities of a problem solver

➢ Objective thinking ➢ Creative thinking ➢ Holistic thinking ➢ Analytical thinking ➢ Situation description ➢ Involving people ➢ Drawing patterns ➢ Leadership skills	➢ Information gathering ➢ Classifying information ➢ Hypothesis formulation ➢ Hypothesis testing ➢ Eliminating information ➢ Drawing conclusions ➢ Presentation skills ➢ Action planning ➢ Counselling skills

There are problem solvers who know the right time of solving the problem. They solve the problem at right time to reduce their time to solve the problem. But they don't know that they are wasting the much more time of affected parties. Some people don't solve problems but they pile up the problems and wait for the situation to solve the problem. This is a dangerous practice because if significant problems are piled up it may be a disaster. It may require huge resources and special skills that you may not have. So it may lead to further problems. Some people perceive a small magnitude problem as a big problem and create a problem for other people in the institution. They create urgency to solve small magnitude problem. People form opinion about the problem solver that s/he unnecessary creates the urgency. Then they don't come forward to solve urgency problem assuming that it is a meagre problem. Some people solve problems rationally. Others try ready-made solution for all types of problems. Some people solve all problems in a routine way others solve using creativity. Some people own every problem others do not own any problem. Some people try to solve every problem individually others involve peoples in every situation. All these styles are commonly observed in institutions. All styles of problem solving are good styles. The problem solver should learn to choose use appropriate style of problem solving.

5. Models of Problem Solving

It is a human tendency to jump upon the solution without understanding a problem. After putting lot of efforts it is realized that the solution is not working. They also think on what for the solution is being implemented. Resources are wasted in applying the ready-made solutions to any problem. Having the problem and without understanding it second ready-made solution is implemented resulting further wastage of resources and frustration. Problem solving is a complex process. It requires thinking, creativity and analytical skills. In a complex situation thinking and creativity becomes little bit difficult so all problem solving models focus on step-by-step description and solution of a problem.

5.1 Logical Model of Problem Solving

A logical model of problem solving is shown in exhibit 9.3. The brief description of each step is given in subsequent paragraphs.

Diagnose the Situation

The situation of concern or worry is analyzed on the basis of the information, data, facts and figures. On the basis of analysis of the situation the boundaries of the problem are drawn. The problem is defined on various parameters of concern. It is said that well-defined problem is half solved. So honest attempt is made to define the problem. For example the result of students in engineering drawing may be poor. On the basis of the result conclusion cannot be drawn about the learning level of the students. It is tried to define the problem from comparison of the situation with other similar situation. Suppose the result of students is good in applied mechanics both the situations are compared and problem area is defined. It may be any thing may be faulty paper, may be irregular classes, and may be poor quality of instruction etc. The problem area is defined on the basis of information gathered. The clear statement of the problem or problem description is listed well-defined parameters. The description includes its boundaries, who is affected by problem, factors in which the problem exist, what is not a problem, the extent of problem, the person causing the problem etc. and on similar parameters. Numerous techniques for defining a problem are available for use. Some of the indicative techniques are control charts, bar charts, action plans, monitoring plans, trend graphs, co-relation graphs, spider diagram.

Analyze the Problem

Once the problem is defined it is analyzed on various dimensions. The problem is seen holistically and likely causes are generated using creativity methods. Creativity techniques, like Brain storming, Nominal group technique and Delphi are used. All possible causes of the problem are generated. And then based on the information those causes are eliminated which in the group's opinion are not the real causes. Remaining causes are classified into various categories. In a technical institution, possible categories may be students, teaching staff, supporting staff, admissions, curriculum, teaching-learning strategies, examinations, industry-institute interaction etc. The classification of causes mainly depends on the type of the causes. The classification can be represented on a fishbone diagram and problem analysis tree diagram. The other method to represent the causes is Pareto diagram. In this case, causes are prioritized on the basis of frequency of occurrence or intensity of occurrence.

Generate Alternative Solutions

Once the causes are classified appropriately alternative solutions are generated for important causes. The solutions can be evaluated on the basis of decided criteria like possible benefits, negative effects, and resources required. Final solution for each cause can be decided. It may be possible to have one solution for many causes or many solutions for one cause. It all depends on the type and nature of the problem. Once the solution to a problem is finalized it is widely shared for greater acceptability by those who are going to be affected by this solution.

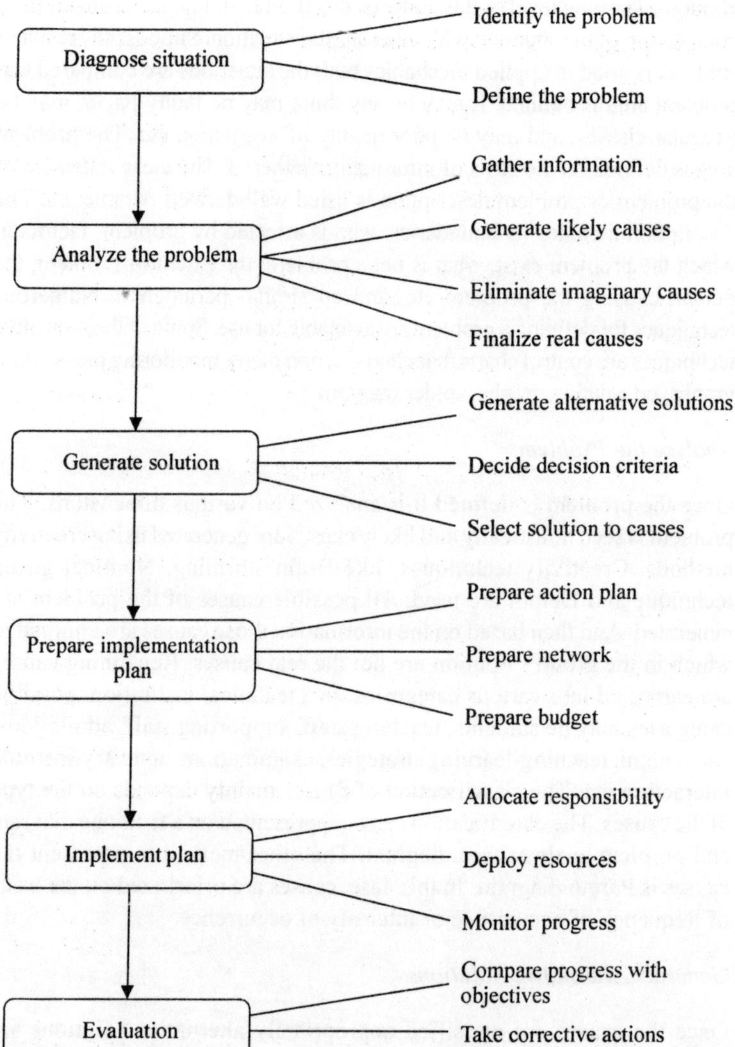

Exhibit No. 9.3: Problem solving model

Prepare Implementation Plan

The problem solver or a team prepares an action plan for making the solution a reality. The action plan can again be prepared in various formats but the simplest form is tabular form. It shows the list of activities, their duration, resource requirements, major responsibility, support requirement and money requirement. The network of activities is also prepared for complex problems to know the duration of implementation and time of resources requirement.

Implementation of Plan

The members of the team organise themselves and take up responsibility mentioned in the action plan to implement the plan. They can jointly or individually implement the plan depending upon the requirements of the plan. During the process of implementation the members also monitor the progress of work and ensure that implementation is in right direction and up to satisfaction level. They also identify and solve small problems occurring during implementation. The implementation continues till the problem is solved. Team members try to ensure that the same problem does not occur again.

Evaluation of a Plan

On implementation of the plan the results are achieved. These results are compared with objectives and corrective actions are taken if necessary. The problem solving experiences are shared and feedback is taken for subsequent problem solving activities. It is assured that problem does not recur.

Logical model of problem solving is useful in solving implementation problems of any plan or projects.

5.2 Process Redesigning

Process charting is another method used to identify the ineffectiveness and inefficiency related problems. The existing processes in the institution are charted as it is and then analysed for ineffectiveness and inefficiencies. The identified causes for ineffectiveness and inefficiencies are removed and the process is redesigned to serve the purpose. The new process is designed in a way to have no redudant, time consuming, material wasting and effort wasting element in the process. Various activities in the process are integrated and simplified in redesign. In designing the process questions begining with what, why, how, when, where, who are frequently asked to make the process sound. The process design approach is described in detail in chapter on management tools and techniques. The process implementers are also trained to implement the process proficiently.

5.3 Competency Statements

To diagnose and identify the learning problems competency based curriculum serves as a plan. It helps to identify and define the learning problems of the students. It helps to decide the remedial measures. If the profeciency level is mentioned along with competency statement the problem of learning can be pin pointed.

5.4 Performance Objectives and Standards

Performance objectives set for indidviduals and teams are helpful to identify the performance gap. The magnitude of the gap is measured and causes of the gap are identified. On the basis of the analysis of the gap objective and constructive feeback is provided to individuals and teams. A complete chapter is devoted on performance appraisal and development in this book.

5.5 Planning Model of Problem Solving

This model is very similar to logical and planning model. The problem is diagnosed on the basis of past performance and future objectives are set in same context. The steps follwed are shown in exhibit 9.4. The major difference between logical model and planning model is that the present situation is extended in future and future is predicted to make the solution sucessful in future. The problem is considered as an opportunity and planning is done for setting future objectives.

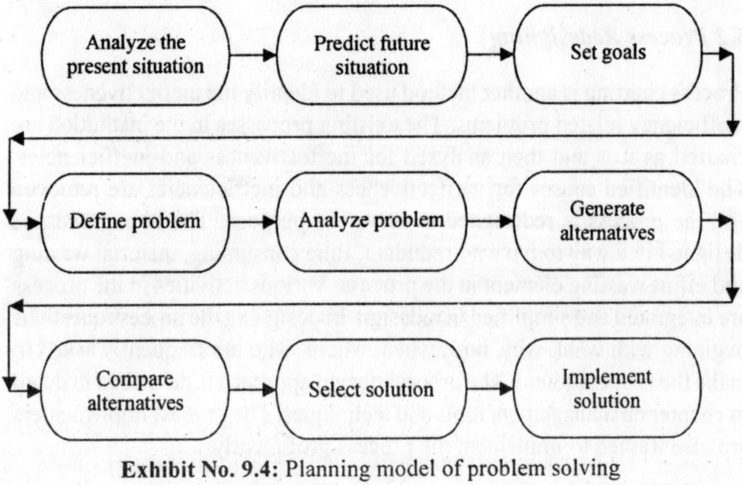

Exhibit No. 9.4: Planning model of problem solving

5.6 LEGUP Model

This model is a very good model to solve behaviour related problems of the employees and students. LEGUP is an accronium used for listening, exploring, goal setting, underpinning and pursuing. The problem solver listens the problem presented by the problem owner. The problem owner may be superior, subordinate, collegue or student. The problem solver try to appreciate the problem from problem owner's point of view. S/he exibits the listening skills to appreciate the problem. Then the problem solver and the problem owner explore the problem together to establish its real nature and to decide the course of action to solve the problem. They jointly set the concrete problem solving goals to bring the change or tackle the problem. The problem owner needs support to solve the problem and achieve the goals for this purpose s/he may need support, guidance, training etc. from the problem solver. The problem solver provides adequet support to problem owner to implement the decision. This step is called underpinning. Implementation of the solution in persuit of goals is tracked by the problem owner and problem solver. They continuously exchange feedback. This process is termed as pursuing.

6. Approaches to Problem Solving

Different situations require different approaches to problem solving. Terry has classified these approaches in five categories. The five approaches are stated in exhibit 9.5 and brief description of each approach is given in subsequent paragraphs.

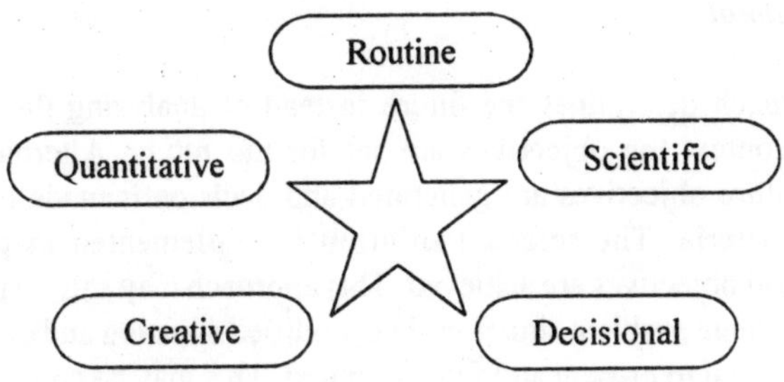

Exhibit No. 9.5: Approaches to problem solving

6.1 Routine

Routine problems are related to behaviour of the people. Problem such as late coming, partially performing the work, wasting time, inefficient ways of working, carelessness, etc. are generally faced in the institution. These problems can be solved using routine ways. Many institutions have manuals to deal with such problems. Standard procedures can be charted to prevent and solve such problems. People are familiar with routine problems. They know the problem as well solutions. They should immediately apply the solution and get rid of the problem. Institutions functioning professionally identify the problem and generate the solution in such a way so that the routine problem is burried forever. They use the information technology or permanent physical setting or alternatives to solutions. For example a teacher doesn't attend the institution without informing. This is a common and routine problem in the institution. In such situation the institution organizes session on entrepreneurship, personality development, environment awareness, etc. and one faculty member is available for this purpose on full time basis.

6.2 Scientific

Scientific method is used for problems that are being faced for the very first time and significant in nature. The problem solver understands the problem on the basis of information gathered. S/he formulates hypothesis and tentative solutions are generated. The hypothesis and tentative solutions are tested systematically and thoroughly. S/he arrives at the solution based on experimentation and applies the solution to the problem. If the problem is partially solved or the solution is not cost effective or time effective further testing is carried out and perfect solution is found out.

6.3 Decisional

This approach determines the future instead of analyzing the past. In problem context the objectives are set for the future. Alternatives to achieve future objectives are generated and decision is made based on decision criteria. The selected solution is implemented in problem situation and objectives are achieved. This approach may solve a problem or it may change problem situation. The modified situation and objectives may be relevant to present and future context. This may be considered as process approach of planning and problem solving.

6.4 Creativity

Institution faces new, complex, and unfamiliar problems. In some situations the problem solver may not know the problem and its solution. The only known thing is concern or victimization from the problem. Creativity methods are used for clarifying the problem and generating solutions to such problems. The creativity of the people is used to generate unique, new, different and innovative ideas to solve the problem. Positive, imaginative and different method is used to solve the problem. Creativity methods such as brain storming, nominal group technique, cognitive mapping are used for generating ideas.

6.5 Quantitative

Quantitative methods are useful in solving the problems that can be expressed in quantitative terms. Problems such as the results of the students in term end examination, low contact hours, wastage of money, calculation of profit, investment decision in new academic programmes, placement of students etc. can be expressed in quantitative terms. Quantitative problems can be analyzed and targets can be set for improvement. Statistical methods and tests can be used to define and solve the problem. In educational institutions statistical tests such as mean, mode, median, standard deviation, Z-test, T-test, correlation, Chi Square are predominantly used. Cost benefit ratio, return on investment and opportunity cost methods are used for identifying and solving financial problems. Student teacher ratio, space utilization factor, equipment utilization factors and similar ratios are used to identify and solve the problems related to resources.

7. Tools and Techniques of Problem Solving

A wide spectrum of tools and techniques is available to solve different problems. These tools and techniques are listed in exhibit 9.6. The use of these tools and techniques is also listed for each step of the problem solving. The detailed description of problem solving tools and techniques is given in chapter on management tools and techniques.

8. Benefits of Problem Solving in a Team

Two heads are better than one. And more than two is even better. If the problem solving and decision-making process is to be effective, it pulls together the skills, knowledge, experience, and opinion of team members. It produces a solution that is greater than that of the sum of its parts. Problem solving requires two major skills that are creativity and analysis.

Exhibit No. 9.6: Use of tools and techniques in problem solving

Diagnose the situation	**Analyze the problem**	**Generate solution**
Plan Gantt chart SWOT analysis Monitoring schedule Control charts Bar diagram Pareto analysis Performance standards Competency statements Norms Rules Policies	Cause and effect diagram Process flow-charting Problem tree analysis Creativity techniques Comparison charts Information gathering tools Modelling Observation Spider diagram	Solution diagram Process flow-charting Solution tree Creativity techniques Comparison charts Information gathering tools Modelling Observation Spider diagram Bench marking

Develop plan	**Implement plan**	**Monitoring**	**Evaluation**
Action plans Gantt chart Network Process charting Resources deployment chart Responsibility chart Budget	Action plans Gantt chart Network Process charting Resources deployment chart Responsibility chart Budget	Monitoring schedule Budget Resources deployment chart Responsibility chart	Objectives Evaluation criteria Process evaluation Success analysis

A good quality problem solving takes into account all of the facts and makes good use of the information. It is a logical choice with sound reasoning behind it. The second element to a good problem solving is the commitment of the people who have to carry it out. Problem solving may be effective and innovative, but if people don't have commitment to carry it out then it is a futile exercise. On the other hand, a poor problem solution that everyone gladly implements is just as wasteful and counter productive. Problem solving in team has numerous benefits over individual problem solving. The benefits of team problem solving are listed in exhibit 9.7.

Exhibit No. 9.7: Benefits of problem solving in a team

➢ Each member brings new and novel idea to the problem ➢ Large pool of information ➢ Common understanding of the problem ➢ Understanding the problem holistically ➢ Effective communication during problem solving ➢ Increased motivation to solve problem ➢ Constructive creativity	➢ Unique solution to a problem ➢ Common consensus to solution ➢ Commitment to solution ➢ Pool of resources for implementation of solution ➢ Collective learning of team members on problem solving skills ➢ Satisfaction of social and psychological needs

9. Common Problems of Technical Institutions

Technical institutions share common problems in general. For many problems solutions are available but because of lethargy people do not come forward to solve the problems. Some of the indicative problems are listed in exhibit 9.8.

Exhibit No. 9.8: Problems of technical institutions

Problems from employers point of view about students	➢ Students do not possess competencies so lot of investment in training of students ➢ Lacks managerial skills—planning, organising, communication, problem solving, leadership, coping with pressure etc. ➢ Commitment for organisation is low
Problems from institution point of view about students	➢ Do not take interest in study ➢ Entry behaviour is low ➢ Not disciplined ➢ Unwilling to accept learning challenges ➢ Use shortcut methods
Problems from institution point of view about teachers	➢ Less exposure to business world ➢ Lack of interest in innovative and challenging work ➢ Lack of research background ➢ Lack of self-initiatives ➢ Work traditionally ➢ Don't want to put extra efforts ➢ More concerned about salary and incentives

(Contd.)

(Contd.)

Problems from students point of view about teachers	➢ Traditional methods of teaching ➢ Busy in other work thereby affecting teaching ➢ Teach simple topics and leave complex topic for us ➢ Lack of integration of learning with the practice ➢ Very few practical examples
Problems from institution point of view about university	➢ Curriculum revision is not frequent ➢ Late admission ➢ Conventional pattern of examination ➢ Delay in result declaration ➢ Instructional resources are not provided by university
Problems from teachers point of view about institution	➢ Lack of autonomy ➢ Paucity of resources ➢ No incentive for unique and different work ➢ No encouragement for doing different things ➢ Traditional way of functioning ➢ Corporate culture missing ➢ Shortage of funds ➢ Lengthy procedures and rigid rules ➢ Administrative work

10. Guidelines for Problem Solving

As stated earlier, institution faces varied nature of problems. It requires professional approach to solve problems. Some indicative guidelines are listed in exhibit 9.9.

Exhibit No. 9.9: Guidelines for problem solving

➢ Do serious planning for all significant and new objectives ➢ Encourage planning at individual, group and departmental level ➢ Inbuilt problem identification and problem solving mechanism in the implementation process ➢ Have well designed systems, processes and procedures for performing activities	➢ A solution to solve one problem should not lead to another problem ➢ Do not apply same solution and problem solving approach to all problems ➢ Have well designed roles ➢ Do not first have solution and search problem for its application ➢ Promote use of participative methods

(Contd.)

(Contd.)

➢ Promote creativity in the institutional functioning ➢ Use creativity techniques to solve problems ➢ Have effective communication systems ➢ Identify the problem at the earliest stage and confirm that it is a problem ➢ Consider a problem as an opportunity for improvement ➢ Analyse the problem from different dimensions and its interdependent point of view	➢ Solve attitudinal problems differently ➢ Promote the use of proactive, positive and practical approaches ➢ Promote the concept of problem owner and s/he should put major efforts to solve problem ➢ Empower people to solve problems ➢ Promote sharing of problem but not shirking from problem ➢ Develop capacity and capability of people for problem solving using collective approaches and reflection

11. Summary

Problem solving is a reactive approach. This approach can improve the efficiency of functioning of the institution to a certain extent. One should learn to diagnose the problem and solve it for the benefit of the students and institution. To solve a problem variety of skills are required but two basic skills are prominently used that are creativity and analysis. It is assumed that problem solving should be carried out using well-established systematic methods like logical or planning approach. Variety of tools and techniques can be used to make the problem solving process easier. These tools and techniques are graphical, models, logical, statistical and simulations. It is said that the root cause of the problem should be identified and solved to remove the problem forever. It is not necessary to have solution of all the problems within the institution. One should approach to stakeholders to get the problem solved. Problems should be solved in such a way so that they do not recur in future.

12. Activity

As a teacher in technical institution you should use creativity techniques to solve problems. Using creativity techniques you can solve many problems before it surfaces out. You can solve the problems with minimum efforts and resources. You can assess your creativity on parameters listed in the table given on the next page. Please honestly mark your extent of involvement on following parameters.

How Creative are You as a Teacher

Sl. No.	The extent to which you are involved in	Extent			
		High	Medium	Low	Nil
1.	Reading books related to your discipline and related disciplines				
2.	Visiting industries and obtaining practical training				
3.	Attending seminars, conferences, symposiums organized by industries				
4.	Accepting industrial problems to solve with the help of students				
5.	Writing books on subjects which are emerging and interdisciplinary				
6.	Conducting researches in a specialized area of technology				
7.	Encouraging students quality circles for learning				
8.	Co-curricular activities of the institution				
9.	Designing variety of assignments, problems, case studies, puzzles, projects for the students				
10.	Organizing seminars, conferences symposiums, interaction sessions for teachers and students on technical and other topics				
11.	Using variety of teaching learning methods in classroom, laboratory and industries.				
12.	Using variety of media and media mix to make the teaching learning process joyful and interesting				
13.	Organizing creativity sessions on various topics of interest				
14.	Using students as a resource person in teaching learning process				
15.	Thinking how to improve the efficiency and effectiveness of teaching learning process				
16.	Visiting industrial fair, information technology fair, and show case conferences				
17.	Accepting and completing new, unique and different projects				
18.	Managing mob of the students and negotiating with them on issues raised by them				
19.	Going out of the set rules and procedures and helping students for learning				

(Contd..)

(*Contd.*)

Sl. No.	*The extent to which you are involved in*	*Extent*			
		High	*Medium*	*Low*	*Nil*
20.	Frequently noting down improvements in teaching learning process that can be implemented in the future				
21.	Providing written and verbal feedback to every student individually for improving the performance				
22.	Evaluating the progress of the work on fixed and additional criteria				

REFERENCES

Charles, J. Margerision (1974). *Managerial Problem Solving*, McGraw Hills Company Limited (UK).

Gerald F. Smith (2000). *Quality Problem Solving*, Prentice Hall of India Private Limited, New Delhi.

Steve Smith (1999). *Solve That Problem*, Kogan Page India Private Limited, New Delhi.

10

Decision-Making

Objectives: The readers will be able to:

1. State the need and importance of decision-making.
2. Describe the concept of decision-making in technical institution.
3. Explain the importance of prioritisation of decisions.
4. Explain the classification of decisions.
5. Describe various decision-making models.
6. Explain various styles of decision-making.
7. Explain factors affecting decision-making process.
8. List guidelines to be followed to take the decision.
9. Assess self decision-making behaviour for improvement.

1. Introduction

Every person takes decision in day-to-day functioning. Some decisions have immediate implications and others have long-term implication. Problems are related to past but decisions are always related to future. Decisions are taken to solve the problems and decisions are also taken to decide future course of action. Problem solving and decision-making both are carried out in the present. Decision-making is a key to management functions. Decisions are taken for planning, organizing, influencing and controlling. Effective decisions lead to success and ineffective decision may lead to crisis and chaos. Decisions always deal with uncertain situations. No one can guaranty about the success of the decision. As a manager, teacher and officer people spend great deal of time in decision-making. Their major chunk of performance depends on the quality of their decision. So their performance is evaluated based on their effectiveness on decision-making. It means they cannot escape from decision-making process. If they procrastinate the decision-making they are in great trouble because the problem or situation may aggravate or they may lose a good opportunity. One should learn and develop decision-making skills to save her/his position in the institution otherwise someone else will take her/his position of decision-making.

2. Difference between Problem Solving and Decision-making

The problem solving and decision-making appears to be same to many people but there is a remarkable difference between the two processes. The difference between problem solving and decision is shown in exhibit 10.1.

Exhibit No. 10.1: Difference between problem solving and decision-making

Sl. No.	*Criteria*	*Problem*	*Decision*
1.	Related to	Past	Related to future
2.	Information on situation	Facts and data available	Predicted
3.	Purpose	Problems are solved to maintain existing performance Short-term gain	To set future performance goals and achieve them Growth, development and excellence Long-term gain
4.	Time of carrying out process	Present	Present
5.	Approach	Analysis of past Reactive Cause and effect known	Forecasting of future Proactive End known in the form of goals and objectives

Decision-making is choosing or selecting an alternative from gathered or searched alternatives. To solve the problem we need to take decision. Problem solving must precede decision-making because the decision must be based on the best understanding of the past and present situation. Information on causes of problems and an understanding of possible future problems are necessary for an effective decision. Effective decision-making will often require inputs from problem. The problem solving and decision-making functions are performed in the present. But problems are caused because of past and decision are taken for the future. The time of problem solving and decision-making and their relationship is shown in exhibit 10.2

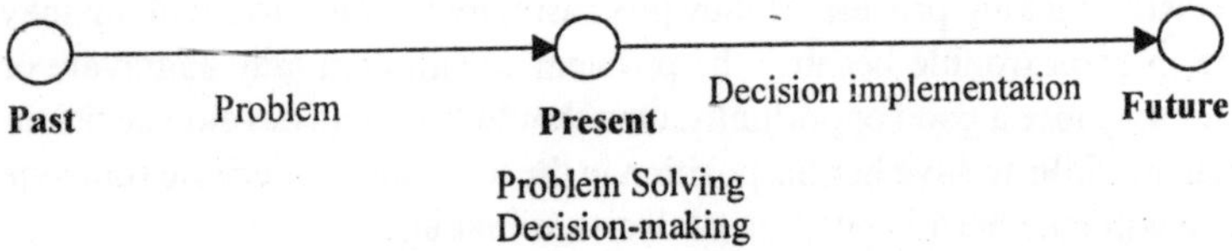

Exhibit No. 10.2: Time of problem solving and decision-making and their relationship

3. Concept of Decision-making

The decision-making is a process of thinking and deliberation to choose one from available alternatives. For example, a teacher decides not to take class, the management decides to introduce a new programme, a student decides to learn from books instead of attending class of a teacher, the management collaborates with sister institution to share resources, the management decides to out source maintenance, security and photocopying work.

4. Classification of Decisions

Decisions can be classified as programmed decisions and non-programmed decisions. Programmed decisions are taken in routine type of situations that occur often. A standard procedure can be developed to deal with such problems. Just like routine maintenance of machines, conducting examination, admitting students, organizing a study tour, organizing a sports meet, publishing a college magazine, organizing a social service camp etc. When the institution faces non-routine and different kind of situation it requires unique solution and that is why non-programmed approach to take decision in a situation is preferred such as starting an undergraduate programme in emerging discipline, meeting the challenge to fill up the seats in existing disciplines, total revision of the curriculum, entering in a business venture, offering online educational programmes, offering distance learning programmes, starting educational programmes for physically challenged people, starting new post-graduate programmes, starting integrated programmes, undertaking research work in new areas etc.

5. Decision-making Models

In earlier days people use to make the decisions on the basis of their intuitions and experiences. Now decision-making is no more an intuition or art it is a science as well. Numbers of decision-making models have evolved in the past in different contexts. Some significant models are described in subsequent paragraphs.

5.1 Janish and Mann Model of Decision-making

The decision-maker should follow the seven steps suggested by Janish and Mann to make good decision. If decision maker omits the steps it would affect the quality of decision. The seven steps are listed in exhibit 10.3.

Exhibit No. 10.3: Seven steps of decision-making

The decision-maker, to the best of his/her ability and within information processing capabilities:

1. Thoroughly canvasses a wide range of alternative courses of action
2. Surveys the full range of objectives to be fulfilled and the values implied in the choice.
3. Carefully weighs whatever is known about the costs and risks of negative consequences as well as the positive consequences that could flow from each alternative.
4. Intensively searches for new information relevant to further evaluation of the alternatives.
5. Correctly assimilates and takes account of any new information or expert judgment to which s/he exposed, even when the information or judgment does not support the course of action initially preferred.
6. Re-examines the positive and negative consequences of all known alternatives, including those originally regarded as unacceptable, before making a final choice.
7. Makes detailed provision for implementing or executing the chosen course of action, with special attention to contingency plans that might be required if various known risks were to materialize.

5.2 Problem Solving Model

As described earlier in this chapter that decisions are taken to solve the problem. The problem is defined and analyzed by the problem solver.

Then alternatives are generated to eliminate the causes of the problem. Out of generated alternatives decision is made based on some criteria for implementation. The decision is validated and implemented by the problem solver or by a team. This model is described in chapter on problem solving.

5.3 Rational Decision-making

Rational decision-making is an economist approach to decision-making. The decision-maker first decides upon the objectives of decision-making and priority among the objectives. S/he generates the alternatives based on the information and evaluates the alternatives on their positive as well as negative implication with reference to the accomplishment of the objectives. S/he makes a choice for the alternative that maximizes the attainment of objectives. This is a quantitative method of decision-making process and number of quantitative tools such as break-even point and decision tree, inventory tables is used. Theory of rational decision-making is based on certain assumptions such as: clear understanding of goals and their priority, complete knowledge and information about situation and decision-making is available, decision-maker is competent and empowered to take decision and explicit decision-making criteria are available.

5.4 Heuristics

Many people do not go in details of the situation and objectives to be accomplished. They recognize the situation requiring decision and based on their hunches they take the decision from available alternatives. The decision is also taken based on experiences without going in details. This method of decision-making became popular because people have no time to go in detail and collect information. They also do not know systematic method of decision-making. The people who use this style are highly creative, self-centred and egoist type of person. Intuition method of decision-making is prove to be good in situations of urgency and low significance.

5.5 Kepner Tregoe Model

Kepner Tregoe developed the first method of decision-making. It is a structured process of decision-making. It is a five step- model of decision-making as shown in exhibit 10.4.

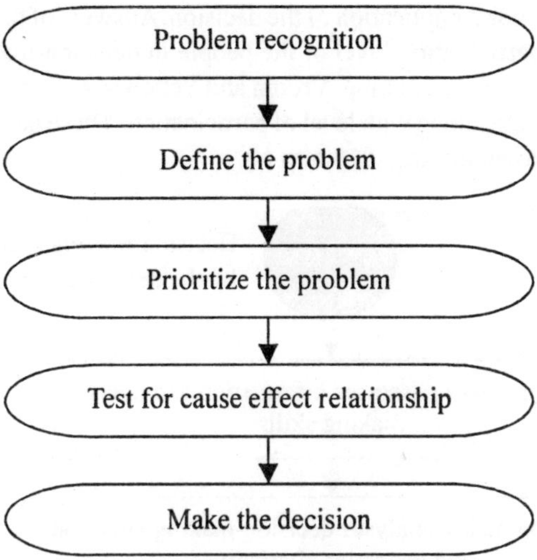

Exhibit No. 10.4: Steps of decision-making model

Kepner Tregoe first described that the existence of the problem should be recognized and it should be defined properly comparing with other non-problem performance. The deviation should be fixed. The problem should be clearly defined asking questions such as what is the problem? Where is the problem? How much is the deviation? When it has occurred? The problem should be compared with other problems in the institution and decide its priority on the basis of its significance. Then the problem should be analyzed to identify the causes and generate solution for removing the causes. The alternatives should be generated and evaluated against their positive and negative impact on the performance. Then final decision should be taken on the basis of the merit.

5.6 Vroom Yetton Model

Vroom and Yetton have worked on styles of decision-making and involvement of people in the process of decision-making process. They worked on quality of decision, acceptance of decision and style of decision making to optimize the quality of decision. They have suggested seven questions to be asked by the decision-maker for a decision-making situation. These questions are related to: quality of alternatives, quality and adequacy of information, structureness of the situation, acceptance of the decision by the implementers, sharing of the problem by the decision-maker and implementers and implication of the decision. Answers of these questions decide the participation level of the people in decision-making process and style of decision-making. Vroom and Yetton suggested five styles of decision-making along with level of participation. These decision-making styles are shown in exhibit 10.5 to 10.9.

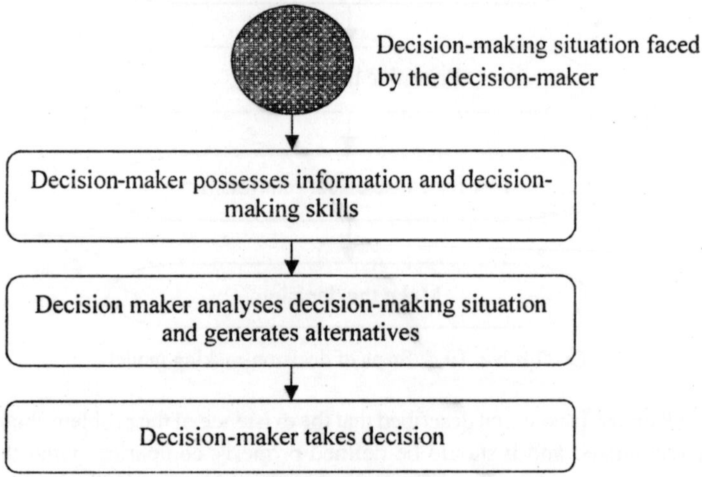

Exhibit No. 10.5: Autocratic style of decision-making with no opportunity for participation

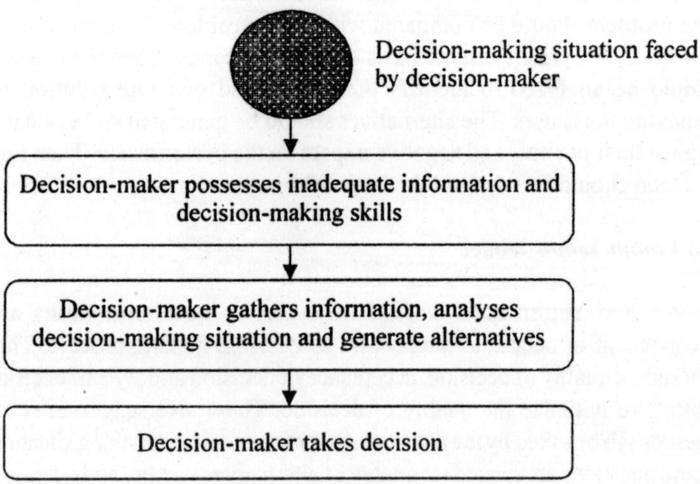

Exhibit No. 10.6: Autocratic information seeking style of decision-making with no opportunity for participation

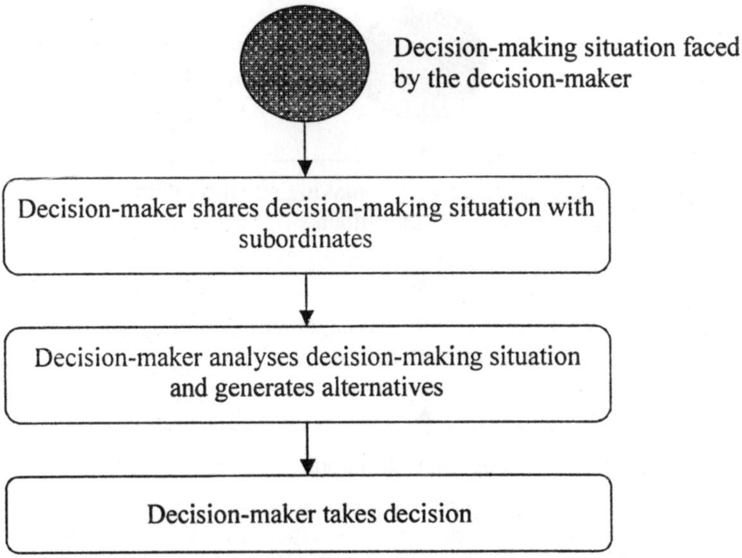

Exhibit No. 10.7: Consultation style of decision-making with no opportunity for sharing the decision

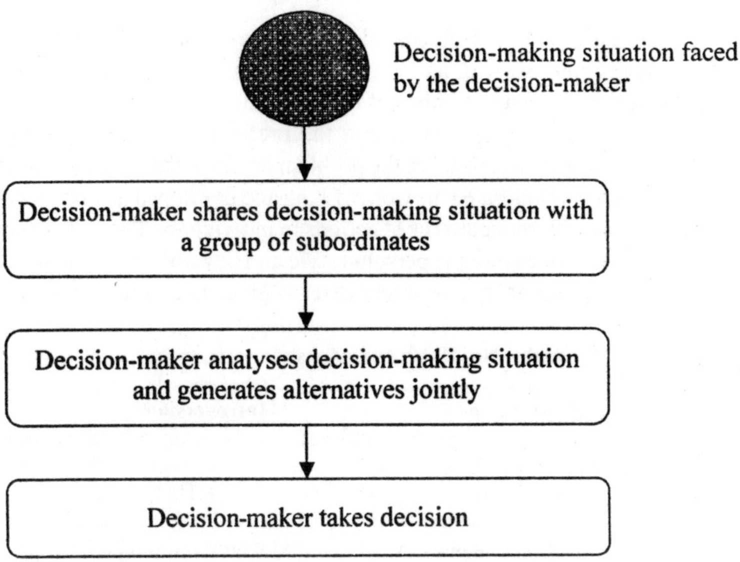

Exhibit No. 10.8: Negotiation style of decision-making with no opportunity for sharing decision problem

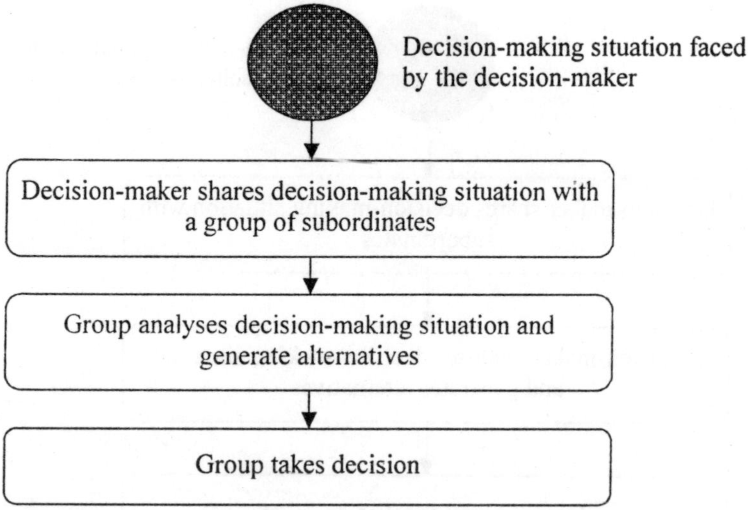

Exhibit No. 10.9: Democratic style of decision-making with opportunity for sharing the decision

6. Problem Solving and Decision-making Personal Style

The personal style of a problem solver or decision maker has profound effect on problem solving and decision-making. Carl Gustav Jung has described that there are number of basic instincts or derivers of action within human beings. He stated that the preference of human beings determine the approach to solve the problem and take the decision. Later on Briggs-Myers elaborated the work of Jung and developed an instrument to identify the different patterns of actions in individuals. The instrument is widely used to measure the personal style and develop the individuals. A brief description of style characteristics is given in exhibit 10.10.

Exhibit No. 10.10: Personal style preferences

Preferred perception of the world	**Extraversion** Individuals develop relationship with people and interact with them to gain energy and know their expectations. Individuals adopt their actions to fulfil others expectations.	**Introversion** Individuals depend on their own energy, beliefs, and values. They possess in-depth knowledge and decide their actions on own preferences.

(*Contd.*)

Preferred way of thinking in information	**Sensing** Individuals gather information using senses. They are practical and realistic. They are concerned more about present and they believe in concrete things.	**Intuiting** Individuals are futuristic. They gather information from speculation, theories, and principles. They believe in creativity and innovation.
Preferred way of processing information	**Thinking** Individuals are rule-bound they make rational decisions and use logic in analyzing situations.	**Feeling** Individuals are subjective. Their behaviour is governed by ethics, values and beliefs. They rely on relationships.
Preferred approach to decision-making	**Judging** They make the decision in planned way. They take quick decision and are always interested in outcomes of the decision.	**Perceiving** They are interested in collecting more data and alternatives. They try to delay decision-making. They are flexible and adaptive.

This model is very helpful in diagnosing the personal problem solving and decision-making style and improving on the same. There are two important steps in problem solving and decision-making. They are information gathering and information evaluation. One should use balanced approach in sensation and institution while gathering information. Similarly one should use balanced approach between thinking and feeling while evaluating the information.

While dealing with the problems of the employees and students in the institution one may require to extraversion, sensation and judging style. On the other hand for making a decision for some new programmes one may need to use introversion, intuition, feelings and judging. It all depends on the type of the situation decision-maker is facing. Decision-maker and problem solver should not go by own preferred style but they should try to diagnose situation and adopt appropriate style.

7. Factors Affecting the Decision-making Process

Decision-making process is affected by many factors in educational institutions. The quality of the decision depends of factors considered in decision-making process. Some of the indicative factors are listed in exhibit 10.11.

Exhibit No. 10.11: Factors affecting decision-making process

➢ Number of people affected by the decision (faculty members, staff members, students, employers etc.) ➢ Revenue to the institution ➢ Time available to take the decision ➢ Time required to implement decision ➢ Quality of information available to decision maker ➢ Government rules and regulations	➢ Decision for long-term benefit or short-term benefit ➢ Acceptability to decision ➢ Availability of resources to implement the decision ➢ Level of efforts required to implement the decision ➢ Risk involved in decision ➢ Personality of the decision-maker

8. Guidelines for Decision-making

Decision-making is a science and effective decisions enhances the quality of products and services of the institution. The decision-makers in the institution should be trained to take the effective decisions. Apart from this certain guidelines should be followed while making the decision. These guidelines will vary for different institutions. A list of indicative guidelines is given exhibit 10.12.

Exhibit No. 10.12: Guidelines for effective decision-making

➢ Empower people to take decisions ➢ Establish time limits for various types of decision-making ➢ Encourage people to make systematic decisions instead of casual or *ad hoc* decisions ➢ Take decision based on facts ➢ Take important and significant decisions first ➢ Inculcate the culture of delegation and decentralization ➢ Seek consensus of affected parties before declaring the decision ➢ Analyse the major risk involved in decision implementation	➢ Have courage to take the decisions ➢ Plan methods, procedures and activities to implement the decisions ➢ Keep aside your emotions while making the decision ➢ Pull creativity of people for taking decisions in new and unfamiliar situation ➢ Use experts and experienced people in taking complex decisions ➢ Don't limit your thinking to institutions limitation while taking the decision ➢ Avoid jumping to conclusion ➢ Differentiate between behaviour related and non-behaviour related decision

9. Summary

Decision-making is a human function. Everyone has to take decisions everyday. Decisions are made in the present. Decisions are made to solve a problem or to create something new grabbing an opportunity. Decisions are always taken for the future and decision-maker does not generally know future. The future can be predicted. The decision-maker should use scientific methods of decision-making to ensure effective decision. There are two types of decision-making situation: routine and non-routine. In routine situation decision-making is comparatively simple in comparison to non-routine situations. Decisions may be quantitative based on data and information. Decisions may be qualitative dealing with the behaviour of the people. Qualitative decisions are difficult to take. Head of the institution plays a very important role in decision-making process. S/he can use five styles of decision-making as suggested by Vroom and Yetton. These styles are autocratic, autocratic information seeking, consultation, negotiation and democratic. There are various models and approaches of decision-making that can be used appropriately to take the decisions. Various tools and techniques add value to decision-making process. Participation of the people is very important in decision-making process if they are affected by decision.

10. Activity

Assess Your Decision-making

As a decision-maker in technical institution you encounter many decision-making situations. Some situations are simple and others are complex. Some situations you face but you are not authorized to make the decision. Some situations you don't face but you are authorized to take the decisions. Some situations of decision-making you like and other you don't but you are required to take decision. You can assess your decision-making behaviour on parameters listed in the table given below. Please honestly mark your response on following behaviour parameters:

Decision-making Behaviour

Sl. No.	*The extent to which you are involved in*	*Extent*			
		High	*Medium*	*Low*	*Nil*
1.	Problem solving				
2.	Taking major decisions in the institution				
3.	Taking minor decisions in the institution				

(*Contd.*)

(*Contd.*)

Sl. No.	*The extent to which you are involved in*	*Extent*			
		High	*Medium*	*Low*	*Nil*
4.	Delegating the decision-making power				
5.	Consulting others for problem solving and decision-making				
6.	Avoiding crisis decisions				
7.	Predicting the future situation for decision-making				
8.	Formulating new and different objectives				
9.	Feeling the failure of decision				
10.	Procrastinating decision making				
11.	Focusing on solution of a problem				
12.	Focusing on problems rather than solutions				
13.	Having alternative solutions of a problem				
14.	Preparing plans of the institution				
15.	Jumping to conclusions				
16.	Involve people in decision-making				
17.	Detaching yourself from the problem situation while making decisions				
18.	Acquiring new knowledge, skills and attitudes for problem solving and decision-making				
19.	Implementation of decisions made by you				
20.	Implementing decisions made by others				
21.	Creativity and different approaches to decision making				
22.	Reducing time, resources, money and resources in taking and implementing the decisions				
23.	Making decisions under pressure of time				
24.	Making decisions in uncertainty				
25.	Generating alternatives to a problem				
26.	Implementing contingent plans				
27.	Setting the priorities				
28.	Solving the same problem again and again				
29.	Thinking to maximize the utilization of institutional resources				
30.	Criticizing the decisions made by others				
31.	Complaining about lack of power to take decisions				
32.	Detaching your personal feelings from decision situation				
33.	Making decisions without much thinking and information				
34.	Assessing the impact of the decisions you have made				
35.	Follow the decision style of a particular person				
36.	Resolving the conflict after making decision				
37.	Rejecting the decisions made by others				
38.	Training others to solve problems and take decisions				
39.	Presenting the alternative solutions to your team members				
40.	Defending the decisions made by you				

REFERENCES

James L. Gibson, John M. Ivancevich and James H. Donnelly (1997). *Organizations*, Business Publications, Inc, Irwin-Dirsey Limited Georgetown, Ontario.

William, F. Glueck (1980). *Management*, The Dryden Press Hinsdale, Illinois.

11

Communication

> ***Objectives:*** The readers will be able to:
>
> 1. State the importance of communication.
> 2. Describe the concept of communication.
> 3. Explain the purpose of communication.
> 4. Explain the elements of communication strategy.
> 5. Describe various types of communication processes.
> 6. Explain communication model.
> 7. List barriers to communication.
> 8. Describe the use of communication in educational processes.
> 9. Test effectiveness of communication in the institution.

1. Introduction

Communication plays a vital role in governance and management of institution. The functions and activities cannot be performed in absences of effective communication. Effective and efficient communication in the institution can prevent many problems, confusion, chaos, crisis and quarrels. At the same time it can enhance the efficiency in integrated functioning of the institution. Many institutions prepare a plan for communication along with strategic, perspective and annual plans to ensure right communication at right time. In educational institution communication is considered to be the life-blood for the growth and development of it. In educational institutions the whole business of academics is based on communication. Often an example of a very knowledgeable and talented professor is quoted who possesses no communication skill and in spite of her/his strengths s/he could not perform her/his job effectively and efficiently.

2. Concept of Communication

Communication in education institution has a significant role. Communication is a basic process of interaction between people who are both transmitters and recipient of the information. It is a key to success in social interaction. The communication is defined as an exchange of ideas, emotions and feelings for achieving specific purpose or goal. It means two or more persons are involved in communication process having common purpose or goal. They exchange ideas, feelings and act accordingly till the purpose is achieved.

3. Purpose of Communication

Communication is a process and it is a means to end. It is situation specific and decided on the basis of purpose of the situation. In educational institution it has purposes listed in exhibit 11.1.

Exhibit No. 11.1: Purpose of communication

Within the institution

- ➢ Share the vision, missions and goals of the institution among institutional members
- ➢ Share the plans of the institution to obtain commitment for implementation and obtaining resources
- ➢ Avoid conflict, confusion, quarrels, and crisis to create healthy work environment
- ➢ Solve problems amicably to reduce waste of time, money and efforts
- ➢ Take decisions effectively and efficiently to achieve objectives without stress
- ➢ Produce effective, efficient and joyful learning for the employees and students
- ➢ Enhance interpersonal relation in the institution for working in a team and avoid delay in the performance of the activities
- ➢ Appreciate, recognize and reward the efforts of the employees to reinforce desirable behaviour
- ➢ Save time, energy and efforts in coordinating, collaborative and networking type of tasks
- ➢ Support management functions of the institution for effective implementation of plans

(*Contd.*)

(*Contd.*)

- Comply the instructions of the management and provide feedback on the progress
- Gain commitment of team members on various tasks and listen their problems related to the task
- Stop rumours
- Counselling the employees and students for selecting right career and observing desired behaviour

With stakeholders

- Market the product and services of the institution to relevant stakeholders and receive business from them
- Make available correct and timely information to the students, clients, customers, and beneficiaries of the institution to project correct corporate image of the institution
- Exchange information for mutual benefit with stakeholders
- Collaborate, network and cooperate with stakeholders for joint ventures
- Help stakeholders to take decisions related business with the institution
- Enhance the corporate reputation of the institution in the society

4. Elements of Communication Strategy

The process of communication has many elements and these elements need to be perfectly designed to formulate an effective and efficient communication strategy. The elements of communication strategy are shown in exhibit 11.2.

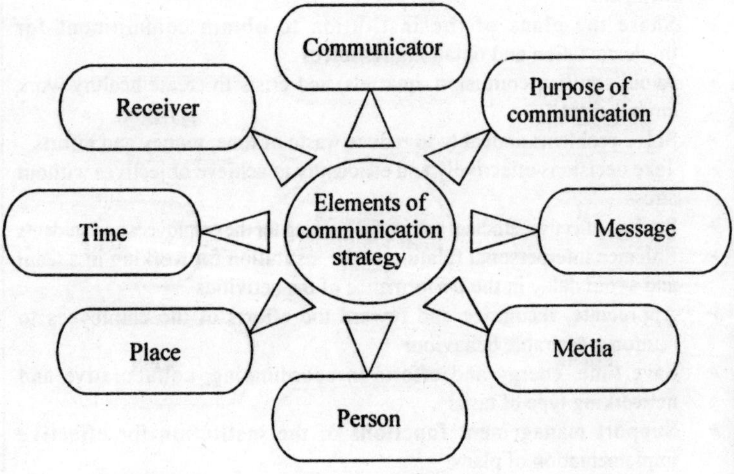

Exhibit No. 11.2: Elements of communication strategy

4.1 Communicator

Communicator is a person who originates the communication process with a purpose. Communicator decides the person who can help in achieving the purpose and establishes relation with the identified person through communication process. To ensure effective and efficient communication s/he should posses a wide spectrum of skills and attitudes to design the communication strategy and carry it out. S/he should possess distinct characteristics to be professional communicator. An indicative list of characteristics of the communicator is shown in exhibit 11.3.

Exhibit No. 11.3: Characteristics of the communicator

An effective communicator should:	
➢ have clear purpose of communication ➢ have clear, strong and balanced voice ➢ have expertise in subject-matter ➢ have patience and tolerance ➢ be a good listener and recognize the recipient that wants to say something ➢ be acceptable to the receiver ➢ dressed properly ➢ appreciate the feelings of the receivers ➢ be precise, concise, simple and concrete in communicating the message ➢ have ability to express ➢ formulate the message for communication that is understandable to the receiver ➢ evaluate the message from its validity, reliability and correctness point of view ➢ identify, design and select appropriate media to effectively communicate the message ➢ effectively use the media	➢ gain attention of recipient ➢ express the message and feeling in right way ➢ create open and supportive environment for communication ➢ be able to design and use alternative strategy of communication ➢ conduct evaluation of communication process continuously ➢ be able to use variety of media and modes to communicate the message ➢ be able to manage the time ➢ use appropriate symbols, signs and body language during the process of communication ➢ be able to manage informal communication ➢ understand the needs, interest, priorities and mood of the receiver ➢ assess the ability, interest and mood of the receiver

4.2 Purpose of Communication

The purpose of communication should be specific, clear, measurable, attainable, time bound and realistic. It should be defined first by the communicator before starting any activity related to communication process. The clear purpose helps the communicator to design and decide other elements of the communication process effectively and efficiently. The purpose of the communication works as a base for designing and implementing communication process. A communicator should give more time on deciding and self-clarifying the purpose.

4.3 Message

The communicator generates ideas, feelings and emotions to design a message to be communicated to the receiver. S/he designs appropriate message using verbal, non-verbal and emotional symbols. The message is validated with the purpose of the communication and level of the receiver. If it fits to purpose and level of the receiver it is communicated using appropriate media. To be effective, the message should have characteristics listed in exhibit 11.4.

Exhibit No. 11.4: Characteristics of a good message

It should be: ➢ aligned to accomplish the purpose of the communication ➢ brief, clear and conscious ➢ interesting to receiver ➢ designed in a language understandable to the receiver ➢ digestible by the receiver ➢ attractive ➢ as per demand and requirement of the situation ➢ based on facts and figures	➢ influential to receiver ➢ strong enough to communicate the intent ➢ create anxiousness and sustain interest of the receiver ➢ culture and context specific ➢ direct ➢ vivid ➢ in consonance to culture of the receiver ➢ well designed: means attractive beginning, meaningful middle and pin pointed end

The message plays a very important role in the functioning of the institution. People try to interpret it in variety of ways and variety of context. The message may be designed in variety of forms as well. Some of the forms of messages are listed in exhibit 11.5.

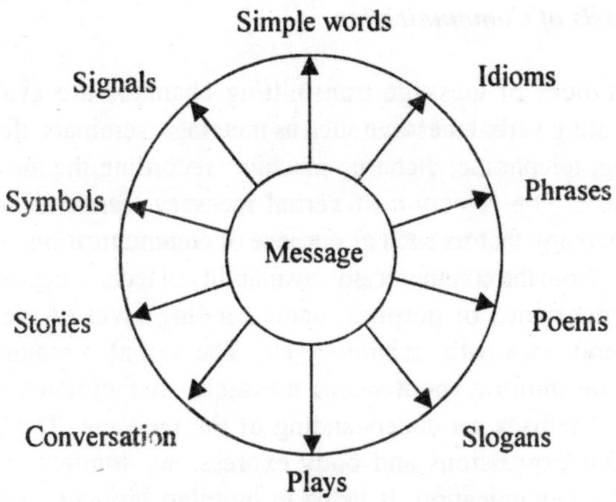

Exhibit No. 11.5: Forms of message

4.4 Media

The message in words can be monotonous and unappealing to the receiver. Use of media adds immense value to a message in the form of colours, graphs, pictures, proportion of shape and size of the picture, symbols, contrast of colours and so on. It is worth to mention old saying here—a picture is worth than thousand words. Media provides multi sensory effect to the message and it uses more than one senses of the receiver. It uses the most powerful sense that is sight. A wide spectrum of print and written media is available to convert the message in media. A list of media that is commonly and frequently used by educational institutions is shown in exhibit 11.6.

Exhibit No. 11.6: List of media

➢ Handouts	➢ Proposals	➢ Photographic albums
➢ Assignments	➢ Posters	➢ Transparencies
➢ Notes	➢ Charts	➢ Models
➢ Letters	➢ Graphs	➢ Bulletin board
➢ Pamphlets	➢ News letters	➢ Power point presentations
➢ Case studies	➢ Journals	➢ Video films
➢ Manuals	➢ Maps	➢ Computer aided learning packages
➢ Textbooks	➢ Photographs	➢ Multimedia
➢ Memos	➢ Hoardings	➢ Simulations
➢ Reports		

4.5 Channels of Communication

Various choices of message transmitting channels are available for communicating verbal message such as meetings, seminars, discussions, counselling, telephonic, dictating machine, recording the message, and using e-mail. The selection of verbal message transmitting channel depends on many factors such as purpose of communication, distance of the receiver from the communicator, availability of technology, availability of time, importance of purpose, understanding level of the receiver, her/his friendliness with technology etc. The verbal communication is good for transmitting spontaneous messages. It facilitates to receive immediate feedback on understanding of the message. The emotional touch, facial expressions and body expressions dominate the verbal process of communication. It helps in building intimate and personal relationship with the receiver.

Number of transmitting channels are available for transmitting messages in pictorial form such as video projection, power point presentations, demonstration, simulation, role play, exhibition, seminars, conferences, meetings, e-mail, teleconferencing, video conferencing etc. The verbal and non-verbal communication can be done using these channels. The message can be transmitted lively, attractively and in sequenced manner to continuously seek the attention of the receiver. It brings live environment in the institution. The written record of the message can be useful for various purposes. It can be reused and explored further. It can be improved also. The limitation is that it requires equipments, power and trained persons to design and use the messages and channels.

4.6 Person

There are situations in which the communicator has no link and relationship with the receiver in that case communicator has to take the help of the mediator person who is known to both. The mediator helps both the parties to come together and complete the communication process. The communicator selects the mediator. The mediator should posses equally good communication skills otherwise the message may get distorted. The mediator should be acceptable to the receiver also. S/he should be willing to become mediator. This mediator helps to effectively communicate initially and later on communicator and receiver may communicate directly.

4.7 Place of Communication

Place of the communication has very important place in the process of communication. One cannot give any message at any place. The instructions to students can be given only in the classroom. Instructions to employees can be given in the meeting or in the chamber of the director or at appropriate place but not publicly. The practical can only be performed in laboratory or workshop. So considering the purpose of the message and type of the message an appropriate place is selected for transmitting a message.

4.8 Time of Communication

Time of message is also very important. To bring the impact of the message it should be given at right time. The curriculum and textbooks should be available to students on very first day of their admission: delay in time may waste their time. It may create learning problems also. The date of examination should be declared well in advance otherwise students would demand for postponement of examination. The planning for the academic session should be carried out before the date of beginning of the session otherwise it may lead to confusion and conflict. Time is very important in communication process. It is said that right message should go at right time to have an impact of it.

4.9 Receiver

The receiver receives the message using the appropriate combination of five senses, namely seeing, hearing, tasting, touching and smelling. The receiver tries to decode the message s/he has received to give it meaning in her/his context. S/he may find the message irrelevant, having different meaning than the intent of the communicator, or incomplete etc. In this case s/he would not behave as desired by the original communicator. The receiver may have different mood, interest, emotions, thinking, and approach to the message communicated. In many situations the receiver is not under the control of the communicator in such situations the communicator cannot do anything except making the request again and again to cooperate.

5. Types of Communication Processes

The communication is classified in many ways based on different criteria. The communication depends on the organization structure of the educational institutions. If the structure is hierarchical it can be defined as top down and bottom up communication. The instructions move from top to down and action on instruction is communicated from bottom to up in the structure. The limitation of this type of communication approach is that it is very slow and message may get distorted during the process or it may lose its importance. In such system of communication, the institution can only sustain the performance but it cannot bring improvement because novel and unique ideas find no place in this process. The upward communication is limited to desire of the top management. Significant and undesired activities are never reported from bottom to top. It is formal approach of communication. In this channel both written and oral communication modes are used.

The organization structure also provides the facility for lateral communication to coordinate various inter-departmental activities. But it suffers from the authority problem. The lateral positions generally do not use the lateral channel unless the higher authority instructs them. That also causes delay and limited communication in the organization. Apart from top to down and lateral communication, diagonal communication is also required to carry out some activities. In hierarchical structure because of authority problems communication gets delayed and it requires intervention from the top. It can be concluded that in hierarchical institutions the communication is very formal, limited and takes its own time. The organizational structure should facilitate the formal and informal communication to perform the tasks effectively and efficiently. If the communication were not effective and efficient in spite of resources, capabilities and capacities of the people the task would not be performed. Teams' structure is suitable in educational institutions that facilitate effective communication within and outside the institution.

It is described in the chapter on management that informal groups are formed by the members of the institutions and even by students. Variety of informal groups does exist in technical institutions. These informal groups satisfy variety of needs of its members. Informal communication has got its own importance in any organization and for that matter in technical institutions as well. In some situations the informal communication is stronger and has importance over formal communication. If formal communication is weak, the informal communication takes its place in its own way to satisfy the needs of the people. There are more chances of rumours, confusions and conflict with the management having uncontrolled informal communication. The teams' structure helps to satisfy the needs such as relationship, personal problem solving, sharing information, sharing resources and clarifying doubts. It helps to use informal communication to facilitate formal communication. In educational institutions multi-channels of communication should be used to spread the message effectively and efficiently. That means right message at right time in right way. The actions should be in consonance with message otherwise people would take it for granted that messages are communicated for formality but actions would take place in traditional way.

6. Communication Model

A simple communication model is shown in exhibit 11.7. There are two persons in the process of communication, i.e. communicator and receiver. The communicator takes some actions to communicate the message and the receiver takes some actions to understand the message.

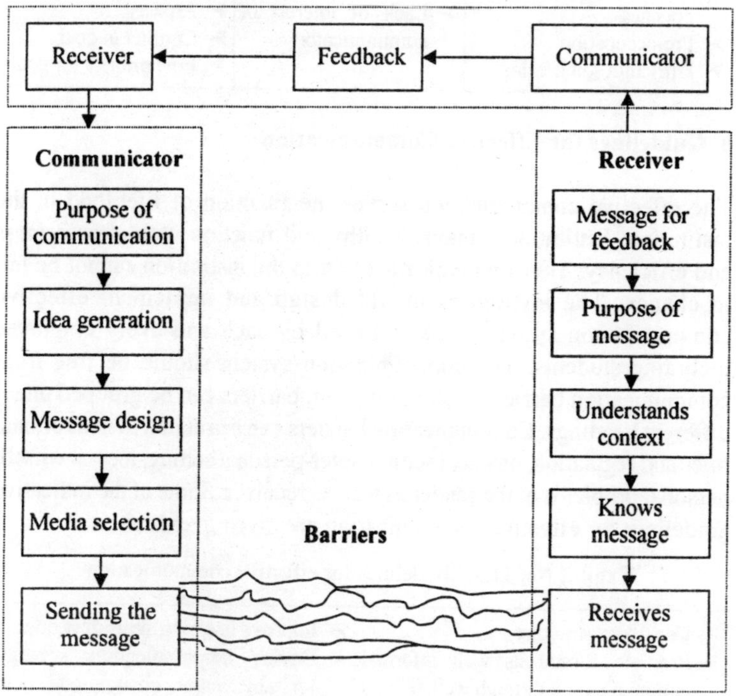

Exhibit No. 11.7: Communication model

7. Barriers to Communication

Numerous barriers to communication are found in the institution because of its faulty design. These barriers are related to organizational structure, authority, work place, role description etc. There are numerous barriers to communication. All the barriers do not appear in every situation of the communication. An indicative list of barriers is given in exhibit 11.8.

Exhibit No. 11.8: Barriers to communication

➢ Incomplete knowledge in subject ➢ Lack of skills ➢ Lack of attitudes ➢ Information overload ➢ Difficulties in expression ➢ Time of communication ➢ Lack of trust and openness ➢ Pre-occupation ➢ Difficulties in hearing	➢ Technical Illiteracy ➢ Vocabulary ➢ Beliefs ➢ Ethics ➢ Emotional disturbance ➢ Dress ➢ Perception ➢ Lack of interest of communicator	➢ Unacceptability of the communicator ➢ Culture ➢ Semantics ➢ Information filtering ➢ Customs ➢ Insufficient message ➢ Physical obstructions ➢ Anxiety ➢ Conflict in goal ➢ Low priority for goal

8. Guidelines for Effective Communication

The effective communication serves the function of lifeblood in the institution. Institution remains healthy and function with effectiveness and efficiency. The communication within the institution cannot be left to chance. The institution should design and implement effective communication system to be followed by each and every employee including students. The communication system should be free from communication barriers. Communication barriers can be grouped under different headings. Communication barriers can be related to institutional rules and regulation, physical setting, inter-personal setting, message itself, personal problems of the sender as well as receiver. Some of the indicative guidelines for effective communication are given in exhibit 11.9.

Exhibit No. 11.9: Guidelines for effective communication

➢ Use teams structure ➢ Promote formal as well informal communication through well defined channels	➢ Improve listening skills of people ➢ Devise communication strategy for any major change and new projects

(Contd.)

➢ Use multiple channels of communication ➢ Empower people to take decisions and communicate ➢ Practice plan based communication ➢ Avoid use of complex terms and messages ➢ Improve communication throughout the institution using various modes of communication ➢ Inculcate a climate of mutual trust, confidence and openness ➢ Provide necessary background of the situation for communicating the message ➢ Ensure accurate and effective communication using direct, short, personal and timely approaches of communication ➢ Make available information required by various stakeholders in written form to save time ➢ Repeat the message till it makes full impact	➢ Plan punishments and other hard decisions carefully and communicate properly ➢ Increase opportunities for open interactions ➢ Create an environment of providing and receiving constructive feedback ➢ Use facts in communication process ➢ Keep the employees informed ➢ Use different styles of communication appropriate to purpose of communication ➢ Promote upward communication as much as possible in the institution ➢ Remove and replace incorrect communication with correct communication immediately ➢ Create valid and reliable data base that can be used for various purposes including ensuring effective communication ➢ Every year conduct communication audit

9. Use of Communication in Instructional Processes

In educational institutions, the institutional communication has got its own importance but more important is the educational communication conducted in classrooms, laboratories and discussions. Teachers should be trained to use effective methods of instructions and use effective styles of communication. Teachers should encourage students to start communication and lead the communication process. This is possible in situations in which teachers use student centred learning methods. Students take the responsibility of learning and they approach to the teachers having specific problems of learning. Teachers should develop variety of leaning resources that can be directly used by students for learning purposes. These resources will involve students in reading and studying. Teachers should remove all the barriers so that students can reach to them at any time for any problem. Teachers should improve listening skills to specifically understand the learning problems of the students. They should also learn the strong and positive methods of offering constructive feedback to students. In the process of instruction students learn communication skills from their teachers. They should never talk loose with the students but they should have great fun in the instructional processes. Teachers should remove all the distractions in the classroom and laboratory before starting the session. They should discus the subject matter with ease. The learning through instructions should be natural and without any heaviness. They should be kind to students to sustain their interest in learning. They should encourage students to speak out their doubts and feelings.

10. Summary

Communication plays a vital role in the governance and management of technical institutions. Effective communication contributes for the growth and development of the institution. It prevents problems, confusion, conflict and quarrels in the institution. It ensures effective decision-making and implementation of decisions. Effective communication is essential for instructional processes. The learning of the students is wholly dependent on the effective communication. Communication is a basic process contributing to perform other major functions in the institution. Communication can be defined as exchange of ideas, emotions and feeling for achieving specific purpose or goal. There could be different purposes of communication processes in the institution. The purpose would vary from situation to situation and person to person. The institutional communication can be classified on three major headings such as communication within the institution, communication for academic purposes and communication with stakeholders. Communication within the institution requires a well-defined strategy in congruence with the goals and purpose of the institution. The communication strategy is designed considering various elements such as communicator, purpose of communication, message, media, persons involved in communication process, channels of communication, place of communication, time of communication and receivers of messages. Each element is given due weightage for ensuring effectiveness of the communication. The barriers to communication are many and different. In different situations different barriers become active. These barriers are considered bottlenecks and need to be removed during the process of strategy design itself. Multi-channels of communication should be used to ensure effective communication in the institution. Teams, structure should be used to promote formal and informal communication in the institution. The authority should be decentralized and people should be empowered to provide quick response to the situation. The institution should ensure that there is no scope of rumour in the institution. Even if wrong communication takes place it should be corrected immediately and effectively with right message. The academic business is the core business in the institution. All the teachers should be trained to ensure effective communication in teaching learning process. They should be asked to encourage communication process from students' side. They should be learner centred and all the time they should ask one question that is 'can students take initiative and active part in the process of learning'? The traditional responsibility for learning should shift from teacher to students. Then only learners would be proactive in communication process.

11. Activity

11.1 Test Effectiveness of Communication in Your Institution

The effectiveness of the communication in educational institutions can be tested using following rating scale. Ask randomly selected representatives of faculty members, staff members and students to fill up this rating scale. Compile, tabulate and interpret the data to ascertain the effectiveness of communication.

Effectiveness of Communication

Sl. No.	*The extent to which the employees*	*Extent*			
		High	*Medium*	*Low*	*Nil*
1.	Are involved in crafting the vision, mission and strategic plan				
2.	Share values, ethics, beliefs and norms				
3.	Prepare plans participatively				
4.	Document the experiences				
5.	Design clear, specific, brief, and effective communication strategy				
6.	Know authority, responsibility and accountability for communication				
7.	Prepare themselves for effective communication				
8.	Plan meetings, briefings, conferences, seminars, creativity sessions, problem solving and counselling				
9.	Classify and record information				

(*Contd.*)

(*Contd.*)

Sl. No.	*The extent to which the employees*	*Extent*			
		High	*Medium*	*Low*	*Nil*
10.	Ensure accurate and timely information				
11.	Use formal and informal channels of communication				
12.	Build healthy relationship for effective communication				
13.	Are confident in communication				
14.	Interact in healthy environment				
15.	Structure communication process				
16.	Use appropriate body language				
17.	Use appropriate style of communication				
18.	Timely communicate				
19.	Manage time during communication				
20.	Exhibit listening skills and empathy for each other				
21.	Find amicable solutions to problem				
22.	Remove communication barriers				
23.	Are willing to learn				
24.	Provide and receive feedback				
25.	Are involved in conducting communication audit				

11.2 Test Your Communication Skill as a Teacher

A good teacher should ensure effective and efficient communication to produce effective learning. Test your communication skill as a teacher responding on statements in following rating scale:

Test your Communication Skill as a Teacher

Sl. No.	*The extent to which you are involved in:*	*Extent*			
		High	*Medium*	*Low*	*Nil*
1.	Preparing lesson plans				
2.	Preparing learning plans for laboratory				
3.	Preparing learning plans for industrial visits and industrial training				
4.	Selecting and preparing instructional resources for promoting self-learning				
5.	Defining technical terms to bring conceptual clarity				

(*Contd.*)

(*Contd.*)

Sl. No.	*The extent to which you are involved in:*	*Extent*			
		High	*Medium*	*Low*	*Nil*
6.	Encouraging students to take up library assignments, industry assignments and internet assignments				
7.	Selecting and preparing media to explain abstract concepts				
8.	Assigning live problems to students to generate alternative solutions				
9.	Organizing industrial visits to observe real life practices				
10.	Organize industrial trainings to have feel of real life work				
11.	Asking students to prepare and make small presentations in the class rooms and laboratory				
12.	Holding group discussions, role plays and action learning				
13.	Active listening of problems of students				
14.	Encouraging students in sharing learning experiences and feeling				
15.	Asking simple but leading questions to test learning				
16.	Providing a slot of time to students to speak out				
17.	Observing the behaviour of the students on well defined criteria				
18.	Creating encouraging environment for two way communication				
19.	Seeking feedback on your communication style and communication				
20.	Noting down the experiences related to communication				
21.	Feeling restless, impatient and eager to end the communication or session				
22.	Loosing confidence during instructional process				
23.	Imparting in stereotyping instructions to students				
24.	Having favourable attitude for positive learning				
25.	Reading reference books and journals				
26.	Writing the text books for students, teachers and practicing engineers				
27.	Surfing internet to down load latest instructional resources				
28.	Organizing seminars, conferences, symposiums and competitions				
29.	Understanding body language and appropriately using it				
30.	Providing constructive and positive feedback to students				

REFERENCES

Bateman and Zeithaml (1990). *Management Function and Strategy Irwin,* Homewood, II, Boston.

Leon, C. Megginson, Donald C. Mosley and Paul, H. Pietri (1989). *Management Concepts and Applications*, Harper & Row, Publishers, New York.

12

Conflict Management

Objectives: The readers will be able to:

1. State the concept of conflict.
2. Describe the types of conflict.
3. List the general causes of the conflict.
4. State the benefits of conflict.
5. State disadvantages of conflict.
6. Design conflict management strategies.
7. List guidelines for managing conflict.

1. Introduction

Conflict is an inevitable part of any organization. It takes place between human beings. Everyone in the institution experiences it. It has an impact on personal life and professional life of people. It may have constructive or damaging effect on personal as well as professional life of people. The extent of conflict may be less or more. It may be between two persons or among many persons. It may be limited to the institution or it may be connected with outside persons. The reasons and sources of conflict may be varied and many. It all depends on specific situation within the institution or outside the institution.

The conflict is purposefully created to generate something new, innovative and different. Conflict is not always bad for the institutions. Healthy and constructive conflict is desirable for the growth and development of the institution. Well-designed created conflict helps to bring the best of the person even in worse and unfavourable situation. It can sparkle the internal needs of the person to achieve something different and unique. It creates challenge to do something better and different. Created conflict foster creativity and innovation in the institution. It helps to bring issues, preferences and potential of the people on the surface.

2. Concept of Conflict

Conflict is a dynamic process that takes place between two parties. Both the parties involved in the process perceive, think and feel that they are negatively affecting the goal accomplishment, interests, feelings, rights, benefits, egos, status or something they deserve. It may be considered as difference of opinion and values. Unnecessary and undesired conflict takes place in institutions having no professional governance and management. There is no vision, values, norms and ethics. The culture of institution is unhealthy to work and people fight on meagre and trivial issues.

3. Dichotomy about Conflict

The conflict management has been a subject of interest of many managers, academicians and researchers. In different contexts and situations number of assumptions have been made and tested but the conclusions could not be generalized. In the literature dichotomy exists on conflict management. The dichotomy is listed in exhibit 12.1 and briefly described in subsequent paragraphs.

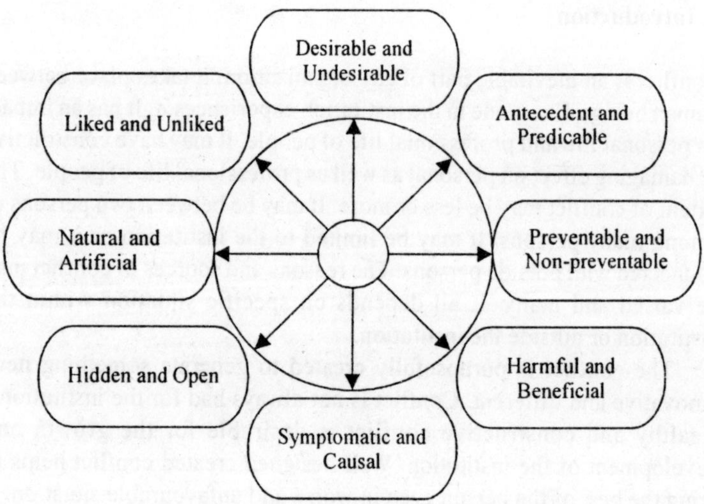

Exhibit No. 12.1: Dichotomy about conflict

3.1 Desirable and Undesirable

Human beings have different types of needs such as need for accomplishment, need for power and need for affiliation. They design strategies to fulfil their varied needs. They try to implement designed strategies and face many challenges, barriers, competitions, problems, confrontations etc. leading to conflict. No institution can be perfectly designed conflict-free. Even automated organizations have human beings and therefore conflict. Whether you desire it or not it exists in the institutions. There is no question regarding undesirable conflict. But people think that conflict is harmful for the individuals and groups and even for the organization so it should be minimized. Yes, steps should be taken to minimize it. When it exists in the institution it has to be appropriately managed at right time in right way. It should be channelised for the benefit of all.

3.2 Antecedent and Predictable

In the institution planning is carried out to accomplish the goals. Strategies and activities are designed for effective implementation. One can very easily predict the likely conflict based on previous experiences. If the activities are in routine, it is easy to predict the conflict. But if there is an issue in it people become wise through gaining experiences from previous situations. The loser parties would design new strategies to gain their benefit. The institution is required to change because of changing demands of the stakeholders. In such changing conditions it is very difficult to predict the conflict. In such situations outcome of the changed action and its impact on the people can be predicted. Then the amount and extent of conflict can be predicted and actions can be designed to minimize the conflict. The institution can frame clear policy on use of resources, authority, distribution of incentives and so on.

3.3 Preventable and Non-Preventable

Conflict can be prevented using professional management approaches. The governors and managers should possess conflict management skills. They should have time and resources to apply the skills to prevent it. If the conflict is predicted it is the predictor who perceives conflict but in reality it may not be a conflict. The time and energy spent on designing conflict prevention strategy would be futile exercise if it does not occur. In most situations it is very difficult to predict the conflict so it is better to use reactive approaches to manage the conflict at early stage of conflict. The apprehension of conflict may lead to maintain *status quo* in performance and no improvement or change is planned.

3.4 Harmful and Beneficial

There are two different views often presented on conflict. One view considers that conflict is harmful for the institution and its employees. It affects the institution and individuals negatively. Some of the indicative negative effects of conflict are listed in exhibit 12.2.

Exhibit No. 12.2: Negative effects of conflict

➢ It destroy the morale and team work ➢ It creates, tension, stress, anxiety, frustration, discontent, guilt, mistrust and hostility in people ➢ It leads to unhealthy politics ➢ It affects the culture and climate ➢ It is risky and disastrous	➢ It creates unnecessary competition among people ➢ It wastes time and energy of the people ➢ It promotes rumours and creates uncertainty and instability ➢ It leads to another conflict ➢ It lowers down performance of the people

There is another view to conflict that is positive view. According to this view constructive conflict is necessary in the functioning of the institution. Constructive, positive and designed conflict is beneficial to the individuals, groups and institution. The indicative benefits are listed in exhibit 12.3.

Exhibit No. 12.3: Benefits of constructive, positive and designed conflict

➢ It reveals important things ➢ It fosters creativity and innovativeness ➢ It promotes constructive criticism thereby improving performance ➢ It promotes healthy opportunities for mutual learning ➢ It brings out weaknesses of systems, procedures, policies, rules, regulations and way of working ➢ It helps to evolve conducive climate	➢ It promotes involvement of people in change initiatives ➢ It promotes healthy competition to achieve goals ➢ It promotes effective communication ➢ It invites people to try their potential to achieve challenging goals ➢ It helps in reducing wastage and misuse of resources ➢ It helps to turn down trivial things

3.5 Symptomatic and Causal

It is said that the conflict is symptom of a problem and not the cause of the problem. Therefore, it is difficult to resolve the conflict. It requires higher level of skills and attitudes. On the other hand there is a view that the conflict can be predicted and prevented that means the causes of the conflict can be identified and removed. Whatever it may be, one thing is clear that conflict is related to behaviour of the people and it is very difficult do modify or change the behaviour.

3.6 Open Conflict and Hidden Conflict

Conflict is considered to be open when it surfaces and characterized by overt controversy, arguments, hostility, defiance, fighting etc. It is observable and one can predict the nature, type and extent of conflict from the behaviour of the conflicting parties. It is a state of unequilibrium between conflicting parties. The observers to the conflict try to withdraw from the situation as soon as possible. On the other hand hidden conflict is not observable. It can be predicted from its symptoms. The symptoms like stress, disinterest in performance, poor decisions, fault finding, negative approach to issue under consideration, complaining, buck-passing, defensive behaviour, etc. are distinctly observable. The open conflict is above the surface can be observed and felt by people. The hidden conflict is like an iceberg that is not observable but can be fatal to the functioning of the institution. The open and hidden conflict is shown in exhibit 12.4.

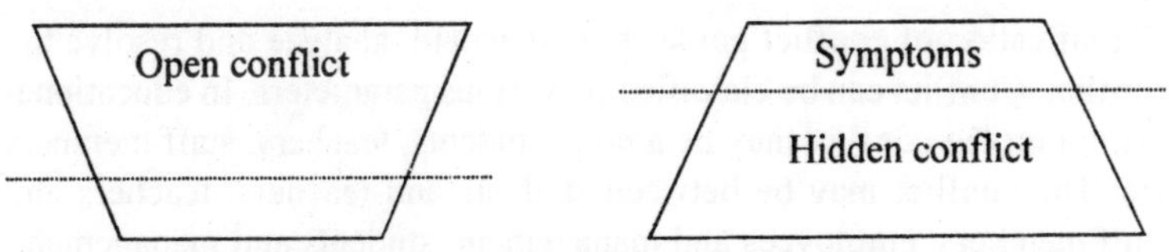

Exhibit No. 12.4: Open and hidden conflict

3.7 Natural and Artificial

The conflict observable in the institution in its normal functioning is a natural conflict. It may be healthy as well as unhealthy. It requires tremendous efforts to resolve natural conflict because it has deep roots. On the other hand artificial conflict is designed and introduced in the processes. It is introduced with a purpose. Purpose may be identifying a better goal, alternative solution to a problem and so on. A trained person to arrive at something, which is not known, or to make the situation interesting creates it. Artificial conflict is created and introduced in the situation naturally. It is used in learning games, role-play, action learning, problem solving, decision-making, planning, innovating, designing change and innovation.

3.8 Liked and Unliked

No one in the institution likes to remain tensed, stressed, and uncomfortable. So no one likes unhealthy conflict. But it is there whether you like it or not. So everyone in the institution should learn to deal with the conflicting situation in a healthy way. People would like the conflict if it were designed, constructive, positive, beneficial, and enjoyable. Think about a teacher who divide the class in two teams and asks each team to prepare questions and answers on one topic and at the same time asks another team to prepare questions and answers and asks both the teams to assemble for asking questions to each other under some rules. There is a reward for the winning team. See the enthusiasm of the team members for preparing the topic and asking questions to opposite team. At the same time the opponent team is also well prepared. The philosophy of healthy conflict works here and all positive points of the conflict can be observed.

4. Types of Conflict

Classification of conflict guides to understand, analyze and resolve the conflict. Conflict can be classified on various parameters. In educational institution the conflict may be among students, teachers, staff members etc. The conflict may be between students and teachers, teachers and staff members, employees and management, students and management, staff and students etc. There may be conflict between institution and any group or the institution and outsiders, for example conflict between institution and university, institution and suppliers, institution and employers of the students etc. When conflict takes place between two persons only it is called interpersonal. Inter group conflict springs from competition. People compete with each other for recognition, authority, power, resources, status etc. Satadeve, Gupta & Shivagunde (1995) studied the nature of conflict in five polytechnics through 12 conflicting situations

Exhibit No. 12.5: Conflict analysis results

Case	*Nature of conflict*	*Parties involved*	*Major causes*	*Central issue of conflict*	*Style adopted by conflicting parties*	*Effectiveness of style*	*Outcome and strategy adopted*	*Effects on system*
Educational visit	Inter-personal	Principal, HOD and students	Personality clashes Leadership Rigid procedures	Changed programme of educational visit	Principal – confrontation HOD – Diffusion Students – confrontation Principal's appeasement, confrontation with HOD confrontation Principal's withdrawal	Partially effective	Conflict resolved Surrender by Principal	Adversely affected
Role ambiguity	Inter-personal	Lecturer vs lab assistant	Role ambiguity Personality clashes	Role ambiguity	Lect – confrontation Lab. assistant diffusion, confrontation Lect – confrontation, force withdrawal	Partially effective	Resolved transfer of LA	Adversely affected
Shadow of seniority	Inter-personal	Lect vs Lect and students	Power struggle, personality differences and prestige issue	Charge of HODs post	Lect – confrontation four times	Not effective	Not resolved	Adversely affected
Walking wound	Inter-personal	Principal vs Lect	Negligence in duty Personality clashes Leadership style	Transfer Lect.	P – confrontation Lect – resignation P – confrontation Lect – confrontation	NE NE E E	Not resolved	Adversely affected

(*Contd.*)

(*Contd.*)

Training needs of supervisor	Inter-personal converted to inter group	Workshop Supt vs charge man and class IV	Power difference Clashes of interest Resources control and role ambiguity	Poor performance of subordinates	WS Negotiation FM confrontation WS confrontation CM and class IV confrontation Principal and WS withdrawal	NE NE NE E E	Resolved transfer of class IV and charge man	Adversely affected
Subject allocation	Inter-personal converted to inter-group	HOD vs Lect and class IV	Leadership style job dissatisfaction	Subject distribution	Lect confrontation HOD appeasement Lect confrontation HOD confrontation Lect and class IV confrontation and forced withdrawal	E E NE E E E	Resolved transfer of HOD and Lect	Adversely affected
Problem of tuition	Inter personal converted in inter-group	P vs HOD and Lect.	Status inconsistency change in practice Egoism and personality clashes	Tuition practices	P negotiation P confrontation HOD confrontation P confrontation Forced withdrawal	NE NE NE NE E	Resolved transfer of principal	Adversely affected
Incharge principal	Inter personal converted in inter-group	P vs HOD and students	Power struggle Difference for leadership Power style egoism Personality clashes	Struggle for power	HOD confrontation S confrontation P arbitration HOD confrontation P resignation forced withdrawal	NE NE NE E NE E	Resolved bringing in regular principal	Adversely affected

(*Contd.*)

(*Contd.*)

Mind your language	Inter-personal converted in inter group	Lect vs Typist	Dignity personality clashes Bad language	Defamation	Lect and supporter confrontation Typist and supporter confrontation Principal intervention, arbitration	NE NE E	Resolved arbitration and negotiation	Not affected the climate
Jeep Phobia	Intra-group	Lect vs Driver and his group	Lack of confidence Change in practice	Driving practice	Driver and his group confrontation Lect diffusion	NE E	Resolved adopting motivational approach	Positive effect
Institution car	Between two organizat-ion	Principal vs DM	Sharing resources egoism Lack of communication	Acquisition of car	P confrontation DM confrontation P resignation P arbitration	NE NE NE E	Resolved intervention from higher authority	Adversely affected
Strikes	Inter-group and intra-group	Students vs Principal and Lect	Resources allocation change in practice Power struggle leadership style	Curbing students freedom and autonomy	P confrontation students confrontation P arbitration Forced withdrawal Lect confrontation Students confrontation Lect compromise Forced withdrawal	NE NE NE E NE NE NE E	Resolved transfer of Principal and HOD	Adversely affected

E – Effective, NE – Not effective, Lect. – Lecturer, P – Principal, DM – District Magistrate, LA – Lab Assistant, WS – Workshop Superintendent, Fm – Foreman, Cm – Chargeman, HOD – Head of Department, S – Students.

and found that in four cases interpersonal conflict occurred, in five cases conflict initiated at interpersonal level and then spread to inter group level, in two cases it was intra group conflict and in one case it was inter organizational conflict. Major conflicts occurred at principal and head of department level because power, status, authority and responsibility are more crucial at higher level. A summary of nature of conflict, parties involved, major causes central issues of conflict, styles adopted by conflicting parties, effectiveness of style, the outcome of the strategy and effects on the system are listed in exhibit 12.5.

5. Stages of Conflict

Pondy has described five stages of conflict. These stages are shown in exhibit 12.6.

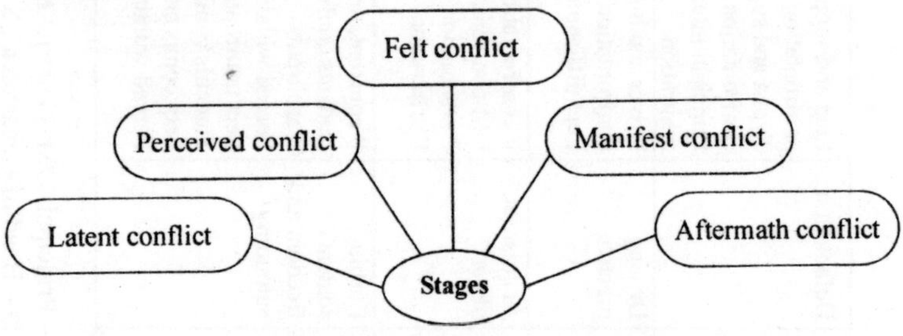

Exhibit No. 12.6: Stages of conflict

5.1 Latent Conflict

It is related to competition over resources, drives for power and divergence of goals. People want to use the available resources to perform the activities with ease and effectiveness. If the resources in the institution were limited people would try to grab them. For example every teacher wants to use overhead projector and power point presentation to make the teaching learning process colourful and interesting but there is paucity of these equipments. Certainly there would be competition to grab the resources and it may lead to conflict. Competition to acquire resources may get converted to ego conflict or authority conflict or importance conflict. People want freedom and autonomy to take decisions and perform activities. They don't want to be controlled or supervised. They don't want to approach superiors for trivial things and superiors waste their productive and purposeful time.

They want empowerment for most of the job functions they are performing. Divergence of goal may occur because of priorities of the institution. The priority of the department may be conducting regular classes to assure quality of instruction and good result of the students in the term end examination in the university. But the priority of the institution may be conducting full time continuing education programmes for the employees of one company that absorb more than 20 per cent passouts of the institution. The company may pay heavily for these programmes adding to revenue of the institution. The management of the institution insists on conducting continuing education programmes on priority basis. The department delays it because the regular classes may suffer, resources may not be available for the continuing education programmes, paucity of time and so on. The latent conflict may be there because of combination of above causes.

5.2 Perceived Conflict

It is the conflict perceived by the one or both the parties to the conflict but in real life situation there is no conflict. It is the perception of conflicting parties. It may be due to lack of communication or miscommunication or misunderstanding or due to rumour. The person feels the conflict because s/he has such personality or position. S/he may not be satisfied with her/his performance and perceive conflict with stakeholders or beneficiaries. For example, a teacher is not confident on her/his quality of teaching and always worries about conflict on poor result with management.

5.3 Felt Conflict

The conflicting parties feel the conflict in the given situation. They appreciate that there is a conflicting situation and both the parties undergo tremendous tension, anxiety and uncomfortness. Think about a situation of recruitment in which there is only one post of professor and more than one internal candidates and external candidates have applied. All the internal and external candidates have almost equal qualification, capability and capacity to become professor. One can imagine the felt conflict of internal members. They would not like to come together and talk to each other on any institutional issues. The conflict would be felt till the result of the recruitment process is declared. Later on the conflict may take another shape.

5.4 Manifest Conflict

The conflict is surfaced fully and conflicting parties use variety of tactics to make the conflicting situation in their favour. The parties to the conflict may become violent and uncontrolled to some extent in such situation. The institutional norms, ethics, rules, regulations and authority do not work effectively and efficiently in such situations. People are at unrest and don't want to listen each other. The conflicting parties blame each other for the conflict and they claim that other party is behaving deliberately to promote the conflict. The manifest conflict results in non-cooperative and withdrawing behaviour. The interpersonal conflict may spread through out the institution. The management of the institution should deal with manifested conflict in a safe and serious way at early stage. Various conflict-resolving strategies are used to resolve the conflict. These strategies are described in later part of this chapter.

5.5 Conflict Aftermath

Conflict aftermath has variety of shapes and versions. If the conflict was resolved in a healthy way to the satisfaction of conflicting parties it would have less damage on the relationship between the conflicting parties. Conflicting parties will come back to the normal position. If the conflict is suppressed using authority and it is still active like volcano it may erupt at any time bringing much damage to the conflicting parties and whole institution.

6. Sources of Conflict

In educational institutions sources of conflict are many in comparison to other organizations because of more number of human processes and less use of machineries for achieving institutional objectives. The indicative sources of conflict are listed in exhibit 12.7.

Exhibit No. 12.7: Sources of conflict

➤ Conflicting expectations ➤ Different priority to institutional goals ➤ Uneven distribution of authority ➤ Inter-disciplinary work ➤ Unclear responsibility ➤ Undefined rules, regulations and procedures ➤ Institutional structure	➤ Performance evaluation and rewards ➤ Short-term versus long-term benefits ➤ Money saving versus investing ➤ Allocation of important work ➤ Role related conflict and stress ➤ Scarce resources ➤ Task interdependencies ➤ Poor communication

6.1 Conflicting Expectations

In educational institutions conflicting expectorations arc commonly found. Students want the examination should be postponed because the curriculum has not been covered due to late admission. The university wants that academic calendar should be followed and examination should be conducted as per schedule. Teachers expect students to come prepared to class but students complaint about paucity of time. Students expect that teachers should discuss practical aspects of concepts and principles but teachers have no exposure to industrial world or it is not in the curriculum or there is no time to discuss the application part. Teachers and staff members expect compatible salary package and incentives from the management but management wants the teachers and staff members professionally perform. The management assures them to give good package on consistently outstanding performance over a period of time. Management has different priorities than personal priorities of the teachers and staff members. Teachers and staff members want to peruse their career doing variety of activities but management want them to perform the activities that are on institutional priorities. Government wants that the institutions should charge reasonable fees from the students but the institution needs money for the growth and development. There are numerous situations in which conflicting expectations exists in the institution. The example of conflicting expectation is shown in exhibit 12.8.

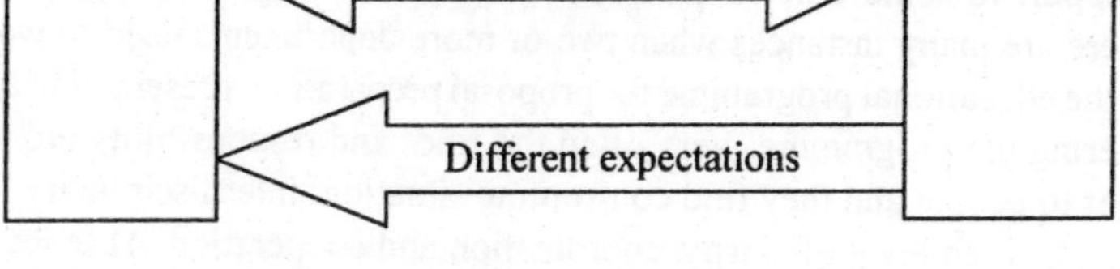

Exhibit No. 12.8: Conflicting expectations

6.2 Different Priorities to Institutional Goals

The governing body wants that the institution should function on full range of activities that can be performed by the institution but there may be insufficient teachers, staff members and resources. The institution may not have capability to perform on full range of activities. It may lead to conflicting situation between governing body and management of the institution. The faculty members may be interested in starting postgraduate and Ph.D. programmes but the management may be interested in starting undergraduate programmes in new and emerging disciplines. The teachers want their students to secure good marks in final year examination but students want good placement and they prepare for placement and not for obtaining good marks in subjects. They devote more time on interview, discussions and studying management topics. Different internal and external stakeholders have different priorities leading to conflicting situation.

6.3 Distribution of Authority

The faculty members and staff members may get the role of their choice but if they do not get appropriate authority they cannot perform the role effectively and efficiently. Since they perform the role so they want to use the authority in their own way. But in this situation the authority hold by superiors so they are required to follow the instructions of the superiors although they are responsible for the same. Such conditions put them in a conflicting situation. The authority may be overlapping and there may not be agreement between the persons holding the authority.

6.4 Interdisciplinary Work

Number of new and emerging disciplines are having common and interdisciplinary subjects. The institution wants that existing department should teach the interdisciplinary subject but existing department don't want to work under any other department. Parent department don't want to report to some other department in which it has got specialization. There are many instances when two or more departments need to work on the educational programme for proposal preparation, presentation and offering the programme. Very often the roles and responsibility are not clear to people and they find confronting situation. Interdisciplinary job requires high level of clarity, coordination and cooperation. Absence of which may lead to conflict.

6.5 Unclear Responsibly

It is very difficult to define the roles and responsibility of individuals and teams in changing environment. The poorly defined roles and responsibility lead to conflict. In traditional institutions also the job is defined but not the role. People perform the job but their stakeholders want them to perform role. The gap between job and role leads to conflicting situation. There may not be sufficient work for positions in the institution so persons working on these positions are deployed for other tasks. Reporting at two places may lead to confusion and conflict.

6.6 Undefined Rules

The policies, rules and regulations are not properly defined in the institution. Undefined rules, regulations, and policies lead to conflicting situation even in trivial situations. The informal norms for effective working are not defined and shared that leads to subjective and biased approach to situation leading to conflict. In some institutions policies, rules and regulations are available but they are irrelevant in today's context. In some situations rules are followed and in others not leading to mistrust in the rules as well as in decision makers.

6.7 Institutional Structure

In many situations, the institutional structure becomes the source of conflict. The structure of the institution and authority system do not support the effective and efficient performance of the activities. On the other hand everyone wants effective and efficient work specially the students, their employers and external stakeholders. The resources are distributed authority-wise but somebody else performs the work. The performer has to approach the authority holder for decisions and resources. It irritates the performer and s/he enters in conflict with the authority holder. The performer has to justify every time for obtaining resources and cooperation of the authority holder.

6.8 Performance Evaluation and Rewards

Same criteria for comparing the performance of the departments, teams and individuals are used but they function in different environment and for different objectives. The performance of a teacher who has been performing routine activities for years is compared with the teacher undertaking research work. Or teaching a subject, which requires continuous learning and it is proved that the traditional teacher is performing better. Such wrong comparison leads to conflict with the management. It also creates negative effect on behaviour of other teachers involved in carrying out innovative works. If rewards are not linked to performance but are based on some other criteria they lead to interpersonal conflict. Subjective evaluation system and comparative evaluation system of performance lead to severe conflicts.

6.9 Short-term versus Long-term Benefits

Some people believe in short-term benefits and work for the same. They want immediate rewards and feedback on performance. Their way of working may not be correct and leading to long-term disadvantages to the institution. There would always be conflict between people desiring short-term advantages with people desiring long-term advantages. People believing in long-term advantages would promote strategic thinking and strategic plans that enhances corporate reputation of the institution.

6.10 Money Saving versus Investing

There may be conflict on issue of money saving *versus* investing between the promoter of the institution and management of the institution. The promoters would like to gain profit from the institution on the other hand the managers are the professionals they would like to take the institution to academic heights investing more and more. Professional managers would like to provide excellent services to the students on the other hand the promoters may press them to cut down the expenditure leading to financial conflict.

6.11 Allocation of Important Work

The management may allocate the institutional work unjudiciously to faculty and staff members. If the work is assigned to incompetent people then the expert in that area may resent it. If important works of the institution are allocated to a few selected persons rest of the people may enter in great conflict with management as well as people holding important works. Rest of the people will not cooperate them. It is true for trivial work as well.

6.12 Role Related Conflict and Stress

If the role of individuals and teams are not properly designed it may lead to role conflict. Udai Pareek has described that role space has three main variables that are self, the role under question and the other roles s/he occupies. Any conflict amongst these is referred to as role space conflict. The conflict under role space take the form of self-role distance, intra-role conflict and role stagnation. If the expectations of role are different from the self-concept the person will feel self-role distance conflict. For example, a person has joined as a faculty because of personal factors but it does not match with the attitude and aptitude of the person s/he will feel conflict. Individuals have to perform variety of roles demanding for diverse competence, attitude and aptitude. Some of the roles may not match to her/his ability or interest. S/he may not have time to perform the role also. Such roles create intra-role conflict. Individuals do work on a particular position for a longer time and after that they get promoted. They feel insecure and uncomfortable because of many reasons. In such situations they feel role stagnation conflict. If a person occupies many roles such as teacher, chairman of professional body, editor of professional journal etc. s/he may feel inter role conflict. When the individual is not clear on her/his role s/he feels role ambiguity. When different stakeholders have conflicting expectations the role occupant feels role expectation conflict. When too many expectations are there from the role occupant that is beyond her/his capacity to satisfy is called role overload conflict. When others are performing the role of the individual the person feels role erosion conflict. When adequate resources are not available to role performer s/he feels resource inadequacy conflict. When the role holder is given a peripheral role s/he feels role isolation conflict.

6.13 Scarce Resources

When the resources in the institution are scarce or they are too much controlled by the management such situations affect the performance of the people leading to conflicting situation. In academics every one would like to engage forenoon sessions because every one feel fresh in the forenoon. Here time is scarce resource for teachers. It may lead to conflicting situation. Allocation of a subject of own choice, good classrooms, computers, projects, positions, and privileges are considered to be scarce resources in educational institutions.

6.14 Task Interdependencies

There are many tasks, which require the cooperation of many individuals and groups. The performance of the task depends on the performance of the previous component. For example, the success of continuing education programme is dependable on training needs analysis, curriculum design, curriculum validation, instructional resources, training programme conduction, and evaluation of the outcome. Apart from this it also depends on commitment of the trainees. The training programme coordinator is dependent on many individuals and teams for the success of the programme. He may face conflict at any stage from any person. The relationship between level of interdependencies and level of conflict is shown in exhibit 12.9.

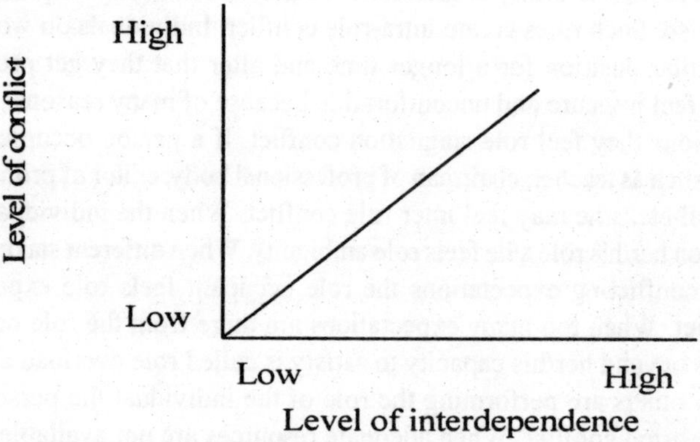

Exhibit No. 12.9: Relationship between interdependencies and conflict

6.15 Poor Communication

The communication in the institution should be effective and efficient. Poor communication or delay in communication or communication gap may lead to severe conflicting situations. It may create confusion leading to conflict. The informal channels of communication may get activated and variety of rumours may take a better shape to shadow the formal communication. Loose talk and corridor talk may create conflict in the institution.

7. Conflict Management Process

Conflict management is a complex and risky task. If it not managed then it is more risky and leads to crisis and chaos in the institution. The concerned person should understand the conflicting situation based on reliable information. S/he should collect sufficient information on conflicting parties, their background, issue of conflict, extent of conflict, history of conflict, her/his authority and responsibility to resolve conflict, rules and regulations related to the situation, previous experiences etc. s/he should find out the relationship between the conflicting parties. S/he should also find out whether s/he is a right person to intervene. Then s/he should intervene. The steps of conflict resolving process are listed in exhibit 12.10.

Exhibit No. 12.10: Conflict resolving process

7.1 Diagnose the Situation

Gather information on conflicting parties, beginning of the conflict, main issues of conflict, their views on conflict, parties affected by conflict, consequences of conflict, etc. Collect the information from the people who have observed the conflict. If the information is available in the records study the documents. The information may be related to perception and opinion also. The conflict resolver should separate out the facts and figures from the perception and opinions.

7.2 Define and Analyze the Conflict

The conflicting situation is defined in terms of its boundaries, parties involved, conflict initiation process, views of the parties to conflict, harm to each party, expectation of each party, sources of conflict, level of conflict, damage caused by the conflict to other parties who are not involved in conflict and to institution, time taken by the conflict to surface out, significant stages of conflict and identification of root cause of the conflict. In analyzing the conflict the conflict resolver should remain in close contact with both the conflicting parties. If situation requires s/he should bring both the parities on one platform to spell out the conflict and find out root causes of the conflict.

7.3 Design Conflict Resolving Strategy

Design alternative conflict management strategies. If conflict-resolving strategies are already available select appropriate strategy considering institutional practices, authority and previous experiences. Select appropriate conflict management style, establish effective communication with conflicting parties and others. In generating conflict management strategy the conflicting parties should be involved if situation permits.

7.4 Implement Conflict Resolving Strategy

Implement the conflict resolving strategy to manage the conflict in healthy way. During the implementation of the designed strategy some modification may be necessary because of the situation. The conflict resolver keeps close watch on effectiveness of the strategy and assesses the impact of the strategy.

In many situation the conflict can be resolved using strategies such as using authority, or modifying the rules, or opportunity is created, or the conflicting situation is changed, or the goal is put on low priority, or the assignment is given to some body else, or the reward is abandoned, of both the parties are granted equal authority, or some rotational arrangements are made or norms are revised, or norms are decided, or some urgency is created, or both the parties are withdrawn from the situation and both are assigned some challenging work in which they consume their energy and have no time for conflict, or both the parties are geographically separated. Numerous alternatives are available with the conflict resolver to stop, resolve and prevent the conflict. In many institutions if complex, bigger and wider conflict prevails they revisit their vision, missions, goals, values, norms, ethics, beliefs, and strategies. They bring drastic changes in the core business of the institution and way of doing the business.

7.5 Evaluate the Impact of Strategy

Conflict resolver should evaluate the impact of conflict resolving strategy. They can learn new conflict resolving skills and sharpen old skills. It also boosts a confidence in them to face and resolve the conflict. If they are successful in constructively resolving the conflict they certainly get publicity and strengthen their power to resolve conflict. The new learning on conflict management should be documented.

8. Conflict Management Styles

Numerous styles of conflict management have proposed by psychologist and management experts. Likert and Likert, Blake, Shepard and Mouton,

Hall, Tommas, Pruitt and many other writers have studied the conflict management on different dimensions and proposed their points of view. Udai Pareek has described the work of experts and his own in his book *Managing Conflict and Collaboration.* Thomas has suggested four styles of conflict management that is avoiding, accommodation, competition and collaboration.

Udai Pareek has proposed a superb model of conflict management. He has considered two groups that are our group and out-group. He proposed that the perception of the out-group should be used for understanding the conflict. He described the behaviour on two dimensions that are avoidance oriented and approach oriented. He suggested four styles of conflict management for avoidance-oriented approach that are resignation, withdrawal, diffusion and appeasement. Similarly he suggested four styles of conflict management for approach mode that are confrontation, compromise, arbitrate and negotiate.

Satadeve, Gupta & Shivagunde (1995) studied the conflict management style of 78 faculty members of five Polytechnics of Maharashtra State and found that the most preferred style is negotiation. This style is supported by compromise style. The order of other styles is shown in the exhibit 12.11. They have studied twelve cases of conflict in different institutions and found that although the negotiation and compromise are the preferred styles but these styles were not used in resolving real life conflict. In most cases confrontation style is used which escalated the conflict to greater intensity.

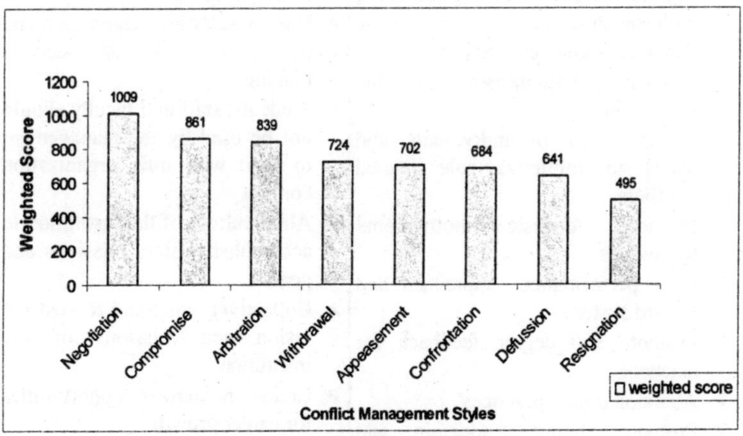

Exhibit No. 12.11: Conflict management style of polytechnic teachers

9. Guidelines for Conflict Management

The conflict can be prevented to a greater extent using proactive and preventive measures in the institution. Even if conflict takes place it can be detected, diagnosed, analyzed and resolved before it brings negative effect on the performance of the institution. Some indicative guidelines for preventing and managing conflict are listed in exhibit 12.12.

Exhibit No. 12.12: Guidelines to prevent and manage conflict

➢ Empower people for decision-making and problem solving under broad framework ➢ Promote participatory governance and management of the institution ➢ Promote working in teams ➢ Have well functioning problem solving, grievance handling and counselling mechanism in the institution ➢ Organize creativity sessions on various themes to steam out the feelings of the masses and generate innovative solutions ➢ Have regular briefing on new initiatives ➢ Sign memorandum of understanding with stakeholders ➢ Promote healthy competitions ➢ Inculcate voluntarism in the institution ➢ Design roles of individuals and teams to minimize role related conflicts ➢ Promote intrinsic motivational techniques ➢ Use performance appraisal and reward system ➢ Promote 360 degree feedback for teachers ➢ Abandon *adhoc* practices ➢ Promote shared leadership and rotation of job	➢ Evolve and practice shared norms ➢ Use appropriate style of conflict management for specific situation ➢ Enhance collaborative and cooperative activities ➢ Train people in conflict prevention and healthy conflict management ➢ Promote personally development and adjustment skills ➢ Give fair treatment to conflicting parties ➢ Deal with the conflict at early stage before it damages relationship ➢ Use consultative, negotiation and democratic style of decision making ➢ Students, staff and faculty should not be used by the management to fight with intèr organization conflict ➢ Align culture of the institution to accomplish vision, missions and goals ➢ Collectively visit and re-visit the vision and missions of the institution ➢ Create numerous opportunities for career growth ➢ Create win-win situation

10. Conflict Management Skills

The leaders and managers in educational institutions should develop knowledge, skills and attitudes to prevent and resolve conflict. They should also have skills to foster healthy conflict for the growth and development of the institution. The conflict management skills are shown in exhibit 12.13.

Exhibit No. 12.13: Conflict prevention and management skills

➢ leadership skills	➢ people skills
➢ problem solving skills	➢ decision making skills
➢ communication skills	➢ team building skills
➢ negotiation skills	➢ behaviour shaping skills
➢ visualizing skills	➢ counselling skills

11. Summary

Conflict is an inevitable human activity. Conflict management is essential in educational institutions because human interactions are many. Conflict can be diagnosed, analyzed and resolved amicably in the institution during its early stage. Conflict can be prevented in the institution following good practices of management such as shared leadership, shared values, effective communication, role design, job enrichment and working in a team. Conflict prevention is much better than resolving the conflict. If not managed it may take horrible shape and situation may go beyond control.

Conflict enhances creativity and constructive criticism also. It can be used in the institution by design to foster creativity for designing new and innovative strategies. Conflict can be used to test the acceptability of change in the institution. It can be used in learning process to harness the potential of the students for producing learning and self-responsibility in learning. Healthy conflict encourages employees to excel better for the growth and development of the institution.

12. Activity

Read the case study on climate in government polytechnic Mahanagar and find the answers to questions mentioned in the brief at the end of the case study.

Climate in Government Polytechnic, Mahanagar

Background

In August, 1993 Mr. Bhinde, Principal of Government Polytechnic, Mahanagar was transferred to Directorate of Technical Education (DTE) Office as Deputy Director. Mahanagar Polytechnic runs 5 diploma programmes out of these three are Electronics related (Electronics, Telecommunication and Industrial Electronics) Programmes. Other two programmes are conventional Civil and Mechanical Engineering. Though there are five sanctioned posts of head of departments, only two were filled up. Mr. Shinde was head of department Civil and Mr. Khare was head of department Electronic. Though Mr. Shinde is young, he is senior to Khare and hence Principal Bhinde handed over charge of Institute to Shinde.

Mr. Shinde and Mr. Khare are crucial characters to this case. Mr. Shinde is BE (Civil) and obtained degree in 1983. Just immediately after passing degree in engineering he joined technical education system as Lecturer in a new polytechnic situated in backward area of the state. He belongs to backward community and he was selected head of department Civil in March 1991 by Public Service Commission. He got posting in same polytechnic as head of department after his selection. He was transferred to Mahanagar Polytechnic in January 1993. His age is around 35 years.

Mr. Khare has been working in Mahanagar Polytechnic since 1988. In 1988 he was senior most lecturer in Electronics Department and hence worked as Incharge head of department. In January 1992, he was also selected head of department Electronics and got posting in the same institute. He had completed Master of Engineering in 1988 (Part time Post Graduate Course). He is looking after academic work of Electronics related three branches.

Shinde is incharge (I/c) Principal with financial power and authority of regular Principal. Khare is much elder and much experienced than Shinde, and he had a superiority complex. He never accepted Shinde's leadership. Khare was looking after three departments (Electronics related) and Shinde decided not to interfere in his department's academic work.

Khare never provided support of cooperation to Shinde. Moreover he was always engaged in criticizing Mr. Shinde and opposing his action and schemes. Khare is very arrogant, dominant and autocratic in his behaviour. Nobody in the institution has good relationship with Khare, even the Lecturers from his department do not like him. Shinde's nature is altogether different. He is soft spoken an easy going. He never interferes in other work. Moreover he has less confidence in his action so he never takes any bold step. He made most of the decision by taking consent of others related to the decision. Mr. Khare's son, Sunil was a third year student in Electronics discipline in the Institute. He is neither Class Representative (C.R.) nor General Secretary (G.S.) still he leads a large group.

Event one January, 1994: In second week of January 1994 Mr. Shinde called meeting of staff members and students representatives to discuss about the annual social gathering programme to be celebrated in first week of February. Khare did not show any interest in discussion. Still being a senior faculty he was made head of 'reception committee'. Other senior staff members were also given different responsibilities. In the same meeting it was decided that this year for smooth running of programme, no student would be allowed inside auditorium without identity card for any programme. This decision was taken keeping in mind last years crowd of outside persons and students.

3rd February 1994 (at 9.45 A.M.): This was the first day of social gathering, an inauguration programme was to be started at 10.00 A.M. Chief Guest of programme was in Principal's cabin. He was General Manager of a large-scale industry in the city. At entrance of auditorium, Mr. Karnik, Lecturer in Chemistry was checking the identity cards of incoming students. A group of 6 students of 3rd year Electronics wanted to enter in hall without identity card. Mr. Karnik disallowed them to enter. They directly approached to Khare who was doing some work in his room and narrated the story. He knew all of them by face, hence gave a chit in name of Karnik to allow them in auditorium. Karnik still refused the entry. He asked them to get the permission from Principal Shinde. Students went back to Khare and narrated the incident. Khare came down with students at auditorium. His anger was beyond control. He scolded Mr. Karnik.

Khare: How do you dare to look upon my instructions? These students belong to my department. You young people learn to honor seniors.

Karnik: Sir, but Principal instructed me to send students without identity card to him for his written permission. Hence I asked them to go to Principal. I am not disobeying you, Sir.

Khare: So what? I am also head of department and equally important. You cannot disregard my note. You non-technical fools don't have a brain. You cannot use common sense. His instructions were to curtail the crowd not to prevent students of our institution from the function.

Karnik: Please mind your language Sir. I am not your subordinate. You cannot talk like this to gazetted officer. And whatever you want to say, say to Principal.

Khare: Principal, that silly Shinde. Who do not know even to write a single line correctly, who is good for nothing and you call him Principal?

Now, Khare lost his temper and was out of control. He asked the students to follow him and went to Principal's cabin without seeking permission (Chief Guest is still there along with some other staff members).

Khare: Listen. Mr. Shinde, your adherents are beyond your control. If you cannot control your guys why do you sit on this chair? Are you really capable of running this institute? (facing others). This fellow who cannot take any decision on his own, who cannot talk in English and write an errorless letter, can run institute like this only. Nobody follows your instruction here and nobody bothers to your orders. It is better for you to get transfer to a small place. Leaving students behind he went to his home. Shinde was shocked and surprised with this sudden attack giving no opportunity to retaliate. Even he was not aware about the incident and heads and tail of Khare's aggressive talk. He asked the students about Khare's behaviour. Students narrated the whole incident. He gave them permission for entry. But it created vary embarrassing situation for him (because all this melodrama took place in presence of Chief Guest). Shinde requested Chief Guest to move to auditorium for inaugural function.

At 10.15 A.M. inauguration function started. Chief Guest, Mr. Shinde, General Secretary and Gymkhana V.P. Mr. Rao were on stage. Meanwhile Mr. Khare's son Sunil came to know about the incident at the door of auditorium by his classmate. Someone told him that, Shinde scolded and insulted his father and he had gone to home. He mobilized students against Principal and chemistry lecturer. He gathered a large group of students from Electronics and other branches and persuaded them to come out of the function. All of a sudden in mid-course of function a big group of students under leadership of Sunil started going out of auditorium shouting slogans against Principal loudly. Many more students followed them in confusion, and others followed them to see. Something strange outside.

Programme got disturbed for few minutes. Lecturers available in hall tried to control students requesting them not to leave the hall. But in this stage of utter confusion about 90 per cent of the students went out. Only 40 to 50 students who were mostly girl students were present in the hall. Mr. Shinde came out himself to convince students. He requested them to come in hall, but students shouted slogans against him and started mocking and abusing him. Shinde called Class Representatives and General Secretary to convince students but even they could not persuade them. Sunil and his group demanded that Mr. Karnik and Mr. Shinde should apologize to Mr. Khare, for insulting him in public. Karnik and Shinde refused to do so, and then the programme was conducted in a almost empty hall hurriedly. This created very embarrassing situation for all present in hall and brought disgrace and ignominy to institute. Programme turned out in very poor show in the presence of Guests.

At 11.30 AM: Immediately after programme Mr. Shinde called a meeting of all teachers. He discussed the matter of Mr. Khare, his son's nuisance at programme and the strategy regarding checking Identify cards. All faculty members condemned the behaviour of Mr. Khare and his son unanimously. All faculty members promised Mr. Shinde to stand on his side for any action he takes against Mr. Khare and his son. After this meeting Mr. Shinde called student representatives to discuss the issue with them and to chalk out strategies to avoid such critical situation in next programmes. General Secretary and Class Representatives promised Mr. Shinde that they would keep close watch on Sunil's activities during other programmes, and maintain the discipline. Sunil and his group decided to boycott the other programmes. Few of the Sunil's close friends were involved in some activities (like drama, etc). They announced not to participate in any programme. Due to such eleventh hour announcement, some programmes were cancelled. It disturbed the whole gathering.

Mr. Shinde issued a memo to Khare blaming him for misbehaving, misguiding and provocating students for undesirable activities. Moreover he reported to Director Technical Education to take disciplinary action against Khare. He narrated all events to Director Technical Education on telephone. Consequently Director Technical Education also issued explanation letter to Mr. Khare. Soon after this event Mr. Shinde took control from Khare of other two departments. Senior most lecturers were made incharge, Head of Department. Though, Shinde had issued orders to handover charges to senior lecturers, but Khare did not do so. All the happenings in the institution was the burning topic of discussion.

28th February, 1994: Shinde wanted to go on leave for three weeks in March. He decided to give charge of institute to a Senior Lecturer from Civil Engineering department. Accordingly, order was under typing in office. This was reported to Mr. Khare by one of the office staff. So Mr. Khare met with Principal.

Khare: Mr. Shinde, this institute is not your own estate. You cannot run it on your whims. You must follow the rules.

Shinde: But, what went wrong.

Khare: Don't become innocent. You are going on leave from tomorrow and you are handing over charge of Principal to Mr. Shironi who is simply Lecturer. You cannot do that. After all I am HOD.

Shinde: It is my decision. And I am going only for 20 days so I have power to decide to whom I should give charge.

Khare: If you will do this then I shall move to court. I will not sit silent; after all you are snatching my rights.

Shinde called office superintendent and seek his advice on this matter. He advised that, Khare should be given charge. If you don't want to give him charge, permission from Director Technical Education is required. Shinde rang Directorate of Technical Education, from there; he came to know that Director is out of Head Quarter for two days. Under such circumstances Mr. Shinde handed over charge to Mr. Khare on next evening. Very next day Mr. Khare visited Chemistry department at 10.30 A.M. sharp, he found Mr. Karnik and other staff members have not come in the department. Immediately he drafted a show cause letter for Mr. Karnik. When at 11.15 A.M. Mr. Karnik entered in his department he found a memo on his table demanding explanation and half day casual leave. Mr. Karnik was sharp enough to understand the hidden message. He applied for half-day casual leave.

In those twenty days of Principalship Mr. Khare used to take rounds of institute in a day. He issued warning letters and show cause letters to 25 persons including Class IV staff. People immediately changed their habits and started coming in time. Some of them did so because of fear and others to avoid unnecessary trouble. Mr. Khare also cancelled the order issued by Shinde in which Head of departments charge was given to two lecturers (Telecommunication and Industrial Electronics Department) and took its control in his hands. People in institute were surprised to observe the changes in the behaviour of Mr. Khare. Two years back in November 1992 he was made incharge Principal by Mr. Bhide when he was on leave for one month. That time Khare was not so malignant and malicious.

21st March, 1994: Mr. Shinde resumed his duties on 21st March. He found lot of work is piled up on his table. On same day he got a letter, signed by all office staff, complaining about Mr. Khare. There was no letter from teaching faculty but most of them complained orally about Khare's autocratic behaviour. Mr. Shinde called Mr. Khare in his cabin.

Shinde: Mr. Khare, I received this letter from office staff, complaining about your rough and rude behaviour and insulting treatment (gave his letter to read out).

Khare: I want to keep discipline in office and institute. These people are habituated to come late and run away before 5.00 P.M. I fired only those who were found missing from their duties during office hours. In my period institute was like a best institution. You should have seen it. You can learn from me how to control people and maintain discipline. If they had any problem from me they should have talked to me. I think you might have provocated them to write against me. So that you can find some excuses to write against me. But mind well, Mr. Shinde, I will not keep mum. I will inform Director that you are most inefficient and ineffective principal who cannot even control the peon on his door.

Shinde: Don't tell me anything about my efficiency. These files and hundreds of letter still waiting for reply is the proof of your efficiency.

Khare: I signed all the letters put on my table only letters related to policy matter were kept aside for your decision. Moreover I have to look after work of three departments. Principal is not supposed to do clerical work sitting in his office. I preferred taking rounds of institute rather than inserting my head into the files.

Shinde is neither bold nor a dashing. He could not make his mind about any action on the letter of staff against Khare. He thought better to keep it pending. Moreover he found himself helpless to take any action against Mr. Khare. Mr. Khare was always in search of an opportunity to create problems in institute and used to criticize Mr. Shinde. Due to Mr. Shinde's polite behaviour teachers and other staff members hardly cared for his orders and warnings (Shinde do not want to use coercive strategies because he thought his tenure is temporary and till regular Principal comes in). Because of this attitude of Shinde, commitment for work and discipline in general was invisible in the institute.

Meanwhile Director Technical Education received three anonymous letters complaining about indiscipline and disorder in Mahanagar Polytechnic because of Shinde's incapability. In May 1994, Mr. Sharma very Senior Principal, and two Head of departments (one for Mechanical Department and one for Applied Electronics) had joined this Institute.

Brief

1. Identify symptoms of unhealthy climate in Mahanagar Polytechnic during Shinde's Principalship.
2. Based on such identified symptoms, identify causes of unhealthy climate.
3. What strategies Mr. Sharma should adopt to make the climate healthy?
4. Design the strategy to promote healthy climate in your institution?

REFERENCES

Pondy, L.R. (1967). *Organizational Conflicts: Concepts and Models*, *Administrative Science Quarterly*, September 1967.

Rao, V.S.P., Venkaiah, V. and Srilatha, P. (1991). *Organizational Conflict*, Discovery Publishing House, New Delhi.

Satadeve, D.C., Gupta, B.L. and Shivagunde, R.B. (1995). *Case Studies on Conflicts in Polytechnics and Adopted Styles to Resolve Conflict*, Technical Teachers Training Institute, Bhopal.

Udai Pareek (1982). *Managing Conflict and Collaboration*, Oxford & IBH Publishing Co., New Delhi.

Udai Pareek (1993). *Making Organizational Roles Effective*, Tata McGraw Hills Publishing Company Limited, New Delhi.

13

Crisis Management

Objectives: The readers will be able to:

1. State the concept of crisis.
2. Explain the characteristics of the crisis.
3. Describe the sources of conflict.
4. Explain crisis management strategies.
5. Diagnose level of crisis.

1. Introduction

Crisis management is a topic that needs to be addressed in this book because the crisis has entered in technical education institutions as well. Many institutions are facing crisis situation and they are helpless. Crisis in educational institutions can be considered as threat to its survival, basic question on its business, stoppage of its core activities, relevance of quality of services, no finance to run the institution, no demand for passouts so thereby no employment, non-availability of professionally qualified faculty, even non-availability of professional governing body members and director for the institution, frequent strikes, frequent disruption of academic activities etc. The crisis is different from conflicts and problems in the sense that they are manageable and affect the quality of passouts to a very meagre extent and that too for a very short period of time. The quality of the passouts is not permanently and continuously affected by problems and conflict. Conflict and problems are not considered as threat to survival of the academic business of the institution but crisis is considered as threat to survival. Crisis is considered to be very dangerous for any organization it should be dealt seriously and cautiously.

2. Characteristics of Crisis

Crisis can be diagnosed on the basis of its distinct characteristics. An indicative list of characteristics of crisis is given in exhibit 13.1.

Exhibit No. 13.1: Characteristics of crisis

- It affects the whole institution and that may be the concern of all the institutions in the state or country. For example, any private company not employs the passouts of a particular technical institution would affect the employment of passouts of other institutions in the state. Similarly if a particular country does not employ the passouts of a particular discipline it would affect the employment of passouts of other disciplines.
- It affects the academics of the institution. Because of crisis the academic activities suffer to a larger extent and continuously. Thereby losing market reputation and face another crisis of less admissions and even no admissions. Thereby closer down of the institution.
- It requires huge resources and efforts to fight the crisis. Thereby affecting other activities of the institution. It means crisis creates another crisis or significant problem.
- It creates huge stresses before, during and after. People perceive stress because they foresee crisis so they lose confidence and thereby they have less energy to fight with conflict. During crisis they give up and wait for the damage. Even they deliberately welcome damage so that after damage they can decide other course of action. After crisis they cannot forget the suffering from crisis. It consciously remains in their memories, dreams and thinking.
- It negatively affects the institutional members, promoters, beneficiaries and clients for a longer duration. The relationship gets disrupted. People do not want to come together and discuss the issues. Everyone take his share and move away from the crisis situation. For example, recognition of one institution is cancelled by the statutory body thereby no admissions, no finance, no salary and operating expenses, corporate image diminished and closure of the institution. Promoters suffered because of huge wastage of resources. No employment to employees because they had been employees of the institution which has closed down. No placement of students because of closure of the institution. Everybody suffered from crisis.

3. Sources of Crisis

Educational institutions are considered to work in open environment. There are number of stakeholders affecting the academic and non-academic business of the institution. There are number of stakeholders who are significant and they can create crisis in the institution. The adverse effect of stakeholders over a period of time may get compiled and create a crisis situation. The employees of the institution do not feel the magnitude of it because they are involved in various dimensions. They do not feel the slow impact of it. Abrupt change in government policy or employers market may lead to sudden crisis. Crisis may be a result of wrong decisions of management or governing body. So conflict may be a result of cumulative adverse effect over a period of time or it may be sudden. Crisis may arise because of actions of external stakeholders or internal stakeholders. It may arise because of wrong decisions. The indicative list of sources of crisis and nature of conflict is listed in exhibit 13.2.

Exhibit No. 13.2: Sources of crisis and their nature

Stakeholder	*Type of crisis created*
Government	No permission for opening the institution leading to wastage of huge resources No permission for starting new educational programmes leading to growth and development of the institution. Also poor utilization of infrastructure and resources No funding leading to poor quality of academics Policy decision affecting functioning of the institution leading to crisis
Statutory body	No permission for starting new programmes No accreditation of the programme Change in rules affecting the business of the institution
University	Outdated curriculum leading to low employment of passouts from a particular university Lengthy procedures and delayed procedures lead to missed opportunity for employment of passouts
Employers	No employment or underemployment Pressure for specialization in particular area leading to investment requirements
Potential students	Consistently poor admissions affecting the image of the institution Admission of low grade students requires more faculty time leading to uneconomical functioning
Promoters	Withdrawal from the business leading to unemployment and social crisis No new investments leading to obsolescence No modernization of infrastructure No professional development of core faculty and staff

(*Contd.*)

(*Contd.*)

Stakeholder	*Type of crisis created*
Employees	Non-availability of professional faculty and staff Strikes Poor interest in academics of the institution Mass retirement or heavy and frequent turnover Wastage of resources and low utilization of resources
Students	Poor interest in study Passouts opt for other professional programmes Massive dropouts Retraining cost of passouts is very high They do not shift in other jobs or enterprises which has nothing to do with their education
Location	Location of the institution is not proper
Sister institutions	High level of competition, conflict and challenges from sister institutions
Foreign universities and private training centres	Taking major share of students in the name of employment guarantee, quality of education and flexible programmes

4. Crisis Management Strategies

Crisis management strategies can be grouped in two categories. First category is proactive management of the institution that is crisis prediction and prevention. Second category is reactive management that is managing the crisis on its occurrence.

Proactive Management

The institution vision, missions, goals and strategies are designed considering internal strengths and weaknesses. Weaknesses in the functioning of the institution are removed and implementation of strategies is carried out. The culture of the institution is aligned to achieve the goals, missions and vision. An effective and efficient control mechanism is used to monitor the progress of the plans. Checks are designed for critical activities of the institution and closely observed. Immediate corrective actions are taken in case of any indicator of crisis is noticed. The serious scanning of external and internal environment of the institution is carried out every year. On the basis of results of the scanning adjustments are regularly made in the business and functioning of the institution. The major changes in the environment are detected and their effect on the business of the institution is predicted. As described in chapter on problem solving and conflict management the problems and conflicts are detected at early stage and resolved. Effective decisions are taken considering all the conditions. Institution has a buffer of faculty, staff, money and alternative strategies to cope up with the crisis situation. Institution undertakes risk analysis exercises every year and before implementing major changes. Institution has strong, collaborative and cooperative networking with stakeholders. A professional consultant works for the institution to provide professional advice.

Reactive Management

The institution functions traditionally. Routine planning is carried out every year that is completely based on the previous year plan. In other words it is a copy of previous year plan without value addition. Same nature of problems occur every year and solved in same way. Problems are solved when they take complete shape. It is true with the conflict management as well. The decision-making process is very slow and procrastination is a common habit at all levels of decision-making. The monitoring and control system is very weak. It is carried out as ritual activity. Almost nothing is done to initiate any change even if it is desired till complete pressure built up. The major problems, conflicts and poor performance is not taken seriously. Feedback and improvement and assurance system is non-existent. It is claimed by the institution that they have solved many problems in the past and managed all types of crisis. It is also claimed that institution has capacity to solve any problem. No contingency plan is prepared and situations are dealt as they appear. Reactive mode is used dealing with stakeholders so almost no correspondence, cooperation and collaboration with government, employers and potential students. It is assumed that the institution has infinite life and no body can close it down. In general no owning of the institution and its purpose. People work for salary and to pursue their ability and interest. Ambition, enthusiasm, determination, dedication and resolution generally not observed in people and their activities. In such institutions the crisis take its toll thereby individuals and groups suffer.

5. Summary

Crisis is considered to be the threat to the survival of the institution or any institutional programme. Crisis in educational institutions may occur because of external stakeholders or internal stakeholders. It can occur in any form such as no admissions of students, no finance for the growth and development of the institution, strikes, lack of professionalism leading to poor quality of services, no employment or underemployment of passouts, severe problems and conflicts in the institution affecting the whole institution. There are two approaches to conflict management proactive approach and reactive approach. Preventive measures are taken to crisis management in proactive approach. Management concepts, theories, tools, techniques and models are extensively used to predict and prevent the crisis. Safety net is used in all major activities of the institution to have control on them. Problem solving and counselling mechanism is established in the institution to have control over problems and conflicts. Reactive approach of crisis management is used after the crisis has occurred it takes its toll. In such approaches crisis management approaches are used based on the situation of the conflict. Use of reactive approaches deteriorate and even worsen the situation in two ways. It consumes huge and important resources of the institution. It affects other activities that are going well because their resources are withdrawn for crisis management. So creating another problem or conflict or inefficiency.

6. Activity

The level of crisis in educational institutions can be tested using following rating scale. Ask randomly selected representatives of faculty members, staff members and students to fill up this rating scale. Compile, tabulate and interpret the data to ascertain the level of crisis.

Test Level of Crisis in Your Institution

Sl. No.	*The extent to which the institution faces following incidents*	*Your extent of agreement*			
		High	*Medium*	*Low*	*Nil*
	Output				
1.	No employment of passouts				
2.	Under employment of passouts				
3.	Passouts undertake other jobs than their education				
4.	Passouts establish enterprise not related to their education				

(*Contd.*)

(*Contd.*)

Sl. No.	*The extent to which the institution faces following incidents*	*Your extent of agreement*			
		High	*Medium*	*Low*	*Nil*
	Stakeholders				
5.	Employers don't conduct campus selection				
6.	Employers don't put any demand				
7.	Employers complain about poor quality of passouts				
8.	Employers complain about retraining of passouts				
9.	Employers don't want to give support in the form of scholarship, sponsorship, consultancy and joint venture				
10.	Sister institutions are creating high level of competition, challenges and standards of academics				
11.	Conflict of students with neighbourhood				
12.	No accreditation of programmes				
13.	No or negligible consultancy				
	Students				
14.	Students take no or poor interest in study				
15.	Students take tuitions				
16.	Students dropout rate is very high				
17.	Students go for strikes or frequent mass absenteeism				
18.	Students have numerous academic and non-academic problems				
	Faculty and staff				
19.	The ratio of student *versus* faculty members is more than 10				
20.	Students are indulged in party politics				
21.	Mass retirement of high profiled faculty				
22.	Faculty members don't use professional approach				
23.	Severe problems of faculty members are pending				
24.	Staff members don't use professional approach				
25.	Severe problems of staff members are pending				
26.	No opportunity for career advancement				
	Processes				
27.	Use of information technology is very poor				
28.	Procedures take too much time leading to frustration				
29.	*Ad hoc* and faulty decisions				
30.	Record management is manual and poor				

(*Contd.*)

(*Contd.*)

Sl. No.	*The extent to which the institution faces following incidents*	*Your extent of agreement*			
		High	*Medium*	*Low*	*Nil*
29.	Use of casual approaches				
30.	Frequent rumours				
31.	No concerns of management for problems, grievances, conflicts, complaints, suggestions and feedback				
	Resources and infrastructure				
32.	Inadequate lab, workshop, library, internet facility				
33.	Inadequate facilities for sports and cultural programmes				
34.	Inadequate facility for women and physically challenged people				
35.	Outdated curriculum				
36.	Outdated teaching learning resources				
37.	Budget deficit to run the regular activities				
	Potential students				
38.	Consistently poor admissions				
39.	Admission of low grade students				
40.	Struggle for filling the seats				
	Governance and management				
41.	Incompetent and undesirable people in the board				
42.	Lack of vision and strategic direction				
43.	Unprofessional approach				
44.	Politics on trivial issues				
45.	Prejudice approach				
46.	No interest in business of the institution				
47.	No new, creative and different pool of ideas and experience				
48.	Bureaucratic approaches				
49.	Poor participation in significant activities				
50.	*Ad hoc* approach				
51.	Poor monitoring, control and evaluation				
52.	Use of directive approaches				
53.	Poor leadership				
54.	Centralized decision-making and authority				

REFERENCE

Thierry C. Pauchant and Ian I. Mitroff (1992). *Transforming the Crisis Prone Organization*, Jossey-Bass Publishers, San Francisco.

14

Time Management

Objectives: The readers will be able to:

1. State the concept of time management.
2. Explain the benefits of time management.
3. Draw the distribution of time on various activities.
4. List the time wasters.
5. Describe the strategies of time management.

1. Introduction

Time is a precious resource. It cannot be saved, stored and transferred. The management of the institution is extremely complex process. In technical institution time management is very important from the students' point of view. The semester starts at a fixed time and ends with examination on predefined dates. In the available time the course has to be completed and examinations are to be conducted. Once the time gone it is gone forever. One cannot regain it. If the time is effectively utilized more skills can be imparted in students. If the time is not effectively and efficiently utilized it affects the time management of hundreds of students. The concept of time management should be practiced in the institution from the students' points of view. The institution can manage time for the fast growth and development. The faculty members can do many productive works for the growth and development of the students in the available time. In technical institution academic activities are dependent on activities of many people. People involved in these activities affect the time utilization of remaining ones. Therefore, time management should be seen from greater perspectives. The effective time management can convert the time as a resource for everyone working in the institution.

2. Benefits of Time Management

Number of benefits of time management are observed in technical institutions. Some of the significant benefits are listed below:

2.1 Benefits to Institution

The institutional activities can be performed effectively and efficiently. More contribution of the faculty and staff members can be ensured. The number of complaints can be reduced. The institution has more time for planning, creativity, innovation and positive change. It means better time management. It brings spiral effect to the process of time management. The better time management leads to less crisis and time related problems. Good practices of time management are based on scientific methods of working in which use of management tools and techniques are very common. That promotes facilitative institutional behaviour for time management.

2.2 Benefits to Faculty

Faculty members are the key functionaries in the institution. Their time is precious for the institution and students. There time can be easily converted in terms of money. It is much more than money in learning situation. They prepare future professional. They can save their own time and time of others using better time management practices. Better time management leads to less tension for them and students. Teachers can save time using appropriate methods of teaching learning. They can use saved time for further saving the time. They can work on other innovative activities related to their professional development and development of the students. They can use saved time for generating revenue for the institution and self. Faculty members can utilize the saved time for developing multi-skills and preparing themselves for the future. Better management of the time promotes self-satisfaction and self-fulfilment.

2.3 Benefits to Staff

Time management of staff members helps them to deal with students' pressure and other pressures coming to them. They cooperate with the students and faculty members. They get more time for their development. Institution cannot employ supporting staff for each activity. The staff members can be deployed for more number of activities and they can be remunerated appropriately. They get more satisfaction.

3. Distribution of Time on Various Key Activities

The time of different persons working in the institution is distributed on various activities. The time distribution profile of the institution can help to improve time management practices in the institution. The time profile can be plotted on parameters listed in exhibit 14.1.

Exhibit No. 14.1: Parameters-time distribution profile of the institution

Sl. No.	*Parameter*	*Percentage of time spent*
1.	Academic	
2.	Development of teaching-learning resources	
3.	Research	
4.	Extension	
5.	Consultancy	
6.	Continuing education programmes for others	
7.	Managerial	
8.	Administrative	
9.	Financial	
10.	Self-development	

4. Time Wasters

The present time distribution for each activity can be charted and the time wasters for each activity can be identified. It is very difficult to recognize the time waster because people are used to them. Recognizing the fact that there is wastage of time in a particular activity. Strategies can be designed to eliminate or minimize the wastage of time. There are numerous time wasters and they occur in variety of forms. These time wasters not only consume more time but they adversely affect the quality of product and services, efficiency and effectiveness and culture of the institution. Some indicative parameters are listed in exhibit 14.2.

Exhibit No. 14.2: Time wasters

- Working on trivial activities because of lack of prioritization
- Lack of use of scientific methods in curriculum design leading to unorganized curriculum in logic, flow, content and prerequisite
- Lack of lesson planning by the teachers leading to causal approach of teaching learning
- Lack of resources planning for conducting teaching learning process leading to devoting more time in arranging resources than teaching learning process
- Lack of preparation for conducting teaching learning process leading to use of ineffective methods of teaching learning
- Lack of planning in organizing learning events leading to confusion in learning
- Poor communication leading to disinterest in learning process and consuming more time to clarify the issues
- Lack of transferring responsibility for learning to students leading to eleventh hour preparation by students
- Lack of involvement of students in learning process leading to poor commitment of students
- Use of scientific methods in teaching process missing leading to consumption of more time for easy topics and no time left for difficult topics
- Causal approach in dealing with learning problems of the students leading to frustration
- Poor problem solving and decision-making mechanism leading to resentment against management
- Roles and responsibility of teachers, staff members and students are not defined properly leading to inefficiency and wastage of resources
- No advance information for different activities leading to confusion, uncertainty and conflict
- Attempting too many activities at a time resulting in no concrete achievements
- Impatience leading to indecisiveness and causal approach of approaching the situation
- Taking tuitions or involved in outside activities leading to poor quality of services in the institution
- Personal disorganization leading to haphazard way of working
- Poor reading habits leading to confusion and frustration at the time of recall of information
- Fear of failure leading to lack of initiative and confidence
- Buck passing leading to game playing and unnecessary conflict
- Frequent turnover of the faculty and staff hampering the implementation of plan

(*Contd.*)

(*Contd.*)

- Lethargy
- Negative attitude
- Poor control over processes leading to poor quality of products and services
- More freedom to students without responsibility for learning leading to indiscipline and politics
- Lack of teamwork or ineffective team work leading to costly processes
- Inability to use potential of faculty, staff and students leading to inefficiency and frustration
- Lack of use of teaching-learning aids in teaching learning process leading to disinterest in the subject
- Poor support for academic activities consuming more time for organizing resources
- Poorly organized learning in laboratories, workshops and industries leading to disinterest of students in learning process
- Absence of good quality learning material for students leading to dependence on teachers
- Too many grievances of faculty members, staff members and students leading to withdrawal from innovative activities
- Grouping, classification and clubbing things are missing leading to delay in decision-making and reporting
- Lack of positive thinking leading to *status quo* in performance and decline in performance
- Lack of creativity leading to no change in business of the institution
- Lack of value addition practices leading to inefficient way of performing
- Poor self-evaluation practice leading to no improvement in performance
- Contour productive work habits leading to unhealthy environment to work
- Initiation inertia leading to no change and development
- Willingly accepting every task leading to overloading
- Inadequate financial power leading to delay in decision-making and providing resources
- Lengthy procedures consuming time and creating frustration for clients and customers
- Inadequate infrastructure leading to poor performance
- Non-availability of funds leading to expansion of the business of the institution
- Delay in decision-making by competent authority
- Below status work leading to disinterest and frustration
- Biased approaches leading to politics and cliques
- Interruption during the class leading to disinterest in teaching learning process
- Eleventh moment postponement of activities leading to confusion and wastage of efforts

(*Contd.*)

(*Contd.*)

- Unplanned vacation by faculty and staff creating problems and crisis for others
- Inappropriate methods of assessment of learning of the students and absence of constructive feedback leading to anxiety
- Students don't know the holistic picture of the subject leading to disinterest in the subject
- Causal way of producing learning without correlating and explaining interrelated concept
- Absence of meaningful learning leading to half hearted learning by students
- Too many meetings leading to no time for core business
- Strikes of faculty members, staff members and students deteriorating the quality of teaching process
- Fire fighting approach by management of the institution leading to wastage of time, money and efforts
- Students do not possess minimum knowledge required to understand the subject leading to confusion
- Lack of exposure of the tutor to the real world leading to poor transfer of learning
- Lack of commitment of higher authorities for quality of education leading to poor commitment of staff
- Lack of rewards for good time management leading to no improvement
- More emphasis on political activities rather than academic activities leading to poor performance
- Lack of challenge in work leading to shirking and turn over of good staff
- Excessive paper work leading to lengthy procedure and dissatisfaction of customer and client
- Lack of training opportunity leading to use of inefficient methods
- Lack of risk taking leading to no gain
- Poor work culture leading to sustenance of performance without any improvement
- Weak leadership leading to decline in performance of the institution
- Desire for perfection leading to wastage of time and money
- Poor salary leading to dissatisfaction and turnover
- Assuming that students can not learn without teaching leading to more efforts by teacher
- Lack of flexibility in implementing the timetable leading to inconvenience and frustration
- Prejudice approaches leading to inefficiencies and conflict
- Frequent conflict on trivial issues leading to involvement in forming pressure against management and gaining power
- Unscheduled meetings leading to hampering important and significant work of the institution
- Inability to concentrate on the task leading to poor performance

(*Contd.*)

(*Contd.*)

- ➢ Long tea breaks leading to hasty work affecting the quality of services
- ➢ Health problem leading to slow and poor performance
- ➢ No or poor information management system leading to delay and ineffective decisions
- ➢ Poor memory leading to more efforts to do the same thing again
- ➢ Poor accessibility to information leading to delay and poor performance
- ➢ Postponement of difficult and complex tasks leading to management by crisis approach
- ➢ Uninformed enjoyment of leave leading to delay of work and poor performance
- ➢ Committee culture leading to unnecessary discussion on trivial issues
- ➢ No performance appraisal leading to poor performance and dissatisfaction
- ➢ Involvement in activities not related to job leading to poor performance
- ➢ Low level assignments leading to frustration
- ➢ Backlog leading to delay in performance and mistakes
- ➢ No time for planning leading to reactive management approach
- ➢ Poor monitoring and control leading to poor quality and inefficiency
- ➢ Sources of information are not known leading to poor decision
- ➢ Poor record keeping leading to delay in decision making and frustration
- ➢ Unnecessarily spreading the work leading to inefficiency
- ➢ Drop in visitors leading to less time for core business
- ➢ Telephone interruptions leading to inefficiency
- ➢ Working long hours affecting the health and quality of performance in long-run
- ➢ Unplanned students activities leading to poor learning
- ➢ Delay in admission leading to crisis management
- ➢ Delay in declaration of result leading to disinterest in further learning
- ➢ Inefficient transport facilities affecting learning process
- ➢ Failure to influence students for learning leading to poor result
- ➢ Poor follow up actions leading to poor performance
- ➢ Lack of transparency in functioning leading to mistrust
- ➢ Slow learners requiring more efforts
- ➢ Frequent changes in schedule leading to confusion
- ➢ Irrelevant un-planned activities creating confusion

5. Strategies for Time Management

Time management brings great benefits to every one in the institution. At the same time it requires initial investment of time to change time management habits. Time management can be practiced at institution level, department level and individual level. There are numerous strategies that can be used at each level. The indicative strategies are listed in exhibit 14.3 and each strategy is briefly described.

Exhibit No. 14.3: Strategies for time management

➢ Planning and re-planning ➢ Delegation ➢ Resources management ➢ Continuous training ➢ Problem solving ➢ Creativity and innovation ➢ Concentration on significant activities ➢ Self-discipline	➢ Tap strengths and grab opportunities ➢ Computerization of records ➢ Use project approach for new and challenging activities ➢ Documentation of experiences ➢ Deployment and re-deployment of human resources ➢ Analysis of use of time

5.1 Planning and Re-planning

Institution should prepare strategic, perspective and annual plan for development. These plans should be prepared in participative way and clearly communicated to all the institutional members. The vision, mission, goals and objectives of development should be made clear to everyone. There should be fairly good challenge in the goals and objectives. All the institutional departments, sections and individuals should be encouraged to prepare annual plans stating goals and objectives to be achieved by them. All the routine works in the institution should be standardized and computerized to promote effective performance. Resources should be allocated for the standard procedures. Institutional processes should be charted, documented and made available in the library. People concerned with the processes should be trained to carry out the process. Redundant and unnecessary activities should be dropped to save the time. All the activities of the institution should support the core business of the institution that is academics. Proper planning in the institution encourages the people to take initiative to put their efforts to complete the task effectively and efficiently. People can fix their role in the whole business of the institution. The role of the individuals and teams should be clear to them. The role should be appropriately distributed among members looking to there interest, experience and competence. People should appreciate that they are utilizing time for the development of the institution. They can measure their progress against planned activities. They can appreciate that non-achievement of the objectives is because of their non-performance.

Similarly achievement of the objective is self-rewarding. People learn from their success and failures because they can measure their progress against plans. The proactive culture should be promoted in the institution. People should be encouraged to anticipate the situation and prepare themselves for the situation. The institutional members should also be encouraged to prepare objectives to cut down and save time for a particular task. The time saving objectives should be regularly reviewed, revised, modified and augmented. Objectives focusing on time saving enable to design appropriate strategies. For example, a teacher is not getting sufficient time to cover curriculum of a subject assigned to her/him in spite of planning for the semester. S/he can formulate the objective to cover curriculum in 80 per cent of allocated time. S/he would certainly look for better, innovative and creative methods to complete the curriculum. S/he would come out from traditional behaviour and use something different. It would cause new learning to her/him. S/he would develop confidence and practice the behaviour of exploration. For example teachers can prepare plans listed in exhibit 14.4.

Exhibit No. 14.4: Time based plans to be prepared by a teacher

➢ Curriculum planning for all subjects ➢ Subject plans ➢ Lesson plans ➢ Plan for industrial training of students ➢ Instructional material development plan	➢ Research plan ➢ Continuing education plan ➢ Consultancy plan ➢ Research scholar guide plan ➢ Vacation plan ➢ Self-training plan

The description of process of preparing plans is explained in chapter on planning.

5.2 Delegation

Delegation is an art. Faculty members can delegate the responsibility of learning to students. Only thing they need to do is proper analysis of the curriculum. They should become student of the subject and try to learn the subject on their own. They might note the difficulties they face in the process of learning. They can remove the difficulties of learning providing appropriate remedial strategies. They can select one or two books for their subject fairly covering the curriculum and prescribe to students to go through it in a planned manner on a time frame. At the beginning of each chapter the teacher can introduce the topic, its learning objectives and main points of learning. S/he can provide support material for learning. S/he explains students what to learn, how to learn, when to learn, where to learn and how s/he would test the learning outcome. S/he should delegate easy, familiar concepts, concrete concepts, known concepts and things based on facts. On completion of the topic s/he can review learning to reinforce learning and provide constructive feedback to the students. S/he can design and give assignments to apply learning in a given situation. Then s/he can move to next topic and repeat the same method or design a new strategy to produce learning.

S/he can form two teams and ask the teams to study a particular chapter from books and frame questions and their answers. On a fixed day a competition between two teams can be organized to ensure learning. It would give sense of satisfaction to the students and develop skills to face competition. S/he can summarize the learning occurred through competition and fill up learning gaps if any. Next chapter can be input based because it is a chapter dealing with complex concepts. It all depends on the creativity of the teachers, entry behaviour level of students, complexity of the subjects, resources availability etc. Delegation of responsibility for learning in a guided way helps to manage the time of the teachers, learning of students, management of time of students and restricting them to participate in unwanted activities. The teacher can enrich learning process of students delegating the responsibility of learning to students. Using delegating style of learning teacher can gradually promote maturity for learning in students. S/he can make them responsible professional. S/he can naturally develop life skills and learning to learn skills in students.

Delegation requires immense preparation on the part of the teacher. It requires detailed planning, preparation of support material, effective communication with students, timely and right kind of inputs, continuous assessment of learning, creativity and innovativeness, constructive feedback to students, use of variety of methods and media for learning. The teacher is required to play the role of facilitator, guide, mentor, supporter, helper, coach, resources provider, planner, leader, encourager, problem solver, arbitrator, behaviour shaper, instruction designer etc. Delegation strategy develops teachers' professional skills. S/he gets more time for further experimentation and cutting down the time to produce desired learning.

Cocurricular activities and student-centred activities should be delegated to the students and lowest level in the hierarchy. Rest of the activities such as cleaning, security, gardening, maintenance, students' facilities, and hostel mess should be outsourced. One-time events should also be contracted to outside professional companies. The institution should utilize its full energy for the core business.

5.3 Resources Management

The resources required for carrying out learning activities are well known to the teachers and instructors. Some resources are fixed type that is over head projector, power point presentation facilities, magnetic board, chalk board, white board, flip chart, paste it slips, display board, magnetic board etc. in the classroom and discussion rooms. The institution should take initiative and furnish the classrooms and discussion rooms. Similarly resources in laboratories like charts, models, demonstration equipment, norms to work, safety precaution, etc. should be fixed. The laboratory manuals and routine type of experiments can be well set and delegated to laboratory instructor or research scholar. Similarly, resources to various process and activities can be allocated and an open environment should be created to share the resources. In some situation well organized resources save more time.

5.4 Continuous Training of Faculty and Staff Members

The faculty and staff members should be continuously trained to up grade and refine their competencies. Everyone in the institution should get an opportunity to undergo training. Every year the training calendar should be prepared to organize need based training. The institution should make a plan to organize more number of training programmes in the institution. The duration of these training programmes should be short may be half day. All institutional members should get an opportunity to participate in in-house training programmes at some point of time or other. In in-house training programmes general topics like leadership, working in teams, planning, creativity, time management, positive thinking, quality improvement, problem solving, etc. can be included. In-house training programmes should also incorporate specific training programmes for a particular group of persons, for example training programmes for teachers may focus on effective curriculum implementation, discovery learning, use of media and variety of instructional methods, development of print and non-print learning resources, research methodology, use of computer, principles of learning, creating challenges in learning, negotiation, networking with industries and sister institution, knowledge management, learning organization, measurement and evaluation of learning, managing educational projects, extension services etc. can be organized. Again the duration of these programmes can be one to three days. All in-house training programmes should be organized at right time and if possible during lean period of the institution. The enhanced competence of the institutional members makes them naturally work effectively and efficiently thereby saving time.

5.5 Problem Solving Groups

Campus life does not move as planned. There could be variety of problems that may crop up in day-to-day functioning. These problems can be solved using problemsolving groups. Well-defined problem solving mechanism should be established. This system should be informal and people should be encouraged to solve problems at their level. They should be motivated to solve the problem forever. The activities of problem solving groups can be expanded to promote creativity, innovation, variety, expansion of activities, and self-discipline in the institution. The group problem solving approaches promote better time management in the institution. If groups fail to solve the problem then it should be formally taken for solution.

5.6 Creativity and Innovation

Technical institutions are the laboratories for developing creative, innovative, research and thinking habits in engineering students. These habits can only be developed in creative, innovative, research and thinking atmosphere. The technical institutions can promote conducive learning atmosphere by encouraging learning through discovery, experimentation, research, mistakes, thinking, creativity, challenges, de-learning, exploration, games, simulations, actions etc. The teachers and instructors in the institution should be competent to practice above methods of learning in the institution. Use of creative and innovative methods of learning saves time and produce long lasting skills in the students for learning. They can go far beyond their capacity in professional life. There should be good rewards for using creative and innovative methods and practices in the institution.

5.7 Concentrate on Significant Activities

Institutions do not do prioritization of goals and objectives that is why they waste the time of faculty members, staff members and students in spending time on trivial activities resulting negligible impact on learning. Priorities should be fixed at institutional level, department level and individual level. The functionaries should concentrate on activities they are performing. They should not attempt too many things at a time. Rather they can do multiple and variety of tasks serially. For example a teacher can organize input sessions, seminars, presentations of the students, discussions in the forenoon. In the afternoon s/he can guide research scholars, do consultancy work, develop learning resources, organize meetings of the staff members, do research work, do documentation work, writing reports, do planning, meet with clients. The tutorials to solve students' problems can be organized in the evening. The continuing education programmes, training programmes, community development programmes, social activities, visits to industry and clients organization can be organized on Saturdays and Sundays. People should be encouraged to plan the activities on time line in a way to concentrate on the task. The shifting and shuttling from one activity to another should be avoided to concentrate on a particular activity.

5.8 Impose Self-discipline

Self-discipline is the best discipline. It promotes time management practice in the habits of the people. One can be self-conscious to her/his time management habits. Self-governance of behaviour develops confidence to manage the activities according to availability of time. Self-listening for improvement on time management encourages further to do analysis on utilization of time to receive internal feedback for improvement. The efforts to develop self-lead to enormous success in time management. Self-learning ways of time management can never be forgettable. One can easily transfer self-learnt concepts to new situation for time management. One can create a sensor in the mind to monitor the utilization of time. One can develop self-confidence for practicing time management practices taking independent personal decisions on time management.

5.9 Tap Strengths and Grab Opportunities

One can do strengths, weaknesses, opportunities and threats (SWOT) analysis and enumerate the strengths and weaknesses. The strengths can be used to grab the opportunities for time management. The combination of strengths and opportunities can be used to minimize the threats and remove weaknesses. For example, a teacher is not good in oral communication and s/he has to complete the curriculum. S/he is excellent in planning and trained in using variety of training methods. S/he can select those methods of teaching in which minimum input is required.

S/he teaches post-graduate students who are responsible and mature. S/he can easily implement learner-centred methods. S/he can provide an opportunity to bright and experienced students to lead the process of learning. S/he can cover her/his weaknesses using her/his strengths on time management.

5.10 Computerization of All Support Processes

The learning utilization centre, library, students' services, accounts section, stores and purchase, maintenance, sales centre of the institution should be computerized. All routine decisions and activities should be supported by computer database. The institute should prepare the profile of faculty members, staff members, guest faculty, consultants and other significant stakeholders and update it for various academic and non-academic purposes. Similarly, the profile of the students should be maintained to take academic and non-academic decisions. The self-learning computer packages, power point presentations, workbooks and tests should be developed for the students. These packages should be available on-line for particular time.

5.11 Use Project Management Approach for Challenging and New Goals

Project management approach is excellent to save time on new and challenging activities. The detailed schedule of all activities is prepared using scientific tools and techniques. The probability of wastage of time is reduced to a greater extent preparing time scheduled. The monitoring and evaluation of the progress of performance and achievements are tracked on time line. One-time activities should be performed using project approach.

5.12 Flexible Approaches

The planning of time is in the hands of the performer. But during implementation of activities there are many factors that operate and affect the planned activities. These factors are beyond the control of performers. In such situation alternative approaches can be used to best manage the time. For example, students' strikes are not under the control of teachers. In case of strike they should have some productive work to do. The control on electric power is not under the control of teachers. In case of power failure they should be ready to use alternative method of teaching learning. In case of uncertainty people should be ready to use the time effectively and efficiently for some other important activities.

5.13 Documentation of the Events

During the implementation of various teaching learning processes teachers learn many new things. They should systematically document the new learning and experience with a brief description of the situation. Teachers refer variety of reference material for producing learning in the students. They do it for all topics. They should maintain reference record for all topics. First time it takes time but later on the references can be obtained in fraction of seconds. They should prepare a file of the subject they are dealing with and arrange learning resources in the file. The file can be arranged topic-wise or handout, assignment, power point, case study, game, simulation, role play, visit, and laboratory work-wise. It all depends on the subject and style of documenting the things. Many teachers maintain the subject-wise and topic-wise computer folders and update everyday the important happenings and list of learning resources used. Similar records can be maintained for research scholars and other activities. Maintenance of the documents is very useful in saving the time for next cycle. It is very useful to develop the juniors to take up the subjects.

5.14 Deployment and Re-deployment of the Human Resource

The institution should have deployment and re-deployment plan of the human resources. Because of fast changes in the business of the institution and variety of the business deployment and re-deployment of human resources would be essential for time management of the institution as a whole. People can be deployed and re-deployed through continuous training. People should be encouraged by the institution to assume similar jobs in the institution developing specific job related skills.

5.15 Analysis of Use of Time

At the end of the day one should analyse the use of time. Everyday stock taking on time use can help to learn skills of time management. It is a kind of self-feedback on the basis of introspection. Self-feedback is always strong motivator for learning about time management. One can chart good time management and poor time management for a day in the mind or on the paper. S/he can reflect upon the time management strengths and weaknesses. Next day time planning can be carried out on the basis of previous day analysis. Devoting five minutes on time planning and five minutes on analysing the utilization of time can bring big change in time management habits.

6. Time Management Skills

It is said that good management encompasses time management as well. There are number of skills that can be useful in time management. An indicative list of time management skills is mentioned in exhibit 14.5. Time management attitudes are listed in exhibit 14.6.

Exhibit No. 14.5: Time management skills

➢ Planning ➢ Scheduling ➢ Decision-making ➢ Problem solving ➢ Prioritizing ➢ Organizing ➢ Influencing	➢ Thinking ➢ Delegation ➢ Controlling ➢ Communicating ➢ Concluding ➢ Analysing ➢ Experimenting

Exhibit No. 14.6: Time management attitudes

➢ Punctuality ➢ Sincerity ➢ Commitment ➢ Appreciation	➢ Winning attitude ➢ Cooperation ➢ Initiation ➢ Introspection

7. Summary

Time is a precious resource. It needs to be managed effectively and efficiently for doing the core business of the institution. Better time management takes the institution, teams and individuals to all heights. The time can be managed charting the use of time and allocating more time for core activities of the institutions. One can prepare a list of time wasters and try to minimize the time on time wasters. Good management is considered to be good time management. Time management techniques such as planning, prioritization, creativity, delegation, effective decision-making, use of tools and techniques, training, deployment and re-deployment of resources, use of project approach, design and re-design of processes, and self-introspection are commonly used in technical institutions. The time management skills and attitudes should be practiced for better management of the business of the institution.

8. Activity

You have gone through the chapter on time management. You have appreciated the concept of time management. You are aware about time wasters. Prepare a list of key activities in which you are presently involved. Identify time wasters in each key activity and amount of time wasted in a day. Set the time saving goals for each key activity and formulate strategies to achieve the time saving goals. An indicative list of major activities is given in the table for teachers. You may not be involved in many activities or given activities may not be key activities for you. You can prepare a separate list of key activities for you. You can complete the assignment in the format given in table.

Table indicating key activities, time wasters, time saving objectives and strategies to be used

Sl. No.	*Key activities*	*Time waster*	*Time saving objectives*	*Strategies to achieve time saving objectives*
1.	Lesson plan preparation			
2.	Class room teaching learning			
3.	Laboratory			
4.	Workshop			
5.	Field visit			
6.	Industrial visit			
7.	Assignment			
8.	Learning problem solving of the students			
9.	Project work			
10.	Research work			
11.	Tests			
12.	Assignment checking and feedback giving			
13.	Learning resources preparation			
14.	Study of the subject			
15.	Searching learning material			

(*Contd.*)

(*Contd.*)

Sl. No.	*Key activities*	*Time waster*	*Time saving objectives*	*Strategies to achieve time saving objectives*
16.	Student record keeping			
17.	Administrative work			
18.	Meetings			
19.	Continuing education			
20.	Consultancy			
21.	Community services			
22.	Other activities			

REFERENCE

David Fontana (1993). *Managing stress*, Excel Books, New Delhi.

15

Stress Management

> ***Objectives:*** The readers will be able to:
>
> 1. List the need and importance of stress management in educational institutions.
> 2. Describe the concept of stress.
> 3. Classify the stress.
> 4. Explain the factors affecting personal stress.
> 5. List sources of stress.
> 6. Describe causes of stress.
> 7. Explain stages of stress.
> 8. Describe effects of stress.
> 9. List guidelines for preventing and managing stress.

1. Introduction

The technical institutions are undergoing tremendous and unprecedented change to cope up the environmental pressures on it. The faculty, staff and students are experiencing increased demand for professional approach in teaching learning process. Teachers have to do variety of work on a wide spectrum of a role, which is dynamic and changing. At the same time they have to update themselves to impart latest knowledge and skills to the students. Similarly the staff members have to perform variety of tasks using computers and information technology because they are working in a dynamic institution striving for excellence. The job in the technical institution is not permanent now it is contractual and its continuity depends on competitive performance. The salary and perks are proportional to the contribution made for the growth and development of the institution. The institution is required to do aggressive marketing for its services and products. In the process of marketing director, faculty members and staff members are intensively involved. Such phenomenon was never observed in technical institutions. There are many other reasons leading to stress in the institution that would be examined in this chapter. The management of the stress in the institution is necessary to ensure healthy climate, physical health and psychological health of the people.

2. Concept of Stress

Stress is defined as a situation in which an individual feels pressed physically or psychologically both because of shortages of time or resources or personal incapacity and incapability. The individual considers the situation challenging and important because it has something for her/him. S/he cannot ignore the situation on account of opportunity inherent in it. It creates sort of pressure to put efforts and fulfil the demand of the situation. Individuals act as per demand of the situation and satisfy their needs. The situation compels individuals to be active, adoptive, creative and energetic. The pressure increases in uncertain and unpredictable situations. The situation creates worry when individuals also perceive risk.

The amount of stress depends on the personality of a person and her/his perception about the situation and demand. A situation may be stressful for a person may be quite normal for another person. One may enjoy the situation and other may be worried. For example, organizing educational tours of students many teachers feel tensed during the tour on various issues such as discipline of the students, train reservations, accommodation, permission to visit industry, health of the students, expenditure etc. On the other hand some teachers enjoy the company of the students and they are always interested to go on educational tours. Think about the behaviour of such teachers if they are deprived from.

3. Types of Stress

Management experts classify stress in many ways. It is classified as eustress and distress. Eustress means positive exhilarating and challenging experiences of success followed by higher expectations. It is positive stimulus which energies, encourages and motivates individuals to accept the challenge and put hard efforts to meet the requirements of challenges.

It is also considered life-saver stress because it engages individuals in enjoyable activities. Individuals become creative, active and ambitious to do something, which they value. For example, a professor has designed and conducted entrepreneurship development programmes for students, passouts of different institutions and unemployed youths. S/he developed some case studies, power points and exercises for developing entrepreneurship abilities in students. When s/he was asked by the Director of the institution to develop a multimedia learning package for engineering students, teachers and unemployed youth, s/he got excited in fact s/he was searching for such opportunity. S/he immediately accepted the assignment and prepared a detailed proposal for developing a multimedia package.

On the other hand distress is disappointment, failure, threat, embarrassment and other negative experiences. Individuals feel tensed, exhausted and depressed under such stimulus. They become indecisive and take ineffective and wrong decisions. They become restless and behave differently. For example, young Director of the institute has asked a professor who had never conducted research study in her/his 30 years of service to conduct research study on recent technology, s/he submitted resignation. Distress is also considered as life destroyer.

4. Factors Affecting Personal Stress

The personality of the person plays a major role in experiencing stress as lifesaver or life destroyer. There are numbers of factors that decide whether the stress is harmful or beneficial for an individual. The behaviour of a person can be classified as Type A and Type B.

Type A personalities: These types of people create challenges for them. They want to work and work. They do not want to relax doing different activities than their professional activities. They are impatient about the results. They want to use every minute as money. They make everything urgent. They undertake many activities simultaneously. They are irritated when people say no to their order even on genuine grounds. They are ambitious and hopeful person. They want to do every thing very fast. They are quality conscious and enter in competition. They accept good challenges willingly. In fact they are work addicts. People having A type personality can absorb any amount of stress in challenging, competitive, uncertain, risky and ambitious situation. These types of people should be identified in the institution and they should be assigned goals and activities that are new, challenging, complex and difficult.

Type B personalities: These types of people are easy going. They are satisfied with whatever they have. They do not emotionally involve in activities. They set moderate goals and achieve them. They enjoy vacation and their personal time. They are very systematic in performing the task. They are realistic people. They take necessary breaks during performing complex activities. They do not publicize their achievements. They participate in activities which give them enjoyment and satisfaction. They have patience even in uncertain and unfamiliar situations. They trust in the competence of the people and team members. They do not undertake numerous activities simultaneously. They create humour at work place and keep the work environment cool. They provide recognition to the efforts made by fellow members.

5. Causes of Stress

There are numerous causes of stress in educational institutions. The stress is not the outcome of single cause but it is a combined effect of many causes. It is also not a result of one time effect. The sources of these causes are listed in exhibit 15.1.

Exhibit No. 15.1: Sources of causes of stress in educational institutions

➢ Struggle for authority ➢ Role ➢ Self-expectations ➢ Expectations of superiors ➢ Over and under work ➢ Poor communication ➢ Poor problem solving, decision-making and frequent conflicts ➢ Inability to perform in challenging and new roles	➢ Emotional involvement with students ➢ Poor incentives and facilities ➢ Lack of autonomy ➢ Poor opportunities for growth and development ➢ Poor time management ➢ More involvement in administrative work ➢ Low risk taking ➢ Non-cooperation from stakeholders

5.1 Struggle for Authority

According to McClelland some people have strong need for power and they feel uncomfortable when they don't have power. They think that they deserve it. They want to enjoy the powers but powers are centralized. For trivial things they have to formally approach to the principal or director that irritates them. When their suggestion is turned down they feel stressed. They have strong needs for power. They want to control the behaviour of others.

Exhibit No. 16.1: Purpose of record management

External stakeholders	Internal Purpose
➢ To get approval of educational programmes from statutory body ➢ To obtain accreditation of educational programmes ➢ To get certificate from professional body ➢ To receive raised funds, resources and guidance from stakeholders ➢ To place students in international and national organizations ➢ To collaborate, network, cooperate and share experiences ➢ To influence potential students and their parents to take admission ➢ To market the services and products of the institution	➢ To take input for planning process ➢ To make effective decisions ➢ To solve problems ➢ To design system and processes ➢ To provide information to members of the institution for various purposes ➢ To save time and reduce waiting time ➢ To do auditing of various processes and think about continuous improvement ➢ To prepare reports for various purposes ➢ To compare the performance ➢ To ensure effective communication ➢ To do inquiry ➢ To keep transparency in functioning of the institution

3. Records to be Maintained by Institutions

The institution should prepare various types of documents to fulfil various purposes. An indicative list of documents along with its purpose is shown in exhibit 16.2.

Exhibit No. 16.2: Records to be maintained by institution

Sl. No.	*Documents*	*Purpose*
1.	Vision document—vision statement, mission statements, shared values, SWOT analysis, vision reach strategies and significant achievements	➢ To communicate the core business of the institution, its ambitions and long-term plans to stakeholders ➢ To get approval, accreditation, certificatetion, recognition, from statutory and professional bodies ➢ To invite stakeholders to collaborate and network with institution ➢ To invite individuals and students to peruse their career with the institution ➢ To use as a tool for decision-making, communicating, improving performance and bringing innovations

(*Contd.*)

(*Contd.*)

Sl. No.	*Documents*	*Purpose*
2.	Information brochure–Vision and mission statements, structure of the institution, programmes and services offered, major achievements, facilities, profile of the resources and faculty, immediate future plans. Different brochures can be prepared for different stakeholders, i.e. potential students, parents, employers, university, professional body, society, visitors, alumni	➢ To use as a communication tool for present and potential clients to market services and products of the institution ➢ To attract students and clients to collaborate on various activities ➢ To enhance corporate reputation of the institution
3.	Profile of the institute	➢ To enhance the validity and reliability of planning and bench-marking purpose ➢ To prioritise the areas of development
4.	Profile of the faculty and staff	➢ To enhance the validity and reliability of planning and bench marking purpose ➢ To prioritise the areas of development of faculty and staff
5.	Policies – Recruitment policy, performance appraisal and development policy, incentives and rewards policy, punishment and retrenchment policy, training and development policy, grievance and complaint handling policy, networking, collaboration and cooperation policy, marketing policy, purchase policy, students policy addressing admission, facilities, rewards, punishments, award of scholarship, freeships, sponsorships, privileges, fines	➢ To decide the authority ➢ To delegate authority ➢ To enhance autonomy ➢ To take decisions aligned to institutions vision ➢ To perform the functions smoothly ➢ To bring transparency in functioning ➢ To settle the litigations and conflicts ➢ To take timely action ➢ To make people aware about functioning of the institution ➢ To promote healthy culture ➢ To save time on unnecessary deliberations ➢ To reduce *ad hoc* and causal approaches ➢ To save overall time on convincing people about decisions

(*Contd.*)

(*Contd.*)

Sl. No.	*Documents*	*Purpose*
6.	Rules and regulations – For major areas of functioning of the institution such as academic, managerial, administrative and financial including authority	➢ To promote smooth performance of the institution ➢ To ensure effective communication ➢ To minimize the scope of rumours ➢ To prevent chances of inconvenience
7.	Plans – Strategic plan, perspective plan, annual plan, project plan, purchase plan, maintenance plan, staff development plan, curriculum revision plan, instructional resources development plan, recruitment plan, academic plan, monitoring plan, capital budget, operational budget, maintenance budget, development budget,	➢ To ensure planned development of the institution ➢ To ensure effective and efficient working of the institution ➢ To minimize confusion, potential, problems and risk ➢ To fix responsibility and obtain commitment of people ➢ To identify and solve implementation problems at earliest stage
8.	Information brochure for students – Use of library, use of internet, examination rules, cultural programmes, sports, scholarship, freeship, sponsorship, fee structure, norms for academic activities, guidelines for completing assignments, practical, project work, seminars, hostel rules, guidelines for industrial training, rules for attendance and internal tests, punishments etc.	➢ To save the time of faculty and staff to provide repetitive information ➢ To make students responsible for their acts ➢ To assure effective communication ➢ To avoid conflicting situation ➢ To assure quality in learning ➢ To mentally prepare students for putting variety of efforts for learning ➢ To prevent crisis situation on the part of lack of information ➢ To inculcate the habit of self discipline ➢ To develop right attitude of systematic management
9.	Procedures Standard major procedures in core business of the institution like curriculum development, instructional resources development, examination,	➢ To save the time of faculty and staff doing same activity again and again ➢ To assure effective and efficient performance ➢ To assure quality in learning ➢ To prevent crisis situation

(*Contd.*)

(Contd.)

Sl. No.	*Documents*	*Purpose*
	industrial training of students and teachers, admission, cultural events, sports events, purchase, recruitment, giving awards, collaboration, undertaking consultancy work, conducting research work, conducting continuing education programmes	➢ To inculcate the habit of self-discipline in performance ➢ To develop right attitude of systematic management ➢ To minimize waste ➢ To bring continuous improvement ➢ To promote accountability ➢ To allocate resources timely ➢ To promote utilization of resources
10.	Forms for various purposes such as leave application, leave record, transmittal slip, indent form, message, dispatch request, supplies requisition, payment voucher, petty cash voucher, students attendance record, internal assessment record, progress card, scholarship application, leave application, medical claims, travel claim, honorarium, etc.	➢ To minimize the time taken to perform routine activities ➢ To make procedure simple, precise and concise ➢ To maintain uniformity ➢ To avoid delay in action ➢ To gather complete, accurate, desirable information at first time
11.	Check lists Admission, examination, teaching learning process, maintenance of equipment, cleanliness, security, organizing meetings, seminars and conferences, minimize wastage, economy in functioning etc.	➢ To ensure the quality of performance of the process ➢ To promote self-evaluation ➢ To avoid crisis situation ➢ To minimize waste ➢ To promote utilization of resources

4. Problems in Record Management System

The institution should decide the documents to be prepared for various purposes. There should not be unnecessary documents in the institution otherwise they make the document handling difficult. If you often face problems mentioned in exhibit 16.3. You should improve the record management system.

Exhibit No. 16.3: Problems in record management

Sl. No.	*Problems*	*Extent of problem*		
		High	*Medium*	*Low*
1.	Information difficult to obtained due to complexity of the record management system			
2.	Incomplete and outdated information is available			
3.	Duplication of record management			
4.	Records are not classified on the basis of priority			
5.	List of records is not available			
6.	Casual way of maintaining records			
7.	No uniform procedure for record keeping			
8.	Takes long to retrieve information because of non-coding or confusing coding, drawer full of documents, inappropriate location, computer full of information, no systematic saving of the documents etc.			
9.	Information is not validated before it is recorded			
10.	Responsibility for record keeping is not fixed			
11.	People do not know about record management			
12.	Proper resources and equipment, and material are not available to manage the record			

5. Method of Improving Record Management System

Every year the institution should review the need and relevance of the documents. For improving record management in your institution you can use matrix shown in exhibit 16.4.

Exhibit No. 16.4: Improving document management process

Sl. No.	*Questions*	*Students*	*Teachers/ Staff*	*Section*	*Principal*	*Stake-holders*
1.	What are the records?					
2.	Where should be they filed?					
3.	Who uses the records?					
4.	How often they use?					
5.	How are they used?					
6.	How are the records referred to?					
7.	What is the size of each record?					
8.	How many of each record are filed?					
9.	Who else has copies of the record?					
10.	What is time for destroying the record?					
11.	Is it managed in hard copy or soft copy?					

The purpose of record management should be defined clearly. The purpose could be as mentioned in exhibit 16.1. The output of the format of record management should be decided to ensure right information at right time. The information should be available on finger tip and within no time that is the beauty of record management system. To make the record management system purposeful and meaningful a step-by-step analysis and design of the record management system should be carried out. The logical steps are shown in exhibit 16.5 with a brief description.

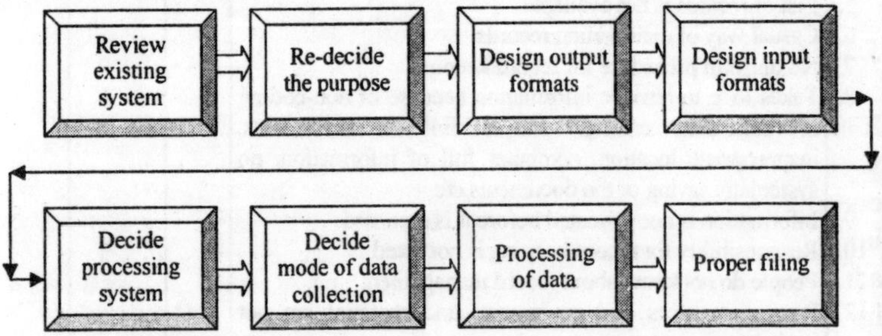

Exhibit No. 16.5: Process of improving record management system

5.1 Review Existing System of Record Management System

The record management system should be reviewed in order to make it useful and purposeful. It should be reviewed on the points mentioned in exhibit 16.3 and some other significant points relevant to institution. The basic purpose of record management review is to examine whether it is serving the purpose or not and if yes what is the effectiveness and efficiency of the system? If the system is not 100 per cent effective and efficient it should be redesigned or redefined or modify to fulfil the purpose. The record management system becomes redundant or obsolete or irrelevant because the purpose has changed or new technology has come or new methods have been designed. It is desirable to review the record management system every year.

5.2 Re-decide the Purpose of Record Management System

Every year new dimensions to business are added or the data become obsolete and redundant or the purpose changes so that the purpose of the record management should be redefined. Every time one should always ask a question what is the purpose of the record? If a satisfactory answer to this question is not found there is no need to manage the record. The purpose of record management should be crystal clear. If there is a purpose then only the type, form and method of record management should be decided. Each record and document should be prepared to serve a specific purpose. It means the information provided in one document may be useful for another document for different purpose. So duplication of information should be avoided creating a database.

5.3 Decide Output Formats

It is necessary to decide output formats of documents to be prepared for various purposes. The output format should be easy to read and comprehend, precise, simple, and attractive. If possible the output information should be graphical, pictorial and in summary form. It should add value to take decision. For example, the document is prepared to influence the potential students to take admission, the most desirous information is previous year placements and their salary status. The second thing could be faculty profile and third thing could be facilities available in the institution.

5.4 Decide Input Formats

The next step is to feed inputs to the process so that it serves the purpose of record management. The input formats aligned with output formats are designed. So that valid and reliable information can be collected timely and input formats are made ready for processing. The formats should fulfil the requirement of the purpose and out put formats. The validity and reliability of the information should be checked before entering it in the input formats.

5.5 Decide the Processing System

The data processing system should be decided. The processing of the data would be done keeping in mind the output formats. The processing can be done manually or electronically. If it is being done electronically appropriate software should be selected or designed. The software should be tested and installed. The responsibility of processing the data should be allocated to a person. S/he should be trained to process the data and prepare the output document.

5.6 Decide Mode of Data Collection

The input and output format guides to data collection process. There could be many formats, which are directly filled by the information originator. The students can provide the information related to them. The formats can be designed considering the respondents limitation. Similarly the teachers and the staff members can provide their personal and other information available at their end. Accountants can provide the information related to expenses and budget. So data can be collected respondents wise designing the formats to be filled up by them. The original source of data should always be used instead of secondary sources. The permanent nature of information should not be collected again and again other-wise it would irritate the information provider and waste the time and resources. Right information at right time in right way from right person should be collected. It means the information provider should know in advance what information in what form, at what time, to whom information is to be provided. So s/he can manage the information accordingly. So far mode of the information collection is concerned it can be collected manually using formats or it can be collected electronically using lane facility.

5.7 Processing of Data

The information collected from various sources in various formats should be compiled in the input formats. The compilation work should go along with data collection process if possible to save the data entry processing time. The responsible person for its authenticity should check the data before it is entered in the input formats. The data should be processed and the output should be prepared in desired form. If it is electronic copy it should timely reach to the person to serve the purpose. If it has to go in hard copy it should be properly arranged, bonded and submitted.

5.8 Proper Filing

The soft copy and hard copy should be filed in a way so that it can be easily retrieved. It should be properly indexed and arranged. Hard copies should be properly arranged so that it is safe, easy to retrieve and handle. The space to store hard copies should be safe, free from moisture and direct sunrays. It should be locked for ensuring the confidentiality if necessary.

6. Information to Stakeholders

Information to stakeholders is provided in many forms. The record management system is very useful to generate information for stakeholders in any desirable forms. The database created is very useful to prepare any kind of document for the stakeholders. Generally the information to different stakeholders is provided in different form. It may be in the form of a report, proposal, simple document, leaflet brochure, memo, voucher, statement, notice, letter, power point presentation, multimedia presentation etc. Institutions should keep ready information for different users of services and products of the institution. The general information about the services and product should be available at the reception of the institute.

7. Summary

Information is considered to be a resource and need to be appropriately managed for the smooth functioning of the institution and marketing its products and services to the stakeholders. Information is maintained in the form of records soft or hard form. The right information should be available at right time to take major development decisions and solve problems. In absence of effective and efficient information system the institution may miss major opportunities and face severe problems. The functioning of the institution may be *ad hoc* and causal. Records are also used for various purposes such as obtaining approval for starting a programme or getting accreditation from statutory bodies. Records are used for obtaining loan and assistance from stakeholders in the form of a cash and kind. By managing information, the institution can lead in many fields. It can save time, money and efforts in searching and compiling the information when required. Ready-made softwares can be used by institution to manage the information. It should be ensured that the information should be valid, reliable and accurate before it is stored. It should be available on fingertip whenever desired by the management. The faculty and staff members should be trained to manage the records in desired formats. They should provide it as and when desired by management. The information and record management system of the institution should be reviewed every year because it would change as per changes in the business.

8. Activity

Design a record management system for your institution and test it on criteria, such as time saved, frustration reduced, reduction of wastage, ease in coordination of the information gathering activities, marketing the product and services, and influencing the customers and client.

REFERENCE

How to Manage Hand Book (1995). Excel Books, New Delhi.

PART IV
MANAGEMENT OF CHANGE AND INNOVATIONS

17

Management of Change

Objectives: The readers will be able to:

1. State the need and importance of management of change.
2. List the types of changes.
3. Describe the change process.
4. List the reasons of failure of change.
5. Explain the significant changes introduced in technical education system in last decade.
6. List the tools and techniques to manage the change.
7. Define the focus of change.
8. State the guidelines to be followed while implementing the change.

1. Introduction

Change is a natural process. As described in chapter on planning, the institution works, in an open environment and numerous changes are taking place everyday in the environment. In technical, economic and social field the change is taking very fast. The institution is required to adopt the changes taking place in the environment to make its services relevant and to assure its existence. Adoptive change is necessary for every institution but in competitive environment adoptive change is not sufficient to lead in the technical education. There is a need to introduce planned change. Planned change means deliberate change introduced in the goals, business and functioning of the institution so that the institution can cope up with any change taking place in external environment. The institution prepares itself to develop capabilities and capacities for growth, development and continuously improve its performance. Planned change is implemented in entire institution to enable the effective and efficient functioning in difficult time as well.

Change is perceived to be complex, expensive, painful, unpleasant, disruptive, and something to be avoided. But this remains the fact that change affects every one. It creates threat to authority for someone or it brings opportunities for some, or it challenges the way of working of people, or it requires resources. Whatever it may be it should focus on satisfying the learning needs of the students and changing needs of the stakeholders.

2. Types of Change

Change can be classified as adoptive change and planned change. The difference between adoptive change and planned change is described in exhibit 17.1.

Criteria	*Adoptive change*	*Planned change*
Approach	Reactive	Proactive
Corporate image of the institution	In tune with social change	High level of respect in industry and society
Methods of change	Most of traditional methods	Most of the innovative methods
Thrust	Incremental development	Achieving excellence
Values and culture	Adoptive	Aligned to vision
Resistance	Significant resistance	Resistance is addressed through involving people
Speed of change	Slow to medium	Radical change
Focus	Present	Future
Area of change	Whole institution or one dimension of functioning	Integrated change in whole institution

Exhibit No. 17.1: Types of change

Most of the organizations have practiced adoptive change that means they have introduced change as per need of the environmental demands. It is again a kind of reactive approach. It cannot be considered good approach because the change is first introduced in industry there it is established and later it is introduced in educational institutions. It is a long process and institutions lag behind the industry and society. It loses credibility because it does not give new things to the industry and society. Planned change on other hand is thinking about new technologies, methods and approaches, testing them and giving them to industry and society.

Another classification of change is observed in its approach in implementation. Step-by-step change is introduced in many institutions, which is gradual and firm. This approach is also called evolutionary. In this approach of change the significant impact of change is not visible. This approach is considered to be feasible when there is more uncertainty for success and change implementers are unable to predict the situation requiring the change. The other approach is radical change meaning thereby total and immediate change in the way of working. These changes are being popular in present time because fast change in technology and economy. The technology and way of working are becoming outdated with the advent of new technology. Radical change requires high level of initial efforts but at the same time it pays much in terms of money and corporate image. People remain in dilemma whether to go for evolutionary change or radical change. It should be decided on the basis of situation requiring change.

3. Change Process

Planned change is comparatively easy to design and implement because it is designed participatively involving the change implementers and affected parties. They appreciate the need of the change and justification for introducing the change. They also appreciate that change is for betterment of the well-being of the institution and individuals. They know that the painful change brings improvements in their institutional life in a long run. In traditional approaches of change the changes were conceived and imposed by the top management because of the need. People used to resist it because it was considered unnecessary and imposed. In contemporary time institutional members participate in governance and management of the institution so they are more aware about the importance of change. They themselves bring many innovative ideas to the institution for implementation. They consider the change as an enjoyment and challenge. They know that they can remove boredom, stagnation, monotony, de-motivation, frustration and dullness through change only. Change will bring new opportunities for them in various forms. They would learn new things, do different things, get promotion, get more freedom to work, enjoy status, become influential, and have a pride in life.

People in growing and developing institution consider change positively. They think change will open up new avenues for them. They see the change positively and welcome it. They do it because of their values and ambitions for continuous enjoyment. They love their institution and the change. They do not resist change because they have fear of failure. But they share the apprehension of failure with institutional members. The planned change is initiated in planned way. The steps of planned change are stated in exhibit 17.2. The steps of planned change are briefly described in subsequent paragraphs.

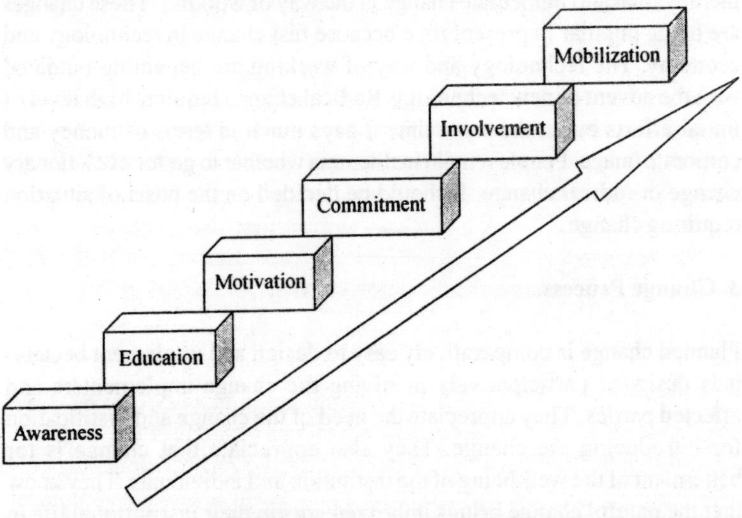

Exhibit No. 17.2: Change process

3.1 Awareness

Number of informal and formal discussions, creativity sessions, meetings, seminars, conferences, in basket exercises, focus group discussions are organized in the institution on design of the change. Various tools and techniques are used to conduct the sessions to make them focused and result oriented. The result of the sessions is collective learning for all the participating members. In discussions people come out with their views, fears, ambitions, commitments, owning and approach for the planned change. This could be done during planning process itself. The change takes hazy shape through collective learning. People become aware about the external and internal environmental changes in the institution.

3.2 Education

The next step is education of people about the future picture of the change. The interaction on the change continues till the concrete picture of the change is collectively created. The pros and cons of change are deliberated widely and conclusions are drawn. The picture of the change is painted with benefits, growth, development, excellence, challenge and similar flavours. Institutional members are encouraged to share the colourful picture with larger population. They are encouraged to invite more ideas on the picture to add beauty to it.

3.3 Motivation

The picture of the change invites people to design ways and means to achieve it. It also motivates people to organize in order to achieve it. People explore alternative ways using their creativity and collective wisdom. They find ways that never been tried in the institution. They get motivated with the process of thinking and modelling of the change. Once the ways and means are finalized collectively to achieve the painted picture people think about minute details of the activities to be performed.

3.4 Commitment

It is said that cradle to grave approach brings commitment of the people for the change. At this stage consensus seeking techniques are used to obtain general agreement of the people for the change and change strategies. They consider that the change is a dynamic process and they are the driver of it. They own the change foreseen collectively. They see their own benefit in the change. They also confirm that the change will not adversely affect them. They mentally, emotionally and physically prepare themselves to put their potential for implementing the change.

3.5 Involvement

People get involve in implementing the change with full energy and enthusiasm. Their energy and enthusiasm should not be distracted by rules, resources shortage, negative remarks and arrogant behaviour of the superiors. They should be encouraged, facilitated and guided by the experienced persons and experts. The mistakes committed by them should be ignored and positive achievements should be duly and openly recognized. The implementation problems of the people should be quickly solved. The change should flow with full-blown and at a very fast speed.

3.6 Mobilization

The implementation of strategy should continue till the crafted change is achieved. The collective implementation creates challenges for the people to mobilize their resources, experience and expertise for achieving the collective goal of the change. Collective efforts bring joy and satisfaction to individuals. They feel pride in extending their own resources because everyone appreciates it and everyone is contributing in same way. It brings spiral effect. In the rolling change another change can be planned and implemented. This cycle of change goes on without external fuel and people enjoy the journey of change sharing the joy and bitter experiences of it. Everyone in the institution becomes the prime mover of the change process.

4. Reasons for Failure of Change

This is the basic theme to understand. People have tried variety of changes pouring huge money in the institution and later on came to know that the change could not bring any impact in quality of education. The reasons of failure were many. Few indicative reasons are listed in exhibit 17.3.

Exhibit No. 17.3: Reasons of failure of change

➢ Focus of change was not core business of the institutions that is academics ➢ The need of change never felt by people working in institutions even by institutional head ➢ It was forced change ➢ The current, existing and burning problems of the institution were not addressed and change was initiated ➢ The change created huge liability for institution, for example maintenance of building and equipment that were not required at all ➢ The assumptions of the change were not tested and were faulty ➢ No attempt was made to translate the assumption in reality	➢ The measure of success of change was financial expenditure ➢ People were not involved in the design of the change and they found it unnecessary ➢ The focus of change was not focused to future ➢ It was centralized change implemented in bureaucratic manner ➢ The goals and objectives of the change were decided at top ➢ The change was based on hunches, concern and worries of people ➢ The change is designed in pieces and in isolated manner ➢ The beliefs and values of senior management was traditional ➢ The change focused on traditional disciplines

5. Change Programmes Introduced in Technical Institutions

Number of change programmes has been introduced in technical education system in last decade. Some innovations have been introduced in whole system and some in selected institutions. Some of the significant innovations are briefly described in subsequent paragraphs.

5.1 Strengthening Technician Education System through World Bank Assistance

This project was implemented in two phases in polytechnics of the country. The major focus of the project was capacity expansion, quality improvement and efficiency improvement.

Capacity Expansion

Under capacity expansion new diploma programmes introduced in polytechnics to cater the growing needs of polytechnic passouts in new and emerging areas. The infrastructure is created to start the new programmes in polytechnics. The new infrastructure includes construction of building, expansion of existing building for classrooms, laboratories, library, computer laboratory, workshop, administrative block, canteen, boys and girls hostels, etc. Most modern equipment, learning resources and implements were purchased. The distance learning programmes are offered by the state to cater the continuing education needs of the persons working in industry. The programme was completely competency based and flexible.

Quality Improvement

Under quality improvement autonomy was granted to polytechnics to implement innovations to improve quality. Under quality improvement component individual polytechnics were granted autonomy to implement variety of need based projects in their institutions. Most of the polytechnics have implemented one or two major innovations in their institutions. For example, most of the polytechnics have introduced flexibility in curriculum offering. Multi-point entry and credit system in diploma programmes was introduced successfully. The impact of multi-point entry and credit system on quality of passouts can be seen in Gujarat and Maharashtra state. The Gujarat experience is worth to adopt in the whole technical education system. In Maharashtra state the concept of lead centre was successfully introduced to develop instructional resources on latest technology in various disciplines. The lead centres not only developed innovative instructional resources but also trained most of the teachers on technological and educational technology developments and its use. Quality circles were introduced to solve work related problems in the institution in all areas of functioning of the institution. Few institutions introduced competency based diploma level curriculum and implemented it successfully. Under the component of quality improvement most of the teachers and instructors were trained in industries to acquire knowledge and skills on latest developments in the respective disciplines. They were also trained to use the knowledge and skills acquired for improving teaching learning process. These trained teachers prepared learning resources using the principles of educational technology for using in teaching learning process to save the time in instructions and to create interest of the students. Apart from industrial and educational technology training senior faculty members were trained in management and managing innovations in their institution. Many institutions have worked on other projects also such as total quality management, enhancing contribution of faculty, reengineering and enhancing the participation of women. The institutions have conducted numerous workshops, training programmes, seminars, and conferences to diffuse experiences of innovations.

Efficiency Improvement

Under this component the board of technical education and directorate were strengthened to support and facilitate the changes in institutions. Some centralized and common innovations in administration and examination system were introduced to improve the efficiency of the whole system. To make the examination system more valid and reliable boards developed question bank and item bank and introduced examination reforms in the whole state.

5.2 The Canada-India Institute-Industry Linkage Project

The Canada-India Institute-Industry linkage project was implemented in the country with a goal to make the technical education more responsive to the changing socio-economic environment by developing practical and effective linkages and partnership between selected technical institutions, directorate of technical education, business and industry. Under the project, contributions were made for developing human resources in the areas of curriculum development, management of systems, continuing education, staff development, industry linkages, empowerment of women, time management and replication of experiences. National and State lavel conferences were organized to share the experiences among the participating institutions and industries.

5.3 Technical Education Quality Improvement Programme of Government of India

This programme is implemented with an aim to improve quality of technical education system. The emphasis is to make the system dynamic, demand driven, quality conscious, efficient and forward looking to respond to rapid economic and technological developments occurring at national and international level. The institutions have been under this programme on the basis of minimum eligibility criteria and selection criteria. Through this programme culture of relevance, quality and efficiency is promoted in technical institutions. The lead institutions are getting major assistance and at the same time networked institutions are developing under the guidance of lead institution. Lead and networked institutions are learning collectively for excellence. The programme focuses on four activities, they are as follow:

Developing Academic Excellence

Under this activity creativity and innovation is promoted in the institution. Institutions have crafted their vision documents through participation of internal and external stakeholders. The potential of existing resources and potential resources would be utilized to achieve excellence. The academic excellence is being achieved through making the curricula more relevant, introducing reliable evaluation system, improving teaching learning process using methods and media and increased access to laboratories and workshops. There is a provision for enhancing the commitment of the teachers for institutional activities, innovations and research. There is a provision of learner centred activities and participation of students in purposeful projects. Teachers and students are being encouraged to make creative and innovative contribution to technical education system.

Networking

The second activity is networking with other institutions for variety of purposes such as sharing resources and experiences, faculty and staff development, curriculum development, undertaking joint research work and consultancy projects, information dissemination, and inculcating competitive spirit for development. Undertaking joint faculty development programmes and faculty exchange programmes. The students also receive benefit of network institution by selecting and studying the elective subjects offered by network institutions, utilizing library, laboratory and lectures of faculty. The institutions conduct joint academic programmes and provide opportunities for collective learning for faculty members and students.

Services to Community and Economy

The third activity in the programme is services to community and economy. Under this activity institution offers need based continuing education programmes in the area of their specialization for industry, community and other organizations. The institution creates awareness on application of technology to improve effectiveness and efficiency in existing practices in industry and society. It provides technical support services for maintaining the tools and equipments. It is the primary responsibility of the institutions to contribute for socio-economic development of the community.

Developing Management Capacity

The fourth activity in the programme is developing management capacity. Under this activity the senior faculty is developed to implement change and innovations envisaged under the programme. They are exposed to new and unique innovations carried out in technical education system and other fields. They are encouraged to promote research work on development of technical education system as a whole. Institutions have also taken up tracer studies and action researches. The senior faculty is trained to take effective decisions. The consultancy work, resources generation work and quality improvement work is initiated in the institution. The focus for developing management capacity is decentralized decision-making and shared leadership.

5.4 Accreditation

The All India Council for Technical Education (AICTE) has established the National Board of Accreditation (NBA) in 1994 to evolve procedure for quality assessment in technical education. The board has issued a manual for accreditation of quality of programmes offered by technical institutions. The basic aim of accreditation is to assure the quality of programmes offered by the technical institutions in the country. The purpose of accreditation is listed in exhibit 17.4.

Exhibit No. 17.4: Purpose of accreditation

➢ To help the institution to know its strengths, weaknesses and opportunities ➢ To identify internal areas of planning and resource allocation ➢ To enhance funding for quality activities ➢ To initiate innovations in academics ➢ To provide valid and reliable information on quality of education offered ➢ To promote networking, collaboration and cooperation among sister institutions	➢ To recognize the innovative achievements of institutions ➢ To benchmark the quality of education and various parameters on which the institution functions ➢ To inculcate the healthy competition among institutions ➢ To continuously improve the quality of passouts ➢ To strive towards the attainment of excellence

The National Board of Accreditation has developed evaluation process for accreditation. It has developed eight criteria to evaluate the principal features of the institutional activities and programme effectiveness. It has divided each criterion on various parameters to objectively assess the performance. The eight criteria are listed in exhibit 17.5. The NBA has developed formats to be filled up by institutions for obtaining accreditation. The formats are user-friendly and institutions can easily fill up the formats. The process of obtaining the accreditation is transparent and the institutions can self-evaluate their status before applying to NBA for accreditation. Many institutions in the country have obtained accreditation certificate for their programmes satisfying the quality requirements. The list of the accredited programmes and institutions is also available on the web site of AICTE. The NBA accreditation has increased the awareness of institutions and stakeholders for maintaining the quality of education. It has created healthy environment for improving the quality of education. The details provided in manual are guiding points for institutions to improve quality in institutional functioning.

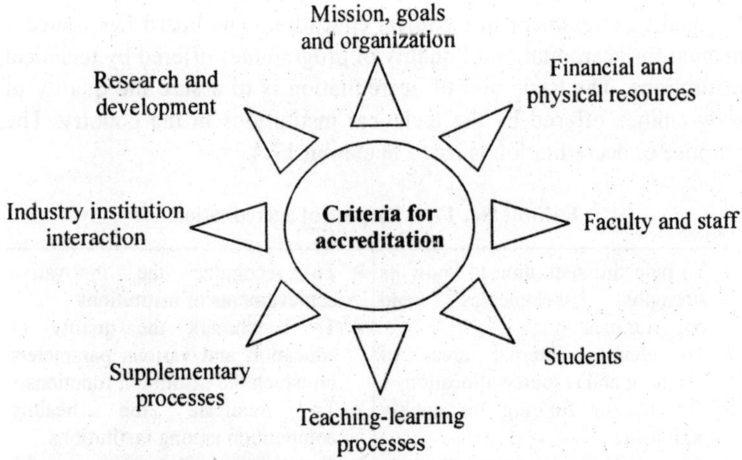

Exhibit No. 17.5: Eight criteria for accreditation

6. Tools and Techniques for Change Management

Number of tools and techniques have been used in the past in different organizations to implement the change successfully. The painful change is implemented successfully in many organizations. Tools and techniques applicable to technical institutions are described briefly in subsequent paragraphs.

6.1 Force Field Analysis

Kurt Lewin has proposed this technique. It is based on the principle of equilibrium. There are two types of forces act in any situation under consideration for change driving forces and resisting forces. If the driving forces are powerful and the people appreciate it they would certainly drive the change process. If restraining forces are more powerful they would resist the change efforts and the change may not be successful in the given situation. There may be a possibility that restraining forces may get aggravated when facilitating forces are manipulated. It is considered good for healthy change management. The intensity of restraining forces can be calculated and remedies can be designed to keep them under control. The force field analysis is helpful to know all the facilitating and restraining forces along with their intensity to change process. Generally force field exercise is carried out participatively so it provides the real picture of the forces. During the process of force field analysis discussions take place on various issues related to the forces. Observing and listening these discussions, one can estimate the commitment of people for the desired change. The force field analysis provides concrete clues to design change strategies. Force field analysis is used during creating awareness, education and motivation about desired change process. A force field analysis of introducing learner-centred approaches is shown in exhibit 17.6.

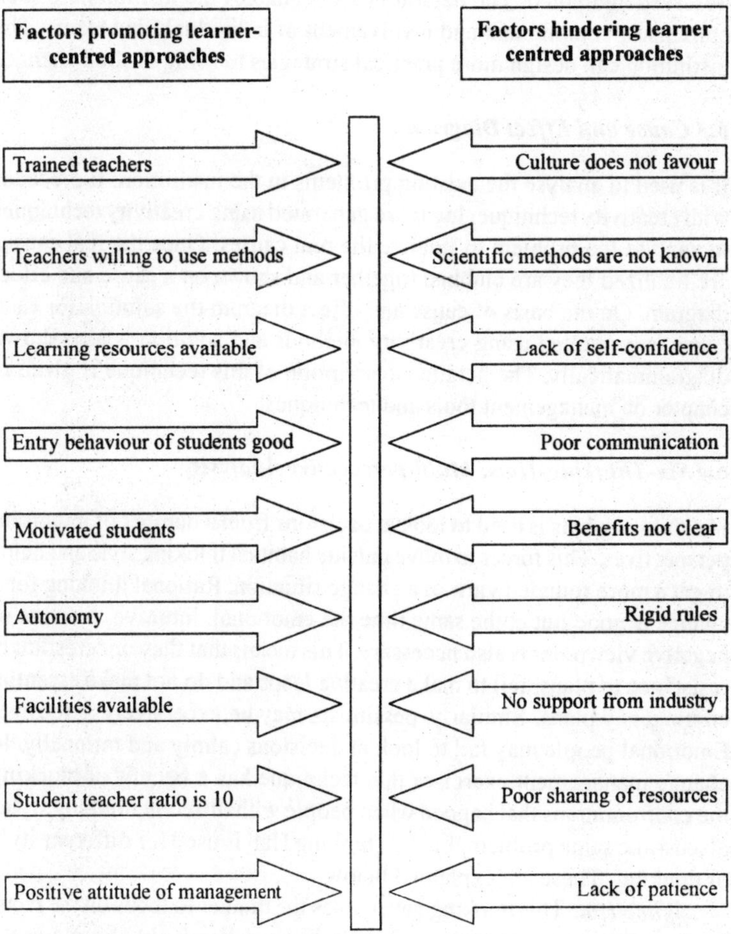

Exhibit No. 17.6: Introducing learner-centred approaches

6.2 Creativity Techniques

Creativity techniques are useful to draw a clear picture of desired change. Use of creativity techniques enables the institution to reveal the views of the people on their level of understanding of change, level of resistance, level of interest, level of opposition, level of confusion, level of consensus, level of enthusiasm and level of involvement. The creativity process is carried out in natural environment so the feelings of the people can be observed and noted. The natural process enables the institution to seek consensus, commitment and involvement of individuals and teams. The institution can design more practical strategies to bring desired change.

6.3 Cause and Effect Diagram

It is used to analyse the existing problems in the institution. It precedes with creativity technique. Ideas are generated using creativity techniques to analyse the problem to finalize the real causes. Once the real causes are finalized they are clubbed together and shown on a cause and effect diagram. On the basis of cause and effect diagram the solution for each cause is generated using creativity methods and solution is also shown diagrammatically. The detailed description of this technique is given in chapter on management tools and techniques.

6.4 Six-Thinking-Hats: Multi-perspective Analysis

Six-thinking-hats is used to look at decisions from a number of important perspectives. This forces to move outside habitual thinking style and helps to get a more rounded view of a change situation. Rational thinking for a change is good but at the same time the emotional, intuitive, creative or negative viewpoint is also necessary. This means that they underestimate resistance to plans, fail to make creative leaps and do not make essential contingency plans. Similarly, pessimists may be excessively defensive. Emotional people may fail to look at decisions calmly and rationally. In change management exercises this technique has a benefit of blocking the confrontations that happen when people with different thinking styles discuss the same problem. Each 'Thinking Hat' is used for different style of thinking. These are explained below:

White Hat: This thinking hat enables the thinker to focus on the facts, figures, data and information. People learn collectively about current situation having discussion on available data. People try to analyze the situation requiring the change understanding its past and present status.

Red Hat: 'Wearing' the Red Hat, the feelings and reaction about the change situation can be analysed. It may be possible that the problem may be a perceived problem and it may not be a problem in reality. Or people may perceive it differently. The analysis of feelings of people helps to deal with behavioural and cultural aspect of the change.

Black Hat: 'Wearing' the Black Hat negative aspects of change are analyzed. The change strategies are analysed from obstacles, barriers and resistance point of view. Black Hat thinking is important because it helps to find out what is not important. It allows for eliminating or altering, or countering the barriers.

Yellow Hat: The Yellow Hat helps to think positively. It is the optimistic viewpoint that helps to see all the benefits of the change and the value in it to the institution. Yellow Hat thinking helps to keep going when everything looks gloomy and difficult.

Green Hat: The Green Hat stands for creativity. This is where the institution develops creative solutions to a problem. It is a freewheeling way of thinking, in which there is little criticism of ideas. A whole range of creativity tools can be used.

Blue Hat: 'Blue Hat Thinking' stands for control. This is the hat worn by people leading the change process. When running into difficulties they shift to Green Hat thinking and find the appropriate solution. When contingency plans are needed, they will ask for Black Hat thinking, etc.

7. Focus of Change

In the past variety of changes have been introduced in the technical institutions focusing on various dimension of functioning of the institution such as more utilization of resources of the institution, change in procedures, change in policy and rules, change in relationship, change in way of working, change in procedure of collecting information etc. The change is desired in peripheral areas of functioning of the institution but it would not bring much impact on the academic performance of the institution. Institutions have invested in buildings, laboratories, examination system but it is interesting to note that they are implementing old age curriculum. The world has changed even the books are out of print because the technology is out of practice but institutions are implementing same curriculum. What is necessary is to change in technical institutions is to revise the curriculum continuously as per requirements of the employers and needs of the students. The change model in academics is shown in exhibit 17.7.

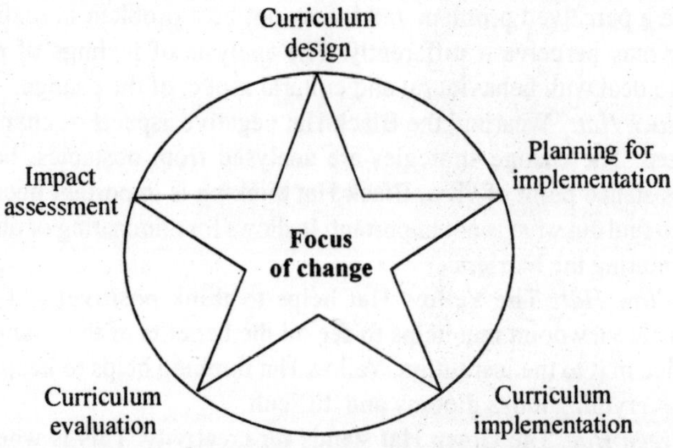

Exhibit No. 17.7: Change model for technical institutions

7.1 Curriculum Design

Every change initiative should start with the curriculum design, revision, refinement and change. It means the inputs to curriculum should come from the employers, technological changes, students and entrepreneurs. The curriculum should be designed using principles of educational technology, educational psychology and education management. It should be designed using scientific methods. Instead of having long irrelevant subject based approach, competency based approach should be followed. This approach to change is relevant, simple, and easy.

7.2 Planning for Implementation

Planning for implementation of curriculum should be carried out at the beginning of the session. The teacher should do planning on competency attainment basis and not on time basis. It means detailed planning should be done on competency development, learning methods, learning exercises, field or industrial training, hands on experience, learning resources and assessment techniques. Time is not so important a factor in competency development. The changes in the infrastructure, laboratory, library, learning resource centre, teacher training, teacher performance evaluation, record management and finance should be carried out accordingly.

7.3 Curriculum Implementation

The curriculum should be implemented as planned. It requires the competent teachers supported by infrastructure, learning resources, laboratory, library, learning resource center etc. These sub-systems should support the implementation of curriculum and attainment of competency. The changes and adjustment in peripheral processes and activities should be initiated accordingly. The implementation and formative evaluation will go hand in hand to ensure attainment of predefined proficiency level in each competency.

7.4 Curriculum Evaluation

The achievements of the competencies stated in curriculum should be evaluated on various parameters such as adequacy of inputs, effectiveness and efficiency of curriculum implementation processes, use of resources, wastages, mistakes, cooperation of stakeholders, experiences gained, shortcomings on the part of teachers and students, response of the students, level of competency attainment by all students etc. The curriculum evaluation process would provide inputs to curriculum design and implementation process for initiating further changes.

7.5 Impact Assessment

Employers can assess the impact of the passouts learning and they can provide feedback to institution on the competencies of the students. Institution on its own can assess the impact of learning on parameters such as improving the profitability, quality, business, research, development, wastage reduction, enhancing corporate image of employer's organization. The impact assessment, tracer study and action research methods are used to assess the impact and get feedback for curriculum design.

8. Guidelines for Introducing Planned Change in the Institution

The change is always introduced for better future of the institution. At the same time it should not be so painful in the present that people find it impossible. Individuals and teams in the institution should see many good things in it for them in the present as well in the future. The general guidelines for introducing planned change are listed in exhibit 17.8.

Exhibit No. 17.8: Guidelines for introducing planned change

Before change

- Create an environment in which people appreciate a problem or feel a need of change
- Often discuss such issues in meetings and notice the reactions of the people
- Promote use of creativity techniques to analyse the problems or issues
- Promote interaction of faculty and staff members with better performing institutions
- Promote principles of learning organization
- Promote organization of collaborative training programmes with stakeholders
- Study the behaviour of individuals and teams
- Provide exposure to new developments
- Invite suggestions of people for improvement
- Analyse the problems and complaints received in past
- Do comparative study on performance of students with other institutions and within the institution
- Address the personal development and growth issues appropriately in the change
- Bring on surface the doubts, apprehensions, perceptions and beliefs of people
- Prepare people to anticipate change and be ready for it

During design of change

- Decide the issues or problems or crisis requiring solution
- Decide the title of theme of change to be implemented
- Organize discussion sessions, meetings and creativity sessions on above issues
- Use change design tools and techniques
- Seek suggestions of all stakeholders for improving quality of passouts
- Document the outcomes
- Discuss the outcome and inform relevant persons about the common consensus or conclusions
- Discuss the concerns of people
- Seek full participation of people for major change
- Project completed picture of change to institutional members, teams and other stakeholders
- Acknowledge the creative suggestions of people
- The change should be aligned to vision and missions of the institution
- Design change management strategy and seek consensus
- Estimate and assure the resources required
- Prepare plans for implementing strategies
- Identify potential problems, major pitfalls and develop contingent plans
- Establish problem solving mechanism

(*Contd.*)

(*Contd.*)

- Create holistic picture of change to show that it is elegant and attractive
- Discourage quick fix
- Raise the expectations of implementers
- Keep the design simple, precise, attractive and feasible

During implementation of change

- Show interest and commitment in change
- Promote self-initiation and proactive activities
- Empower people to take decisions and develop ownership for implementing the decision
- Encourage people to use their full potential
- Take priority activities first
- Promote working in teams
- Encourage integrated and collaborative efforts
- Encourage shared leadership
- Ignore mistakes of people
- Publicize and project positive outcomes of change progress
- Solve problems and resolve conflict immediately
- Remove procedural and authority related problem
- Use information technology
- Use effective communication, negotiation and influencing techniques
- Promote flexibility in implementation
- Encourage process ownership
- Work continuously on change
- Use action research and process planning approach
- Review the progress
- Inbuilt rewards for achievements in implementation
- Provide constructive feedback

During evaluation of change

- Evaluate the change on pre-defined criteria
- Publicize the success
- Share the shortcomings and encourage people to remove them
- Continuously change with changes in environment
- Celebrate the success
- Publicize the learning and experiences

9. Summary

Change is a continuous process. It is necessary because technical institutions have to function in open environment and change is taking place in the environment at a very fast rate. There is significant change observed in globalization of economy, education, rapid technological changes, way of doing the business, competition and challenges. Similarly changes are taking place in the technical education system as well. The old faculty is retiring, new institutions are coming up in a big way, high turnover of faculty and staff, pressure for quality of education etc. Only those institutions will survive, grow and develop in future those have culture in which the change can thrive. There are two types of changes that always take place in educational institutions – one is adoptive and other is proactive. Adoptive change can maintain the status of the institution in the society but it cannot enhance the corporate image and make leader institution in the system. A six-step model of change process can be used to design and implement the change. The steps are awareness, education, motivation, commitment, involvement and mobilization. Number of changes implemented in technical education in last decade to name a few strengthening technician education, Canada-India industry-institution liaison programme, accreditation of institutions, quality improvement programme of government of India etc. Number of tools and techniques such as visioning, force field analysis, participation, creativity techniques, cause and effect diagram and project management are available for designing and implementing change in technical institutions. These techniques are useful to effectively implement the change in the institutions. The focus of change should be on academic activities and not on peripheral activities. The change should be introduced in right way at right time to take the advantages of it. That means the institution should act proactively to design and implement change. It should be far ahead than other institutions in technology and methodology. The change should be implemented in a planned way. There is no need of separate planning for change it should be the inbuilt part of the planning process carried out every year.

10. Activity

Organize an open forum in your institution of a half-day duration to know the views of students, staff and faculty members on what change, to what to change and how to cause the change. If possible involve representatives of the employers of passouts of your institution.

REFERENCES

James, A.F. Stoner (1992). *Management*, Prentice-Hall of India Private Limited, New Delhi.

Karp, H.B. (1996). *Change Leader*, Jossey-Bass, Pfeiffer, San Francisco, California.

18

Performance Appraisal

Objectives: The readers will be able to:

1. State the need and importance of performance appraisal.
2. Describe existing system of performance.
3. List the purpose of existing performance appraisal system.
4. Describe the deficiencies of existing performance appraisal.
5. Explain the recent concept of performance of appraisal.
6. Describe the purpose of recent performance appraisal system .
7. List the characteristics of performance appraisal system.
8. State problems of performance appraisal system.
9. List the strategies of overcoming problems of performance appraisal system.
10. Describe the methods of performance appraisal system.
11. List the parameters of performance appraisal for various significant functionaries of the institution.
12. Describe the model of implementation of performance appraisal in technical institution.

1. Introduction

The National Policy on Education, 1986 had given considerable stress on improving quality of technical education. It considers the teachers as the pivot of the system. The teachers have to perform multiple roles such as teaching, research, consultancy, development of instructional resources, administration, student services, acquisition and development of expertise in their chosen field of specialization. In order to promote the excellence in technical education, the national policy on education recognizes the need to perform such multiple roles by the teachers. The National Policy of Education also stipulates the introduction of performance appraisal system for teachers, which will make the teachers accountable for their work. It states that a system of teachers evaluation should be open, participative, and data based. It should create reasonable opportunities of promotion to higher grades.

The academic performance of the institution depends on the performance of the faculty members, technical support staff, librarian and other significant members involved in carrying out the academic business of the institution. Especially faculty members are considered to be the backbone of the academic activities. Their performance is crucial to shape the behaviour of the students. The performance of the key persons should be traced, monitored and measured to ascertain the quality of education. Looking to the changing scenario of technical education life long learning is becoming important in the technical institutions. The performance evaluation system followed in many institutions is not based on scientific methods of planning and evaluation. Now there are variety of performance appraisal models based on scientific principles are available and in use. These models can be adopted and used in technical institutions. The performance of other members of the institution is key to support the activities of the institution.

There is a need of the process that continuously monitors the progress of performance qualitatively and quantitatively. This is necessary for the growth and development of the employee or a team and at the same time for achieving the results. The growth and development of a team is possible in the appraisal situation where progress is monitored and underlying causes are identified for the poor performance or excellent performance. These causes are used to improve the performance of individuals and teams. Individuals and teams constantly innovate methods for improving the performance. Now-a-days use of information technology has become mandatory to enhance the performance of individuals and teams.

The faculty and staff members of technical institutions have been traditionally discharging their duties and responsibilities for a long time. All India Council for Technical Education (AICTE) has suggested the job description for faculty and staff members. This job description is indicative and may not be complete looking to the specific requirements of the institution. It happens because different institutions are having their own vision, mission and goals that may require its members to perform variety of roles, there may be constant change in the role of its members. Number of processes take place in different areas of functioning of an institution to accomplish the vision and mission. It is not necessary that all faculty members perform all the jobs prescribed by AICTE equally. Teams' structure is becoming important in contemporary time rather than working individually. There is a need to derive the role of different position holders as well as teams keeping in view the roles proscribed by AICTE, stakeholders' expectations, institutional requirements and individual requirements. Role so derived should be appropriately allocated to the individuals and teams according to their competencies, capabilities, experience and willingness. Individuals and teams' performance should be measured on goals or objectives set by them against these roles.

2. Existing System of Performance Appraisal

The existing system of performance is based on theory X assumptions. These assumptions are listed in exhibit 18.1.

Exhibit No. 18.1: Theory X assumptions

- ➢ The average person inherently dislikes work and will avoid it if possible
- ➢ Because of the dislike of work, most people must be coerced, controlled, directed, and threatened with punishment to get them to perform effectively
- ➢ The average person lacks ambition, avoids responsibility, security and economic rewards above all else
- ➢ Most people lack creative ability and are resistant to change
- ➢ Since most people are self-centred, they are not concerned with the goals of the organization

In existing system of performance appraisal, performance is assessed in dimensions such as knowledge, capability, suitability, leadership, capacity, and physical fitness. Personal traits such as; honesty, sincerity, dependability, integrity, punctuality are considered. The present system is neither open nor data based. The results of the appraisal are not communicated to appraisee so it doesn't contribute to improve the performance. Moreover the performance appraisal is carried out by superiors that has nothing to do with learning of the students or satisfaction of the stakeholders.

3. Use of Existing Performance Appraisal Reports

The scope of the existing performance appraisal system is very limited in technical institutions. Some of the uses are listed in exhibit 18.2.

Exhibit No. 18.2: Uses of existing performance appraisal

- Confirmation after completion of probation period on the basis of good performance
- Giving special and prestigious projects to competent and experienced people
- Placement to superior positions following selection procedure
- Transfer within the institution or to other institution
- Issue warning in case of undesirable and illegal behaviour is found
- Initiation of disciplinary process and imposition of punishment

The use of existing performance appraisal is dependable on the mercy of superiors. They can use it in the manner they desire because it is subjective.

4. Deficiencies in Existing Performance Appraisal System

There are number of deficiencies reported in existing performance appraisal system in technical institutions. Some of the significant deficiencies are listed in exhibit 18.3.

Exhibit No. 18.3: Deficiencies in existing performance appraisal system

➢ One way ➢ Vague ➢ General ➢ Not quantitative and qualitative ➢ Self-appraisal is not very well organized ➢ Biased and based on opinions ➢ Based on traits ➢ Lack of transparency ➢ One time activity ➢ Weak link to career advancement ➢ Inadequate opportunity to work in areas of interest ➢ Non-realization of employees needs	➢ No guidelines for adverse comments ➢ Lack of feedback ➢ Assessment on the basis of subjective information ➢ Subjective ➢ Lack of trust ➢ Results are not used for planning ➢ Lack of openness ➢ Inadequate participation of appraisee ➢ Absence of agreed criteria for appraisal ➢ Based on past performance ➢ Not used for development purpose

5. Emerging Concept of Performance Appraisal

The concept of performance appraisal is based on theory Y assumptions. These assumptions are listed in exhibit 18.4.

Exhibit No. 18.4: Theory Y assumptions

➢ The expenditure of physical and mental effort in work is as natural as play or rest ➢ People exercise self-direction and self-control in the service of objectives to which they are committed ➢ Commitment to objectives is a function of the rewards associated with achievement	➢ The average person learns, under proper conditions, not only to achieve but to seek responsibility ➢ The capacity to exercise a relatively high degree of imagination, ingenuity, and creativity in the solution of organizational problems is widely distributed in the population

Performance appraisal technique has been used for a long time in various forms. Its definition and purpose changed time-to-time. The assessment and evaluation of individuals and groups performance was given different names by different authors. Some of key points recently given by various authors and practitioner related to definitions and concepts of performance appraisal are listed in exhibit 18.5.

Exhibit No. 18.5: Key points of performance appraisal

Performance appraisal is ➢ a judgment of individuals' behaviour and certain related personal characteristics as manifested in her/his work. ➢ an instrument for developing morale and attitudes to achievement and result orientation, both in individuals and in work groups. ➢ assessment of an individual's strengths and weaknesses in specific areas of her/his work responsibilities and duties. ➢ an appraisal of the performance of an individual in her/his assigned duties and responsibilities. ➢ well-designed self-learning process leading to step by step correction and improvement in the performance. ➢ undertaken in order to develop competence related to role at work. ➢ used to improve the human performance on significant and core business dimensions. ➢ a real constructive feedback to individuals and teams for improvement ➢ a base for training, counselling, guidance and coaching for individuals and teams. ➢ an opportunity of learning for superiors and subordinates for bringing continuous improvement. ➢ organized, systematic and regular process for human resources development.

(*Contd.*)

(*Contd.*)

➢ a summarization of past performance, considerations of present and decision on future direction. ➢ a process through which an individual employee's behaviour and accomplishments for a fixed time period are measured and evaluated. ➢ a systematic and objective way of judging the ability of an employee in performing her/his task. ➢ analysis of causes of performance to reinforce positive causes and remove negative causes. ➢ assessing potential of individuals and teams for future improvement. ➢ a systematic method of obtaining, analysing, and recording information about a person that is needed for deployment. ➢ useful in human resources recruitment, human resources planning, human resources researches, human resources development and human resources recognition. ➢ a two-way discussion between appraiser and appraisee on plan and outcome.

It is necessary to understand the concept of performance considering what is not performance appraisal. The non-examples of the performance appraisal are listed in exhibit 18.6.

Exhibit No. 18.6: What is not performance appraisal

➢ The management telling the employee what s/he did wrong ➢ A secret report that the employee never sees ➢ Another name for disciplinary interview	➢ An attack on the employee or a character assassination ➢ A salary discussion ➢ Interview for promotion ➢ Explanation call on undesired behaviour

6. Purpose of Performance Appraisal

The performance appraisal serves variety of purposes for individuals, groups and organization. This system focuses on development of individuals and groups. The purpose of performance appraisal system for institution is listed in exhibit 18.7 and for individuals is listed in exhibit 18.8.

Exhibit No. 18.7: Purpose of performance appraisal for institution

The performance appraisal is useful for: ➢ Participative and integrated planning for development of the institution	➢ Identifying existing and potential problems ➢ Job design and job enrichment ➢ Improving quality of academic services and product

(*Contd.*)

(*Contd.*)

➢ Realistic planning incorporating the competence, capability and resources of the institution ➢ Obtaining commitment for work ➢ Increasing productivity ➢ Deciding rewards ➢ Training needs analysis ➢ Deciding promotions ➢ Empowerment of individuals and teams ➢ Enhancing corporate reputation ➢ Improving work related relationship ➢ Responding to changing needs ➢ Resolving disputes related to performance on the basis of records ➢ Sustaining the performance ➢ Removing performance obstacles, such as inadequate resources, cultural problems, non-cooperative attitude	➢ Allocating funds for training of faculty and staff ➢ Redeployment of employees ➢ Documenting performance record ➢ Succession planning ➢ Recognition of merit ➢ Drawing the profile of the institutional members ➢ Effective communication ➢ Harnessing the untapped potential for developmental research and innovative work ➢ Introducing change and innovation ➢ Role clarity and accountability ➢ Collective learning about the business of the institution ➢ Distinguishing the performance of individuals

Exhibit No. 18.8: Purpose of performance for individual

The performance appraisal is useful for: ➢ Self-improvement ➢ Self-evaluation ➢ Career development ➢ Improving relationship with students and stakeholders ➢ Identifying strengths and weakness ➢ Exploring new opportunities for development ➢ Identifying self-potential ➢ Seeking cooperation from superiors, peers and subordinates	➢ Improving self-confidence ➢ Increasing job satisfaction ➢ Identifying training needs ➢ Identifying resources requirement to perform the role effectively and efficiently ➢ Time planning ➢ Knowing desired and undesired behaviour ➢ Setting performance improvement objectives ➢ Clarifying the roles and responsibility ➢ Collaborative learning ➢ Providing more autonomy to work

7. Characteristics of Performance Appraisal System

The performance appraisal system should be designed to serve its intended purposes. The performance appraisal system should have characteristics listed in exhibit 18.9.

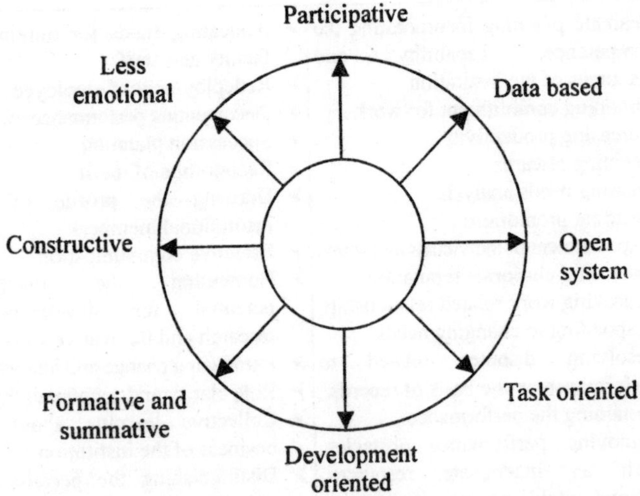

Exhibit No. 18.9: Characteristics of performance appraisal system

7.1 Participative

Performance appraisal should be participative. All the interested persons should be involved in the performance appraisal. In the language of total quality management internal as well as external customers should be involved in performance appraisal. The involvement of related persons should be from beginning itself. The post holder or a particular team sets objectives to be accomplished at the beginning of the academic session. This is right time when the related persons should be involved for setting performance standards and evolving effective strategy to reach the goals. Participation of related persons from beginning of the session will enhance the commitment of all parties for providing resources and help. Continuous interaction of the related persons is the key to success of performance appraisal system.

7.2 Data Based

The performance of an individual or a group should be evaluated on the basis of factual data and performance standards set during the planning stage. The objectives are set for the semester or a year. In the process of objective setting all the significant stakeholders are involved. Name of some of the plans are mentioned in the chapter on planning and time management. One can take the data from the various plans prepared in different areas of the functioning of the institute. The performance objectives should fulfil characteristics such as; clear and comprehensive, specific to the performance, measurable quantitatively and qualitatively, deliverable, in tune with the institution objectives, challenging, attainable, development oriented and observable. For all the significant performance objectives strong and direct indicators are generated so that during the implementation of the activities progress can be measured objectively. As indicated by Alto (2000) there are number of benefits envisaged by using indicators. The benefits are listed in exhibit 18.10.

Exhibit No. 18.10: Benefits of indicators

➢ Have an element of empowerment ➢ Enables performer to monitor results ➢ Make informed decisions based upon reliable performance information ➢ Diagnose problems and act quickly ➢ Learn from experience and integrate lessons learned ➢ Redundant activities can be abandoned	➢ Establish explicit links between project activities, outputs and results derived ➢ Provide a common frame work to discuss performance ➢ Learning about successful strategies there by successful endeavours can be repeated and mistakes avoided ➢ Experience can be shared and institutionalized

As performance appraisal is data based. Data on performance is generated for measuring objectives through indicators. Indicators help in making decisions regarding improvement in performance. This is based on the principle if we can measure performance, it can be manipulated. The position holder will record the data continuously in a systematic manner, which will provide her/him continuous feedback regarding the progress of the work. This kind of documentation will be an evidence of progress.

7.3 Open System

The open system of appraisal not only prevents doubts and apprehensions about the performance report but it also avoids the possibilities of grapevine communication. People learn from good examples and mistakes of others. Open system helps to build up trust in interpersonal relationship. It provides an opportunity to exchange views on performance.

7.4 Task Oriented

The performance appraisal should measure the accomplishment of objectives or results. It should be task or job or role based. The task-based objectives should be prioritized and performance should be appraised on significant tasks. Low importance should be given to the personality aspects.

7.5 Development Oriented

The performance appraisal should contribute for development of individuals, groups and organization. It should not be used for harassing or curbing the creativity of individuals and groups. It should provide inputs for development of individuals and teams.

7.6. Formative and Summative

As described in the guideline document that formative performance will help individuals to receive constructive feedback for continuous improvement in the performance. It will also help the individuals, departments and institutions to identify development needs and design training programmes to fulfil the needs. On other hand summative appraisal will help in assigning grades, motivating good performers and assigning them challenging and prestigious jobs.

7.7 Constructive

The performance appraisal is introduced in an institution for enhancing its effectiveness in delivering the goods and services. The introduction of performance appraisal in an institution is possible when it is constructive and focus on improvement of the performance. The system of appraisal where there is no fear of punishment.

7.8 Less Emotional

The system of appraisal based on facts and data is helpful in providing constructive feedback. It avoids the chances of incorporation of emotional parameters such as very old employee, performed very well during the crisis time, honest person, relative of influential person, never oppose the decisions of management and so on.

8. Problems in Performance Appraisal in Technical Institutions

Everyone wants to succeed and climb up the ladder and this is possible only when the superior helps. The performance appraisal system can be successful only when there is counselling. In an open system such as technical education the assessment of performance is difficult. Problems in introducing and implementing performance appraisal system and their broad solution in technical institutions are listed in exhibit 18.11 and exhibit 18.12 respectively.

Exhibit No. 18.11: Problems in implementation performance in technical institutions

Sl. No.	*Problems*	*Explanation*
1.	Shortage of staff	Shortage of staff at all levels in technical institution may affect the effective implementation of performance appraisal
2.	Resistance of change	Staff may show resistance to accept the new system due to lack of understanding and awareness
3.	Central tendency	The nature of performances may adopt the median in rating the performance
4.	Leniency of the appraiser	Because of temperament, some are generous or conservative, leading to inaccurate appraisal
5.	Error of similarity and contrast	Comparison of present performance with past performance
6.	Halo effect	Impression about a person on one or two dimension of work influencing the judgment
7.	Strong likes or dislikes of appraiser	The appraiser may be blind believer of something and if s/he found the performance of her/his liking s/he may high rate the performance than appraisee deserves
8.	Logical errors	Coming out with a logical explanation for the impression instead of data base judgment
9.	Proximal errors	The previous rating influencing the present judgment
10.	Mutual mistrust	The appraiser and appraisee do not trust each other
11.	Lack of detailed planning	Failure on the part of institution to clearly articulate goals and the relative importance attached to each

(*Contd.*)

(*Contd.*)

Sl. No.	*Problems*	*Explanation*
12.	Favouritism and nepotism	The appraiser may favour appraisee because of some distinct qualification and rate high. The distinct feature may not relate to performance on task
13.	Lack of opportunities for training	The faculty and staff development programmes in specific area may not be available
14.	Appraiser personal bias	Appraiser may be biased for something and if s/he found that indicator s/he may favourably rate high
15.	Too much paper work	For keeping the record of each and every incident and the performance level, lot of paper work is needed. This may be a problem for maintaining proper records.
16.	Rigorous planning	Performance appraisal requires rigorous planning, sufficient time and expertise
17.	Initially time consuming	Due to unawareness of the system it requires more initial time
18.	Huge demand of resources	People take an opportunity to grab resources through this system
19.	Support and guidance from superiors	Expertise may not be available in the institution to support and guide performance appraisal system
20.	Improper deployment of persons	May create vacuum or resistance
21.	Recent behaviour bias	Appraisal tends to be based more on recent performance than on the performance over the entire rating period.
22.	Inflation of rating	There is a tendency to inflate rating, which at times, happen over a period of time, or it may even happen at all times with some.
23.	Strictness bias	The strictness bias is just the opposite to leniency bias. It results from appraisers being too harsh in their evaluation of performance. Sometimes the strictness bias results because the appraisers want other to think that s/he is a "tough judge" of people performance. Both leniency and strictness errors more commonly occur when performance standards are vague

Exhibit No. 18.12: Some common strategies to overcome performance implementation problems

Sl. No.	*Problem*	*Strategies*
1.	Shortage of staff	➢ Part-time arrangement ➢ Guest lecturers ➢ *Ad hoc* appointments ➢ Promote self-learning ➢ Pursue for filling the vacant post ➢ Job enrichment of supporting staff ➢ Automation of office ➢ Sub-contract ➢ Collaborate with other institution
2.	Resistance to change	➢ Arrange awareness programmes ➢ Arrange training ➢ Introduce reward or incentive system ➢ Set realistic goals ➢ Involve staff in goal setting ➢ Take commitment of staff
3.	Central tendency	➢ Make the system data base ➢ Evaluate separately on each factor ➢ Playing safe must be avoided by proper training ➢ Taking appraisers in confidence
4.	Leniency of appraiser	➢ Proper training of appraisers ➢ Creating a culture of fairness and openers ➢ Bring to notice of appraiser the effects of improper appraisal ➢ Appraisal is for development and not for punishment
5.	Error of similarity and contrast	➢ No past records should be provided to appraisers ➢ Present performance should be compared with planned objectives ➢ As far as possible introduce objectivity in appraisal system
6.	Halo effect	➢ Appraisal of performance and not of personality ➢ Consideration of each appraisal factor separately and one at a time, carefully, accurately and objectively.
7.	Strong likes and dislikes	➢ Make rigorous planning ➢ Decide the performance levels and proficiency level in each factor ➢ Each factor should be considered
8.	Logical errors	➢ Keeping record of performance in each factor ➢ Create management information system ➢ Use simple formulas

(*Contd.*)

(*Contd.*)

Sl. No.	Problem	Strategies
9.	Proximal errors	➢ Each year new targets should be fix up ➢ Proper training of appraisee as per her/his need should be provided for improving the performance ➢ Provide guidance and counselling facility
10.	Mutual mistrust	➢ Take into confidence each employee ➢ Appraisal is for development not for punishment ➢ Make appraisal objective as far as possible ➢ Make appraisal reports open to all
11.	Failure on the post of institution to clearly articulate their goals	➢ Prepare institution development plans ➢ Decide priorities among the different activities and goals ➢ Strategic planning of activities ➢ Clearly identify the needs
12.	Favouritism, nepotism etc.	➢ Educate the appraiser on the purpose of performance appraisal ➢ Data base appraisal ➢ More objectivity ➢ Discourage favouritism
13.	Lack of programmes/ opportunities of faculty development	➢ Plan well in advance ➢ Decide possible ways of getting trained the persons at different places ➢ Organize in-house programme
14.	Raters personal bias	➢ Make performance data base ➢ Introduce more objectivity ➢ Create good management information system
15.	Too much paper work	➢ Use simplified formats ➢ Automation of office ➢ Use of software ➢ Training of personnel
16.	Vigorous planning	➢ Make long and short-term plans ➢ Keep minimum possible factors ➢ Be realistic in setting goals ➢ Make the work of appraiser structured and simple ➢ List the critical factors of performance
17.	Initially time consuming	➢ Plan well ➢ Carry out potential problem analysis ➢ Train the faculty and staff members before introduction of performance appraisal system ➢ Introduce performance appraisal system step-by-step

(*Contd.*)

(Contd.)

Sl. No.	*Problem*	*Strategies*
18.	Requires lot of resources	➢ Initially go for activities which require less resources ➢ Plan for resources procurement ➢ Prepare plan for internal revenue generation ➢ Timely prepare proposal for resources requirements
19.	Support and guidance from superiors	➢ Convince the superiors that their support is needed to make the performance appraisal system successful
20.	Deployment of persons	➢ Prepare deployment plans ➢ Involve staff in the preparation of plans ➢ Consider the interest of staff

9. Performance and Motivation

The performance is based on various theories of motivation. Performance appraisal focuses on promoting self urge to excel better using scientific tools, techniques and methods. Self-motivation can be increased using psychological and management aspects of motivation. As stated earlier in this chapter performance appraisal is based on Y theory of motivation. It is also based on the theory of goal setting. Individuals and teams involved in setting their own goals for performance will commit to it and put efforts to accomplish the goals because it is their dream and they would like to translate the dream in reality. They think that there is something worthwhile in the goals. The goal contributes towards development of the institution and it is the desire of employees as well. Employees pursue their own interest, hobby, and ability of setting their own goal. As the work progresses they get self-feedback on the progress of work. Self-feedback on the progress of the work is much stronger and motivating than external feedback. They get sense of satisfaction that in turn motivates them to further excel better to complete the work and achieve goals.

Performance appraisal is also based on theory of reinforcement. The individuals and teams are involved right from the planning process to completion of the task. They know each and every aspect of the work. Their achievements are appreciated, recognized, and rewarded by the management of the institution. Their undesirable behaviour is modified using constructive feedback. They feel that they are treated equally responsible and failure to perform is not a punishment but it is because of their deficiency and institution is providing support to modify the behaviour.

Performance appraisal is also based on theory of expectancy. The expectations of the self, team and stakeholders are clearly set in terms of goals and objectives. There is a challenge in the expectations. People are encouraged to enhance their willingness through guidance and support from the management. The associated rewards to achievement of the objectives are also clear to them. These rewards are spelled out during the time of performance planning. They are also spelled out in the policy of the institute.

Performance appraisal is also based on theory of job enrichment. Individuals and team prepare the performance plan. They know about the challenges involved in achieving the goals. At the same time they are granted full autonomy to work in their own way and achieve results. They get all necessary resources and support from the management. They receive feedback from the management at the end of every semester or a year. A sort of healthy competition is created in the institution to raise the level and quality of performance.

Performance appraisal is also based on theory of equality. Individuals and teams are encouraged to set and pursue different objectives in different areas and they are rewarded on the basis of the achievements and not on the basis of completion of so many years of service. Varieties of rewards are introduced to encourage employees to perform better and receive the reward.

Performance appraisal is based on theory of empowerment. People are empowered to work in the area of their choice at the same time area of importance of the institution. They are provided full freedom to prepare the performance plans and implement them. Management of the institution provides full guidance and support to achieve the objectives. Their performance related problems are solved periodically and constructive feedback is provided when demanded or required. People are fully empowered to do experimentation, research and excel better for the satisfaction of the students, employers and other stakeholders. People are encouraged to take risk and work in uncertainty. Management of the institution has trust in their competence and performance.

10. Methods of Performance Appraisal

There are number of methods of performance appraisal prevalent in different organizations. A brief account of significant methods is given in subsequent paragraphs.

10.1 Merit Rating

Usually in this method, criteria are listed and each criterion is given a rating depending on the quality of performance, for example, excellent, very good, good, fair, and poor. The criteria used vary enormously from one scheme to another. There are two major disadvantages of merit rating. First, the criteria are normally subjective and therefore difficult to measure. The subjectivity in measurement frequently results in friction between the boss and the subordinate. Second, most managers are inclined to tick the middle of the scale rather than extremes of good or bad. So most of the subordinates are appraised as "average".

10.2 Written Statement

The biggest difference between the merit rating and the written statement is that the people doing the appraisal are required to write their views-not just put a tick against the criteria under consideration. This has great advantage of making the appraiser to give more thought to what s/he wants to say to it. However, the ultimate success of this method again depends on the criteria and the questions asked and answered. Also, the criteria are still largely subjective. In some cases, merit-rating and written-assessment schemes encourage to write down assessments without talking to the subordinate.

10.3 Management by Objectives

To minimize the difficulties of 'personality' and therefore subjectivity, the management by objectives was introduced. Management of objectives encouraged people to set objectives of their preferences and design strategies to achieve them. It helps subordinates to ask for appropriate resources and support from management of the institution. It is good way to seek approval of the management on the objectives. Since the objectives are measurable quantitatively and qualitatively so at the end of the semester or year one can prove the level of performance achievement.

10.4 Target Setting

Some organizations measure the performance of individuals through a system called target setting a simpler form than management of objectives.

This works best when boss and subordinate regularly discuss priority for action. Targets are then set for the subordinate, and achievements are likewise reviewed on a regular basis, that is, six monthly or quarterly basis.

11. Development of Performance Formats

The performance appraisal for individuals and teams is carried out using well designed formats. The format may be same or different for different faculty members and staff members. It all depends on the business of the institution. It is suggested that format for faculty members should be same. Similarly format for staff members should also be same. The parameters of the format for faculty members and staff members may vary. The institution can also design a comprehensive coded format and respective members of the faculty and staff may use the relevant parameters for performance planning and assessment. The format of performance measurement should be designed cautiously keeping in mind the characteristics listed in exhibit 18.13.

Exhibit No. 18.13: Characteristics of formats of performance appraisal

The format of performance appraisal should:

- cover core parameters of performance of the institution, teams and individuals.
- enlist objective parameters.
- focus on end results of performance as well as process.
- specify significant behaviour parameters that may be in the form of values, beliefs, ethics, norms and other cultural and institutional dimensions.
- be simple to understand, easy of fill, less time to fill up and simple to communicate.
- encourage to do rigorous planning.
- be easy to track the performance and take feedback on progress.
- promote objective interpretation of data and performance.
- measure all dimensions of performance with proportionate weightage
- promote valid and reliable data collection.
- promote participation of people in planning, implementing and evaluation of results.
- benchmark for results on various parameters indicated in the format.
- be developed respondent-wise.
- not embarrass the appraisee and appraiser .

12. Parameters of Performance Assessment

The parameters of performance assessment vary from institution to institution. The parameters can be categorized on various dimensions of institutional functioning and thrust of development. Kumar (1996) has prepared the validated list of activities carried out in the technical institutions. He has listed 24 activities mentioned in exhibit 18.14. He classified activities 1 to 8 as teaching, activities 9 to 14 as research, activities 15 to 18 as extension and activities 19 to 24 as other activities.

Exhibit No. 18.14: Activities performed by teachers of engineering institutions

1. Classroom teaching 2. Practical work 3. Demonstration 4. Tutorials 5. Fieldwork 6. Evaluation work – internal and external 7. Remedial instruction 8. Counselling 9. Guidance for research 10. Paper publication-research and review articles 11. Reports of innovative practices 12. Curriculum development 13. Publication of books and project reports 14. Consultancy 15. Taking part in community work – flood and draught relief, peace, humanism, small family norms, National Cadet Core, National Literacy Mission etc.	16. Organization of camps for helping old age people, for eye operation, spectacles etc. 17. Organizing orientation programmes for teachers, workers, farmers, industrialists regarding new developments 18. Organizing blood donation camps 19. Taking part in co-curricular activities like examination duties, admission work, organization of workshops, seminars, debates, picnics and cultural activities 20. Organizing games, sports, hostels etc. 21. Membership of various bodies/ committees on education and national development 22. Organizing placement programme of students for internship 23. Membership of professional bodies, societies etc. 24. Editorship of journals, magazines etc.

Khedkar, Tarnekar and Kothari (1999) suggested five major areas for performance appraisal of technical teachers. They have classified these areas under teaching, research and development, admission work, consultancy, faculty exchange and continuing education. They further divided these broad areas in sub areas and assigned weightage to each sub-area. They have suggested relative distribution of weightage for Head of department, Reader, Assistant Professor and Lecturer under each area. They have suggested 50 per cent weightage for teaching, 10 per cent for research and development, 10 per cent for admission work, 10 per cent for consultancy, and 10 per cent for faculty exchange programme for lecturer of post-graduate institute. However, Umale and Gupta (2002) conducted research in the area of performance appraisal in technical education has recommended that 50 per cent weightage for academics, 20 per cent weightage for research, 20 per cent weightage for administrative and 10 per cent weightage for development and extension activities should be given to appraise the performance of the lecturers. It has also recommended that 50 per cent weightage should be given to the appraisal marks assigned by self, 20 per cent to head of department, 20 per cent to students, and 10 per cent to principal of the institution. This study was conducted for teachers of polytechnic colleges. However, institutions can decide the weightage to be given to parameters and to the appraiser and make it clear to all the internal and external stakeholders of the institution. The weightage for different teachers may be different looking to the job responsibility of individuals.

The formats are designed on the basis of educational outputs, processes, and inputs. The performance can be measured on the basis of achievement on outputs, processes and inputs. The behaviour component can be measured separately on behaviour parameters.

The institution should prepare guidelines for performance appraisal. In this document the key areas of performance for individuals and teams can be mentioned. The individuals and teams can select the activities and objectives from there. They can prepare the plan to achieve set performance targets. The institution should do benchmarking for significant and key areas. That would establish minimum target for everyone to choose. The guidelines for performance appraisal should be based on the vision document of the institution.

Factors Responsible for Performance Appraisal of Teachers

Umale and Gupta (2002) have found out factors responsible for performance of teachers in polytechnic institutions. These factors are classified in two categories that are individual and institutional. These factors are listed in exhibit 18.15 and exhibit 18.16 respectively.

Exhibit No. 18.15: Rank order of performance appraisal factors for individuals by principal, head of department and lecturers

1. Teacher competence	8. Proper planning and coordination
2. Knowledge	9. Communication skills
3. Attitudes towards work	10. Expertise
4. Confidence in work	11. Job satisfaction
5. Commitments in the work	12. Good health
6. Abilities to perform the task	13. Support by family
7. Creativity and innovation	

Exhibit No. 18.16: Rank order of performance appraisal factors for institution by principal, head of department and lecturers

1. Team sprit	8. Environmental opportunities
2. Feedback from stakeholders	9. Opportunities provided to individuals to demonstrate competence
3. Institutional climate	
4. Student quality	
5. Staff development planning and implementation	10. Grievances handling system
	11. Fulfilment of personal goals
6. Selection and promotion criteria and policies	12. Transfers
	13. Recognition by peers and others
7. Physical facilities and resources availability	14. Financial incentives

13. Performance Appraisers

All significant stakeholders appraise the performance of the individual. For example, for a faculty member self, head of the department, peers, subordinates and students, should appraise the performance. Client organization and other important stakeholders can further measure the performance of the faculty member.

All appraisers should be trained in assessing and evaluating the performance. They have to play a significant but delicate role during the process of appraisal. On the basis of performance appraisal they should be able to provide constructive feedback to appraisee for improvement on performance. They should be able to identify the development needs of the appraisee. If immediate boss is the appraiser s/he should give appropriate rewards for the excellent performance so that desired behaviour is sustained and improved in future. There could be difficulty in understanding between an appraiser and appraisee. The understanding should be maximized during the process of appraisal. More emphasis should be given on facts and data during the process of appraisal. One should not indulge in feelings and intuition. The outcomes of the appraisal process need to be recorded and communicated to the appraisee to build trust and confidence. The appraiser should act as a good facilitator to improve the performance during formative appraisal process. If the appraisee is facing some problems during the process of appraisal these should be tackled properly.

The appraiser should be good motivator. During the critical stage of performance appraisal s/he may assist and help the appraisee. During the performance stage s/he may act as a good trainer, coach and mentor instead of demonstrating the supervisory or policing role. The appraiser should be able to act as a source of energy and inspiration for the appraisee. In fact appraiser and appraisee act together right from the beginning when the process of planning takes place. Appraiser needs to be a good listener and at the same time s/he should be good in preparing the summary and presenting the mirror image to appraisee. During the formative process of appraisal the appraiser should make all the resources available in absence of which the appraisee is unable to perform in a desired manner. S/he should be impartial and fair in her/his act of appraisal. The process of appraisal can only take place successfully if there is open and effective communication. There is no accusation or blaming from both the sides. The appraisers should act as good role model. When colleagues carry out appraisal they do not point out the areas for improvement. They admire the performance of the fellow member. This practice harms the whole purpose of performance. When superiors carry out performance appraisal they point out their expectations rather than eliciting strengths and weaknesses.

When subordinates carry out performance appraisal they make complaints regarding not making available the requisite resource in time and poor leadership. When customers carry out performance appraisal they point out gaps in services and product. When students appraises the performance of the teachers they complaint about low marks received by them in the tests and practical rather than emphasizing on how to improve teaching learning process. They never appreciate the good points in a teacher and her/his style. Different types of appraisers appraise the performance from their point of view. This may give incomplete picture of performance appraisal. Someone should present the holistic picture of appraisal. All the appraisers should be trained to do performance appraisal otherwise the whole purpose of performance may go in vein. They can be trained in building relationship with appraisee, communication skills, filling the prescribed formats, analysing the performance records, drawing conclusions, giving feedback in positive way, and understanding the reactions of the appraisee during the process of feedback. In summary the appraiser plays a positive role in improving the performance of the appraisee. The appraiser should use guidelines stated in exhibit 18.17 during the process of providing feedback to appraisee.

Exhibit No. 18.17: Guidelines for providing feedback

➢ Be sensitive to the mood of the appraisee ➢ Use acceptable sentences ➢ Be clear and specific ➢ Focus on performance and desired behaviour ➢ Express suggestions in positive way ➢ Provide timely feedback	➢ Be brief and objective ➢ Provide opportunity to clarify doubts ➢ Explore opportunities for development ➢ Focus on strengths as well as weaknesses ➢ Use simple sentences ➢ Listen to appraisee ➢ Be respectful

14. Appraisee

People who feel good about them tend to perform well. Those with a good self-image need not be defensive. They can focus on achieving new goals at higher levels of performance. They are likely to be more pleasant, interested, flexible, cooperative and supportive to others.

How to Receive Constructive Feedback for Improvement

When receiving constructive feedback, the goal of appraisee should be to help the appraiser to provide information about her/his performance and behaviour. The appraisee should appreciate that the appraiser has put lot of time, energy and efforts to observe the performance and records to find out the performance related strengths and weaknesses. S/he has organized the information to provide constructive feedback to the appraisee. Without their efforts appraisee would not have an opportunity to act on it. Let the appraiser provide the feedback and the appraisee can note it down without any reaction. Later on the appraisee can reflect on it and design strategies for improvement. The appraisee can follow guidelines suggested in exhibit 18.18 while receiving the feedback.

Exhibit No. 18.18: Guidelines for receiving feedback

➢ Keep an open mind ➢ Listen to understand ➢ No interruption ➢ No reaction ➢ Clarify your doubts	➢ Keep reality in perspective ➢ Express your appreciation ➢ Discuss strategies for improvement ➢ Ask for guidance ➢ No personal blame on appraiser ➢ Show interest in feedback

15. Models of Performance Appraisal

There are various models proposed by experts over the years. Some of the models are described briefly in following paragraphs:

15.1 360-Degree Feedback

All the stakeholders measure the performance of an individual or a team. They measure the performance on quality of services and behaviour of the performer. They measure performance using scientific tools and techniques. They measure in detail the behaviour and competencies shown by the individual and group in achieving goals. They promote empowerment and trust in the institution. Every stakeholder measures the strengths and areas of development of appraisee. The stakeholders measure the behaviour of the individuals and teams objectively. The feedback of the stakeholders is used on development, team building, validation of the training, organizational development and raising remuneration.

15.2 Key Performance Area Model

Each member in the institution identifies the key job area and formulates objectives to be achieved on the basis of these areas. Superiors and collegues validate the objectives. On the basis of these objectives individuals prepare a plan for implementation. Thy spell out the significant activities, time frame, resources required and support required. Individuals also indicate performance criteria in the plan. The plan is prepared for a year. Superiors and performers validate the plan and criteria for performance appraisal. Individuals implement the plan and monitor the progress. They solve the implementation problem during formative appraisal. Superiors and subordinates carry out the terminal appraisal jointly at the end of the year. The results of the appraisal are used for preparing training plan, rewarding individuals, counselling poor performers, giving inputs to next year plan.

15.3 Three-phase Appraisal Model

Three-phase appraisal model is developed at SBM Polytechnic Bombay and is reported by Shah (1991). This model proposes introductory phase, formative phase and developmental phase. This model systematically spells out the stages of performance appraisal and various steps to be followed in each phase. The major activities proposed in this model are criteria specification, goal setting, performance analysis and review. Format for performance appraisal of the faculty member is also suggested in the paper.

16. Performance Appraisal Implementation Model

The performance appraisal in the institution should be implemented systematically. The major steps of implementation of performance appraisal system in institution are stated in exhibit 18.19 and briefly described in subsequent paragraphs.

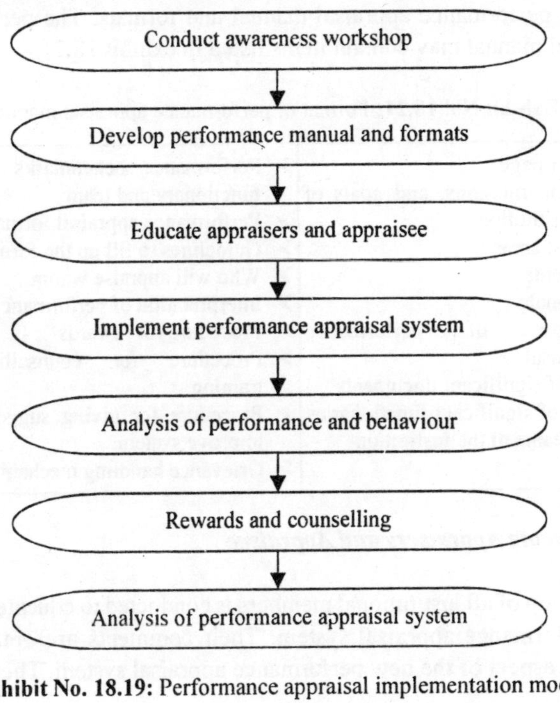

Exhibit No. 18.19: Performance appraisal implementation model

16.1 Conduct Awareness Workshop

The institution should conduct awareness workshop for all the internal members of the institution. The indicative agenda for the workshop are listed in exhibit 18.20.

Exhibit No. 18.20: Agenda for awareness workshop

➢ Concept of performance appraisal ➢ Benefits of performance appraisal ➢ Method of performance appraisal ➢ Formats for performance appraisal ➢ Method of data collection ➢ Record keeping for performance appraisal	➢ Performance reporting ➢ Feedback on performance appraisal ➢ Inputs such as counselling, training, coaching, system improvement etc. after appraisal ➢ Rewards

16.2 Develop Performance Manual and Formats

A workshop of selected representatives of all groups is conducted to develop performance appraisal manual and formats. The performance appraisal manual may contain items listed in exhibit 18.21.

Exhibit No. 18.21: Format of performance appraisal manual

➢ Cover page ➢ Vision, missions, and goals of the institution ➢ Thrust areas ➢ Contents ➢ Rationale ➢ Purpose of performance appraisal ➢ List of significant documents ➢ Role of significant functionaries and teams of the institution	➢ Performance benchmarks for each functionary and team ➢ Performance appraisal formats ➢ Guidelines to fill up the formats ➢ Who will appraise whom ➢ Interpretation of performance ➢ Procedure for rewards ➢ Procedure for counselling and training ➢ Procedure for giving suggestions to improve system ➢ Grievance handling mechanism

16.3 Educate Appraisers and Appraisee

A workshop of all institutional members is conducted to educate them on new performance appraisal system. Their comments are obtained on practical aspect of the new performance appraisal system. Their doubts are clarified and commitment is obtained for implementation. The agenda for performance appraisal education workshop are listed in exhibit 18.22.

Exhibit No. 18.22: Agenda for performance appraisal education workshop

➢ Explanation of the manual ➢ Procedure of the appraisal ➢ Format filling trial ➢ Appraisal process and its schedule	➢ Clarifying difficulties ➢ Training of counseller ➢ Demonstration of counselling ➢ Demonstration of feedback offering

16.4 Implement Performance Appraisal System as per Schedule

Complete the Performance Plan: The process of performance appraisal starts at the beginning of the academic year says in the month of June. The institution provides the format to all the institutional members and groups to fill up the formats on the basis of institutional and individual plans. The performance plans are prepared on the basis of inputs mentioned in exhibit 18.23. After a week time the institution/department may organize the presentation of individual plans to validate and refine the plans. Plans are approved in the presentation session itself.

Exhibit No. 18.23: Inputs for performance plan

➢ Vision and mission ➢ Strategic plan ➢ Perspective plan ➢ Annual plan ➢ Priorities for next year ➢ Previous year appraisal reports ➢ Team plans for projects ➢ Departmental plans ➢ Thrust areas ➢ Benchmarks ➢ Training plans ➢ Employability and feedback from stakeholders ➢ National/State goals	➢ Results of potential assessment tests such as carrier advancement interview and psychometric tests ➢ Individual plans: • Curriculum planning for all subjects • Subject plans • Lesson plans • Plan for industrial training of students • Instructional material development plan • Research plan • Continuing education plan • Consultancy plan • Research scholar guide plan • Vacation plan • Self-training plan

Implement the Plan: Individuals and teams work on the plan throughout the year. They maintain records of the progress. They note important achievements against performance plan. Performers and the management jointly solve the implementation problems. If additional targets are assigned to individuals and teams they are included in the plan. They note down the significant learning took place and major barriers faced to implement the plan. Individuals and teams carry out implementation of plan. Process listed in exhibit 18.24 are carried out during the implementation of performance appraisal system.

Exhibit No. 18.24: Processes to carry out plan

➤ Develop performance plans on the basis of above listed plans ➤ Provide resources to implement the plans ➤ Provide training, guidance and support ➤ Solve individual and team performance problems ➤ Encourage individuals and teams to perform as per plan ➤ Ask individuals and teams to maintain records of achievements against performance indicators ➤ Conduct regular department/ inter-departmental meetings	➤ Assist individuals and teams to do monitoring of progress ➤ Fill up the formats at the end of the year ➤ Do self assessment ➤ Ask all other relevant stakeholders to do assessment in the prescribed format ➤ Do appraisal in the environment of mutual trust and confidence ➤ Submit the assessment to head of the department ➤ Head of the department submits the complied appraisal report to the director of the institution ➤ Take review every month regarding progress of the work

Presentation on Achievement: At the end of the academic year the individuals, teams and departments are asked to make presentation on achievement of the planned targets. They make the presentation on the points listed in exhibit 18.25.

Exhibit No. 18.25: Presentation on achievement

➤ Performance plan ➤ Modifications made during implementation ➤ Problems encountered during implementation ➤ Causes of problems encountered ➤ Achievements	➤ Learning during implementation ➤ Inputs for next year plan ➤ Relationship with people ➤ What improvements should be made in the system to enhance individual and team effectiveness ➤ Question answer during presentation

Once the presentation of the appraisee is over the appraisers can submit their appraisal about the appraisee to the head of the department. For example, for a lecturer 30 per cent peers and supporting staff associated to the appraisee can be asked to provide feedback in the prescribed format. These appraisers maintain record of the appraisee through out the year on the parameters prescribed in the format. Ten per cent students can be asked to provide feedback in the prescribed format.

16.5 Analysis of Performance and Behaviour

The head of the department compiles the feedback information for the departmental members and analyse the performance data. The performance of teachers can be analysed on the results of the students. A comparative chart is prepared to show the comparison of results of students on different subjects in the institute. The concerned teachers can be rewarded for best performance or counselled for poor result. Similarly the performance is analysed against the plan, performance parameters and benchmarking. S/he interprets the data of the department and draws conclusions for common training, coaching, mentoring, counselling. S/he also draws conclusions to bring improvement in the system to make it more effective and efficient to remove hurdles and barriers to performance. S/he prepares the plan to provide constructive feedback to individuals and groups for improving the performance.

16.6 Rewards and Counselling

The head of the institution gives rewards to excellent performers. The varieties of rewards are given to outstanding performers in the institutions. These rewards are declared in the reward policy of the institution. The outstanding performers get open recognition for excellent performance. The counselling is carried out of poor performers. The head of the department or expert counsellor carry out counselling of individuals and teams. The counselling is carried out to improve specific skills or behaviour or both. S/he uses professional counselling techniques to carry out the counselling. Emphasis on positive thinking and positive attitude is given during counselling process. The counsellor uses positive, constructive and strong techniques for counselling.

16.7 Analysis of the Results of the Performance Appraisal

The reports of all the departments are submitted to the director of the institution. S/he analyses the repots and prepares a compiled report at institution level. This report is used for the purposes stated in exhibit 18.26.

Exhibit No. 18.26: Use of performance appraisal report prepared at institute level

➢ Discuss achievements and deficiencies at institution level with all the institutional member ➢ Celebrate success ➢ Distribute the rewards to outstanding performers ➢ Identification of developmental needs, training needs, opportunities for motivation	➢ Plan and arrange for individual and team feedback, counselling, coaching and training in case of deficiencies ➢ Give inputs to training plan ➢ Give inputs to next year plan ➢ Report to governing body ➢ Communicate to stakeholders

17. Assessment Centres

A trained team of three to five people in the institution uses the scientific methods of assessment to assess the potential of groups and individuals. Variety of psychometric tests, interviews, peer ratings, simulation and action learning exercises are carried out to assess the potential of individuals and groups. The assessment results are used for signing new contracts, organizing new training programmes, starting new programmes and so on.

18. Summary

Performance appraisal is a recent concept of assessing the performance of individuals and teams. The existing performance appraisal system in institutions is poorly designed and does not focus on assessing the performance of the people. Rather it emphasises on traits of the people. It does not encourage people to develop their competencies. It is used for punishing the people. The new performance appraisal system emanates from the plans of the institutions and roles of the individuals. It focuses on performance and development of the people that is based on the needs of the plan and role of the people. New performance appraisal system is open, data based, transparent, participative, objective, task oriented, formative and summative. It focuses on development of people and based on theory Y of motivation that is people are creative, innovative, self-motivated and responsible. The new performance appraisal system is based on positive thinking and reward system. The new performance appraisal system emphasises on assessing the performance of the individuals and teams by all significant stakeholders including students.

The new system can be designed and implemented in the institution following the principles of management and involving people. The performance appraisal formats are designed for each position and appraisers of that position. For example, for the post of lecturer there would be separate formats such as self-appraisal format, format for superiors, format for subordinates, format for peers and format for students. Each appraiser assesses the performance of the person related to her/his stake and provides constructive feedback for improvement. The feedback is considered to be very important for the individuals and groups for improving the performance. The institution can take common steps such as counselling, mentoring, training for the development of the individuals and teams.

19. Activity

Activity 1–Formats of Performance Appraisal

Formats of performance appraisal for lecturer are given on subsequent pages. These formats can suitably modified and refined to match the requirement of the institution and individuals. These formats are prepared for self-appraisal, appraisal by superiors, appraisal by peers, appraisal by subordinates and appraisal by students. Modify the formats and use them for your institution.

Performance appraisal for teachers

Name of the teacher: ....
Designation: ....
Name of the institute: ....
Duration of appraisal: ....

A. *Self-appraisal*

1. Performance of engaging lectures

Sl. No.	*Class/ Course*	*Subject taught*	*No. of lectures target*		*No. of lectures actually engaged*		*Reasons for shortfall*	*Remarks*
			I term	*II term*	*I term*	*II term*		

2. Performance of engaging practical

Sl. No.	*Class/ Course*	*Subject taught*	*No. of lectures target*		*No. of lectures actually engaged*		*Reasons for shortfall*	*Remarks*
			I term	*II term*	*I term*	*II term*		

3. Attendance of students

Sl. No.	*Class/ Course*	*Subject taught*	*Average Percentage of students attended in class*		*Reasons for less attendance, if any*	*Remarks*
			I term	*II term*		

4. Performance of Results (Theory subjects)

Sl. No.	*Class/ Course*	*Subject taught*	*No. of students*		*No. of students obtained marks*			
			Appeared	*Passed*	*Above 75%*	*60-75%*	*40-60%*	*Below 40%*

5. (a) Whether teaching plan was prepared? Yes/No
   (b) If yes whether same was implemented Yes/No
   If no give reason
   (c) Whether teaching aid was used during class Yes/No
   (d) If yes, mention type and number
   (i) Overhead projector transparencies
   (ii) Models
   (iii) Charts
   (iv) Power point presentations
   (e) If no give reason
   (f) Teaching aid prepared for the year

Sl. No.	*Type*	*Number*

(g) Number of extra classes conducted
(h) Number of students guided in project
(i) Nature of guidance given

6. Examination Work

Sl. No.	*Type of work*	*Planned*	*Completed*	*Reason for non-completion*
1.	Question paper setting			
2.	Answer book assessed			
3.	Worked as external/internal examiner			
4.	Invigilation duty			
5.	Others			

7. Visits

Sl. No.	*Particulars*	*Planned*	*Attended*	*Reason for shortfall*
1.	No. of field visits			
2.	No. of educational visits			
3.	Short tour			
4.	Long tour			

8. Details of publications

Sl. No.	*Type*	*Planned*	*Achieved*	*Reason for shortfall*
1.	Technical paper			
2.	Books			
3.	Workbooks			
4.	Handouts			

9. Training for self-development

Sl. No.	*Type*	*Planned*	*Attended*	*Reason for shortfall*
1.	Short-term courses			
2.	Long-term courses			
3.	Seminars			
4.	Conferences			
5.	Delivering speech in other institute			

10. Member of professional organization

Sl. No.	*Name of organization*	*Position held*

11. Have you win any Award or Honors?

12. Student Guidance and Counselling

Sl. No.	*Particulars*	*Planned*	*Achieved*	*Reason for shortfall*
1.	Guidance to students about books and literature			
2.	Guidance about higher education/career planning			
3.	Guidance about job opportunities/entrepreneurship			

13. Internal Revenue Generation

Sl. No.	*Activity*	*Target*	*Achieved*	*Type of involvement*	*Reason for shortfall*

14. Co-curricular activities

Sl. No.	*Type*	*Planned*	*Achieved*	*Reason for shortfall*
1.	Organization of cultural programme			
2.	Sports			
3.	Contribution to maintaining students discipline			
4.	Worked as a resource person			

15. Maintenance work

Sl. No.	*Type of work*	*Planned*	*Achieved*	*Reason for shortfall*
1.	Preventive maintenance			
2.	Breakdown maintenance			
3.	Any other			

16. Administrative work

Sl. No.	*Name of work*	*Describe*
1.	Contribution to conduct Gymkhana activities	
2.	Worked as a social gathering in-charge	
3.	Worked in admission work	
4.	Activities related to cooperative store	
5.	Activities related to canteen	
6.	Rector/Warden	
7.	Election work	

17. Meeting with subordinate staff

Sl. No.	*Planned*	*Held*

18. Details of assistance provided to Head of Department for departmental work
19. Number of hours worked after office hours (average monthly)
20. Contribution to any other Government activities

Signature, Name and Designation of Lecturer

Performance Appraisal of Lecturer

B. *By Head of Department*

1. Percentage of lectures engaged against proposed posts
2. Average passing percentage subject-wise

Sl. No.	*Subject*	*Percentage*

3. Capacity to get work done by subordinate
4. Relation with colleagues and the public
5. Integrity and character
6. State of health
7. Willingness to work on computer
8. Number of days not reported to duty in time (punctuality)

9. Number lectures missed due to unauthorized absenteeism
10. Area in which improvement is required
11. Training needs
12. Do you agree with the self-appraisal
    (If not state specifically the remarks with which you do not agree)
13. Which of the following qualities can be seen
    (a) Dedication
    (b) Commitment
    (c) Punctuality
    (d) Intelligent
    (e) Discipline
    (f) Promptness
    (g) Innovative
    (h) Cooperative
14. Other performance

Signature, Name and Designation of the Appraiser

Performance Appraisal of Lecturer

C. *By Principal*

1. Number of complaints received, if any

HOD	*Peers*	*Students*	*Subordinate*	*Office*	*Parents*	*Industry*

2. Number of appreciation received, if any

HOD	*Peers*	*Students*	*Subordinate*	*Office*	*Parents*	*Industry*

3. Contribution to IRG
4. Special attitudes observed
5. Contribution to institutional development
6. Contribution to student's discipline
7. Suggested area for improvement
8. Overall performance based on appraisal received from head of department/peers/self/subordinates/students according to your opinion.

Signature, Name and Designation of the Appraiser

Performance Appraisal of Lecturer

D. *By Peers*

1. Number of occasion agreed to adjust Lecture/practical when requested
   Number of times opposed Number of times agreed
2. Number of occasions supported in extracurricular activities when approached
   Number of times opposed Number of times agreed
3. State the extent of following qualities observed in lecturer at work
   (a) Dedication
   (b) Commitment
   (c) Punctuality
   (d) Intelligent
   (e) Discipline
   (f) Promptness
   (g) Innovative
   (h) Cooperative

Signature, Name and Designation of the Peer

Performance Appraisal of Lecturer

E. *By Students*

Course and year: ....
Subject: ....
No. of students in class: ....
No. of contact hours/week: ....

A. *Classroom instruction*

Sl. No	*Items*	*Describe*
1.0	**Planning and organization**	
1.1	Teaching is well planned	
1.2	Objectives made clear	
1.3	Time used effectively	
1.4	Subject matter organized in logical sequence	
1.5	Thorough with subject matter	

Sl. No	*Items*	*Describe*
2.0	**Presentation/Communication**	
2.1	Uses simple, clear language	
2.2	Ensures students attention, interest	
2.3	Provide examples of concepts	
2.4	Uses diagrams/sketches for effective communication	
2.5	Ask questions to test understanding	
3.0	**Students participation**	
3.1	Ask questions to promote interaction	
3.2	Encourages students questioning	
3.3	Ensures learners activity in the class	
3.4	Ask thought provoking questions	
3.5	Encourages note taking by students	
4.0	**Media/Methods**	
4.1	Uses variety of teaching techniques	
4.2	Uses variety of media	
4.3	Chalk board work clean and systematic	
4.4	Provides useful printed notes	
4.5	Encourages use of library	
5.0	**Class management**	
5.1	Engages classes regularly	
5.2	Engages classes punctually	
5.3	Maintains discipline	
5.4	Gives times to individuals	
5.5	Covers all topics	
6.0	**Assignment**	
6.1	Provides useful assignments	
6.2	Conducts tests	
6.3	Returns assignments in time	
6.4	Provides constructive feedback on assignments	
6.5	Fairness in assessment	
7.0	**Overall performance**	
8.0	**Comments (if any)**	

B. *Laboratory instructor*

Sl. No.	*Item*	*Describe*
1.0	**Planning and organization**	
1.1	Well organized in terms of time and equipment	
1.2	Experiments relevant to curriculum	
1.3	Equipments/Instruments operational	
1.4	All prescribed experiments conducted	

Sl. No.	*Item*	*Describe*
1.5	Encourages questioning	
2.0	**Guidance**	
2.1	Provides clear directions	
2.2	Demonstrates procedure	
2.3	Available in laboratory for guidance	
2.4	Encourages questioning	
2.5	Provides instruction sheets	
2.6	Promotes discovery learning	
3.0	**Laboratory assignment**	
3.1	Appreciates concise, useful laboratory reports	
3.2	Emphasizes scientific reasoning	
3.3	Examines and returns assessed assignments in time	
3.4	Provides useful feedback on reports	
3.5	Assessment/Grading fair	
4.0	**Management**	
4.1	Engages classes regularly	
4.2	Engages classes punctually	
4.3	Maintains discipline	
4.4	Encourages initiative	
4.5	Gives individual attention	
5.0	**Overall performance**	
6.0	**Comments** (if any)	

Activity 2 – Performance Appraisal System

S.Z. Polytechnic is an autonomous polytechnic. It is a 40 years old polytechnic. This polytechnic offers 10 diploma and 5 post-diploma programmes in conventional and hi-tech disciplines including information technology. The Polytechnic has received huge resources from Central and State Governments for modernization and updating the facilities from time-to-time. It was also considered under Strengthening Technical Education project assisted by World Bank. Prof. B.L. Gupta has recently taken over the charge of the Principal. He is surprised to see the huge resources lying under utilized including the human resources. Prof. Gupta is Technical Teachers Training trained and he knows various management techniques to increase the utilization of resources. He believes in harnessing the potential of human resources. He thinks that if human resources are utilized properly utilization of other resources will improve automatically. Prof. Gupta has attended a week duration-training programme in Technical Teachers Training Institute, on enhancing faculty contribution. Prof. Shivagunde was the coordinator of the programme.

Prof. Shivagunde preached that there are number of factors, which can be redesigned for encouraging faculty members to excel better. Some of the factors he preached are listed below:

- Challenging work
- Interesting work
- Variety of work
- Freedom for action
- Responsibility
- Sense of accomplishment
- Opportunity for persons growth and development
- Recognition of achievements
- Friendly atmosphere and good working conditions
- Vision for the future
- Dynamic and shared leadership etc.

Prof. Shivagunde had also promoted the concept that plans should be prepared at institutional, departmental and individual level. Plans so prepared should be clear, specific, realistic and flexible. He had promoted the concept of 'Performance Appraisal' during the training programme. He preached that performance appraisal system should be well designed and introduced in the institution. It should be open, participative, data based, objective, transparent and flexible.

Each teacher should prepare individual plan in the beginning of the academic year. This plan should be in tune with the departmental and institutional plan. This idea clicked to Prof. B.L. Gupta, Principal of the Institute and he decided to implement the performance appraisal system in his institute along with other good factors. He called a meeting of head of departments and briefed them about the training programme he attended and shown his determination to introduce the performance appraisal system in the institution. He asked three head of departments of conventional discipline to revise the format of confidential report system. Three head of departments, who are experienced people, designed one format applicable to all levels of faculty and staff members. This format is a little bit modified version of the confidential report system format. They placed the format for approval before the principal. Principal Gupta was busy that moment of time and he was under pressure for organizing society meeting so with minor modification he approved the format and asked three head of departments to get it printed and distribute to all the faculty and staff members. They did so. One head of department out of three head of departments in the committee called all the faculty and staff members of his department. He fired them commenting about their unsatisfactory performance. He warned them and asked them to improve performance in left out period of the year. At the end of the year he appraised the performance of all the faculty and staff members. He assigned fair and good to all the faculty and staff members on all the dimensions of the format and asked them to improve upon the performance otherwise he will not tolerate next year. Two other head of departments have assigned very good to most of the faculty and staff members with few exceptions of good and excellent. Other head of departments did not take much interest in introducing the performance appraisal. They simply graded the performance as they used to do in the past. One head of department called a lecturer Mr. Asati and commented on his performance that he performed excellent but is being awarded good. If he continues to perform excellent next year also then he can be graded excellent. Some of the staff members were shirkers so most of the head of departments graded them fair or good. But one head of department issued show cause notice to one staff member for poor performance. As Principal Gupta received the appraisal report of faculty and staff members well in time but at the same time he received many complaints about head of departments. Some complaints were related to misappropriation of funds and misbehaviour. All the faculty and staff members were against the new system of performance appraisal. They met the Principal with the request to continue the previous system. They also threatened the Principal if their request is not accepted they will go on strike.

Issues for Discussion

Q.1 Was Principal's strategy to implement performance appraisal system okay?

(a) If yes, highlight the strengths of the strategy

(b) If no, state what are the weaknesses?

Q.2 Design suitable alternative strategies to implement performance appraisal system in S.Z. Polytechnic?

REFERENCES

Balu, S.A. (1991). Formative Evaluation of Teachers and Instruction. The Journal of Technical Education, ISTE, New Delhi, Vol. 14 No. 1.

Clive Fletcher, *Appraisal*, Jaico Publishing House, Mumbai.

Deshpande, N.H. (1992). Appraisal Review and Self-assessment ARSA—The Mirror, Evaluating Employee Performance. *Journal of Engineering Education*. Vol. V No. 4

Gp Capt N. Vijaya Kumar. *Performance Appraisal of Senior Level Managers – A Neglected Activity.*

Joglekar, M.V. (1999). Performance Evaluation of Technical Education Institute as a System for Total Quality. *The Indian Journal of Technical Education,* Vol. 22, No. 1

Keswani, C.A. (1991). Performance Appraisal System in Technical Institution, *The Indian Journal of Technical Education,* Vol. 14. No. 2.

Khedkar, M.K. (1999). A Performance Indicator for an Ideal Engineering College teacher, *The Journal of Technical Education,* Vol. 22, No. 1

Kumar, S. (1996). Performance Appraisal of Teachers in Technical Institutions. *The Journal of Technical Education, ISTE,* New Delhi, Vol. 14 No. 1.

Mithani, D.M.(2000). Towards Effective Worker Performance Evaluation: An Important Issue for the New Millennium. *NMIMS Management Review* Vol. XII No. 1.

Naik, B.M. (1991). Performance Planning and Appraisal: Why and How? *The Journal of Technical Education, ISTE,* New Delhi, Vol. 14 No. 1.

Natarajan, R. (1991). *Fundamental Concept of Performance Appraisal and Their Applicability to Faculty Appraisal and Development.*

Patrica King (1989). *Performance Planning and Appraisal,* McGraw-Hill Book Company.

Peter Ward (2004). *360 –Degree Feedback,* Jaico Publishing House, Mumbai.

Prem Chadha (2003). *Performance Management,* MacMillan India Limited.

Raju, G. J.V.J. (1995). Performance Appraisal and Development System, *The Journal of Technical Education,* Vol. 19, No. 2

Rao, C.R. (1991). *Formats for Performance Appraisal, The Journal of Technical Education, ISTE,* New Delhi, Vol. 14 No. 2.

Shah, D.J. (1991). Performance Appraisal and Development System at SBM Polytechnic: A Case Study. *The Indian Journal of Technical Education,* Vol. 14, No 4.

Shukla, R.N. (1998). Errors in Performance Appraisal System, *The Journal of Technical Education,* Vol. 21, No. 2.

Suganthi, L. (1993). *A Novel Performance Appraisal and Development System for Educational Institutions in the Wake of Total Quality Management.*

Tom Boydell and Malcolm Leary (1996). *Identifying Training Needs,* Universities Press (India) Limited.

Tracey, B. Weissw and Franklin Hartle (1998), *Reengineering the Performance Management,* St. Lucie Press Inc, U.S.A.

Vanveri, V.B. (1998). *Accountability of Faculty in Technical Institute by Performance Appraisal.The Journal of Technical Education, ISTE,* New Delhi, Vol. 22 No. 2.

Vedaiyan, S. (1991). *Performance Appraisal System; Objectives.*

Venkata Rao, R. (2000). Graph Theory and Matrix Approach for the Performance Evaluation of Technical Institutions. *The Journal of Technical Education, SITE,* New Delhi, Vol. 23 No. 2.

Venkateswarlu, P. Performance Appraisal and Its Problems. *Indian Journal of Training & Development,* New Delhi, Vol. XXX, No. 2.

19

Learning Organization

Objectives: The readers will be able to:

1. State the concept of learning organization.
2. Explain the need and importance of learning organization.
3. List the dimensions of learning organization.
4. Describe the benefits of learning organization.
5. Describe the assumptions of learning organization.
6. Describe the learning methods in learning organization.
7. Describe the shift required in traditional organization to become learning organization.
8. List the role of the leaders in the learning organization.
9. Assess the perception of the people on learning organization.
10. Prepare a plan to transform existing organization as learning organization.

1. Introduction

It is an organization in which people develop capacity and capability to strive for achieving organizational goals, missions, and vision using processes of continuous learning. It is an organization in which learning, thinking, and analysis of learning is encouraged to create innovative, forward looking and moving ahead organization. It is an organization in which people learn collectively about the business of the organization, its problems and future. They also learn individually and collectively to devise the ways and means to develop continuous learning environment in the organization. People working in the organization know that future of the organization is dependent on their ability, capacity and creativity. They appreciate that the future of the organization is dependent on their continuous learning about the changing business of the organization. They learn and contribute to meet the changing requirements of the organization.

The organization provides opportunities to its employees for learning and development. The organization appreciates that ways of learning for different people are different. The learning organization motivates employees to learn about the changing business of the organization and provides ample opportunities for continuous learning. Employees use their competencies for excellent contribution. The meaning of learning is continuous analysis of the core business and experiences taking place in the organization. Sharing work related experiences with individuals and teams. Experience sharing in the organization creates mutual learning and brings positive changes in the work related behaviour of people. Positive change in work related behaviour produces positive change in the performance of continuously changing organization. In learning organization human resources are the focus for all developmental activities. A relationship between learning organization and people is shown in exhibit 19.1.

Exhibit No. 19.1: Learning organization and people

In learning organization people:	
➢ are considered as resources and not as a burden on the organization. ➢ learn from their mistakes and they take measures not to repeat the mistakes. ➢ do experimentation to produce better results. ➢ are empowered to perform the duties. ➢ are granted autonomy to perform the task. ➢ are considered a source of creative and innovative ideas. ➢ are encouraged to participate in all important decisions related to development of the organization.	➢ are encouraged to question the rationale of important decisions and policies of the organization . ➢ are motivated to question on ineffective strategy or policies. ➢ are encouraged to carry out formative appraisal of the performance and take steps to bring continuous improvement. ➢ are trusted on their performance and capability. ➢ perform the tasks on the basis of mutual trust. ➢ are always ready to break work boundaries to perform new task. ➢ are encouraged to take risk.

2. Dimensions of Learning Organization

Learning organization has varied dimensions in doing business. The significant dimensions of learning organization are stated in exhibit 19.2.

Exhibit No. 19.2: Dimensions of learning organization

➤ Shared vision, missions and goals ➤ Shared values, beliefs and ethics ➤ Strong values for learning ➤ Ample learning opportunity ➤ Learning culture ➤ Use of variety of learning approaches ➤ Flexible learning methods	➤ Effective communication ➤ Collective understanding of changing business ➤ Learning is a part of the business ➤ Rewards are associated to learning ➤ Adequate learning facilities ➤ Feedback on performance

3. Benefits of Learning Organization

There are number of benefits of learning organization. Some indicative benefits are briefly described in subsequent paragraphs.

3.1 Understanding of Organizational Tasks

People appreciate the importance of performing routine, changing, additional, new and innovative tasks. They do prioritization of goals and tasks to obtain optimum results. They understand the importance of bringing improvement and change in the performance. They collectively develop the skills to perform changing tasks. They apply the skills learnt to perform the tasks to produce better results for customer satisfaction. Customer satisfaction brings pleasure and joy to the performers. Collective learning about the business warns the employees to foresee the learning requirements of tomorrow. They prepare themselves to learn for tomorrow before it gets late.

3.2 Able and Dedicated Employees

People learn collectively to acquire competencies to perform the organizational tasks. In the process of collective learning people offer mutual feedback to each other that assures acquiring minimum performance level of work related competencies. Collective learning promotes acquire higher level of proficiency in competency. It promotes higher and deep level of learning through creativity, analysis and reflection. Competent employees are confident employees to take up any kind of business venture. They are prepared to enter in uncertain business environment and take risk for competitive advantage.

3.3 Optimum Use of Resources

People learn collectively to minimize wastage of all types of available resources (man, material, machine, minutes, information and money). They use and reuse the resources to perform the tasks of the organization. They improve the efficiency of the processes continuously reviewing it and enhance resources utilization. Faculty and staff members prominently use the learning utilization center, learning resources development centre and library.

3.4 Effective Communication

During the process of collective learning-effective communication takes place throughout the organization. People get correct information thereby reducing the chances of grapevine communication. People promoting grapevine communication and creating confusion about the organization can easily be identified. People are encouraged to use variety of modes and media to assure effective communication. Right person carries out the communication at right time in right way.

3.5 Healthy Culture

During the process of collective learning mutual relationship becomes strong that promotes spirit of cooperation and coordination. It helps to understand and adopt organizational values. Collective learning about the business of the organization helps to evolve appropriate work culture and institutionalize it. People learn to live in healthy changing culture. They groom the new members joining the institution to live in changing culture. The changing culture directly contributes for customer satisfaction.

3.6 Use of Best Practices

The human nature is to excel better for the benefit of the organization and self. This nature encourages the organization to evolve and adopt best practices related business and work culture during the process of learning. People always try to search the best practices in the world and adopt them to satisfy the needs of the customers and carry out the work with ease and joy.

3.7 Development of Thinking Skills

Collective learning in the organization develops, promotes, expands and refines thinking skills such as positive thinking, analytical thinking, creative thinking, thinking to accept the challenges, thinking to accept the risk, thinking to struggle with the situation, thinking to improve quality of product and services, thinking to innovate, etc. People provide stimulus for thinking and creativity during the process of collective learning. People are encouraged to challenge the existing skills to invent new, different and better skills.

3.8 Development of Human Resources

In learning organization people are involved in continuous learning process that helps their personal development. Their personal development contributes for organizational development and it provides them an opportunity for further development. It creates a sort of spiral effect for individuals and organization both. In learning organization people learn from the business itself. The training is inbuilt in learning organization. Initially formal training may require but after establishment of learning culture it becomes the part of the business.

3.9. Enhanced Image of Organization in Society

Continuous learning brings good image to organization in the society. It becomes the source of motivation for other organizations. They perform with more efforts and energy. Customers get satisfaction from the excellent services of the organization. Sister organizations approach the learning organization for collaboration, cooperation, and networking. Learning organization always has far superior image than its competitors.

4. Learning Organization – Some Assumptions

The concept of learning organization is based on some assumptions. Some of the indicative assumptions are listed in exhibit 19.3.

Exhibit No. 19.3: Some assumptions for learning organization

➢ Employees of the organization are willing and self-motivated to learn ➢ Employees learn for various purposes ➢ Employees are committed to produce better results ➢ Conducive and healthy environment is prevalent in the organization for promoting learning ➢ Organization is committed to provide resources for learning ➢ Different learning styles are used by learners and the organization creates adequate learning opportunities to match learning styles ➢ Learning produces varied outcomes	➢ Customer satisfaction is assured performing better through learning ➢ Employees would transfer learning for the development of the organization ➢ Mistakes committed during the process of learning are not punished ➢ Organization is committed to bring continuous improvement and employees are willing to contribute for continuous improvement ➢ Collective energy, creativity, capacity, and commitment of the employees fuel the process of continuous change

5. Learning Methods in Learning Organization

Methods of collective and individual learning are generally used for learning in the organization. The learning method is selected on the basis of its strengths to produce learning about the business and work culture of organization in specific situation. Some indicative learning methods are briefly described in subsequent paragraphs to produce learning in the organization, if used appropriately.

5.1 Group Creativity Methods

A range of group creativity tools and techniques are available for learning in the organization. Some significant methods such as Brain storming, Nominal group technique, Delphi, Focus group discussion, force field analysis, action learning, multiple role play, mind mapping etc. are used appropriately to collectively improve the performance on various dimensions of the organization. These methods are used for various purposes in the organization. Some of the indicative purposes are listed in exhibit 19.4.

Exhibit No. 19.4: Use of creativity methods in the organization

➢ To develop the shared vision, missions, goals, objectives, work ethics, organizational values, work culture, and vision reach strategies ➢ To set performance standards for products and services of the organization ➢ To enhance organizational commitment to achieve organizational objectives, goals, missions and vision ➢ To develop consensus among employees on significant policy decisions	➢ To generate adequate, appropriate and innovative alternatives ➢ To assess the potential impact of the decision taken ➢ To solve important and sensitive problems ➢ To develop healthy work culture ➢ To design change ➢ To produce purposeful collective learning ➢ To induct new members in the organization

Group creativity techniques are completed in two phases. In first phase, a forum is provided to employees of the organization creating conducive environment in which employees generate creative ideas. In second phase, creative ideas are analyzed considering limitation of the organization and resources. Screened out ideas are considered for implementation. Creativity techniques are used to generate ideas for other management techniques such as force field analysis, U procedure, fish bone diagram, and affinity diagram. The ideas are further analyzed using these techniques.

5.2 Learning from Experiences

Learning collectively why the present processes are not producing or producing good or weak results. Strategies are evolved to refine these processes and add value to them to produce effective and efficient results. In this learning process many learning activities such as micro study of the process, known to unknown, specific to general, simple to difficult concepts of learning are adopted. The refined process is collectively understood and anticipated results are analyzed. In the process of learning capability for risk taking, accepting the challenges and continuous improvement are developed. Work related skills are generally learnt through experiences. People should be conscious for learning while working. The process of learning through experiences is lengthy and may be costly in some situations.

5.3 Learning from Experimentation

Collective experiments are conducted to improve the quality of products and services to satisfy the needs of the customer using scientific methods. New experiments are conducted to minimize wastage of resources and improve the work related competencies. To conduct the new experiments management techniques are used extensively. The popularly used techniques are survey, process analysis, process design, fish bone diagram, relationship analysis, U process, strengths, weaknesses, opportunities, threats (SWOT) analysis, customer supplier charting etc.

5.4 Learning from Complaints

Complaints received about the product and services of the organization can be analyzed to learn collectively to bring improvements. The complaints are attended and removed. At the same time their nature and frequency can be analyzed and strategy can be designed to prevent them to recur in the future. This is possible through collective leaning and collective efforts. Collective analysis of complaints and designing strategy to remove it promote organizational learning.

5.5 Learning from Opportunities

Organization works in an external open environment. Many opportunities are available in the external environment for the growth and development of the organization. The organization learns about these opportunities collectively and grabs them for the benefit of the organization. The potential opportunities include participation in special workshops, seminars, debate, case study, meet, etc. Professional bodies and other promoters of the business sponsor these opportunities.

5.6 Learning from New Technology

To improve the efficiency in the performance use of new technology and techniques are necessary. New technology and techniques are learnt collectively. These are management techniques, information technology, business related technology, education technology, television and internet. Media plays a significant role in creating learning. Use of computer in learning has created added advantage and created lot of flexibility and scope in learning.

5.7 Learning from Competition

In learning organization competition is created for learning. Competition is related to core business of the organization. Specific challenges are created for different teams in the organization to set performance objectives and achieve them. People learn consciously and unconsciously when they work on challenges. After working on each competition reflection sessions on learning are organized for learning of masses. While working on competition people challenge traditional way of working and technology. They explore the deficiencies in the existing practices and think to bring improvements. A sense of urgency is created for fast learning through competition.

5.8 Learning to Learn

This concept is very important in learning organization. Individuals and teams should be conscious to learn from every opportunity. They should learn from the job they are performing. They should analyze the performance and causes lying behind. They should repeat the successful learning from the job on similar jobs at the same time avoid the weaknesses in the future through better learning. They should plan what to learn, how to learn, when to learn, and how to apply previously learnt skills on a new job. People should develop skills to recognize that they learnt new skills consciously and they are going to use these learning skills in the future.

5.9 Learning through Exploration

People should be given ample opportunities to visit other organizations and work there for some time to explore the ways and means adopted in doing the business in other organizations. They should move out and observe what other organizations are doing and why they are doing so. Learning challenges are created to explore the alternative and better ways of working in the organization.

5.10 Learning from Mistakes

Mistakes are good teacher of people working in the organization. Efforts should be made to collect the mistakes and analyse them collectively for learning and not to commit them in future. The greatest punishment for people in the organization is to ask them to analyse their mistakes and tell others how they can avoid committing such mistakes.

5.11 Learning from Struggle

People in the organization complaint about shortage of resources and many other things related to behaviour. They should be put in teams to come out from unfamiliar situation. People will use their creativity and mobilize their resources to come out from the situation. They will develop confidence for resolving uncertain and unfamiliar situations because they have learnt skills of struggling and learning. In many situations struggle becomes the source of inspiration for learning and achieving.

5.12 Learning from Projects

Projects are considered challenging and symbols of status in the organization. Projects are completed in teams. Projects are demanding and require variety of inter disciplinary skills. People should be given opportunities to do projects and learn. People should be encouraged to work on industrial and social projects. They should be encouraged to use learning in other situations.

5.13 Learning from Self

Self-learning attitude should be promoted in the organization. People should be motivated to explore opportunities for self-learning in the organization and outside the organization. The organization should also create learning opportunities for self-learning. A learning centre equipped with self-learning resources should be established in the organization to promote learning. Self-learning is always based on individual needs. It is considered to be purposeful learning by individuals. Learning provides immense satisfaction because it is directly and immediately used on the task. It provides sense of confidence and self-positive image is created. People become confident to express their views in the organization.

5.14 Learning Collectively

The power of synergy is boosted in collective learning. People learn collectively to set organization destination and design strategies to reach destination. They learn to live collectively and dedicate their efforts collectively for the growth and development of the organization. They learn to continuously improve the performance of the organization. Numerous learning methods are available for collective learning in the organization such as action learning, creativity techniques, group discussions, case method, U method, force field analysis, fish bowl, fish bone, tree analysis, role analysis, stakeholders analysis, multiple role play, relationship mapping, business process reengineering, meetings and so on.

5.15 Learning under Guidance of Experienced Person

Learning under the guidance of experienced person reduces the time of learning. It minimizes the repetition of mistakes on performance in the organization. Learning under the guidance helps to receive constructive feedback on the quality of performance. Right guidance on right time is provided by the guide that acts as a source of motivation for improving the performance. Learning under guidance of experienced person helps to know better ways of working and reduce possibilities of committing mistakes. The tips of guide boost up confidence to accept the challenges. Learning under guidance prepares the organizational members to take up the higher level of jobs, new role and different roles.

5.15 Learning through Formal Methods

A vide spectrum of formal training programmes of educational institutions are available to the organizational members for learning new technologies and new skills. People should be encouraged to join formal educational and training programmes as per their needs and interest to bring new ideas and technology in the business. Formal training programmes should be organized in the organization to benefit more number of employees.

5.16 Learning through De-learning

It is necessary to update the knowledge and skills to meet the changing requirements of the business. People should be encouraged to forget old methods of doing the work and encouraged to develop and adopt new skills as early as possible. It is difficult to forget or change the work related behaviour but it is essential in changing environment. The best way to de-learn old behaviour is to work in team and consciously practice new way of working. Think positively and act promptly to use new knowledge and skills.

5.17 Learning through Copying

There are many people in the organization possessing distinct and different skills and talent. Some people are more influential than others, some are creative, some are analytical, some are visionary, some are humorous and so on. Different types of skills are required to perform the different tasks in the organization. Considering the type of the work, one can copy the style and skills of the person best suiting in that situation. One can use her/his wisdom in copying the behaviour or style of role models. It boosts confidence to perform the new task. One should assure that s/he has selected right person and right style for copying otherwise it may lead to disaster.

5.18 Learning through Reading

A library containing literature related to business and culture of the organization should be maintained to provide books and literature to employees. People should be encouraged to write on the experiences gained by them and contribute to literature. They should be encouraged to document the business related thoughts of other people. People have personal collection of books that can be shared on mutual basis. The organization should acquire literature of interest for reading. Technical institutions should have section in their library on education management, education psychology, education technology, education research and so on. They should have latest collection of print and non-print learning resources on technical education. People should be encouraged to read the literature related to technical education.

5.19 Learning from Introspection

People should be encouraged to do introspection and analysis of their performance. They should be asked to note down their strengths and weaknesses. They should be asked to find out ways and means to use their strengths and remove their weaknesses. People should be encouraged to analyse all aspects of approaching and completing the task.

5.20 Learning through Meditation

People should be given an opportunity to do meditation. They go away from the organizational setting and do meditation to improve their thinking power and concentration. They develop skills to tap the full potential of their brain. They are encouraged to increase spiritual power and self-motivation level. They are also encouraged to reduce stress and learn stress coping strategies. They are motivated to enjoy uncertainty.

5.21 Learning from Simulation

People can learn many skills in simulated conditions. Learning through simulation is risk free and provide feeling of real life situation. Simulated situations can be created in the organization to develop particular skills in individuals and teams. There are number of simulation techniques available for producing various types of skills to name a few action learning, game, role play, mechanical simulator, electronic simulator, computer simulator and so on.

5.22 Learning from Autobiographies

There are number of people who contributed for organization building. Their contribution may be unique and significant. People tell stories about their courageous efforts. These contributions should be documented and made available to rest of the members of the organization for learning. Reading autobiographies of great hero of the organization people get charged to do something different and innovative for the organization. People should be encouraged to read the autobiographies of renowned personalities of the world.

5.23 Action Learning

It is a process of collective learning from the real life situation. Situation may be related to problem solving, decision-making, planning, implementing plans, resolving conflict, developing something new, evaluation of performance and so on. During the process of dealing with the situation people collectively learn from the interaction, discussion and reflection on actions taken. During performing they seek intrinsic feedback from action and receive extrinsic feedback from fellow team members. People learn solving real life problems as well as dealing with uncertainties and risks. It produces learning in all the three domains of learning that is cognitive, affective and psychomotor. It prepares employees to accept and meet challenges. People learn skills of thinking to think and challenge their own style of learning through action learning.

5.24 Learning through Performance Appraisal

Plans are prepared and goals of are set at the beginning of the year at organizational, team and individual level. Planning is carried out participatively that promotes collective learning. The presentation of institutional, team and individual plans are organized and validated by the institutional members. People implement plans participatively and cooperatively. They do experimentation during the implementation process and learn new skills. At the end of the year achievements of the goals is analyzed participatively and feedback is provided by superiors, peers, subordinates, customers and stakeholders for improving performance. This constructive and positive feedback is used for next succeeding year goal setting and improving the performance. Analysis of the performance at the end of the year provides sense of achievement and motivates individuals and teams to think about strategies to improve performance. Self-feedback increases confidence and causes self-learning.

6. Paradigm Shift—Traditional Organization to Learning Organization

It is little bit difficult to convert traditional organization in learning organization during the initial stage of efforts but there is no alternative to it. Government or private organization can be converted to learning organization in a planned way. People working at different leadership, managerial and supervisory positions should initiate the direction setting process. They should take the exercise of shared visioning or revisiting the vision statement to set the direction. This exercise should be carried out participatively. They should derive the missions, goals and objectives and prepare strategic, perspective and annual plans involving employees and stakeholders. The strategies should be evaluated and analysed participatively to assure their effectiveness and efficiency. The organization should create learning opportunities for its employees so that they can learn using their own learning style and time to ensure continuous improvement in the performance and bring innovations in work situation. The organization should provide learning opportunity within and outside the organization for collective learning. People working at significant positions in the organization should push and increase momentum for collective learning. They should do so playing a role of trainer, guide, motivator, role model, supporter, coach, evaluator, recognizer, leader, problem solver, conflict manger, learning resources provider, learning opportunities provider, counseller, mentor, etc.

A well-equipped learning centre in the organization should be created to promote collective and self-learning. Good learning resources and a team of facilitators should support this learning resource centre. The organization should fix suggestion/complaint box to encourage people to drop spontaneous suggestions and complaints. The organization should start a newsletter or magazine to share the information and experiences with internal and external stakeholders. Important information should be shared with affected and involved teams using booklets to avoid confusion and miscommunication. There should be electronic circulation for the information and experiences if facility is available in the organization. The full potential of human resources and thereby other resources can be harnessed by organization developing multidisciplinary knowledge, skills and attitudes creating learning organization. It can overcome the problem of shortage of manpower, obsolescence and redundancy. In learning organization people are naturally trained to assume changing role. They are deployed and redeployed. The organization should consider learning as one of the processes of the business and allocate budget and resources for it. The shift required on various parameters is listed in exhibit 19.5.

Exhibit No. 19.5: Paradigm shift from training to learning in learning organization

Criteria	*Training*		*Learning*
Focus	Trainer		Trainee
Learning	Passive learning		Active learning
Philosophy	Principles of training		Principles of learning
Responsibility for learning	Trainer		Employee
Role of trainer	Directive		Co-learner
Motivation	Trainer influence the behaviour of the trainees	⇒	Promote self-motivation for learning
Power	Enjoy expert power		Empower trainees
Emphasis	Curriculum completion		Learning about changing business, innovation, and development
Trainers think	Trainees need to be controlled		Employees have potential to learn on their own
Recognition	Take credit for the success		Share success
Rewards	Extrinsic		Intrinsic
Information	Controlled information		Free flow of information

(*Contd.*)

(*Contd.*)

Problems	Trainer own the problem	Employees own the problem
Communication	Often one way	Multi-channel
Creativity and innovation	Less scope	Foster creativity in learning
	Analytical thinking	Intuitive learning
Perspective	Limited scope	Life long learning
Approach	Trainer centered methods	Employee centered methods
Use of media	Traditional	Multi media
Effect	Growth and development	Learning climate
Force	Supply driven	Demand driven
Way	Formal	Informal
Focus of training	Input	Output
Approach	Generic	Specific and generic both

7. Role of the Leaders in Learning Organization

The role of the leaders to create learning organization is significant and requires different kind of mind set and attitude. First of all they initiate the process of self-learning and collective learning in the organization. They create conducive and healthy learning environment in the organization. They commit to quality of product and services. They strive for customer satisfaction and delight. They give importance to the customers and stakeholders. They predict the uncertainties and remove them through participation of the people. They encourage people to take risk for the benefit of the organization. They dedicate processes, resources and efforts to product and services of the organization. They promote the attitude of continuous improvement and value addition in the organization. They develop knowledge, skills and attitude of people thereby shape the work related behaviour to achieve excellence in the business. They invite employees and stakeholders to challenge the work practices, responsibilities, rules and policies of the organization and seek cooperation to remove all barriers coming to the way of performance. They lead the people through vision and values. They delegate the power and empower people and teams. They believe in and put efforts for the development, progress and promotion of the people. They are pro to change. They perform variety of and multiple roles and encourage others to perform similar roles. The indicative roles of leaders in learning organization are listed in exhibit 19.6.

Exhibit No. 19.6: Role of leaders in learning organization

➢ Guide ➢ Coach ➢ Influencer ➢ Helper ➢ Recognition provider ➢ Trainer ➢ Counsellor ➢ Role model ➢ Problem solver ➢ Direction setter ➢ Visualizer ➢ Value setter ➢ Work culture promoter ➢ Predictor	➢ Team builder ➢ Motivator ➢ Collaborator ➢ Supporter ➢ Evaluator ➢ Leader ➢ Conflict manger ➢ Learning resources provider ➢ Learning opportunities provider ➢ Mentor ➢ Strong spokes person ➢ Change agent ➢ Information provider ➢ Analyser

8. Impact of Learning Organization

Learning organization produces variety of results and impact in the society. Most of the results and impacts are mentioned in the chapter under different heading. A model on impact of learning organization is shown in exhibit 19.7.

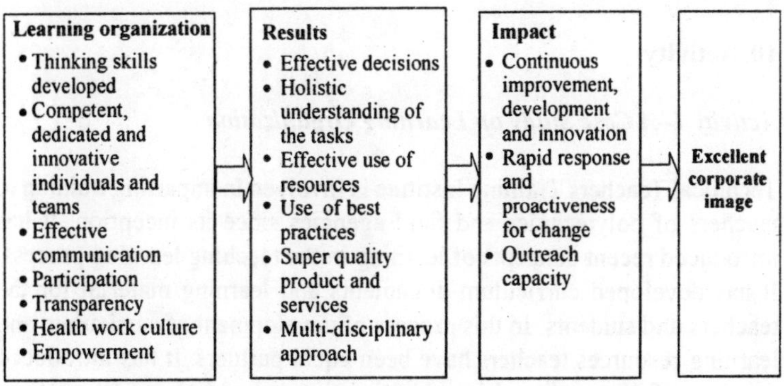

Exhibit No. 19.7: Impact of learning organization

9. Summary

The external and internal changes are taking place on political, economical, social, technological, and educational dimensions at a very fast rate. These changes force the organization to continuously change in business and way of doing the business. The organization should accept the demand of the changes. They should take proactive and positive approach for the change instead of reactive approach. They should focus on core business to satisfy the needs of the customer. The increasing competition in every walk of the life will forcibly throw out the traditional organization from market in a short period of time. The future organizations would need to work on shared vision. They have to work professionally in changing environment. They have to evolve self-renewal work technology and work culture suiting to needs of the environment. They have to do it through participation of people, their commitment for change and learning, making transparent processes, developing capability and capacity of people through self and collecting learning, empowering them for decision-making, and increasing accountability. The organizational structure would require being more flexible and team oriented. The organization needs to be a learning organization in which people continuously and collectively learn the business and tricks of the business. They develop competence to professionally perform the tasks. They have positive attitude for change and changing requirements. The organizations have to recognize the importance of varied learning requirements and learning styles of individuals and groups. They have to promote continuous and collective learning in the organization to survive, grow and develop in the market.

10. Activity

Activity 1–A Case Study on Learning Organization

Technical Teachers Training Institute is involved in imparting training to teachers of polytechnics and field agencies since its inception. It has introduced recent concepts of learning in the teaching learning process. It has developed curriculum documents and learning material for the teachers and students. In this process of development of curriculum and learning resources teachers have been equal partners. It has introduced number of innovation like; multi-point entry and credit system, institutional autonomy, linkages with industries and field agencies, guidance and counselling centres, training and placement centre, learning resources development centre, learning utilization centres, quality circles, engineering experimentation, item bank, management of information system, total quality management, performance appraisal and development system, organizational development, centre for excellence, question bank etc. in polytechnics for improving the quality of passouts. At the same time it has introduced the concept of learning to learn, self-learning, learning for life, discovery learning, learning with pace and time, learning to solve problems, learning through struggle etc. in the polytechnic education. It has supported Government of India, State Government and technical institutions for preparing policy and other significant documents.

The faculty of the institution has been continuously updated itself through variety of modes such as in-house programmes, outstation programmes, taking up prestigious projects, organizing seminars on issues related to technical education, etc. Self-learning and learning on the job is a very common approach used in the institute. Faculty members continuously update themselves through reading books and applying concepts in technical education. The institution has taken major initiative during 90s undertaking a joint exercise of crafting a vision document. The entire faculty members discussed openly on various issues related to institute business. The discussions were organized in small groups on various issues like; future opportunities for the institution, finance, autonomy, potential customers, satisfaction level of the existing customers, government initiatives and policies, potential customers, existing value system of the organization, existing job description of the faculty members, future job description of the faculty members, the way institution is doing business etc. Outcomes of each discussion were presented in the larger group for validation and it was properly documented. These discussions continued in smaller groups and larger groups for a period of one year. The institution crafted its vision document on the basis of the outcomes of discussions that comprises following points:

- History of the institution
- Vision and mission statement
- Strengths, weaknesses, opportunities and threats
- Value analysis
- Broad strategies of the institution
- Capabilities and capacity of the institution
- Existing and future clients of the institution
- Financial arrangements
- Need for human resources development
- Job analysis of faculty and officers
- Criteria for evaluating the performance of the institution, groups and individuals
- Structure of the institution

The institution has discussed this vision document with the Government of India, Board of Governors, Directors of Technical education of various states, industry representatives, teachers of the polytechnics and other significant stakeholders. They offered valuable suggestions and comments on the vision document. After discussion in the faculty meeting these comments have been incorporated and final document is produced. This document is considered as reference document for all purposes. After completion of this process the institution started working in accordance to the vision document. The major change reflected in its way of working are:

- Each faculty member, group, department submits a annual plan of activities in which s/he spells out the training requirements.
- Plans of individuals, groups and departments are discussed in detail in a workshop situation and compiled, discussed, analysed, finalized and submitted to Government of India.
- Each training programme/project is jointly designed by a team of faculty members drawn from various department after due deliberation. Faculty members provide free and frank suggestions on the design of the programme. The programme is designed on the basis of the training needs spelled out by the respective state. The course material is designed and validated by the same team members. The team that has worked on the topic conducts the training programmes.
- Faculty members provide open and constructive feedback to each other for mutual learning. Feedback is taken in a positive way and thanks are extended for taking pains to provide feedback.
- Subsequent programmes are designed on the basis of the feedback received on the previous programme.
- Potential trainees are also involved in the design of the programme when more number of programmes are planned on the same topic.
- Programmes are conducted in variety of modes and small experiments are conducted to test the effectiveness of the new mode.
- The institutional values are strictly adhered by faculty and staff members in completing the task.
- Progress of the work is quarterly reviewed in faculty meetings and reasons for non-accomplishment of targets are found out and solutions are generated jointly. Implications of the solutions are also discussed.

- All the major changes are discussed and welcomed by faculty members. They are ready to take moderate risk to do something new, unique, and different. Generally no punishment is given in case of failure but they are asked to analyse the causes of failure and learn from it.
- Working in a team is very common in institutional functioning. Teams are formed looking to the competence, interest and learning requirements of the faculty and staff members.
- All the faculty members are empowered to take decisions related to academic matters. They use the power without fear and analyse the impact of the decision.
- Different individuals and groups share new experiences with each other informally. The interested members organize informal sessions very often.
- Faculty members pursue the area of interest and they try to learn from the experienced faculty members. They develop in the new area and invite others to develop in that particular area if opportunity exits in that area.
- All the significant experiences are documented and published. Faculty members refer these experiences very often.
- Training and learning process is not limited to the business of the staff development cell but it has become the culture among the faculty members. No formal setting is required for training and learning purposes. Most of the experiences are related to learning and no finance is involved so experienced faculty members also take keen interest in sharing the experiences.
- Many a times it has been noticed during the group meetings that old methods of working has been challenged in the new context. The challenge was accepted and new methods were installed
- Presentation of papers in seminar and other occasion is very common culture of the institution.

The persuasion of the vision document has enhanced the confidence of the faculty and staff members of the institution. Meantime a special committee constituted for the review of the performance of the institution by Government of India has noted that the institution has tremendous potential to serve the other institutions of higher learning in the country so that the services of the institution should be extended to Engineering colleges, Management institutions, Pharmacy institutions and field agencies. The institution has decided to go for ISO 9000 to enhance the corporate reputation. The institution has developed the quality policy and procedure manual for describing the business and way of doing the business to the client and stakeholders. The quality standard for each significant service and product are fixed considering the international standards. Institutional members considering best practices, previous experiences, and use of technology prepare all the procedures jointly. Now apart from vision document, faculty and staff members invariably use quality manual and procedural manual. The result is analysed through indigenously developed software. Corrective actions are taken whenever gaps are found. This has enabled the institution to continually update the quality standards and procedures. The policy and other rules and regulations are changed accordingly.

Brief: Find the answer of following questions in institutional groups

1. What are the characteristics of the learning organization visible in above institution?
2. What are the characteristics you would like to promote and pursue to develop your organization as learning organization?

Activity 2 – Assignment

In this chapter you have appreciated the concept of learning organization. Prepare a plan of your organization to transform it in learning organization. You can prepare the plan in following format.

Sl. No.	*Learning events*	*Purpose*	*Partici-pants*	*Duration*		*Resource persons*	*Responsi-bility*
				From	*To*		
1.	Creativity sessions						
2.	Participative planning						
3.	Experience sharing sessions						
4.	Experimentations						
5.	Complaints analysis sessions						
6.	Opportunity analysis sessions						
7.	Use of technology for learning						

(*Contd.*)

(*Contd.*)

Sl. No.	Learning events	Purpose	Partici-pants	Duration		Resource persons	Responsi-bility
				From	To		
8.	Competition analysis sessions						
9.	Exploration exercises						
10.	Learning challenges						
11.	Learning projects						
12.	Self-learning opportunities						
13.	Team learning exercises						
14.	Guided learning						
15.	Learning simulations						
16.	Meditation						
17.	Performance appraisal						
18.	Action learning exercises						
19.	Case study						
20.	Researches						
21.	Review of policies, rules and regulations						
22.	Collective planning						
23.	Seminars						
24.	Conferences						
25.	Meeting with customers						
26.	Formal training programmes						
27.	Workshops						
28.	Diagnostics						
29.	Interaction with stakeholders and experts						
30.	Learning games						
31.	Problem solving sessions						
32.	Observation opportunities						

(*Contd.*)

(Contd.)

Sl. No.	*Learning events*	*Purpose*	*Partici-pants*	*Duration*		*Resource persons*	*Responsi-bility*
				From	*To*		
33.	Discussions – panel, group, focus group						
34.	In basket						
35.	Quiz						
36.	Industrial training						
37.	e-learning opportunities						
38.	Study leave						
39.	Sabbatical leave						
40.	Advance educational programmes						
41.	Excursion/educational tours						
42.	Secondment of faculty members						

Activity 3–Assignment on Perception of People about the Institution

A list of statements related to learning organization is given. Read statements serially and decide the extent to which it applies to your institution. Mark your response in appropriate column. 4 indicates full weightage and 0 indicates no weightage. If you do not respond to the statement it would be assumed that this is not applicable to your institution.

Sl. No.	*Statement*	*Extent*				
		4	*3*	*2*	*1*	*0*
1.	Training needs are analysed every year and training plans are prepared on the basis of training needs					
2.	Competency based training programmes are designed					
3.	Most of the training programmes are organized in-house					
4.	People are conscious about learning					
5.	Academic interactions are frequently organized					
6.	Self-learning is promoted by institution					
7.	People learn from all learning opportunities					
8.	Learning to learn concept is promoted					

(Contd.)

(*Contd.*)

Sl. No.	*Statement*	*Extent*				
		4	*3*	*2*	*1*	*0*
9.	Faculty and staff members are encouraged to organize learning events such as creativity sessions, seminars, conferences, workshops, training programmes					
10.	Meetings are organized to learn about the academics and discuss academic problems					
11.	Variety of training learning methods are used in training programmes					
12.	Learner centered methods are used in training programmes					
13.	Latest learning resources are procured immediately					
14.	Teachers develop learning resources such as text books, work books, assignments, case studies, video films, computer aided instructions, modules, monographs, concept papers, guide for learning specific topics, etc.					
15.	Teachers do experiments for bringing improvements in academic processes					
16.	Teachers prepare academic plans					
17.	Teachers undertake consultancy projects					
18.	Effective team work prevails					
19.	Open and constructive feedback is accepted by employees					
20.	Use of learning media is very common in institution					
21.	Complaints and academic problems are welcomed by the institution					
22.	Concrete suggestions are implemented					
23.	Performance appraisal and development system is effectively used					
24.	Participatory approaches are used for long-term and short-term planning					
25.	Management and educational tools and techniques are used for planning, implementation and evaluation of educational programmes					
26.	Employees follow values, norms and ethics					
27.	Changes are implemented collectively or in teams					
28.	People are developed to design and implement change					
29.	Learning opportunities such as attending out station courses, in house courses, secondments, sabbatical leave, study leave, fellowship, exchange, industrial training, are easily available					

(*Contd.*)

(*Contd.*)

Sl. No.	*Statement*	*Extent*				
		4	*3*	*2*	*1*	*0*
30.	On the job coaching, guidance, counselling, mentoring is common					
31.	All types of learning is aligned to vision, mission and goals					
32.	Competencies and proficiencies level for all the positions is well defined and known to people					
33.	Full talent and potential of people is used					
34.	Seniors devote time to develop juniors using variety of methods					
35.	Training and learning activities are monitored					
36.	Impact of training and learning is assessed					
37.	People are developed to accept future challenges					
38.	Risk taking for learning is common					
39.	Self-learning centre, learning utilization centre and digital library is fully functional and used					
40.	Training need analysis, training implementation, learning resources development, achievement measurement processes are in place					
41.	Team building exercises are carried out					
42.	Action learning is common in teams					
43.	People think strategically					
44.	Learning from failures and mistake is common					
45.	Communication is effective and efficient					
46.	Interdisciplinary learning is practiced					
47.	People are often deployed and redeployed					
48.	Joint learning events are organized with industry and sister institutions					
49.	Systems and processes are designed, implemented and refined jointly					
50.	Documentation of experiences					
51.	Knowledge, technology, techniques and models are developed					
52.	Easy access to information					
53.	Significant budget is allocated for training and learning activities					
54.	Budget is utilized effectively					
55.	Grants are always available for learning events and innovation					

REFERENCES

Larry, E. Senn and Jhon, R. Childress (1999). *The Secrete of Winning Culture*, Prentice Hall of India Pvt Ltd. New Delhi.

Michael, J. Marquardt (2003). *Action Learning in Action*, Jaico Publishing House Mumbai.

Michael, J. Marquardt (2003). *Building the Learning Organization*, Jaico Publishing House Mumbai.

Pat Hedges (1997). *Increasing Profitability by Effective Use of Learning*, Kogan Page. London.

Pater Lassey (1998). *Developing a Learning Organization*, Kogan Page Limited, London.

Peter Senge (1994). *The Fifth Discipline, Field Book*, Nicholas Brealey Publishing, London.

20

Reengineering

Objectives: The readers will be able to:

1. State the concept of reengineering.
2. Describe importance of reengineering the processes in technical institutions.
3. Describe the principles of reengineering.
4. Explain reengineering implementation models.
5. Describe tools and techniques used in reengineering.
6. List the hardware requirements to reengineer the processes.
7. Enlist main processes in technical institution that can be reengineered.
8. Describe the guidelines to be followed for reengineering.

1. Introduction

The customers are the main focus of any business whether it is production or service organization. The needs of the customers are satisfied by organizations through performing various processes. In educational institutions students are the immediate customers and their employers are the distant customers. The needs of the employers are satisfied by the students and needs of the students are satisfied by the educational institutions. Educational institutions provide academic services in the form of instructions and products in the form of instructional resources. Products and services are created using many academic and non-academic processes. Academic processes are the main processes and theses main processes are dependent on numbers of non-academic processes. The processes can be reengineered to make them effective and efficient. The time, money and resources can be saved that can be used for productive services. In reengineering initiatives the traditions and existing process are challenged. The institute set very high level of goals to redesign the processes. the structure of the institution is redesigned to support the core processes.

2. Concept of Reengineering in Educational Institutions

Michael Hammer has proposed the concept of reengineering. He defined reengineering as 'the fundamental rethinking and radical redesign of business processes to achieve dramatic improvements in critical, contemporary measures of performance such as cost, quality, service and speed'. Joe Peppard has defined reengineering as an improvement philosophy. It aims to achieve step improvements in performance by redesigning the processes through which an organization operates, maximizing their value-added content and minimizing every thing else. He stated that business process engineering approach could be applied at an individual process level or to the whole organization. The main focus of reengineering is process and minimization of non-value added items in the process. The improvement scale in the process is radical change. It emphasizes on processes leading to satisfaction of the customers. All the processes in the organization are streamlined to produce outcome and redundant process are eliminated. Variety of tools and techniques are used to redesign the organizational processes. All types of organizations in the world adopted this concept of reengineering for survival and success of their business. The concept of reengineering should be appreciated holistically before its implementation. So it is necessary to appreciate what reengineering is not. Reengineering is not events listed in exhibit 20.1 only.

Exhibit No. 20.1: Reengineering is not only events

- application of software to improve efficiency of various academic and non-academic processes
- automation of academic and non-academic processes
- changing the structure of the institution as per requirements
- taking casual initiatives to improve things
- solving day-to-day problem
- delegation of power down the line
- introducing new courses in the institution
- collaborating with sister institutions and employers of the passouts for mutual benefit
- introducing new policies in the institution

In context to educational institution the concepts has great importance on following parameters.

- cost of professional education is very high and it requires high attention of the planners and providers of the professional education. The cost parameters can be addressed by adopting concept and principles of reengineering.
- quality of education needs to be assured to develop desired competencies in the students to take up suitable employment.
- service in terms of organizing the instructional process in a way to meet the learning requirements of the students. It requires lot of flexibility in terms of duration of course, learning methods, learning material, time of learning and choice of learning and methods of assessment from students' point of view.
- speed is a major concern in the process of learning. Students with different entry behaviour and learning capability admitted in the institution but they have to progress with same speed that creates problems for slow learners and fast learners. Another important issue related to duration of the programme it takes four years to produce a professional by the time the technology and processes get changed in the employers' organization. The period of four years need to be reduced significantly to meet the changing requirements of the employers.

The issues related to cost, quality, service and speed can be appropriately addressed through reengineering the academic and supporting processes along with organizational structure of the institution.

3. Principles of Reengineering

The principles of reengineering are defined by Michael Hammer and later on adopted by many organizations. In fact the reengineering is total change in mindset of the people performing the activities. If a teacher is questioning the need of the teaching in faculty meeting she is thinking fundamentally to change the way of instructional strategies. If another teacher is questioning the 5 days working and 10 to 5 timetable she is thinking about bringing radical change. There could be such thinking that challenges the existing practices and their needs. Reengineering initiatives should be based on certain principles. Some of the indicative principles are listed in exhibit 20.2.

Exhibit No. 20.2: Principles of reengineering

➢ Organize work around results, not tasks ➢ Capture data only one time – when it is first created ➢ Allow decision points where work is performed ➢ Incorporate controls into information processing	➢ Make people who use a process do the work ➢ Work in parallel instead of sequentially, then integrate results ➢ Treat geographically dispersed resources as one ➢ Focus on process that contribute 80 per cent to results

4. Reengineering Implementation Models

Numerous models have been successfully used by various organizations to implement reengineering in their organizations. A brief description of these models is given subsequent paragraphs.

Jayaraman and his colleagues have suggested five-step model of implementing reengineering. The step one in their model is developing a process vision and determining process objectives. The vision should focus on fulfilling customers' needs and add value to services and products. It should provide competitive advantages to the institution. The processes should be derived on the basis of the vision and should specify the quantitative and qualitative improvements. The second step of this model is defining the processes to be reengineered. The start and end points of the main processes are defined and process measures are clearly stated. The owners of the processes are identified to ensure process implementation. The processes should add value to the customer. The third step in the model is understanding and measuring the process performance in terms of cost, quality, time and speed. The measurement leads to dissatisfaction with present level of performance. Fourth step in the model is identifying the information technology levers. The information technology is used to speed up and simply the process. The fifth step in the model is designing and building a prototype of the new process. In this step fine-tuning of the process reengineering is carried out and ownership of the process is created.

Cheryl Currid and Company has suggested three approaches to reengineering. These approaches are streamline, integrate and transform. Streamlining is carried out to make the process simple, fast and better. It is an improvement process in itself without bringing a radical change. This approach doesn't require much effort. Integrating approach is related to integrate the discrete processes in the organization and making them unified. This approach requires little bit more efforts than streamlining approach. Third approach is transforming. It is related to complete evaluation of the core business of the organization. The entire business of the organization and ways of doing the business are given a fresh look. This approach requires lot of efforts and radical change initiatives.

Cheryl Currid and Company has suggested four A's approach to implement the reengineering in the organization. First A is describes activate the reengineering philosophy in the organization. In this phase the reengineering efforts are initiated. The change process is planned and preliminary work is carried out including the acceptance and agreement of the people working in the organization. Implementation teams are formed and awareness workshops are conducted throughout the organization. The core business processes are mapped out. The vision and mission statements of the organization are crafted or refined. Second A describes analyse. In this phase the vision and mission statements are finalized and the processes are finally charted. The existing processes are charted, the scope of each process is finalized and barriers are removed. The team members are made capable and deployed for carrying out the process. Third A describes annihilate. Many creativity exercises are undertaken to perfectly design the process, check the process, develop a prototype, test it and refine it. Old paradigms are challenged and new paradigms are evolved in the organization. The study of similar organizations is carried out to know the different way of doing things. Fourth A describes assimilate. The new paradigms are tested and the change is implemented throughout the organization. The change process is supported and efforts are made for continuous improvement. The impact of the change process is assessed and the change is institutionalized.

5. Reengineering Tools and Techniques

Reengineering of educational institution is not a simple task. There is no ready-made or quick fix solution, even reengineering goals are not known from other institutions. The reengineering initiatives can be speeded up using variety of tools and techniques. A wide spectrum of reengineering tools and techniques is available for application in educational institutions. The institutions have a choice to select suitable tools and techniques suiting to their purpose and requirement. A brief description of some of the tools and techniques is given in chapter on management tools and techniques. A family of tools and techniques is shown in exhibit 20.3 and brief description is given in subsequent paragraphs.

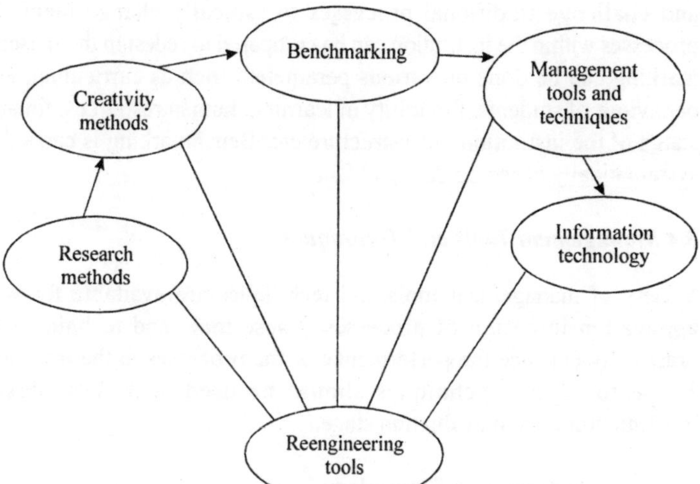

Exhibit No. 20.3: Reengineering tools and techniques

5.1 Research Methods

Various research methods like descriptive, *ex post facto*, content analysis, experimental, co-relational, snap study, tracer study, impact analysis etc. are used to study and reengineer the core business of the institution. These studies provide research base for initiating, designing, implementing and sustaining the reengineering initiatives in the institution.

5.2 Creativity Methods

Various creativity methods like brain storming, nominal group technique, cognitive mapping, ranking, matrix mapping etc. are used to generate new, innovative, unique and different idea about the core business and ways of doing the business. Creativity methods are useful right from the beginning of the reengineering process to the end of the journey. The concept of reengineering is based on radical rethinking which is not possible without intensive and deep use of the creativity methods.

5.3 Benchmarking

It is a technique to highlight areas for improvement in the institution. The institution can compare its processes with better performing institutions and challenge traditional processes to radically change them. The processes within the institution can be compared to redesign them. Benchmarking can be done on various parameters such as curriculum, entry behaviour of students, flexibility in learning, human resources, financial status of the institution, infrastructure etc. Benchmarking is carried out systematically based on data and facts.

5.4 Management Tools and Techniques

Variety of management tools and techniques are available for wider application in design of processes. These tools and techniques can drastically enhance the performance of the processes in the institution. These tools and techniques should be used at process design, implementation and evaluation stage.

5.5 Use of Information Technology

This is the era of information technology. Information is the main base for any educational institution. The information technology is widely used in reengineering initiatives. It is a means to increase the speed, improve the quality and reduce the cost of academic and non-academic business of the institution. The appropriate use of information technology enables the institutions to broaden the geographic coverage of the business. The distance learning programmes and on line programmes using internet is the concrete examples of the benefits of the information technology. The extent and reach of the students and clients to educational institutions has increased many fold because of information technology. It has created a greater scope for flexibility with respect to time, boundary, learning style and selection of educational programmes. Application of information technology in educational institution has increased the validity and reliability of the decisions as well. In educational institutions the information technology is useful in reengineering initiatives in following ways:

- Database for quick application is available for curriculum design, revision and modification.
- Learning packages on latest knowledge and skills are available for wider use. They provide opportunity of flexible learning and cater the needs of students taking admission with different entry behaviour.
- Assessment tests based on psychological principle are available to assess the progress of learning with flexibility.

- Data base support for taking academic and non-academic decisions within no time.
- Online admission, learning and assessment is available.
- The need of a teacher is reduced to a greater extent because of variety of mode of learning is possible.

6. Hardwares to Carryout the Work

Varieties of hardwares are available to carry out the academic and non-academic processes. Everyday new hardwares are introduced in the market. The institutions take the advantage of new equipment to speed up the process and increase the validity and reliability of the results. An indicative list of hardwares and their purposes is given exhibit 20.4.

Exhibit No. 20.4: Reengineering hardwares and their purpose

Sl. No.	*Hardwares*	*Purpose*
1.	Computer	➢ Networking ➢ Online learning ➢ Online assessment ➢ Quick communication ➢ Data base ➢ Quick decisions ➢ Multi-tasking ➢ Sharing ➢ Information to public ➢ Easy monitoring and evaluation of processes and results ➢ Presentations ➢ Inventory management ➢ Reduce paper work
2.	Electronic and mechanical simulators	Creating real life feeling Developing skills and attitudes
3.	Voice system ➢ Voice mail ➢ Interactive voice response ➢ Fax	Answering the questions and queries of the students and clients Time saving for client and institution Effective and efficient communication
4.	Document management system	Effective management of documents Effective and efficient communication Easy retrieval of information

(*Contd.*)

(Contd.)

Sl. No.	*Hardwares*	*Purpose*
5.	Group wares	➢ Meetings ➢ Video conferencing ➢ Information sharing ➢ Work sharing ➢ Examination of students ➢ Guidance and counselling ➢ Problem solving
6.	Multimedia	➢ Marketing the business of the institution ➢ Flexible learning ➢ Learning about real life practices ➢ Purposeful learning ➢ Learning about things which is not possible even in real life

7. Factors Affecting Process Design

There are numerous factors affecting the design of academic processes. Some of the indicative factors are listed in exhibit 20.5.

Exhibit No. 20.5: Factors affecting design of academic process

➢ Lack of information on design and implementation of academic processes ➢ Lack of knowledge of developments in the employers organization ➢ Lack of information on entry behaviour of students ➢ Unawareness about tools and techniques of reengineering ➢ Inertia on the part of the management to bring radical change ➢ Lack hardwares and softwares to support the instructional process ➢ Teachers are not trained to use information technology and modern concepts of education	➢ No rewards for innovative work ➢ Rigid organizational structure ➢ Lack of funds for modifying the infrastructure ➢ Requires high level of initial efforts in the beginning ➢ Bureaucratic way of managing institution ➢ Lack of collaboration with sister institutions and employers organization ➢ Benchmarks are not available ➢ High dependence on university ➢ Rigid rules and regulations ➢ Lack of pressure from students and employers

8. Main Processes of Technical Institutions

Reengineering is a systematic approach to improve the academic and supporting processes in institution. The meaning of academic processes in technical institution is to transfer learning to meet the learning needs of the students and thereby satisfying the needs of the employers. The meaning of reengineering the academic processes is to make the learning purposeful, joyful, flexible and interesting with lees efforts on the part of teachers and students, in less time, at less cost. Every thing done in the academic processes to add value to purposeful learning of students is considered reengineering. The value addition should not be minor but it should be major. It should set the challenge for other institutions. It should create sense of urgency and importance for the teachers and students. It should enhance the image of the institution in the society. It means the reengineering efforts on academic processes should bring good name in the society. The institution should be known for its professional approach to education. The goals of reengineering the academic processes are shown in exhibit 20.6.

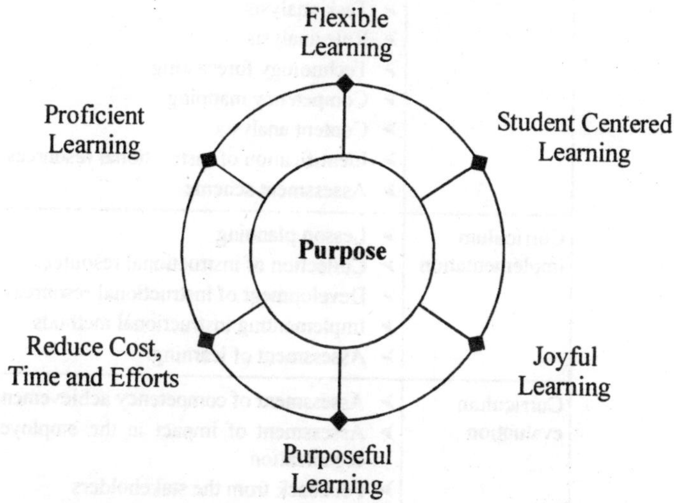

Exhibit No. 20.6: Purpose of reengineering academic processes

The main processes of the institution are listed and existing processes are charted out to know their effectiveness and efficiency. The main process that is academic process is redesigned to satisfy the needs of the students, employers and other stakeholders. The main process is designed by a dedicated team. While designing the process the outcome is kept in the mind. The process is designed using the tools and techniques described in this chapter and other chapters. The redesigned process is validated by large number of people and it is further refined on the basis of their feedback. Once the main process is designed other supporting processes are designed to facilitate main process of the institution. The resources are committed to main process and supporting processes. The institutional structure is tuned to implement the redesigned processes. People are trained to implement the processes. Main processes in technical institutions are listed in exhibit 20.7.

Exhibit No. 20.7: Main processes in technical institutions

Academic processes	Curriculum design, revision, modification	➢ Entry behaviour analysis ➢ Impact assessment ➢ Curriculum evaluation ➢ Feedback received from stakeholders ➢ Job survey ➢ Task analysis ➢ Role analysis ➢ Technology forecasting ➢ Competency mapping ➢ Content analysis ➢ Identification of instructional resources ➢ Assessment scheme
	Curriculum implementation	➢ Lesson planning ➢ Collection of instructional resources ➢ Development of instructional resources ➢ Implementing instructional methods ➢ Assessment of learning
	Curriculum evaluation	➢ Assessment of competency achievement ➢ Assessment of impact in the employers organization ➢ Feedback from the stakeholders
Administrative processes	Admission of students	➢ Advertisement ➢ Receiving applications ➢ Screening applications ➢ Conducting entrance test ➢ Declaring the list of eligible candidates ➢ Giving admission

	Recruitment of staff	➢ Job profile ➢ Advertisement for recruitment ➢ Scrutiny of application ➢ Calling for test ➢ Taking test ➢ Declaring list of selected candidates ➢ Making them join
	Record keeping	Students records Staff records Expenditure record Inventory record Purchase records Assets records Examination record Various plans of the institution like strategic plan, perspective plan, maintenance plan, annual plan, project plan, academic plan etc.
Managerial process	Planning	Various plans of the institution like strategic plan perspective plan, maintenance plan, annual plan, project plan, academic plan etc.
	Monitoring	Academic Managerial Administrative Financial
Financial	Budget	Non-recurring Recurring
	Monitoring	Schedule
	Revenue generation	Plans
	Audit	Plan

9. Guidelines for Implementing Reengineering in Technical Institutions

It should be noted that reengineering initiatives depends on many factors such as type of the academic activities, purpose of the institution, quality of employees, commitment of governing body and management of the institution, location of the institution and performance of the institution. Main guidelines for implementing reengineering philosophy in technical institutions are listed in exhibit 20.8.

Exhibit No. 20.8: Guidelines for implementing reengineering philosophy in technical institutions

- The reengineering initiatives should begin from the governing body and management of the institution instead of academic staff or administrative staff
- The shared vision, missions, goals, values and processes need to be effectively and efficiently communicated throughout the institution to establish the urgency, importance and need of reengineering
- Empower individuals and teams to take decisions to bring improvements in the processes. They should be empowered to think radically and experiment new ideas
- Clarify and effectively communicate the purpose of reengineering to the internal and external stakeholders
- Elevate the ambitions and motivation level of the individuals and teams to commit resources and energy to redesigned and implement the processes
- Set high level of performance level goals for core processes that is academics. The goals may be related to introducing flexibility in learning with respect to time, choice and assessment
- Involve students and employers in reengineering initiatives right from the beginning to win their confidence and commitment
- Use principles of education psychology, technology and management in redesigning the processes
- Commit adequate and timely resources to carry out the process without obstacles. Dedicate the resources for core processes in the classroom and laboratory to minimize the time in organizing the resources
- Use information technology generously in the process design and implementation. Update the process using information technology
- Establish guidance and counselling cell in the beginning to solve individual problems and keep high motivation level of process owners
- Promote radical thinking throughout the institution to minimize the likelihood to go back to previous practices
- Use media and software to carryout academic and non-academic process. Develop management information system to support the decision-making, communication and reporting.
- Carry out networking at all levels of the institution to share the information and experiences
- Design compatible, complementary and supporting processes to carry out the academic processes effectively and efficiently
- Redesign processes from students and employers point view and see the process holistically. Keep it simple, clear and communicable

(Contd.)

(Contd.)

➢ Define terms used in reengineering initiatives and make them clear to all individuals and teams. Use interdisciplinary teams for process implementation ➢ Try to minimize rules and regulations and work under broad policies and guidelines that facilitates the smooth implementation of processes ➢ Think about bringing improvements in the process rather than improving the performance. ➢ Use media and methods in implementation of instructional processes. Network with organizations developing media and methods for instructional purposes ➢ Hire experts for various purposes rather than training and deploying the existing staff. They will do work professionally and would not disturb the process implementation ➢ Improve communication in the institution using variety of modes of communication. There should not be any confusion, conflict and quarrel on account of ineffective communication ➢ Frequently evaluate all plans and reset the priorities according to the demand of the situation ➢ Deploy all resources of the institution for implementing the processes. It means resources should be dedicated to the processes and not to the persons ➢ Win the heart and soul of the staff members for implementing process reengineering initiatives ➢ Develop patience for achieving the results. The institution may be doing many things first time so there may be some confusion and delay in the result. Keep on moving removing the barriers and confusions. ➢ Focus on changing the values, beliefs and attitudes of people performing the processes

. Summary

eengineering is all about redesigning the processes, structure and sources of the institution. Reengineering is a fundamental rethinking d radical redesign of processes of the organization to accomplish goals at are connected to the customers. Reengineering initiatives should duce the cost, time, and effort to perform the process. They should add gnificant value to the product and services to the customers. A wide ectrum of tools and techniques is appropriately used to reengineer the ocess. Use of information technology plays a vital role in reengineering e processes. Numbers of electronic and mechanical equipments are used carryout the process. The validity and reliability of information is enhanced using computers and softwares. Use of information technolog supports the decision-making process. Quick and effective decisions ar possible with the use of information technology. The effectiv communication is assured using various modes of communication. Th academic process and supporting process are listed, charted and analyze through radical rethinking. New processes are designed taking inputs fro education psychology, education technology, education research an information technology. The redesigned processes are validated an installed in the institution for implementation. The motivation of th faculty members, staff members and students is kept high during th implementation of redesigned processes. The reengineering is carrie out throughout the institution that requires courage and patience in th employees and top management of the institution. During th reengineering process certain guidelines are followed to effectivel implement the processes.

11. Activity

Consider the vision, missions and goals of the institution and chart th academic and supporting processes of your institution. Study the charte processes and find out the gaps, overlaps, redundant elements an inefficiencies in the existing processes. Also find out scope for applyi the concepts of education management, education research, educati technology, and information technology in different elements of th processes. Redesign the academic and supporting processes radical rethinking and applying information technology. Involve internal a external stakeholders in the process redesign and validate the redesign processes for implementation. Organize the resources and people carryout the redesign processes. Measure the impact of redesigned proce after one cycle and bring necessary improvements in the redesign processes based on the feedback of the implementers and beneficiarie

REFERENCES

Cheryl Curid and Company (1995). *Reengineering Toolkit*, Galgotia Publicati Pvt. Ltd New Delhi.

Daniel, P. Petrozoo and John, C. Stepper (1998). *Successful Reengineeri* Jaico Publishing House, Mumbai.

Henry, J. Johansson, Patric Mchugh, A. John Pendlebury, William A. Wheeler (1993). *Business Process Reengineering*, John Wiley & Sons, New Yo

Jayaraman, M.S., Ganesh Natarajan and Rangaramanujan, A.V. (1994). *Business Process Reengineering*, Tata McGraw Hills Company Limited, New Delhi.

Joe Peppard and Philip Rowland (1995). *The Essence of Bussiness Process Reengineering*, Prentice Hall of India Private Limited.

Waman, S. Jawadekar (1998). *Redesigning the Business Organization*, Jaico Publishing House, Mumbai.

21

Total Quality Management

Objectives: The readers will be able to:

1. State the need and importance of total quality management.
2. Describe the meaning of quality in technical education.
3. Describe the meaning of total quality management in relation to technical education.
4. List the elements of total quality management.
5. State the factors affecting quality of passouts.
6. Explain the model of total quality management.

1. Introduction

The quality word is used very commonly by most of the stakeholders connected with technical education. People use the word quality loosely because it is not defined appropriately in context to technical education. For example, an undergraduate electrical engineering student is unable to tell about the fault or do the wiring for domestic electricity supply, it is quoted that s/he could not repair a small fault. What has s/he has learnt in engineering college. People do not understand that the person is not trained for doing such jobs. This confusion prevails because the competency profile of the passouts of various engineering programmes has not been defined. Even employers select the passouts and later on they complaint to institutions that passout of the institution is not performing well. When the case is studied it reveals that the employee has been assigned the job for which s/he were not trained in the engineering college.

In past few years the phenomenal increase in advertisement for tuition and coaching of engineering students is a good indication of poor quality of instructions provided in engineering institution. These hidden coaching and tuition taking institutions are doing rework for producing desired level of learning. Students have to spend more time on attending classes in engineering institutions and coaching institutions. That creates lot of stress and time pressure on them. Students have no extra time for self-study and other developmental activities. Their parents have to pay more on the education.

Apart from this students are also joining parallel education, training and coaching programmes related to their profession to obtain jobs in good companies. They join personality development programmes, communication skills improvement programmes, computer programmes and hobby programmes. They also join high technology and advance courses related to their disciplines. This indicates that the technical institutions are not offering adequate curricular and co-curricular programmes fulfilling the needs of the students.

Employers employ passouts from different institutions and there is a wide variation in the assessment process among the institutions. Passouts of one institution may be lucky to have job related knowledge they have gained in technical institution. Naturally they will perform better in comparison to those who have not been trained in a particular subject. Although they are better knowledgeable in other subjects. It is very difficult to select right persons for a particular job on the basis of the contents they have studied in engineering college.

Great variation is found in the passouts of same institution ranging from pass division to honors. This also indicates that the institutions are not quality conscious and the quality assurance mechanism is poorly working or not working at all. It may be inferred that the good result is there because of concern of students about their career. Those who study well on their own get good marks and those who do not get poor marks. Institutions do not pay major role to monitor the progress of the students on learning and reduce variation.

2. Meaning of Quality

Management *Gurus* have defined quality in their own way in different context where they have worked. Definitions proposed by experts are general and common definitions. These definitions help to define the quality of passouts in operational terms so that the quality of passouts can be assured and managed on sustained basis. Some of the important definitions are stated in exhibit 21.1.

Exhibit No. 21.1: Definitions of quality

- Fitness for the purpose – Juran
- Quality should be aimed at the needs of the customer, present and future – Deming
- Quality is the degree of excellence at an acceptable price and control of variability at an acceptable cost – Broh
- The totality of features and characteristic of a product or services that bear on its ability to satisfy stated or implied needs – ISO 8402: Quality Vocabulary
- Ability to meet or exceed customer requirements and expectations – Joseph & Susan Berk

There is a need to define the quality of passout and then take measure to manage it on a sustained basis. Without defining the quality and its parameters one cannot manage it systematically and scientifically. It is very difficult to measure it for various purposes. There is need to have uniform curriculum throughout the country which is competency based and also indicating proficiency level in each competency. It should address the needs of the employers, students and industries in meaningful and measurable terms. Then only institutions can design academic and non-academic processes to produce the passouts possessing specified competencies. There is a need to have certifying agency at national level to certify the attainment of competencies by passouts on well-designed criteria. The certificate of this agency would ensure quality of passouts of technical institutions. The quality of passouts can be compared on uniform criteria also. Employers will be assured that they have selected right professionals and passouts will be confident on their ability.

Technical institutions are professional institutions. They are expected to function professionally. They should translate the needs of the employers, students, their parents and other significant stakeholders in terms of quality of passouts. The definition of the quality of passouts has to be objective and measurable. It should have relevance to present and future demands of the passouts. The quality should have provision of comparison to different groups of students. The quality passouts should be available to employers and society at right time and at fair price. All potential employers should have equal access to passouts. The quality of passouts should be assured through cost economic way.

The quality of passouts can be defined in terms of competencies and proficiency level in each competency. Competency profile for students of each discipline can be drawn and curriculum can be designed to achieve them. The competency profile and the proficiency level will be different for different disciplines. Three types of competencies profile can be designed for each discipline. These profiles are technical, managerial and social competencies. Employers, alumni, students and other significant stakeholders should validate the competency profile. This profile can be used to design the curriculum document that is educational plan for that particular discipline.

3. Definitions of Total Quality Management

It is a process. A process of continually improving the product and services of the institution to better satisfy the needs and expectations of the students, employers, society and other significant stakeholders.

4. Elements of Total Quality Management

The concept of total quality management evolved over the years and experiences related to quality management and improvements have been added to the philosophy of total quality management. A list of significant elements of total quality management is mentioned in exhibit 21.2 and described in subsequent paragraphs.

Exhibit No. 21.2: Elements of total quality management

➢ External customer focus ➢ Continuous improvement ➢ Preventive approach ➢ Universal quality responsibility ➢ Quality measurement ➢ Problem solving through treating root cause ➢ Participation, involvement and empowerment ➢ Team work ➢ Benchmarking	➢ Value addition ➢ Training ➢ Proactive approach ➢ Thinking holistically ➢ Variability reduction ➢ Customer satisfaction ➢ Quality assurance ➢ Reporting ➢ Recognition ➢ Feedback

4.1 External Customer Focus

The major customers of technical institutions are students. Although they do not pay for the services but their parents pay the fee so their parents can also be considered indirect customers. Another group of customers is employers who give employment to passouts of the institution. In this case also employers do not pay to institutions but they pay to students through employment. In technical education this is a very interesting case where the direct customer is not paying to service provider. The whole educational programme is designed for students. The programme is designed on the basis of requirements of their potential employers and their self-needs. To prepare students to take up job or to be self-employed numbers of functions are performed in the institutions. These functions directly and indirectly contribute for the development of the students. There are many functions in which the performers do not come in contact with the students and industries but they support the faculty and staff members to perform the academic functions effectively and efficiently. Without their support academic functions cannot be carried out perfectly. So within institution people and teams are tied in supplier customer relationship. Satisfaction of internal customers is key to satisfy the needs of the external customers. Institutional processes should be designed in a way to satisfy the needs of the internal and external customers. For example the curriculum document should be clear to understand by the teachers and instructors. It should be implementable. Think about a vaguely defined curriculum and try to answer question mentioned in exhibit 21.3.

Exhibit No. 21.3: Answer the questions related to implication of vaguely defined curriculum

➢ What teachers and instructors will teach? ➢ What students will learn? ➢ What interpretation of curriculum employers will do? ➢ What examiners will assess? ➢ What the stores department will purchase to facilitate teaching learning process? ➢ What will be the depth and coverage in testing?	➢ How many complaints do you expect related to curriculum document, its implementation and assessment? ➢ What training will you provide to teachers and instructress to implement the curriculum? ➢ How will you establish validity and reliability in assessment? ➢ How much efforts, time and energy will be wasted to clarify the things?

In the total quality management philosophy every individual or team working in the institution has customer. They should satisfy the requirements of their customer. It is said that quality is produced by various functions in the institution and the quality of service or product is defined by the poorest quality produced by any function. It may take worse shape also because quality may get deteriorate in subsequent series of function.

In case of vaguely designed curriculum document it may affect the total process of implementation and assessment. Thereby affecting the quality of learning of the students and their employment. Imagine that the curriculum is designed scientifically and new concept of competency development is incorporated in the curriculum that is new to faculty and staff members. In this case the implementers are educated and trained to understand and implement the curriculum. They are also trained to assess the learning based on the competency. Similarly other parties are also educated and trained. The crucial point is suppliers should satisfy the needs of the customer.

4.2 Continuous Improvement

Continuous improvement is inherent concept and process in total quality management. Continuous improvement is related to improving the quality of passouts in incremental way. For example, improving the attainment of competencies and proficiency level of the students on various competencies. In present context if the curriculum is content based and marks are awarded, improving the marks of students and average marks of students every year. Continuous improvement may be in the form of adding new competencies as per requirements of the employers and students. Teachers should be encouraged to set continuous improvement objectives in the subjects they are teaching. They should design teaching learning processes and inputs to achieve the continuous improvement objectives. It means continuous improvement objectives should be specific, measurable, attainable, realistic and time bond. Then only they will be able to design teaching learning processes and supporting processes to achieve set objectives. Continuous improvement can focus on time, efforts, way of producing learning, style of learning, causing joyful learning in natural way etc. The continuous improvements objectives can be set in the annual plan or subject plan. A teacher prepares a subject plan in the beginning of an academic year. To start with modest level of continuous improvement objectives should be set so that success can be realized to boost up the confidence. Later on for next year higher-level objectives can be set in this way the journey of continuous improvement continues.

The main aim of continuous improvement is to find the deficiencies, gaps, problems, obstacles and barriers in the process of teaching learning and removing them in such a way so that they do not get repeated again. Apart from tackling the problem one can look for opportunities to improve teaching learning process. For example, use of print, non-print and electronic media to make the learning interesting and to bring the real world in the institution. The remedial and improvement measures would depend on continuous improvement objectives. For example a teacher is interested to improve thc average marks of the students in a particular subject s/he is teaching. S/he should identify the poor performers through continuous tests and find out learning difficulties. S/he should design and provide remedial instructions to bring them up to a minimum level of achievement. To bring continuous improvement in teaching learning processes numerous tools and techniques are available. These tools and techniques can be selected and used by individuals and teams. Commonly used techniques to bring continuous improvement in teaching learning processes are subject planning, lesson planning, use of media, use of variety of teaching learning methods, shifting the responsibility of learning to students, continuously testing the achievement level of the students and remedial actions, use of computer aided instructions, using the fast learners as resource person and so on. Teachers should develop competence to use strengths of teaching learning methods for producing desired level of learning. They should select methods and media suiting to needs of the topic and level of the students. Management and scientific methods are used for other supporting processes of the institution. Most commonly used methods are process flow charting and process design, problem tree analysis, cause and effect diagram, creativity techniques, Pareto analysis, check sheets etc. Use of information technology and computers has significantly improved to increase the efficiency of processes.

4.3 Preventive Approach

This element of total quality management emphasizes to detect and prevent the problems before they affect the quality of processes or products. There is a popular saying on prevention that goes like this an ounce of prevention is worth a pound of cure. There are many techniques popularly used in educational institutions for preventing the factors affecting the quality of passouts. These methods are planning, potential problem analysis, risk analysis, problem solving, performance review, performance appraisal, continuous assessment of students learning, systems analysis, success analysis, flow charting, process design and many more.

4.4 Universal Quality Responsibility

The quality is a responsibility of all individuals and teams working in the institution including the students. It is also a responsibility of suppliers of materials, equipment, and students to the institution. It extends to the parents and industries, as they are also involved in the governance and management of the institution. Total quality management requires commitment of institutional members for maintaining the quality of products and services served to internal as well as external customers. The responsibility for quality is increased using various strategies such as involving people in various activities of the institution, granting them autonomy to maintain and improve quality, delegating them powers to take decisions and empowering teams.

4.5 Measuring the Quality

'If you can measure it you can manage it' holds good in quality measurement and quality management. It means the quality should always be defined in measurable terms. There are two more concepts used in measurement that is validity and reliability. If one subject is considered and achievement level of students is measured on any five or six questions out of eight and internal choice. You are not measuring the achievement on complete subject but on sixty per cent content. Again the passing marks are fifty per cent you are measuring only thirty per cent and certifying. Students are intelligent and they know the 80/20 rule they apply it and study well significant few and omit trivial many topics in the subject. It means there is a scope for even studying less than 30 per cent curriculum and getting certificates of pass. The reliability is also questionable in such cases because the performance depends on luck and guess and not on the coverage of the content and difficulty of content. Is it valid to provide certificate of pass and that too in professional technical institution? Will it satisfy the needs of the employers and students? As mentioned earlier, the needs of the employers and students should be translated in competency statements and proficiency level should also be defined for each competency. Each competency should be developed through teaching learning process and tested and certified. In such case institution can talk and prove objectively that it is functioning professionally and satisfying the needs of the customers. There are many techniques available and used for defining and measuring quality of passouts. The commonly used methods are job survey, task analysis and validation of competencies along with proficiency level. The achievement tests, skills tests and attitude tests can be designed and used to certify the competencies.

4.6 Problem Solving through Treating Root Causes

Problems at various stages of implementation of activities and processes affect the final quality of the product and services. Learning problems of the students in a particular topic may affect further learning. If learning problem is not analysed and solved properly it may affect learning in other connected subjects as well. Consequently whole or part of learning process may get disturbed. The teacher and students jointly identify, define, analyse and solve it. The root cause of the problem may lie in some other subjects that are prerequisite to present subject. There are numerous methods available to identify and solve the problems so that they do not recur. Some of them are content analysis, establishing horizontal and vertical linkages in subjects and topics, defining prerequisites, testing the entry behaviour of students, lesson planning using principles of learning such as simple to complex, concrete to abstract, known to unknown, single skill to multi-skills, multi-skills to complex skills, one-way communication to both way communications, teaching to learning. For other institutional processes planning, problem tree analysis, cause and effect diagram, flow chart, system analysis techniques are used.

4.7 Participation, Involvement and Empowerment

People's participation is one of the significant factors in assuring the success of total quality management movement. Institutional members should think that quality movement is initiated by them. It means they should be involved in total quality movement right from the beginning. They should freely discuss pros and cons of the quality aspect, set the quality objectives, design the strategies to achieve set quality objectives, implement the strategies and evaluate the achievements. Continuous and full involvement of employees in total quality movement assures their commitment throughout the journey of the quality improvement. It becomes their natural habit to produce, improve and add features to quality of products and services provided by institution. Full potential of faculty and staff members can be realized through need based training and empowerment. Trained, competent and empowered people provide competitive edge to institution for continuous quality improvement. Empowered people feel that their position is important in the institution and their contribution is meaningful and necessary for improving the quality. They are not treated like cogs in the wheel. One of the conditions for continuous improvement is continuous learning for enhancing the competence, capability and capacity to bring quality improvement. Continuous and collective learning about the business of the institution and refining it to satisfy the needs of the students and employers is essential for institutions moving towards never ending quality journey. Number of techniques have been used in the past by various institutions to enhance participation and involvement of the people. Some indicative techniques are listed in exhibit 21.4.

Exhibit No. 21.4: Techniques of participation, involvement, and empowerment

➢ Management by objectives	➢ Job enlargement
➢ Attitude survey	➢ Job enrichment
➢ Performance appraisal and development system	➢ Job rotation
	➢ Delegation
➢ Employee development programmes	➢ Decentralization
➢ Team work incentive programmes	➢ Quality circle
➢ Self-management work teams	➢ Focus team
➢ Task force	➢ Suggestion programmes
➢ Reward programmes	➢ Creativity session
➢ Multiple management	➢ Management by committees
➢ Consultative supervision	➢ Shared leadership
➢ Democratic supervision	➢ Training groups

Participatory approaches have tremendous potential and bring variety of benefits when used whole-heartedly. The benefits of participatory management approaches are stated in exhibit 21.5.

Exhibit No. 21.5: Benefits of participation, involvement and empowerment

➢ Quick decisions and enhanced quality of decisions	➢ Shared/collective responsibility
	➢ Distributed work
➢ Quick implementation of decisions	➢ Lower risk
➢ Increased responsibility and accountability for quality	➢ Individuals and teams are ready to face challenges
➢ Enhanced commitment of individuals and teams for quality	➢ Sustained interest in work
	➢ Work does not suffer because absence of a person
➢ Enhanced self-confidence for continuous improvement	➢ Healthy conflict

(*Contd.*)

(*Contd.*)

➤ Enhanced coordination and cooperation among individuals and teams ➤ Improved quality of academic and non-academic processes ➤ Time saving ➤ Increased flexibility in functioning ➤ Continuous training and education of institutional members ➤ Improved performance in core processes ➤ Conducive environment for quality movement ➤ Creative problem solving ➤ Enhanced trust among institutional members	➤ Effective utilization of resources ➤ Effective communication within and outside the institution ➤ Healthy interpersonal relationship ➤ Good discipline ➤ Amicable settlement of disputes ➤ Power equalization ➤ Desired change in behaviour ➤ Practice of democratic values ➤ Motivation to contribute more for quality improvement ➤ Preparation to take higher challenges and job positions ➤ Satisfied employees

The participatory approaches are successful under certain conditions. The institution should note that prerequisite conditions are fulfilled otherwise it may take wrong direction. One more point should be cautiously noted that participation is not solution of all problems of the institution. The situation should be cautiously diagnosed and appropriate approach of participation should be used. Some indicative conditions for successful participation are stated in exhibit 21.6.

Exhibit No. 21.6: Condition for successful participation, involvement and empowerment

➤ Management should be committed to implement participatory approaches ➤ Employees should be trained to do the job professionally ➤ Sufficient time should be devoted by management and senior faculty for participation, involvement and empowerment	➤ Jobs and tasks should be allotted as per interest and ability of the individuals and team ➤ Open atmosphere of trust and confidence should be created ➤ Total philosophy of participation should be implemented

Participation, involvement and empowerment is a philosophy paramount to total quality management. It has to be introduced in planned way in the institution. The successful implementation of participation, involvement and empowerment depends on factors listed in exhibit 21.7.

Exhibit No. 21.7: Factors responsible for successful participation, involvement and empowerment in technical institutions

➢ Trust and confidence in faculty members, staff members and students ➢ Importance of the work ➢ Clarity of task and objectives ➢ Clarity of roles ➢ Opportunities to use knowledge, skills and experiences ➢ Relationship of management with faculty members, staff members and students ➢ Training opportunities and scope for learning new things	➢ Personal and collective responsibility of individuals and teams ➢ Supportive leadership ➢ Effective communication ➢ Team work ➢ Recognition, appreciation and acknowledgement of contributions ➢ Scope for gaining status ➢ Personal, group and work related problem solving ➢ Quantity and quality of rewards ➢ Scope for career advancement ➢ Timely availability of resources

4.8 Teamwork

Working in teams produce synergic effects in the institution. Many quality improvement objectives cannot be attained without teamwork. Teamwork produces both creativity and innovations that are essential and prerequisite condition for total quality management. There are many academic activities that cannot be completed without teamwork. These activities are learning need identification, curriculum development, seminars, projects, problem solving, learning resources development, examination of students, preparing reports etc. Teams are most powerful tool for continuous improvement and collective learning. In total quality management most of the techniques and tools are developed for teams. Teams have introduced a new concept of multi-disciplinary and multi-skills approach to total quality management. For more description on teamwork refer chapter 8 on teamwork.

4.9 Benchmarking

Benchmarking is a process that compares the quality of passouts and services of the institution with the quality of passouts and services of other institution performing well. The institution can benchmark curriculum, contact hours, quality of faculty, resources, inputs to various processes, facilities to the students, incentives to faculty and staff, researches conducted in the institution, consultancy project, budget, and almost every thing. Statutory organizations, professional bodies, employers and students also do the benchmarking. The benchmarking provides the concrete evidence that improvement can be brought in. Bench-marking can be undertaken in many ways within the institution on above parameters. For more description on benchmarking refer chapter 20 on reengineering.

4.10 Value Addition

Value addition is related to increasing the value of products and services offered by the institution. It is also related to offering more facilities to students and stakeholders and its employees. The concept of value addition is based on the notion that there must be a better way. This concept of searching better ways is helpful in adding values to the output, processes and input. Some indicative examples of value addition are listed in exhibit 21.8.

Exhibit No. 21.8: Examples of value addition

Passouts employment	**When they are students – more** facilities in terms of
➤ Better placed in national and multi-national companies ➤ Placed in companies offering better career opportunities ➤ Placed with highest salary ➤ Placed on key positions ➤ Placed on prestigious projects **Teaching learning process** ➤ Use of variety of methods and media to produce expected level of learning ➤ Create opportunities for joyful learning ➤ Opportunity to work on live projects ➤ Opportunity to interact with students and faculty of other institutions ➤ Opportunity to interact with eminent personalities ➤ Accessibility to library of other institution	➤ Free coaching ➤ Personality development programmes ➤ Entrepreneurship development programmes ➤ Preparation for competitive examination ➤ Health check ups ➤ Free sports ➤ Free cultural programmes ➤ Scholarship ➤ Better accommodation ➤ Selected hobby courses ➤ Sponsorship for academic and non-academic activities ➤ Part-time employment ➤ Membership of professional chapters ➤ Share on consultancy projects ➤ Accessibility to internet and electronic media

(Contd.)

(*Contd.*)

➢ Clear expectations form students ➢ Adequate learning resources ➢ Personal academic problem solving ➢ No wastage of time in waiting, vacant periods, transportation, unproductive assignments in the institution ➢ Complete information on various academic activities	➢ Participation in community development activities ➢ Availability of tools, implements, and consumables for conducting practical and project work. ➢ More exposure to industrial environment and live problems ➢ Career counselling ➢ Transportation ➢ Safe drinking water ➢ Proper sanitation

4.11 Training

Training is the base for total quality improvement in the institution. The training of faculty and staff members should be conducted to prepare them for teaching learning profession. A systematic approach should be followed to train them. The training need analysis should be carried out every year and training programmes should be designed and implemented at right time. The continuous improvement, problem solving, problem prevention, value addition, innovations and wastage reduction cannot be thought out without professional training of faculty and staff members. The induction of new teachers and in-service training of existing teachers is essential to fulfil the changing quality demand of the employers and students. For more details on training refer chapter 19 on learning organization.

4.12 Proactive Approach

Proaction is eminently preferable to reaction. Proact means to anticipate events and be in a position to take appropriate action as the right moment arrives. To react means to have no or little anticipation and do something only when something wrong in terms of problem, barriers, obstacles and crisis has occurred. Use of proactive approaches always put the institution in right perspective in right time. The institution can anticipate opportunities and prepare itself to grab the opportunities at right time before it goes away. Difference between proactive and reactive approach is listed in exhibit 21.9. For more details on proactive approach refer chapter 4 on planning.

Exhibit No. 21.9: Difference between proactive and reactive approach

Proactive approach	*Reactive approach*
➢ People anticipate future opportunities for quality improvement ➢ Focus on grabbing opportunities at right time ➢ People are better informed ➢ People are alert to challenges ➢ People are ready to accept change ➢ People are active for professional life ➢ People prevent problems ➢ People think holistically ➢ People are creative ➢ People do continuous planning and re-planning	➢ People analyze past and solve problems ➢ People live passive life ➢ People lack information ➢ People are good in problem solving and crisis management ➢ People are expert in detection of problems ➢ People do situation based thinking ➢ People possess analytical skills ➢ People do one time planning ➢ People adopt causal approach

4.13 Thinking Holistically

Total quality management itself hints for holistic thinking. The situation should be thought out from all the angles and its consequences should be analyzed. For example institution is planning to offer a continuing education programme it should see that training needs have been identified, course material has been prepared, relevant examples from clients company have been picked, financial implication have been examined, availability of faculty ensured, administrative arrangements have been made and so on. Then only total quality can be assured and customer can be satisfied. Thinking holistically approach helps in visualizing the whole picture at the same time seeing the minor details of various elements of the situation. Visualization helps to anticipate the impact of initiatives on the total quality of product or services and at the same time assuring and maintaining the quality of every activity in the initiative.

4.14 Variability Reduction

Variation is found in the marks of students in one subject among subjects and among disciplines. If the variation is more, there is more variability it means there is low consistency in the performance of students. Low consistency affects the over all quality. Variability can be at various stages of educational programmes. It may be in results of the students, teaching learning process, inputs, supporting processes and so on. The quality is directly proportional to variability at various stages of educational programmes. This variability can be reduced using various educational techniques such as pre-test, bridge courses, additional subjects, remedial instructions, recognition of prior learning and so on. To eliminate the variability in processes flow chart, statistical process control, problem solving, system design, performance assessment and 360-degree feedback methods are used. To design variability reduction methods Pareto analysis, rank ordering and matrix approach is used.

4.15 Customer Satisfaction

The basic aim of total quality management philosophy is to satisfy the needs of the customers and stakeholders first time and every time. The needs of the customer may be changing with respect to time. The educational programmes are related to behaviour modification and for every batch of students the amount, range and extent of behaviour may be different. So to satisfy the changing needs the processes of the institution should be well designed but at the same time they have to be flexible and dynamic. There could be variety of expectations of different stakeholders from the institution. These expectations should be identified, defined and satisfied following legal procedures. Stakeholders' analysis, industry institute interaction, collaboration, networking, and coalition techniques are generally used to identify and satisfy the needs of the customers.

4.16 Quality Assurance

Quality assurance is a proactive approach to manage total quality of product and services of the institution. The quality is assured using scientific methods at different phases of education system. Needs assessment, curriculum design, subject plans, lesson plans, continuous assessment and feedback, performance appraisal, competency attainment certification are the techniques commonly used to assure the quality of product and services. Training of faculty and staff members is paramount in assuring the quality of product and services. Another aspect to quality assurance is committing resources including teaching learning resources at right time to perform activities.

4.17 Reporting

Measurement and control are continuous activities in total quality management movement. The data needs to be recorded for future reference and comparison. It is also essential to report and share the success of quality movement with all internal and external stakeholders. The purpose of reporting is to provide the recognition to total quality management movement and learn from success and failure.

4.18 Recognition

Recognition of efforts made by institutional members in achieving quality objectives plays a significant role for further motivation to improve the quality. Theory of reinforcement suggests that desired behaviour should be acknowledged immediately and it should be positively reinforced with appropriate motivators. Institution has a range of motivation to be provided to its employees for the work done to improve quality. The kind of motivation that can be provided is listed in exhibit 21.10.

Exhibit No. 21.10: Motivation to employees

➢ Appreciation letter ➢ Certificate ➢ Presentation of achievements to management and governing body members ➢ Video recording of significant achievement and publicizing it ➢ Gifts ➢ Prizes ➢ Rolling shield ➢ Badges ➢ Mementoes ➢ Invitation on tea or dinner ➢ Coverage in college news letter	➢ Sponsoring for attending conferences, seminars, training programmes, symposiums, quiz, conventions, study tours ➢ Introduction with dignitaries ➢ Study leave ➢ Sabbatical leave ➢ Offering good projects ➢ Key positions ➢ Increments ➢ Promotions ➢ Salary increase ➢ Privileges ➢ Felicitation

4.19 Feedback

Receiving feedback on quality of product and services is essential element of total quality management. It should be an integral part of the total quality management system. This feedback is received from the employers and passouts of the institution. Feedback is also obtained on the performance of internal processes of the institution. Continuous external as well as internal feedback is obtained for improving the performance of the system as a whole and its significant processes. Techniques used for obtaining feedback are baseline survey, success analysis, tracer study, performance evaluation, benchmarking and employer satisfaction survey.

5. Model of Total Quality Implementation in Technical Institutions

In the past number of institutions have taken initiative to introduce total quality management philosophy in their institutions. The model shown in exhibit 21.11 is evolved over the years based on experiences in technical institutions. This model is generic and can be used in any technical institution. The significant steps of the model are briefly described in subsequent paragraphs.

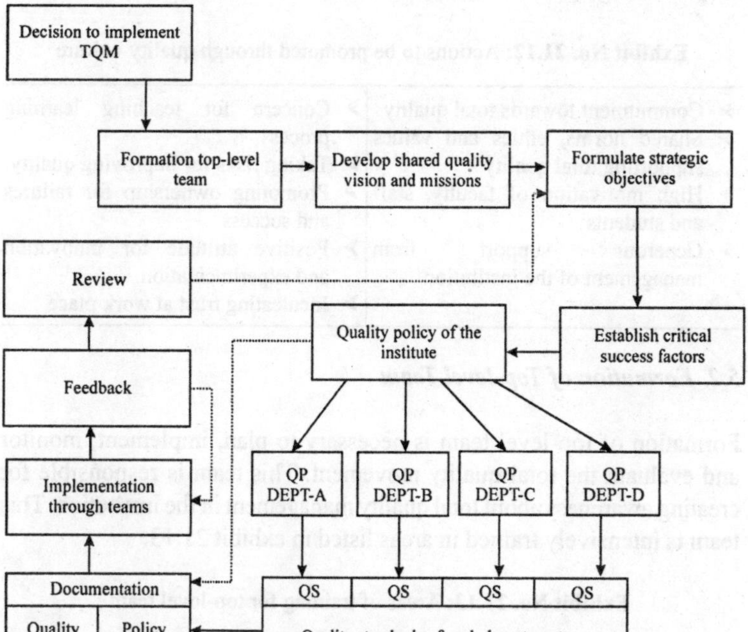

Exhibit No. 21.11: Model of total quality management in technical institution

5.1 Decide to Proceed

Pressure for quality of passouts compelled engineering institutions to opt for implementing quality improvement programmes. The first step towards total quality management is to list the benefits the institution is going to have from total quality management. It is necessary to have commitment of Governing body and Director to implement total quality management in the institute. The governing body and director of the institute will provide resources for total quality management. The decision for implementing total quality management in the institution must be based on careful study on criteria like institutes past performance, resources, funds, infrastructure, staff-student ratio etc. It is suggested to do strengths, weaknesses, opportunities and threats analysis before going for total quality management. The total quality management movement requires quality culture in the institution that needs support of the governing body and director of the institute. The quality culture helps to satisfy needs of the students, parents, and stakeholders. The Quality culture is necessary for promoting actions stated in exhibit 21.12.

Exhibit No. 21.12: Actions to be promoted through quality culture

➢ Commitment towards total quality ➢ Shared norms, ethics and values supporting total quality ➢ High motivation of faculty, staff and students ➢ Generous support from management of the institution	➢ Concern for teaching learning process ➢ Taking risks for improving quality ➢ Promoting ownership for failures and success ➢ Positive attitude for innovation and experimentation ➢ Inculcating trust at work place

5.2. Formation of Top-level Team

Formation of top-level team is necessary to plan, implement, monitor and evaluate the total quality movement. This team is responsible for creating awareness about total quality management in the institution. This team is intensively trained in areas listed in exhibit 21.13.

Exhibit No. 21.13: Areas of training for top-level team

➢ Total quality management philosophy ➢ Total quality management theory and practice ➢ Creation of shared vision and perspective plans ➢ Shared leadership and team building ➢ Total quality management training strategies ➢ Preparation of quality manual and quality policy	➢ Change management ➢ Tools and techniques of quality management ➢ Resources mobilization ➢ Monitoring and evaluation of quality initiative ➢ Seeking participation ➢ Process design ➢ Creativity and innovation

Top level trained team will impart training to each head of department, and selected faculty members, then the trained faculty will impart training in their respective departments.

5.3 Development of Shared Quality Vision and Mission

Development of the institute vision is the crucial step towards total quality management. Ideally, this should take place through creativity sessions during top-level meetings under the guidance of experts. The vision is normally expressed in terms of commitment to quality, responsiveness to users' requirements and desire to achieve more in the future. It must be exciting, clear ambitious, desirable and shared or accepted. The mission statements are expressed in terms of long-term desire for accomplishment of quality. A team of experienced professionals develop mission statements. This exercise can be completed under the guidance of top-level team through series of workshops, meetings and discussions.

5.4 Formulation of Strategic Objectives

Quality vision gives the direction for navigation. Formulating objectives is most important to understand the road for the quality journey. The objectives must be stated in simple and clear manner. They should be written in attainable, measurable, specific and time bound manner. They should fulfil the requirements of the vision. The overall objectives of quality change should be communicated to all institutional members including students.

5.5 Establishing Critical Success Factors

To measure the quality of performance of various processes, departments, teams and individuals' specifications or standards need to be set. It is difficult to set the specifications or standards for all processes but it can be set for overall programme in terms of competencies and proficiency level. There may be various areas of concern or having problems or perceived as process difficulties in the institute. To identify such areas and setting the specifications for quality is establishing critical success factors. The critical success areas may differ from discipline to discipline within the institution. Examples of some of the concerned areas are given below:

- Access to stakeholders
- Customer satisfaction

- Effective learning
- Meeting students needs
- Cost of the quality
- Climate
- Culture
- Leadership
- Safety
- Services for customers
- Shared values

Indicators of above-mentioned areas may be generated and actual practices to be compared against the stated indicators. Indicators must be stated in terms of quality, quantity, time, location etc. These should be observable and measurable.

5.6 Quality Policy of the Institute

The quality policy consists both the vision statement and the mission statements. The faculty and staff members are required to understand, implement and maintain the quality system relevant to their function in respective department. A team of heads of departments, administrative officer, workshop superintendent, director and selected senior faculty members formulates the quality policy. This policy is detailed out for all areas of functioning of the institution. Then this policy document is shared with institutional members and their comments are invited to refine and finalize it. Once the direction of quality change is clear in the form of institute's quality policy and its objectives, the group will select crucial areas for further detailing. The areas may be such as; learning resources, staff development, student amenities, industry institute interaction, continuing education, administration, examination, curriculum development etc. The institute should operate and maintain an effective quality management system. Indicators for each specific objective have to be identified. Systematic monitoring of quality for each critical action stage is to be ensured. Checks and quality tools are applied at appropriate stages.

5.7 Quality Policy at Department Level

The quality policy of the institute and major areas provide guideline to formulate the policy and objectives at department level. The team at departmental level may be formed. The team will formulate departmental policy and specific objectives in tune with the institute policy. Each department must include areas such as classroom instruction, laboratory and workshop experiences, students' projects, formative assessment, students' guidance and support in quality policy. However some departments may include other areas of concern.

5.8 Quality Standards of Department

Teamwork is required to accomplish specific objective. The standards of quality are to be stated for every major activity in each area. The quality standards in terms of minimum acceptable level have to be decided with employers and students. The customer may be external like passouts, parents, industries and other stakeholders of the institution or internal like students, fellow members and other employees. The negotiation with customer is necessaiy before fixing the quality standards. For example quality standards for civil engineering department (provision of room and facilities) may be like

- No class will be subjected to change more than one room in a day
- All rooms will be equipped with sufficient desks, tables to accommodate every member of the class
- The lecturers will report, in writing, any fault of electric switches, fans, wiring and audio-visual aid to the person responsible on the same day
- Every room including chalkboard will be cleaned before the start of working hour.

The acceptance of quality standards of all the employees of the department is the key to implementation.

5.9 Documentation

Documentation is essential part of the process towards total quality management. It is maintained at planning and implementation stage. Results of processes are systematically documented, communicated and shared with institutional members. People must know what they are required to do and what they are doing. This comparison is possible through documentation. The quality document will help to measure and reduce deviation. It is also helpful to take corrective actions to meet quality standards.

5.10 Implementation

Quality action plan is implemented in right spirit to achieve quality. Implementation of activities requires resources at right time that are provided by management of the institution. It has to be ensured early to avoid problems because of resources shortage. Most of the quality improvement activities do not require additional resources. The critical activities are to be given more importance.

5.11 Feedback and Review

Prompt and efficient corrective action is essential to any quality system. When non-conformances or failures are found these must be put right. The ideal is of course to get it "Right First Time". The process of correction should start right from implementation of first activity. It reduces deviation between 'what should happen' and 'what is happening'. Problem solving techniques are used by individuals and teams to solve and prevent the problems. Periodical review of achievement of objectives is done to maintain quality and to set new quality objectives.

6. Summary

Total quality management in technical institution is a new concept. The quality of the passouts is not well defined in measurable and specific terms. The quality parameters are not prevailing that is why people interpret the quality of passouts in their own way. Institutions also offer different curriculum under same title. There is wide variation in courses offered by institutions. The whole programme of technical education can be defined in terms of competencies of passouts and their proficiency level in each competency. The competencies should be validated at national level and minimum proficiency level should be defined. Management *Gurus* have defined quality in various ways relating the quality with customer needs and satisfying them. There are various features of total quality management such as external customer focus, continuous improvement, preventive approach, universal quality responsibility, quality measurement, problem solving through treating root cause, participation, involvement and empowerment, team work, benchmarking, value addition, training, proactive approach, thinking holistically, students and industry involvement, variability reduction, customer satisfaction, quality assurance, reporting, recognition and feedback. Total quality management is introduced in the institution following sequence of steps. The vision of the institution, quality policy, quality standards and monitoring indicators are used to assure and monitor the quality of instructional processes. The total quality is assured using synergy of teams. The achievements are measured comparing the performance against critical success factors.

7. Activity

Design a total quality management system for your institution and get it approved from institutional members and stakeholders.

REFERENCES

Gupta, B.L. (2000). An overview of participatory management approaches and their applicability in the management of polytechnics, *The Journal of Engineering Education*, Vol. XIV, No. 1 July–Sept. 2000.

Jablonski, J.R. (1992). *Implementing TQM,* 2nd ed. Pfeiffer & Co., California USA.

Joseph and Susan Berk (1995). *Total Quality Management*, Excel Books, New Delhi.

Maclean, G.E. (1993). *Documenting Quality for ISO 9000 and Other Industry Standards,* Tata McGraw Hill Publishing Co. Ltd., New Delhi.

Sundra Raju, S.M. (1995). *TQM – A Primer*, Tata McGraw Hill Publishing Co. Ltd., New Delhi.

TTTI Bhopal (1992). Quality Circle Guideline Document for Polytechnics. Seminar Proceedings of the National Seminar on application of TQM approach in Technical Education organised by PDU-ISTE, Bhopal (21-24 November, 1995).

Zairi Mohammed (1991). *TQM for Engineers,* Woodhead Publishing Limited U.K.

22

Networking

> ***Objective:*** The readers will be able to:
>
> 1. State the need and importance of networking.
> 2. Describe the concept of networking for technical institutions.
> 3. List the forms of networks.
> 4. State the purpose of networking.
> 5. Explain the steps of networking.
> 6. Explain the whole system improvement process through network.
> 7. Describe the network activities for technical institutions.
> 8. Explain the process of networking.
> 9. Describe the process of functioning of the network.
> 10. Explain the network activities for technical institutions.
> 11. List the skills required to network.

1. Introduction

Institutions cannot work in isolation. There is a demand for increased variety of services from the technical institutions. Different clients and beneficiaries are putting institutions in great pressure to satisfy their growing and changing needs. There is a demand for greater service choice in each area of functioning of the institution. At the same time there is a pressure for innovative services focusing on quality, speed and accuracy. Different customers, clients, and beneficiaries have different demand for services and products. Similarly there is a great uncertainty in technical education system because its functioning is wholly dependent on the employers market and their market is dependent on the customers. Under such conditions institutions need to develop to cope up changing needs, variety of needs, different needs, growing needs, with quality and time. Institutions may not have capacity to meet the above demands of the clients, customers and beneficiaries. Therefore they need to network for pooling together their capacities and capabilities.

2. Concept of Networking

The network is a way to mobilize the capabilities and capacities of different organizations to satisfy the needs of the customers, clients and beneficiaries and to seize opportunities to grow and develop the business of network partners on mutual basis. The network adds value to products and services of the institution at comparatively low price with ease and comfort. One network is shown in exhibit 22.1.

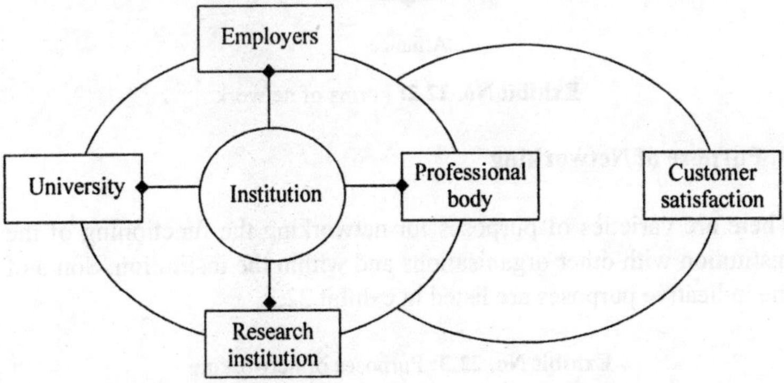

Exhibit No. 22.1: Networking for customer satisfaction

The institution can network with external organizations with specific purposes. There could be one or more than one purposes of networking for each network. An institution can participate in more than one network. It can play central role in one network and network partner role in the other network. The network provides an opportunity to collaborate the best resources of the network partners to excel better. The networking can be done within the institution. The networking can take variety of shapes with external organisations and within the organisation. The networking can be one to one or one to many. It all depends on purpose of the networking. In some situation institution can be the major provider of the services and products and in other it can be the distributor of the services and products of other institutions. The forms of networking are listed in exhibit 22.2.

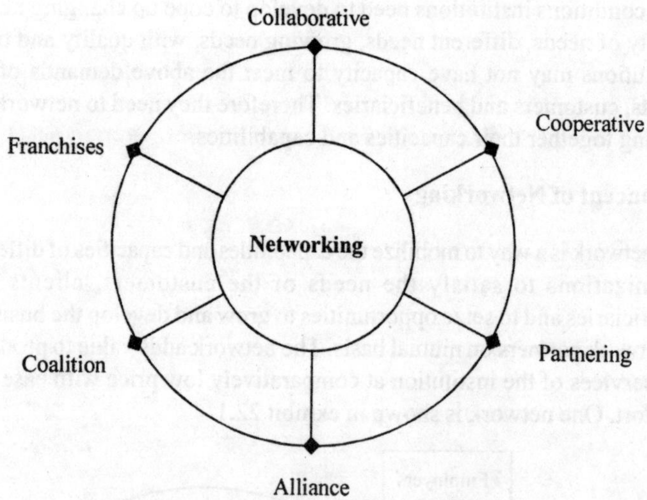

Exhibit No. 22.2: Forms of network

3. Purpose of Networking

There are varieties of purposes for networking the functioning of the institution with other organisations and within the institution. Some of the indicative purposes are listed in exhibit 22.3.

Exhibit No. 22.3: Purposes of networking

Networking with external organisations

➢ To meet the changing, growing, different and variety of demands of customers, clients and beneficiaries ➢ To expand customer base ➢ To ensure quality of product and services ➢ To add value to product and services through creativity, innovation and use of technology ➢ To create win-win situation ➢ To meet the competition ➢ To meet the challenges ➢ To deal with uncertainties	➢ To deal with changing environment ➢ To share information and experiences ➢ To share problems and opportunities ➢ To avoid the duplication of efforts ➢ To pool resources to grab national and international opportunities ➢ To generate resources ➢ To benchmark the product, services and processes ➢ To increase market base ➢ To create new interests and goals ➢ To expand family of institution ➢ To cope up with uncertainties

(*Contd.*)

Networking within the institution

➤ To promote synergic effects ➤ To promote flexibility in working ➤ To accelerate the pace of internal change ➤ To increase the rate of institutional learning ➤ To mobilize resources ➤ To share information and experiences ➤ To share problems and opportunities ➤ To avoid the duplication of efforts ➤ To promote effective communication within the institution ➤ To develop corporate culture	➤ To enhance strengths and reduce weaknesses ➤ To create mutual support ➤ To manage crisis ➤ To reduce wastage ➤ To promote mutual trust ➤ To harness the collective potential of people ➤ To use collective wisdom ➤ To link institutions of similar goals ➤ To harness power of network ➤ To increase access to resources and access to customers

4. Whole System Improvement

The networking among technical institutions and other organisations can improve whole system of technical education, social development and economy development. The networks need to be planned carefully for a particular state and the whole nation. There could be various models of networking with a specific purpose.

Networking for educational programme development: Networking for educational programme development can improve the quality of instructions in the whole system of technical education. The network for each discipline can be developed nationwide. There could be one central agency having responsibilities listed in exhibit 22.4.

Exhibit No. 22.4: Responsibility of central agency for developing programmes

Design of curriculum on scientific basis Industrial survey Technological survey Entry level of students Educational technology **Design of print and non-print instructional material** Development of text books, work books, teacher guide, students guide, laboratory manual, project work, research work, assignments, power point presentations, charts, models, video films etc. Guidance on library, laboratory and classroom setting	**Certification** Assessment scheme, assessment guide, process of award of certificate **Evaluation of the impact of the programme** Tracer study Action research Impact assessment Feedback on the design of the programme Scope for improving the programme

Network for educational programme development is shown in exhibit 22.5.

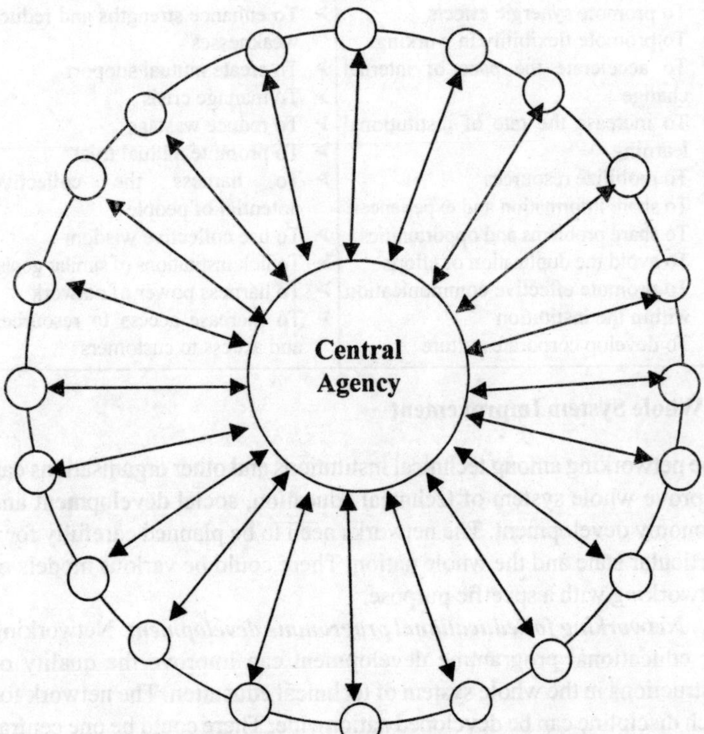

Exhibit No. 22.5: Network for instructional resources development

The network can be formed and developed selecting one centre of excellence in a particular discipline at national level as central agency. Other institutions having comparative strengths in that particular disciplines or components of the discipline can become network partners. The other partners of the network can be research institutions in that discipline, statutory and professional bodies, employers, universities, industries and other agencies having experience and expertise. The central agency can coordinate the educational programme development activity for a particular discipline. It should use cradle to grave approach to design educational programmes involving identified partners. It should develop a strategic plan and responsibility should be distributed to network partners as per their strengths and interest. It should prepare complete package for a particular programme and that package should be followed in all institutions uniformly in that discipline. Using separate network for each discipline uniform programmes can be developed for the whole country. The network partners will develop their capacity and capability participating in these programmes. They will get an opportunity to interact with each other to learn many new things. This way minimum standards of quality of all processes can be assured in the technical education system. Beside it there would be obvious benefits of the network.

The networks can be developed for other purposes such as offering continuing education programmes, consultancy, research and development, community development, developing physically challenged people, development of women, working for deprived section of people, winning the competition at world level in specific field of life such as space technology, production of particular goods, communication, energy, environment etc. The network can be developed on self-sustained basis to earn and serve the institutions in the country. The institutions, employers, industries, entrepreneurs can be customers for network. It is not necessary to develop separate network for each purpose. The existing network should be used for more than one purpose with a vision at national level.

Similarly the networks can be developed among the states and institutions for specific purpose to take advantage of opportunity. The institutions should have internal networks for producing synergic results. The basis of these networks would be different than network constituted at national level. These networks will mainly work for local purposes and innovations including sharing all types of resources and solving local problems. Networks at local level can reduce duplication of resources development and efforts. The purpose of local network should focus on developing, sustaining, and harnessing the infrastructure and talent. It may be related to any purposes mentioned in exhibit 22.3. The local network would certainly reduce wastage of resources and improve utilization of resources for greater cause.

5. Process of Networking

The processes of networking are very simple and easy because it creates win-win situation for network partners. The steps of network implementation are shown in exhibit 22.6 and described briefly in subsequent paragraphs.

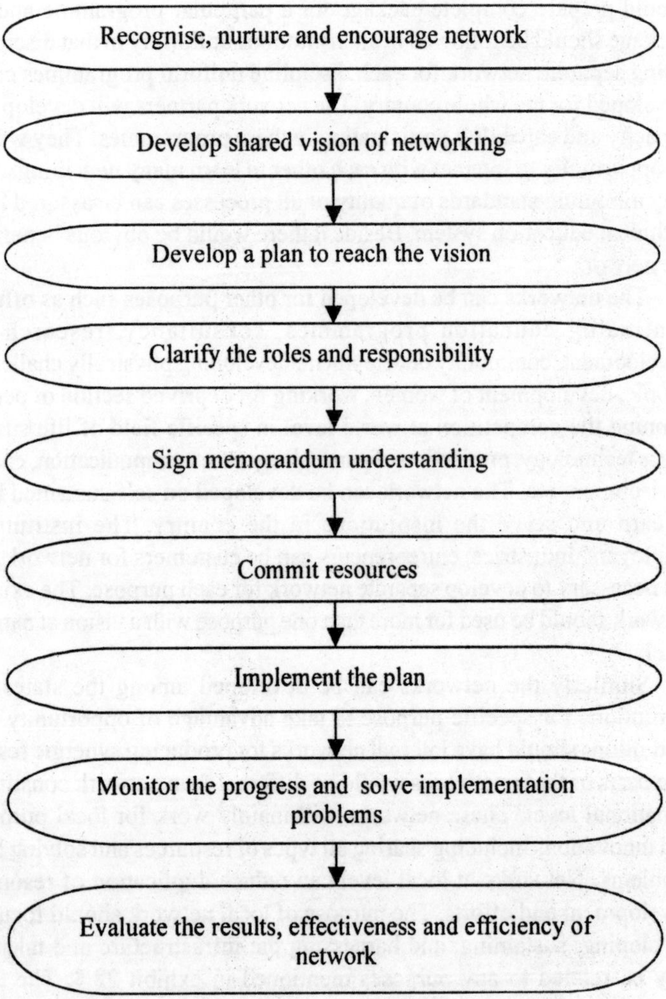

Exhibit No. 22.6: Steps of network implementation

5.1 Recognise, Encourage and Nurture Network

The institution should identify its strengths, opportunities and areas for networking. It should identify the organisations with whom it can do networking for mutual benefit. It should encourage the partners for networking through negotiations. There could be some policy problems related to networking. It should sort out the initial problems and barriers for mutual benefits.

5.2 Develop Shared Vision of Networking

The network partners should collectively interact at different levels and at different times in different ways to craft the shared vision to grab the environment opportunity. The vision should create win-win situation for all partners and customers. There should be super ordinate goals for collective working and individual goals for individual contribution. The shared vision should create ambition, hope and expectations for growth and development of network partners. The shared vision should create opportunity for creativity, innovation, synergy, and collaboration. It should compel network partners to excel their best for the benefit of the network.

5.3 Develop a Plan to Reach the Vision

The network partners should develop a strategic, tactical and annual plan of action to smoothen the performance and fix up the responsibility. The plan should be developed participatively addressing the critical major activities. It should not create rigidity for functioning. The plan should be shared at different levels with the network partners. There should be provision for incorporating the environmental changes in the plan. It should come out from documents and should be in the minds of the implementers.

5.4 Clarify the Roles and Responsibility

On the basis of network plan decide the roles and responsibility of network partners. The network partners should decide the central agency for coordinating and controlling the progress made on the plan. Different network partners should take central role for implementing different major critical activities. One institution can take central major role in one activity and minor role in another activity in same network.

5.5 Sign Memorandum of Understanding

The network partner should sign memorandum of understanding to formalize the process of networking and show their interest working with network. There could be one memorandum of understanding for one network explaining the share of benefits, responsibilities and liabilities of partners.

5.6 Commit Resources

Network partners should commit right resources as per plan at right time. They should come forward with new ideas and problems if any. To maintain the network they should tolerate small network problems. The network should be institutionalised rather than personalized. The best way to commit the resources is to incorporate the network plan in organizational plan. The network partners can develop norms for effective relationship and follow it.

5.7 Implement the Plan

The network partners ensure the effective and efficient implementation of the plan at all levels. The central partner should ensure that every partner completes its part to achieve the objectives. The central partner possesses experiences and expertise in the area of working so it guides and facilitates the process of implementation.

5.8 Monitor the Progress and Solve the Implementation Problems

The central partner should monitor the progress on the plan and solve day-to-day problems of implementation. It should take major decisions related to implementation of the plans. The central partner should also prepare monitoring schedule to smoothen the monitoring process. It should also create a buffer of resources to meet the contingency. If significant changes have occurred in the environment and some activities have become redundant it should bring the facts in the notice of the network partners. Various tools and techniques such as review reports, review meetings, and problem solving workshops are used to monitor the progress of the work and involving partners.

5.9 Evaluate Results, Effectiveness and Results of the Network

The network partners jointly evaluate the achievement of the results and distribute the benefits to network partners as per agreement. Immediate distribution of benefits encourages partners to develop trust in network and enter in new agreements. It is a good learning exercise for network partners. They learn to enhance the effectiveness and efficiency of the network at the same time enjoy the benefits of the network. They can transform the new learning to their non-networked activities.

6. Functioning of Network

The network should have distinct characteristics to function effectively and efficiently. The networks should facilitate the functioning of institutions smoothly and efficiently. It should create scope for growth and development on multiple fronts of the institution. It should promote characteristics listed in exhibit 22.7.

Exhibit No. 22.7: Characteristics of network for effective functioning

➢ Shared vision or superordinate goals ➢ Visionary and transformational leadership ➢ Institutionalisation of agreement ➢ Norms for functioning ➢ Effective communication ➢ Electronic connectivity ➢ Mutual trust ➢ Create win-win situation ➢ Scope for innovation ➢ No duplication of efforts	➢ Fast action ➢ Problem solving and conflict management mechanism ➢ Frequent and open exchange of information ➢ Openly sharing the resources and experiences ➢ Extension motivation ➢ Continuous feedback

7. Network Activities for Technical Institution

Technical institutions can enter in varieties of network with different organisations. The network should facilitate the process of growth and development of network partners. Technical institution without proper design practices the concept of networking. The existing network is live with industries to maintain and sustain the performance. There is a great scope for networking with other types of organizations. These institutions should fulfil the demand in competitive, challenging, uncertain and changing environment. They need to undertake activities listed in exhibit 22.8 for strengthening the technical institutions.

8. Network Skills

Institutions participating in the network should promote network skills in the resource persons. The skills can be developed by the central agency or within the institution. In absence of key skills of networking it would be difficult to nurture effective networks. The key players in the network should develop skills listed in exhibit 22.9.

Exhibit No. 22.8: Activities for network institutions

Joint ventures
- Design of need based programmes
- Development of curriculum
- Design of training programmes
- Design of teaching-learning resources
- Design of research work
- Design of innovative projects
- Undertake joint problem solving
- Explore new market
- Explore new customers
- Increase customers
- Increase publications

Joint learning programmes
- Seminars
- Conferences
- Symposium
- Workshops
- Focus group discussions
- Learning projects
- Exchange of faculty
- Hand holding
- Training programmes
- Chapters of professional bodies
- On the job training
- Educational tours

Sharing
- Experiences
- Resources
- Expertise
- Capabilities
- Faculty and staff
- Knowledge
- Literature
- Culture
- Values and ethics
- Researches
- Power to award degree and certificates
- Customers and clients
- Profit and benefits

Learning resources
- Books
- Handouts
- Manuals
- Trainers hand book
- Power points
- Video films
- Computer aided instructions
- Self-learning packages
- Question papers
- Learning resources development and utilisation centre

Offering
- Continuing education programmes
- Research studies
- Problem solving
- Distance learning programmes
- On line programmes
- Extension services
- Awareness programmes
- Consultancy for technology development, system development and problem solving
- Testing and calibration
- Expertise
- Software design
- Information centres

Challenges
- Growing demand for learning competencies
- Variety of demands for learning
- Improving effectiveness and efficiency
- Reducing the cost
- Increasing relevance
- Removing weaknesses
- Minimising threats
- Increasing access
- Repetitive problems
- Retraining of staff
- Fast changing technologies and methodologies
- Loss of market
- Paucity of trained and experienced faculty
- High turnover of trained and experienced faculty

Exhibit No. 22.9: Key skills for networking

➢ Crafting vision of the network ➢ Strategic thinking ➢ Influencing, convincing and winning ➢ Negotiation ➢ Visualizing big picture ➢ Trust building ➢ Effective communication ➢ Fostering innovation	➢ Converting crisis and problem in opportunity ➢ Concern for others ➢ Concern for quality ➢ Use of information technology ➢ Receiving feedback ➢ Strengthening network ➢ Interdisciplinary skills ➢ Respect for diversity

9. Summary

Networking is a process of harnessing the strengths of the network partners to cover up the weaknesses of them and jointly undertaking activities to achieve a shared vision. The network partners can explore new opportunities for the growth and development of themselves and the system as a whole. Networks provide an opportunity to create win-win situation for every one including customers. Networking is necessary because the demands on institutions are increasing continuously in magnitude and variety. At the same time there is a uncertainty for sustained business in one area of functioning. There is possibilities of unwanted competition among the institution, which may create, lose-lose situation. This situation can be converted in win-win situation through networking. The network partners should be selected carefully considering their capabilities and capacities. The network should be self-sufficient, self-dependent and self-renewable so far its functioning is concerned. It should improve quality of services and products for customers at cheaper rates. It should develop the system as a whole. There are various areas of functioning in which the network at national, state and local level can be developed.

10. Activity

Assess the Effectiveness of Network

A list of questions is given in the format given below. Answering each question you can assess the effectiveness, efficiency and relevance of your network. Based on the level of effectiveness, efficiency and relevance you can take actions to enhance it.

Sl. No.	*Questions*	*Response*
1.	What is the vision of network?	
2.	What is the purpose of the network?	
3.	What flows through network?	
4.	Who control the activities of the network?	
5.	How are the problems and conflicts between network partners resolved?	
6.	Who coordinate the activities of network?	
7.	How are the responsibilities distributed among network partners?	
8.	How are the benefits distributed?	
9.	How are the effectiveness and efficiency of networks evaluated?	
10.	How one can withdraw from the network?	
12.	Are there alternatives if key players withdraw from the network?	
13.	How the network is sustained?	
14.	How the effectiveness and efficiency of the network is improved?	

REFERENCES

Christopher Mabey, Graeme Salaman and John Storey (1998). *Strategic Human Resources Development*, Sage Publication, London.

Kulkarni, D.S. and Dandoti, S.Z. (1996). Strategies to develop institutional linkages with other organisations, *The Journal of Engineering Education*, July 1996.

23

Marketing Educational Products and Services

Objectives: The readers will be able to:

1. State the need and importance of marketing the services and products of technical institutions.
2. State problems of technical institutions related to marketing .
3. Define the concept of marketing in context of technical institutions.
4. List the beneficiaries of products and services of technical institutions.
5. State the attractions to the customers of technical institutions.
6. List the areas of marketing of educational products and services.
7. State the products and services that can be marketable.

1. Introduction

Technical institutions are created to fulfil the technical manpower needs of the society. They are supposed to contribute for the upliftment of the society and economy through technology. They should understand the needs of the society and industry and address them through education and training. They should develop user-friendly technology, safe methods and ease in working. They should improve the quality of life of people. They should act as a think tank for the industry and society so far technological and technical manpower is concerned.

Kotler and Fox mentioned that all institutions operate in students market, faculty market, donor market and a public opinion market. Apart from this technical institutions operate in technological market as well. It has a major responsibility to satisfy the technological, social and economical needs of the society through various services and products. Needs of various stakeholders are varied and different. Kotler and Fox have defined marketing as effective management by an institution of its exchange relations with various markets and publics.

2. Significant Problems of Technical Institutions

Technical institutions function in open environment and have more stakeholders than industry or any other enterprise having diverse and changing expectations. The expectations of significant stakeholders are listed in exhibit 23.1.

Exhibit No. 23.1: Problems and expectations of significant stakeholders

Sl. No.	*Stakeholders*	*Expectations*
1.	Employers	➢ Expect competent passouts with professional approach ➢ Look for technology, training and innovation ➢ Entrepreneurial approach
2.	Students	➢ Varied expectations of low and high entry behaviour groups ➢ Changing expectations, learner centred and practical approaches
3.	Potential students	➢ Complete information about the performance of the institution ➢ Job assurance ➢ Joyful learning
4.	Society	➢ Technical skills up gradation ➢ Transfer of technology ➢ Technical assistance
5.	Parents	➢ Not interested to pay very high fee ➢ Quality education of their ward ➢ Discipline and facilitating academic environment
6.	Alumni	➢ Institution seek feedback and improve performance
7.	Government	➢ Adhere to rules and regulations ➢ Maintain academic standards
8.	Professional body	➢ Adhere to professional norms

(*Contd.*)

(Contd.)

Sl. No.	*Stakeholders*	*Expectations*
9.	Promoters	➢ Are interest in earning money ➢ Not interested in investment ➢ They are in business because other options are exhausted ➢ They are non-professional ➢ They are dependent on traditional retired and faculty who have no experience of managing private enterprise, never faced competition
10.	Governing body	➢ Strive for excellence ➢ Function professionally
11.	Teachers	➢ Fresh graduates having no experience of imparting education, less interested to pursue their carrier in technical institutions ➢ Most of the fresh graduates are not by choice they are by chance ➢ They are not prepared for the educational system ➢ Low paid ➢ More turn over ➢ Not professionally trained and exposed to research, development and learning material development

3. Concept of Marketing

In the educational context Kotler and Fox defined marketing. Marketing is the analysis, planning, implementation, and control of carefully formulated programmes designed to bring about voluntary exchanges of values with target markets to achieve institutional objectives. Marketing involves designing institutional offerings to meet the target market needs and desires, and using effective pricing, communication, and distribution to inform, motivate, and service the market.

The concept of marketing of educational services starts from the needs and wants of the stakeholders. They want students to perform the competencies on a specific job or role. It goes up to supply of competent passouts as per requirements of the employers. The employers may ask for increasing proficiency level and updating the competency of the employed personnel through training and the institution does it through continuing education programmes. In this process the identified competencies and developed competencies are one and same. That means the institution has consciously, scientifically and professionally worked on the needs of the employer and satisfied the needs. At the same time institution has charged for providing the services. In first case it has charged to students and in second it has charged to employers. The institution has to carry out following steps to market the services to the employer for one specific educational programme:

- Speculating that there is a need for institutional services and identifying the employers
- Approaching the employers with competence and capability of institution
- Convincing them that institution has a potential to satisfy their manpower needs
- Identifying manpower requirements and their competencies
- Planning to satisfy the requirements and development of competencies
- Invite students to join programmes
- Implementation of plan
- Evaluation of plan
- Providing the output to employers
- Receiving feedback on employers satisfaction and students satisfaction
- Refining above steps based on feedback

All these steps are the part of the marketing. To implement these steps successfully the institution must have capacity and capability. Otherwise it would fail to satisfy the needs of the employers and students. That will bring bad name to institution and next time it would be more difficult to market its services. That means less business to the institution and less revenue. Over a period of time it would loose corporate reputation and come down to closure stage because no demand for services. Similarly the institutions can enhance corporate image satisfying the needs of the employers and students and may make them permanent customer. Even they would become the sales man for the services of the institution. The employer who is taking one service and satisfied may readily accept other services such as continuing education programmes for their employees, joint projects and problem solving, collaborative research work, and collaborative learning programmes. In this way the institution can expand the spectrum of services with the captive customers.

4. Beneficiaries of Institutional Products and Services

The institution can also develop captive customers. These may be the schools from where the students take admissions in the institution. These may be the employers who employ the passouts of the institutions, towns, which take the services of the institution, entrepreneurs who give the consultancy work and so on. If the institution is able to create captive customers its survival and development is assured. In this regard institutions have done very less work. In fact marketing is required to develop captive customers and beneficiaries. Very few institutions in the country have done marketing to make captive customers. To make captive customers a well-designed marketing strategy needs to be implemented. This strategy requires to be different than normal strategies of marketing. The institution should also explore the possibilities of having floating customers so that in the times of turbulence this customer base can support the business of the institution. The captive customers may have too many and too much expectations from the institution. If the institution is unable to meet their expectations they can shift to floating customers. Institution should also explore likely customers. The likely customers can be converted into captive customers and floating customers. Having all three types of customers the institution can increase its capability and capacity to expand the business. There are unlimited opportunities for the institutions to do business in the educational sectors. The business of the technical institutions is encroached by other higher learning institutions, human resources development cells in industries, training centres and non-government organizations. The institution can capture the encroached market through marketing its services and products.

There is an opportunity to develop new markets in changing economy and technology. The engineering institutions have capabilities to fulfil the changing requirements because it is their core competence. Institutions must learn to design compact, simple, need based, flexible and practice oriented programmes. They should come out from highly time oriented and time bound programmes. So far undergraduate and post-graduate programmes are concerned rethinking should be done at government level but skill up gradation programmes should be highly need based. Similarly research work and projects require highly professional approach to capture the market.

5. Attractions for Clients

Institutions are required to make captive customers for various services and products. These customers need to be sustained. They should be convenience to influence other potential customers to take services of the institution. This is possible in conditions when they get privileged services. Institutions must have attraction for the clients. The attractions may be in varied forms as shown in exhibit 23.2.

Exhibit No. 23.2: Attractions for the customer

➢ Extra coaching in difficult subjects ➢ Linguistic ability development ➢ Personality development ➢ Easy to learn material ➢ Additional facilities in the form of books, computers, learning material, equipment, transport, fee exemption, photocopying, e-mail ➢ Concessional lodging and boarding	➢ Scholarship, freeship, sponsorship, loan ➢ Provision for depositing the fee in instalments ➢ Additional co-curricular facilities ➢ Additional sports ➢ Hobby courses ➢ Free coaching for competitive exams ➢ Assured placement ➢ Opportunity to work on live projects

6. Areas of Marketing of Products and Services of Technical Institutions

Every institution has lot of potential for marketing the services and product irrespective of its location, size and resources. The institution should identify its strengths and identify the opportunities available in market. At the same time institutions should grow and develop excellence in one or two areas of their functioning. They should develop uniqueness in selected areas. In these areas they should try to capture the market through their product and services. There are institutions that have crossed geographic, social and cultural boundaries and marketed their services and products. At the same time there are institutions that are fulfilling specific manpower requirements of specific organizations. There are institutions that have contributed for the development of the community using their technological capabilities. The institutions are required to move out from the campus and explore the academic and non-academic problems of the stakeholders and their ambitions. They should design strategies to fulfil the needs and demands of the stakeholders. They are required to be more flexible, forward looking and out looking. They should share greater responsibility for the development of society and economy. They can do this by marketing their services and products. There are organizations and schools that do not know what they want from technical institutions in such situations institutions should educate the organizations that they have a need and the institution can fulfil their need. The list of marketable products and services of the institution is shown in exhibit 23.3.

Exhibit No. 23.3: Products and services marketable by technical institutions

Sl. No.	*Services and products*	*Market*
1.	Regular educational programmes	Potential students, employers
2.	Continuing education educational programmes	Employers, society, alumni, entrepreneurs, foreign organizations
3.	Seminars, conferences, symposiums, workshops	Organizations of any type in any business
4.	Research	Technological, management, educational, research, product development, impact analysis, system development, consumer survey, market research
5.	Problem solving	Technological, management, educational
6.	Professional chapters	Discipline specific, technical education
7.	Journals	Discipline specific
8.	Learning resources; Video programmes, Multimedia package, Power points, Transparency, Print material — case study, assignments, text books, work books etc.	Discipline specific organizations, other educational and training institutions and human resources development centres in industries, entrepreneurs
9.	Technical assistance	Industries, entrepreneurs and society
10.	Infrastructure Building, laboratories, library, learning resource centre, computer centre, playground, auditorium, conference hall, classrooms, guest house, hostel, etc.	Sister institutions, educational institutions, organizations and society at large

The institution should survey the market and find out the exact scope in that particular area. It should also predict the requirements analysing the trends in the technology and economy. Then it should plan strategy to fulfil the market demand. Marketing the services and product is essential for the survival and growth of the institution. Apart from educational programmes they should do marketing of research, problem solving, training and development, experience sharing, knowledge management, designing and implementing innovations in other organizations. Now many institutions are planning to enter in the business. They want to remain in education, training and do business. They are also providing full range of education, i.e. school to Ph.D. to capture the market to have a base of captive customers. The institutions can implement their programmes through franchises in the country to earn the profit and corporate reputations. The collaborative marketing of product and services is the need of the day in technical institutions.

7. Spiral Effect of Marketing

The institutions are created to serve the society in variety of ways. The institutions get variety of inputs in the form of students, faculty, information and finance. At the same time it serves and fulfils the variety of expectations of the society using its collective strengths. Institutions survive and grow using inputs from the society. If they satisfy and fulfil the needs they continue to get more and more resources. Again using these resources they enhance and expand their services to get more and better input. These cyclic phenomenons multiply after each cycle. If the performance of the institution is poor the cycle brings adverse effect that means after each cycle the institution get less inputs so lesser performance and so on. Institutions using marketing and professional approach get the positive advantage of the cycle.

8. Summary

The marketing of services and product of the institutions is necessary for survival, growth and development of the institution. Marketing of services and product is necessary to meet the growing competition and challenges. The institutions are required to identify their core competence and opportunities available in the area of their core competence. The institutions are required to come out from their campus and need to be proactive to the present and growing needs of the society and economy. There is a tremendous scope for institutions to grab their core competence and fulfil the expectations of the society. The institutions are required to grow and develop for this purpose they require variety of inputs from society. If the institutions satisfy the needs of the society they get more and better inputs from the society. Each institution should think in strategic terms to do marketing of its services and products.

9. Activity

Prepare a list of products and services that you can market to various stakeholders, clients, customers and beneficiaries. You can use following format for preparing the list of products and services.

Sl. No.	*Product/services*	*Stakeholders/client/customer/beneficiaries*
1.		
2.		

REFERENCE

Philip Kotler and Karen, F.A. Fox (1985). *Marking educational services*. Prentice Hall Englewood Cliffs, New Jersey.

24

Six Sigma

Objectives: The readers will be able to:

1. State the need and importance of six sigma in technical institutions.
2. Define the concept of six sigma in context of technical institutions.
3. State the benefits of six sigma.
4. Explain the dimensions of six sigma in technical institutions.
5. Describe the shift required to become six sigma institution.
6. Evolve a model to implement six sigma in technical institution.
7. Explain the problem solving process in six sigma institution.
8. List the tools and techniques used in six sigma institutions.
9. Describe the process of implementation of six sigma in technical institution.
10. List the competencies required to implement six sigma in technical institution.

1. Introduction

Technical education system has not defined the competencies and proficiency level of passouts. Different institutions are implementing different curriculum and there is wide variety in contents of the curriculum. The educational processes are not standardized. There are no standard parameters to compare the competence level of passouts of one institution with passouts of other institution. Even there is a great variation in process of certification. The certification is based on marks and grades and not on attainment of competencies. Even there is a great variation of level of achievement among passouts of same batch, in the same discipline, in the same institution. There are great amount of variability on different dimensions of functioning of the institution. Variation on different dimensions of functions is creating variety of problems such as under employment, no employment, mismatch in employment and qualification, job stagnation in the organization, low satisfaction in job, high turnover in job, salary difference, and many more problems. The rate of dropouts is high that is also causing wastage of resources and blocking the opportunities of other deserving potential students.

Technical institutions produce thousands of passouts every year. The variability among the quality of passouts can be minimized on various dimensions using six sigma methodologies in technical education system and technical institutions. Six sigma assures the commitment of the management for excellence, quality of passouts, continuous improvement, wastage reduction and rapid change management. It helps institutions to reach near perfection in performance improvement of students and its processes.

2. Concept of Six Sigma

The sigma is standard deviation used in statistics to describe variation in the set of data. For example, one of the prestigious technical institutions claims that its passouts of under graduate programme obtain 80 per cent to 100 per cent marks. It means the institution should take all the measure so that all the students obtain 80 per cent to 100 per cent marks. If only 68 per cent students obtain 80 per cent to 100 per cent marks the institution is performing at 2 sigma level. If only 93 per cent students obtain 80 per cent to 100 per cent marks the institution is performing at 3 sigma level. If only 99.4 per cent students obtain 80 per cent to 100 per cent marks the institution is performing at 4 sigma level. If this institution is interested to become six sigma institution 99.9997 per cent students should obtain marks between 80 per cent to 100 per cent. This example is applicable for admission process or for any process also. It is clear from this example that the institution should produce students with declared performance criteria. If the range of the performance criteria is large it is an easy task for the institution but if the range is small it is very difficult target for the institution to achieve. If the range is 90 per cent to 100 per cent it becomes still difficult for the institution to meet the targets. The performance range decides the quality of passouts and the actual number of students obtaining marks in that range decides the quantity of performance. The range of marks is related to requirements of the students or their employers. This was a simple example to explain six sigma in terms of marks obtained by students. The industry may like students to possess certain number of competencies and for each competency a defined proficiency level. There could be other requirements of the industries and students in terms of other job related skills such as communication skills, planning skills, stress management skills, problem solving skills, relationship building skills and so on. The performance is measured in terms of customer requirements. Six sigma helps to design processes to satisfy the requirements of the students and industries consistently. It also helps to compare the effectiveness and efficiency of various processes in the institutions.

3. Benefits of Six Sigma

As described earlier in this chapter six sigma is comparatively new concept in technical education and technical institutions. The six sigma institutions have numerous benefits over traditional institution. Some of the indicative benefits are listed in exhibit 24.1.

Exhibit No. 24.1: Benefits of six sigma in technical institutions

➢ Need based curriculum ➢ Focus on significant few activities ➢ Satisfaction of students for learning competencies ➢ Satisfaction of industries ➢ Improved academic and support processes ➢ Economic functioning of the institution ➢ Fast learning ➢ Time saving ➢ Better placement ➢ Effective communication ➢ Change based on data	➢ Quality of all passouts is assured ➢ Reduced cycle time of educational programmes ➢ More demand for passouts of the institution ➢ Sustained employment of all passouts ➢ Continuous learning ➢ No private tuition business ➢ No extra time required for learning ➢ Better admission ➢ Reduced wastage of resources ➢ Effective teamwork ➢ Development and use of professional skills

4. Dimensions of Six Sigma in Technical Institutions

There are many dimensions of six sigma technical institution. There is a need to understand these dimensions to become six sigma institution. Some of the significant dimensions are listed in exhibit 24.2.

Exhibit No. 24.2: Paradigm shift on various dimensions from traditional institution to six sigma institutions

Criteria	*Traditional institution*	*Six sigma institution*
Focus	Teaching-learning	Students and industries
Actions	Persons	Academic processes
Philosophy	Administration based	Self-management
Motivation	Punishment based	Achievement based
Management	By assumptions and guess	By facts
Power	Lays with management	Lays with teachers and performers
Emphasis	Curriculum completion	Competencies development and attainment of proficiency level
Recognition	Management takes credit for success	Share success with institutional members
Rewards	Extrinsic	Intrinsic
Information	Controlled information	Free flow of information
Problems	No one own the problem Fire fighting	Performers own the problem Problem prevention
Management approach	*Ad hoc* and causal	Proactive
Working style	Individual and committees Isolation	Teamwork Interdisciplinary
Overcoming weaknesses	Training Waiting for good time	Networking, collaboration, cooperation with internal and external stakeholders
Performance focus	May be improvement	Perfection

5. Model of Implementing Six Sigma in Technical Institution

Technical institutions are functioning at different levels of performance. They have varied reputation in the employment sector and society. Each institution is required to evolve its own model for implementing six sigma. A generic model and its steps are listed here for ready reference. For each step the institution has options to use suitable tools and techniques from the available basket.

If the performance of the institution is poor in comparison to other institution and passouts are not getting appropriate placement in industries. There is a problem of less employment, underemployment and inappropriate employment. Seats are lying vacant in the institution. The institution is awarded lower grades by accreditation bodies. Good faculty and staff members are planning to leave the institution. The institution is facing severe academic, financial and non-academic problems. The institution is facing these and similar problems consistently. It requires fresh and complete review of the academic business. It should re-craft the vision, missions and goals. It should redefine the performance goals in terms of placement of students and results of the students. It requires full scale and institution wide change.

If the institution is performing well and its passouts are getting fairly good jobs but some problems are prevalent in one or two disciplines or with some groups of students. There are some problems in carrying out the academic or non-academic processes. In one or two disciplines few seats are lying vacant. There is a problem of absenteeism or negligence related to learning. Such institution may focus on six sigma in problem areas. Such well performing institutions can also look for better opportunities in the external or internal environment. It can expand its experiences in other areas of institutional functioning or throughout the institution. For example, experiences of initiatives taken in examination reforms may be extended in teaching-learning process. Experiences of certification of continuing education programmes can be further extended in formal regular programmes. Problems of confusion during teaching learning may be addressed through curriculum refinement.

If the institution is performing excellent and has excellent corporate image but wants to sustain and improve performance with respect to time. It can use problem solving approach and project approach. The scope of the problem solving would be limited to that particular situation only. The problem is solved using scientific methods. The problem is analyzed to find the root causes. The solution is implemented in such a way so that problem does not recur again. Institution remains vigilant about the opportunities available in the environment and grabs them for the benefit of the institution.

The autonomous institutions would like to adopt approaches that can bring rapid change. The private institutions would like to solve their local problems related to money collection and academic reputation. The government institutions would like to take approaches that can be implemented through existing powers.

6. Problem Solving Process in Six Sigma Institution

It is described through out the book that teams' structure is a suitable structure for growth and development of the institution. It is an approach for solving quality problems also. Teams formed in various functional areas of the institution work on quality and six sigma projects in their respective processes. They carry out process, bring improvements, solve problems, and handle complaints. They grab opportunities for the benefit of the students and employers. Through out the institution a common model can be used to solve the problems. This model is very popular in industries and picking up in educational institutions. The name of the model is DMAIC. In this model D stands for define, M stands for measure, A stands for analyze, I stands for improve, and C stands for control. Institutional teams are trained to use the DMAIC model to solve the problems. Teams get involved right from identifying and defining the problem to implementation of the solution. Team members constantly interact with other individuals and teams affected by problem. If required, they interact with experts to validate the solution. Team members implement the solution and see that the problem is solved and impact is sustained. The advantages of using DMAIC model over other problem solving approaches are many; few of them are defining the problem based on data, focusing on students and industries while solving the problem, analyzing the root causes, participation in the process thereby ensuring commitment of team members, evaluating the results and sustaining the changes. The brief description of DMAIC is given below:

6.1 Define the Problem

The six sigma team works on institutional problems affecting the results of the students and employment of the students. The problems are clubbed and prioritized to be considered for definition. Questions starting with what, how, when, where, who, whose are asked to define the problem. These questions promote understanding of the problems. The problem is explored further and a preliminary plan is prepared stating the justification of selecting the problem, objectives of the problem, tentative assumptions, scope of the problem and role of the team to solve the problem. Number of techniques are available to define a problem. The use of technique is dependent on the type of problem situation. A commonly used technique in six sigma is SIPOC. In this technique S stands for supplier, I stands for input, P stands for process, O stands for out put, and C stands for customer. The SIPOC is used to show the major activities or sub-processes in a business. In this diagram the boundary area of the problem is defined. SIPOC diagram is first prepared to chart existing process and then a new process is charted. The difference between existing process and should be process shows the gap. The gap is expressed in terms of quality or efficiency or relevance or effectiveness or combination of these parameters. The SIPOC diagram for curriculum development process is shown in exhibit 24.3. SIPOC diagram is used for all significant process of the institution to improve the quality of performance of core processes and consequently quality of dependent processes.

Exhibit No. 24.3: SIPOC diagram of curriculum development process

Supplier	*Inputs*	*Process*	*Outputs*	*Customers*
Employers	• Job profile • Technology • Industrial processes • Performance related expectations • Behaviour related expectations • Future competencies requirements • Feedback on performance of employed students	• Job survey • Interview • Expectation analysis • Technology analysis • Culture study • Feedback analysis • Job analysis • Role analysis • Validation	Curriculum document • Rationale • Entry behaviour • Job profile • Role description • National priorities • Hard competencies • Soft competencies • Proficiency level • Teaching-learning units • Horizontal and vertical linkages in contents • Teaching-learning resources and methodologies • List of practical, assignments, projects, and training • Time to complete curriculum and units therein	• Employers • Statutory bodies • Professional bodies • Accreditation agencies • Universities • Institution • Teachers • Students • Parents • Examination bodies • Funding agencies
Schools	• Curriculum	• Curriculum analysis		
Government	• National policy	• Policy analysis		
Teachers	• Professional expertise • Methods • Media • Assessment methods	Content analysis Curriculum planning and development Curriculum document		
Statutory bodies	• Legal information	• Analysis		

(*Contd.*)

(*Contd.*)

Supplier	*Inputs*	*Process*	*Outputs*	*Customers*
Experts	• Format of curriculum • Presentation of curriculum document • Methods • Media • Time	• Curriculum development and validation	• Assessment scheme • Examination agencies • Teacher competencies to teach the subject • Important guide-lines for teachers and students	

6.2 Measure

The actual data and facts about the existing process are collected using appropriate, valid and reliable instruments. These data further helps in defining the problem qualitatively and quantitatively. The data is collected on inputs, processes and outcomes. The output data helps to define the problem perfectly. On the basis of output measures the problem can further be analysed on process part and on input part. These data acts as a base line for comparing the impact of interventions.

6.3 Analyse

The data collected during the measure step are classified and assumptions and hypothesis is made to find out the real causes of the problem. There is likelihood that for some problems data collected are not sufficient and recollection of data may require. On the basis of data assumption or hypothesis is tested. During this step real causes are finalized in the team and communicated to other related persons for validation. Numerous methods of analysing and presenting the problem are available these are creativity techniques, force field analysis, cause and effect diagram, problem tree analysis, socio-diagram, why-why diagram and statistical techniques.

6.4 Improve

This is a next step in DMAIC model. Alternative solutions are generated for the real causes of the problem. Number of techniques are available for generating alternative solutions. Creativity techniques, experimentation, research, survey, observation, fish bone diagram, alternative tree analysis, are commonly used techniques in education institutions. The effectiveness and efficiency of the alternatives are assessed on various well-defined criteria and best feasible and implementable solution is selected for implementation. Before making the final decision it should be compared with the solution or practice existing in other institutions. Then final decision is made. If the solution is going to affect the large population of internal or external customers pilot implementation and testing is suggested. On the basis of the results of pilot testing implementation plan is prepared. The potential problems and risks are analysed. Then the team members carry out full implementation. The management of the institution and other stakeholders provide full support to implementation process.

6.5 Control

Solution or process implementation team develops the monitoring mechanism to trace the progress. Generally monitoring indicators or check points, or tool gates are developed for monitoring and evaluating purpose. The progress is monitored and implementation problems are solved timely. The important data are recorded to prepare the report and assess the effectiveness of the solution. The level of achievement is measured comparing present data and baseline data. Team members evaluate the level of achievements to learn and enjoy the success. The purpose of control is listed in exhibit 24.4.

Exhibit No. 24.4: Purpose of control

➤ to find out extent of realization of objectives ➤ to better plan and solve problems ➤ to better understand the elements of process and their importance ➤ to diagnose the implementation difficulty ➤ to reduce wastage	➤ to reinforce motivation of team members ➤ to enhance trust of the management on capacity and capability of a team ➤ to make effective decisions ➤ to add value in the process ➤ to learn collectively ➤ to deciding responsibility

Once the problem is solved and solution is stabilized team members go for another six sigma problem or opportunity.

The institution can select significant problems that are affecting the students' performance, teachers' performance, satisfaction of industries, satisfaction of society, satisfaction of internal customers and inefficiency of process. Some indicative problems are listed in exhibit 24.5.

Exhibit No. 24.5: List of problems for DMAIC

➢ 30 per cent students are failing in final examination in a particular subject ➢ 5 per cent dropouts from different courses ➢ 15 per cent wastage of resources ➢ resources utilization is very low ➢ almost no research work in the institution ➢ revenue generation through consultancy is low	➢ quality of continuing education programmes is poor ➢ result declaration time is more than one month ➢ routine administrative cases of employees takes more than one week ➢ information system is very poor ➢ awareness of institutional programmes is low in the society and schools

7. Tools and Techniques of Six Sigma

There are numerous tools and techniques available that can be used to improve the quality of academic and non-academic activities of the institution. Institutions can evolve their own techniques for a particular purpose. Institution can use the tools and techniques available in the literature differently, if they serve the purpose. A complete chapter is devoted in this book on tools and techniques to be used for carrying out various processes in the instuition. Creativity is a key to six sigma institutions. All the institutional members should be trained to use creativity techniques for various purposes. This could be the starting point to commit for six sigma. Most popularly used creativity methods are brain storming, nominal group technique, cognitive mapping and Delphi. The need analysis techniques such as students learning needs can be analyzed using survey techniques, job analysis, task analysis, content analysis and curriculum analysis. Curriculum design models for various programmes such as competency based curriculum development and skills based curriculum are used to design the need based and relevant curriculum. Check sheets, rating scales, opinionnaire, interview schedule and observation schedule are used to systematically record the information. Process charting is used to measure the effectiveness and efficiency of the process. Value and non-added value analysis is carried out to know the redundancies, unnecessary decision points, wastage, time consuming activities etc. Existing processes are designed to contribute for internal or external customer satisfaction. Charts and graphs such as pie chart, bar chart, histogram, Pareto analysis, control charts, run chart and scatter diagram are used for classifying, clubbing, analyzing and presenting data for various purposes. Advance statistical tools such as Chi square, *t*-test, *z*-test are used to analyse the results of the students. Research methods such as content analysis, experimental design, *ex post facto* are used to bring process improvement and innovations. Project method is used to solve significant problem or to meet the requirements of a particular challenge, or to face competition, or to grab an opportunity. Stakeholders' analysis is carried out to know the needs of them and design strategies to satisfy their needs. It is also carried out to obtain their favour for six sigma efforts. Force field analysis is used to know the favourable and restraining forces that are responsible for six sigma. It is also used for seeking participation of the institutional members for six sigma. Process documentation is carried out to record the experiences gained during the implementation of the process. This document can be used for various purposes in the future.

8. Implementing Six Sigma

It is easy to conduct awareness programmes, training programmes and motivating institutional members to go for six sigma implementation. The institution should do force field analysis to know the intensity of driving forces and resisting forces. If the intensity and weight of driving forces is high it can immediately go for six sigma implementation. If the resisting forces are heavier than facilitating forces it should wait and think to create conducive environment to reduce the restraining forces and their intensity. An example, of force field analysis is shown in exhibit 24.6.

9. Resource Persons to Implement Six Sigma in the Institution

A team of resource persons is required to implement six sigma in the institution. The team members are trained to plan six sigma strategies and implement it in the institution. They implement six sigma through various teams and individuals working in different areas of functioning of the institution. The six sigma team is thoroughly trained to accept the challenge of six sigma. The team members are trained in need analysis,

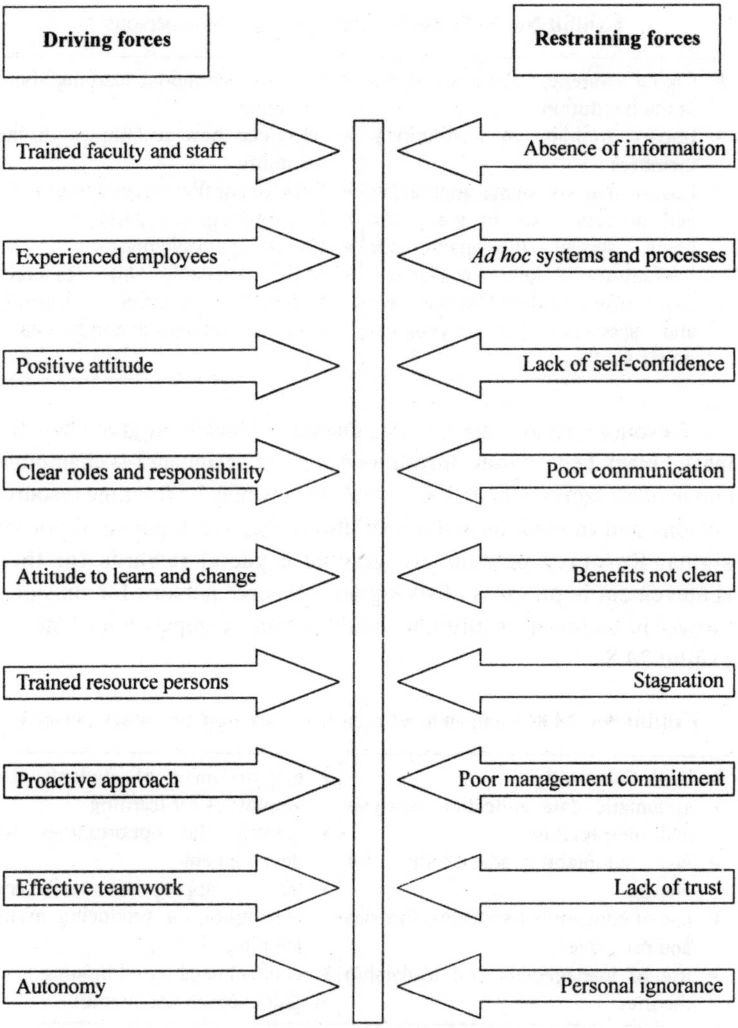

Exhibit No. 24.6: Force field analysis for six sigma implementation in technical institution

curriculum design, process design, problem solving, creativity, education technology, education management, leadership, coaching, project management, planning change management, and on similar topics. These resource persons in the institution fulfil responsibilities mentioned in exhibit 24.7.

Exhibit No. 24.7: Responsibilities of resource persons

➤ Create awareness about six sigma in the institution ➤ Impart training to institutional members ➤ Ensure that six sigma approaches and processes are in place and being spread throughout the institution especially in academics ➤ Keep informed the team members and superiors about the progress on six sigma	➤ Promote continuous learning about six sigma ➤ Introduce new techniques in the institution ➤ Resolve conflicts related to quality ➤ Prepare progress reports ➤ Carryout periodic review ➤ Make available all resources including teaching learning resources to teams and individuals

Resource persons are also designated as black belt, green belt and master black belt. In some institutions they are designated as champions and in other facilitators. In big institution they may be full time resource persons and in medium sized institutions they work part-time for six sigma. Resource persons are granted especial rewards for their achievement in progress of six sigma. Resource persons for six sigma project in technical institution should possess competencies listed in exhibit 24.8.

Exhibit No. 24.8: Competencies required in six sigma resource persons

➤ think holistically ➤ systematic data collection, analysis and interpretation ➤ fast adoptability/adaptability for change ➤ use of educational concepts, theories and principles ➤ use of management and leadership theories	➤ empowerment of students and employees for learning ➤ identify the opportunities for development ➤ use of appropriate tools and techniques for producing joyful learning ➤ conduct need based training ➤ guide, coach and mentor

10. Six Sigma as a System of Governance and Management of Technical Institution

To satisfy the needs of the employers and students the institutional processes should be well designed and implemented perfectly to produce results in terms of results of students learning. The significant persons in the institution especially the teachers and director should be hold responsible for the expected results of the students. The other persons like registrar, accountant, store purchase officer should be hold responsible for supporting the academic process. The performance of the teachers should be measured on the results of the students and accordingly rewards should be given or remedial actions should be taken. The teams structure proposed in this book should be adapted to carryout the processes. Individuals and teams should be hold responsible for non-compliance of the results. The problems, complaints and barriers should be analysed properly and it should be seen that they do not recur in the future. Result producing practices in one department should be adapted in other departments of the institution. The responsibility and power for teaching learning process should be decentralized to teams and individuals. They should be encouraged to deal with all types of requests of students at their own level.

11. Summary

The six sigma is standard deviation used in statistics to describe variation in the set of data. The variability among the quality of passouts of one institution can be reduced using six sigma approach. Six sigma approach in technical institution brings variety of benefits to the institution and stakeholders. The relevance and acceptability of passouts can be increased using six sigma approach. The six sigma institution has number of dimensions such as focus on students and industries, emphasis on academic processes, self-management philosophy, empowered teachers and staff members, proactive approach, problem solving, networking and perfection. DMAIC model is used to solve the problems related to core business of the institution. There are other tools and techniques along with statistical techniques that are used to improve the quality of passouts and reduce variability among the competence level of the students. The institution should undertake force field analysis before implementation of six sigma. If the restraining forces are strong an environment should be created to reduce the intensity of restraining forces. Six sigma process is designed and guided by a team of trained resource persons and every member of the institution participate in reducing the variability in quality of passouts. Institutional members should develop required competencies to implement six sigma in the institution successfully.

12. Activity

Design a model for implementing six sigma in your institution.

REFERENCES

Michael, L. George (2002). *Lean Six Sigma*, Tata McGraw Hill Publishing Company Limited, New Delhi.

Pete Pande and Lary Holpp, *Six Sigma,* Tata McGraw Hill Publishing Company Limited, New Delhi.

25

Ethics in Technical Institutions

Objectives: The readers will be able to:

1. State the need and importance of values, ethics and behaviour in technical institutions.
2. List the purpose of the values, ethics and behaviour in technical institutions.
3. Describe the method of crafting values, ethics and behaviour in technical institutions.
4. Describe the process of establishing the values in the institution.
5. Describe the concept of beliefs.
6. Develop the professional norms for achieving excellence.
7. List guidelines to be observed to evolve values, ethics and behaviour in technical institutions.

1. Introduction

Institutions to survive, grow and develop in changing environment must adapt the values, beliefs, ethics and culture to meet the needs of the students, employers, stakeholders, and society. At the same time they should also meet the needs of the faculty and staff members of the institution. Everyone in the institution takes part in shaping the values. It should not be considered a job of a director or governing body members. The values, beliefs and ethics define the way of working of people individually and collectively. Values are the base of human behaviour. Institutions achieve excellence designing and observing value loaded vision of the institution. Values work as foundation and bed rock for the institutions. The strength of the bedrock decides the life of the institution. Sound values enable the institution to resist the external pressure of the environment. It binds people together for a specific purpose that is shared and attractive. It means values are aligned to vision of the institution. Values without vision and vision without values are illusion. Values control the behaviour of the people and channelize it for collective progress. Values guide the actions of institutional members and teams. Values help people to take right decisions in uncertainties. Values do not naturally develop in the institution. They need to be inculcated and established in institutional functioning.

Values bind people together for a greater cause that is shared by everyone in the institution. Values shape our thinking and behaviour. If institutional members observe right values there is no need to do supervision of activities being performed. They promote self-discipline in working. Values provide a clearer focus for providing feedback on performance of individuals and teams. Values shape the behaviour of the people to excel better. They are very much helpful in creating healthy conflict and minimizing the unhealthy conflict. Institutional priorities are set on the basis of values. All new members joining the institution can easily be socialized. Values built up the atmosphere of trust and trust is the key to success. Values become the code of behaviour for individuals and teams. People know the tolerance limit of dealing with each other. Values need to be carefully derived and practiced in the institution. There should not be any dilemma between derived values and the values in which institutional members work. Values must be practiced consistently. Leaders inculcate desired values in followers through modelling.

2. Purpose of Values

The values serve the purpose of relationship technology in the institution. It works as a greese and oil to improve efficiency in functioning of relationship. It saves the institution from becoming uneconomical and rusted in terms of relationship. It also saves the heating and burning of human elements. It increases the life of the institution and keeps the customers for long time even if the quality of services is comparatively poor. It seeks the commitment of the people for the excellence. Institutions feel the need of values when they are in great trouble. When the senior management consumes most of energy in solving employees problems, conflict and crisis. The purpose of values is listed in exhibit 25.1.

Exhibit No. 25.1: Purpose of values

➢ Climate based on values nourishes the human spirit and brings out the best in every one ➢ Shared values allow for change, innovation and excel better ➢ Provide scope for continuous improvement, reduction in waste and accepting challenges ➢ Values serve as the foundation of relationship ➢ Values guide the work and relationship in the institution ➢ Values help self-management of the people	➢ Values work as bedrock of common thinking, creativity and innovation of the institutional business ➢ Values provide direction in situations of uncertainty ➢ Provide scope for specific and constructive feedback ➢ Contribute to quality of relationships ➢ Create opportunities for culture building training ➢ Provide scope for win-win situation ➢ Socialize new employees naturally

3. Methods of Crafting Values

Normally values evolve in the institution with its birth and growth. The evolved values may not be in tune with the purpose of the institution. Values need to crafted, carved and designed because the institution has to move ahead in cohesive manner. People come from different background and experience in educational institutions and they may be having conflicting values as well. Institutional members may have diverse personal values. That is not the serious issue in value design. There are two sets of values. First is values related to human relationship and other is professional value. The human relationships are required for functioning of the institution. But what is important is professional values. It is observed that most of the institutions have congenial relationship. It is not sufficient for the growth and development of the institution. Institutions need to develop shared professional values to enhance corporate reputation and achieve the vision. Institutional members carve the values collectively. The process of crafting values is very simple. It is carried out in two steps.

Identify existing values: The existing individual and collective values of institutional members are identified using well-designed methods such as discussions, meetings, confidential survey, attitude survey, interview, 360 degree feedback and observations. The individual values and collective values are analysed to know the existing value system in the institution. It is also analysed how the values are contributing for the quality and productivity of the institutional services and how they are adversely affecting. The identified values are classified in two categories that are general values and professional values.

Craft desired values: All the institutional members work in different teams to derive desired values from the vision and missions of the institution. Numbers of creativity sessions are organized and analysis is carried out to finalize the values. The values should focus on academic activities and not on peripheral activities. They should add to professional standards of the institution and should be unique. They should be clear and communicable to the internal and external stakeholders. The new values should be publically shared, put into action and followed in difficult situations.

4. Focus of Values

Values are related to satisfaction of students, employers, community and rest of the stakeholders. Values are set at individual, group and institutional level. These are classified as primary or core or significant or must or essential as well as secondary or peripheral or desirable or want these values should help the institution to shape the relationship of all the employees with the students, employers and stakeholders. Values are also classified as instrumental and terminal. These values could be common values for all institutional members and separate as well for teachers, staff and students. Values support the institutional activities positively and should not be confused with personal values at home and in the rest of the society. Values are also classified on the basis of the professional requirement and relationship requirement in the institution. Institution should set professional values inspiring for achieving professional standards in all areas of functioning. Without clear, congenial and professional values the institution may suffer from inconsistent efforts, because people do not know what level to strive at. The professional values establish a clear level of quality and excellence that everyone can understand and aspire to observe. Institution should also set values inspiring for building healthy relationship in the institution. These values need to be consciously created and nurtured for the institution. These values work as a gum of relationship. This gum binds every individual and team of the institution even in the adverse situation. This can also be called institutional culture on which it thrives and inspire people to continuously improve the performance of the self and team. These values provide natural support to the relationship in the institution. Institutional values are nothing but a game plan to coordinate the efforts of everyone towards achieving the mission and vision of the institution. It encourages every institutional member to express passion towards individual and team objectives. The understanding of these values allows a greater movement toward self-management. Values must be shared and observed from the top level. Values are gradually established in the institution.

5. Process of Establishing Crafted Values in the Institution

The prevalent values in the institution may not be in congruence with the requirements of the vision of the organization. The existing values need to be modified, refined or even completely derived. It is a very complex and time taking process. Taking the inventory of the prevalent values it can be identified that what is to be modified, refined and changed. The value modification, refinement and change process is participatively carried out justifying the need of it. The new value system is discussed, printed and published in all official documents. Everyone in the institution observes all the values. If someone is not observing it constructive feedback is given. Appreciation and recognition is also provided to the persons that are promoting the new value system. If necessary, training is imparted to observe some values which are totally new and difficult to observe. Six monthly or yearly reviews are done to know the impact of the new value system. In some situations resources may require to observe the values. Necessary resources are provided by the organization. A comparative study after a year can be conducted to know the shift in values between previous year and current year. Leaders play a very important role to install new value system in the institution. Right value related behaviour is projected again and again in all meetings, interactions, documents, and communication. The shift in value system requires confidence, patience and coaching.

The director of the institution, senior faculty and staff members should practice the crafted shared values to derive the benefit from it. It should reflect in their decisions and performance of employees. They should act as role model for others to be followed. The most effective role model for values is contained in telling people to follow what senior faculty and officers are following. Leaders need to be tight on values. Values multiply its effect. Values can easily be inculcated in teams. The rules may change as per need of the situation but the values stand. Values stand in adverse conditions. Values should be distinguished from rituals.

6. Beliefs in Technical Institutions

Belief is another important dimension that reflect the overall culture of the institution. Peters and Waterman has described the belief on dimensions such as; enjoying the work, being the best, innovations, risk taking, attending details, importance of people as individuals, superior quality and services, informational communication, growth, hands on management, and recognized institutional philosophy. The beliefs applicable in technical institutions on various functions and processes are listed in exhibit 25.2.

Exhibit No. 25.2: Beliefs in technical institution

Teaching learning processes

We believe in ➢ Competency based education ➢ Use of variety processes ➢ Use of variety of media ➢ Flexibility in learning ➢ Continuous assessment of learning ➢ Offering constructive feedback for improvement ➢ Development of higher level of skills ➢ Personality development of students ➢ Training and development of teachers and technical support staff ➢ Continuous improvement in teaching learning process	➢ Joyful learning ➢ Development of generic skills ➢ Development of entrepreneurial skills ➢ Experimentation to enhance effectiveness and efficiency of teaching learning processes ➢ Hands on experiences ➢ Coaching free education ➢ Better placement of students ➢ Development of technology ➢ Development of appropriate technology ➢ Learning new technologies ➢ Development of instructional material that is easy to learn

Services

We believe in ➢ Community services ➢ Contribution for economic growth of the society ➢ Helping industries to innovate and change ➢ Transfer of technology for betterment of the community	➢ Enhancing technical knowledge, and skills of the society ➢ Sharing resources with external stakeholders ➢ Value addition to services ➢ Creating awareness for safety, health, cleanliness, environment, education and peaceful life

(Contd.)

Institutional functioning

We believe in	➢ Use of Information Technology to enhance efficiency of processes
➢ Growth and development of the institution	➢ Harnessing full potential of all types of resources
➢ Creativity, innovation and change	➢ Minimizing the waste
➢ Discarding obsolete methods and process	➢ Integrity and honesty
➢ Autonomy, accountability and responsibility	➢ Shared leadership
➢ Empowerment of individuals and teams	➢ Respect for individuals
➢ Proactive approaches	➢ Being the best
➢ Effectiveness and efficiency	➢ Personal growth of individuals
➢ Collaborative networking with world class institutions and industries	➢ Generating resources for the institution
➢ Sharing information for mutual benefit	➢ Taking initiatives
➢ Performance based rewards	➢ Accepting our failures
➢ Team work and mutual support	➢ Risk taking
➢ Research	➢ Use of scientific tools and techniques
	➢ Creating win-win situation
	➢ Recognition and appreciation

7. Professional Norms

The values, ethics and beliefs can be translated in professional norms. The norms being followed by institutional members are observed in their activities. Some of the indicative norms are listed in exhibit 25.3.

Exhibit No. 25.3: Professional norms

Sl. No.	*Professional norms*	*Indicators*
1.	Coaching/ private tuition less education	1. Teachers do not take tuitions 2. Students do not take tuition
2.	Proactive approach	1. Vision document 2. Planning is done at every level 3. Institutional plan 4. Departmental planning 5. Subject planning 6. Lesson planning

(*Contd.*)

(*Contd.*)

Sl. No.	*Professional norms*	*Indicators*
3.	Shared leadership	Leaders at different levels
4.	Participation	1. Team work 2. Participatory decision-making 3. Participatory learning approaches – Group discussion, Problem solving, Action learning, Project, Visit, Seminar, Simulation, Symposium 4. Group creativity 5. Group work 6. Teams structure
5.	Innovation and change	1. Creativity sessions 2. Suggestion box 3. Complaint handling 4. Research activities 5. Training 6. Quality circles 7. Curriculum revision 8. Personality development workshops 9. Entrepreneurship development session 10. Interaction with eminent persons 11. Researches 12. Patents
6.	Good Inter-Personal Relationship	1. Use of respectful language 2. Counselling sessions 3. Problem solving groups 4. Complaint handling 5. Picnic 6. Social and family function 7. Parents meet 8. Open feedback 9. Effective communication 10. Transparency in work 11. No rumour
7.	Customer care	1. Meeting with Industry and field agencies 2. Memorandum of understanding with stakeholders 3. Students' meet 4. Carrier guidance to students 5. Guidance and support to establish enterprise or solve problem

(*Contd.*)

(*Contd.*)

Sl. No.	*Professional norms*	*Indicators*
		6. Need analysis surveys 7. Research on performance of passouts of the institute 8. Reception 9. Information brochure on services of the institute 10. Teacher-guardian association meet 11. Problem solving mechanism 12. Placement cell
8.	Overall development of students	1. Personality development workshops 2. Entrepreneurship development workshops 3. Generic skill development workshops 4. Creativity sessions 5. Interaction with eminent persons 6. Training in industry
9.	Placement of student	1. Campus interview 2. Training of teachers and students in industry 3. Directory of employers 4. Alumni 5. Employer meet
10.	Self-development	1. Identifying the strengths and weaknesses – self-assessment 2. Removing the weaknesses – self-development plan 3. Receiving feedback for improvement – feedback sessions 4. Attending training programmes and counselling sessions – training plan 5. Conscious efforts towards self-development 6. Positive thinking
11.	Fair and equal treatment	1. No favour to special class or person – less complaints 2. Respect to all 3. Understanding the needs/problems of the different students and helping them – tutorials 4. Objective and performance based reward system – policy 5. Maintaining confidentiality wherever it is necessary 6. Policies and decision-making criteria are publicly known 7. No difference in words and actions

8. Guidelines for Establishing Right Values, Beliefs and Ethics in the Institution

Establishment of proper values, beliefs and ethics in an institution is a complex task. It requires specific approaches and strategies. Everyone in the institution is required to promote them. The general guidelines are noted in exhibit 25.4 to assure effective establishment.

Exhibit No. 25.4: Guidelines for establishing values, beliefs and ethics

Values, beliefs and ethics should:	
➢ be shared and aligned to vision of the institution ➢ promote intimate relationship with students, employers, industry and stakeholder ➢ focus on satisfaction of stakeholders external and internal as well ➢ be defined and strictly observed ➢ be exhibited in behaviour of the people ➢ be promoted by everyone	➢ become natural part of the behaviour ➢ add value to product and services ➢ facilitate functioning ➢ contribute to achieve excellence ➢ clearly spell out the acceptable and non-acceptable behaviour in the institution ➢ appear in official documents ➢ promote personal pride and self-image ➢ supplement and complement the functioning of the institution ➢ be encouraged positively ➢ bring benefits to individuals and teams

9. Summary

The values, ethics and beliefs of the people contribute to enhance the performance of the institution. If these are crafted in consonance to vision of the institution the actions of the people will naturally contribute towards observing them. These will bind the people together to channelize the collective energy with synergetic effect to achieve the vision of the institution. In absence of clearly defined core values, beliefs and ethics there would be confusion, conflict and unhealthy politics. The institution would have excellent vision and plans but they would never be put in action in right spirit. The values, ethics and beliefs are classified in many ways such as primary and secondary, instrumental and terminal, focusing on external stakeholders and internal stakeholders and so on. Values can be expressed separately for faculty members, staff members and students. They can be stated for various areas of functioning of the institution. They can be expressed for various processes of the institution. They can also be expressed in terms of standards of behaviour. Values should be practiced and observed continuously and consistently by the institutional members individually and collectively.

10. Activity

In the following questionnaire statements related to identification and determination of values are given. These values may be in practice in your institution. You might have prepared vision document of your institution. In order to effectively implement the vision reach strategies you need strong value, belief and ethics base aligned to vision. Please give you honest response for existing values and desired values. The meaning of the weightage is as follows: Practices to a very great extent-4, great extent-3, small extent-2, almost negligible-1, desired to a very great extent-4, great extent-3, small extent-2, almost negligible-1.

Sl. No.	*Values, ethics and beliefs*	*In practice*				*Desired*			
		4	*3*	*2*	*1*	*4*	*3*	*2*	*1*
	Learning								
1.	Focus on learning								
2.	Student centered approach								
3.	Joyful learning								
4.	Flexible learning								
5.	Remedial treatment in learning								
6.	Use of learning principles								
7.	Variety of modes in learning								
8.	Learning takes place in its own pace								
9.	Recognition of slow learners								
10.	Recognition of fast learners								
11.	Recognition for prior learning								
12.	Right habits								
13.	Rewarding								
14.	Constructive feedback								
	Teaching								
15.	Learner centered								
16.	Use of learning principle								
17.	Use of media								
18.	Hands on practices								
19.	Use of appropriate and variety of methods								
20.	Competence development								
21.	Entrepreneurship								

(Contd.)

(*Contd.*)

Sl. No.	*Values, ethics and beliefs*	*In practice*				*Desired*			
		4	*3*	*2*	*1*	*4*	*3*	*2*	*1*
	Research								
22.	Attitude of inquiry								
23.	Development of new knowledge								
24.	Innovation								
25.	Change								
26.	Experimentation								
	Industry, employers and stakeholders								
27.	Service								
28.	Synergic partnership								
29.	Collaboration								
30.	Networking								
31.	Easy access								
32.	Quality								
33.	Effective communication								
34.	Adherence to legal provision								
35.	Improving quality of life								
	Institutional functioning								
36.	Participative decision-making								
37.	Transparency in decision-making								
38.	Use of democratic processes								
39.	Team spirit								
40.	Visionary leadership								
41.	Shared leadership								
42.	Supportive leadership								
43.	Transformational leadership								
44.	Approachable leadership								
45.	Sharing of experiences								
46.	Mutual trust								
47.	Effective communication								
48.	Healthy relationship								
49.	Honesty in working								
50.	Dedication for vision								
51.	Initiatives for change								
52.	Constructive criticism								
53.	Openness								
54.	Can do attitude								
55.	Right work to right person								
56.	Planned and systematic working								
57.	Decentralization								
58.	Empowerment								

(*Contd.*)

(*Contd.*)

Sl. No.	*Values, ethics and beliefs*	*In practice*				*Desired*			
		4	*3*	*2*	*1*	*4*	*3*	*2*	*1*
59.	Risk taking								
60.	Accepting challenge								
61.	Commitment to work .								
62.	Equal opportunities								
63.	Respect for diversity								
64.	Service mentality								
65.	Healthy competition								
66.	Attitude of continuous improvement								
67.	Self-discipline								
68.	Enhancing competence								
69.	Benchmarking								
70.	Accountability and responsibility								
71.	Strategic thinking								
72.	Use of information technology and technology								
73.	Quality of services and products								
74.	Development of individuals and teams								
75.	Flexible and innovative approaches								
76.	Concern for safety								
77.	Concern for environment								
78.	Concern for energy saving								
79.	Profitability								
80.	Cost effective								
81.	Excellence								
82.	Originality								
	Resources								
83.	Minimizing wastage								
84.	Maximizing utilization								
85.	Sharing								
86.	Updating								
87.	Modernizing								
	Finance								
88.	Revenue generation through legal means								
89.	Exploring new sources								
90.	Investment for growth and development								
91.	Long-term returns								
92.	Short-term returns								
93.	Profitability								

REFERENCE

William, R. Trancey, *Leadership Skills*, Amacom.

26

Education Project Management

Objectives: The readers will be able to

1. State the concept of project management.
2. Describe the characteristics of a project.
3. State the benefits of project approach.
4. List the sources of project idea.
5. State the types of projects in technical institution.
6. Describe the various phases of project management.
7. Explain the barriers to project management in technical institution.
8. Describe the logical framework model of project management.
9. Explain the approaches of project design and project management.
10. List the project management tools and techniques.
11. Prepare the project proposal.
12. Describe the role of a project manager.
13. Explain the abilities of the project manager.
14. Describe the methods of developing a project manager.
15. Describe the characteristics of a project manager.
16. Explain the project implementation tools and techniques.
17. Explain the process of monitoring and evaluation of a project.
18. Describe the process of success analysis.

1. Introduction

Technical institutions face number of challenges related to quality of learning outcomes of students. These institutions also face other functional challenges. Now-a-days institutions are facing tough competition with each other. Competitor institutions provide variety of services and attractions to the students. Technology is changing at a very fast rate that demands for continuous up-gradation in curriculum and facilities. This imposes financial and academic liability on the institution. Technological changes are creating challenge for the teachers to upgrade their knowledge continuously. There are developments taking place in educational technology that can be used for curriculum implementation in an effective and efficient way. There are number of opportunities available in the environment for the growth and development of the institution. The institution at right time can grab these opportunities. Internal changes may also require improving the efficiency and effectiveness in the functioning of the institution. Project approach is the answer to all above issues and challenges. Projects with specific purpose can be designed and implemented in the institution.

2. Concept of Project

An educational project focuses on a problem, crisis, challenge, opportunity, competition, need, desired change etc. It is designed to accomplish set of goals related to development, growth, quality, relevance of programmes, expansion of business and efficiency of the institutional functioning. A project can be defined as undertaking a set of activities in a scientific and systematic way assuring efficiency in implementation to achieve defined goals in a fixed time. It is a one-time event in the institution that finishes when goals are achieved. It is designed and implemented by a team of competent professionals. Generally something new is created through projects. It is a practice in some institutions to design and implement projects to solve a trivial problem that is not the purpose of the project approach. Projects should be designed to create examples for other institutions and rest of the world. The complete growth and development can be achieved through project approach in the institution. All the projects should focus on satisfying the needs of the students and industries. Project approach can be a way of working in the institution. The vision of the institution can be achieved using project approach. Institution should aim at quality of learning of students, faculty members and staff members of the institution. It should focus on improving its services for the industries, field agencies and society. It should initiate researches using project approach in the institution.

3. Characteristics of a Project

We have examined definition of a project, and by now we appreciate that projects are distinctive than other routine activities. Main characteristics of the project are listed in exhibit 26.1.

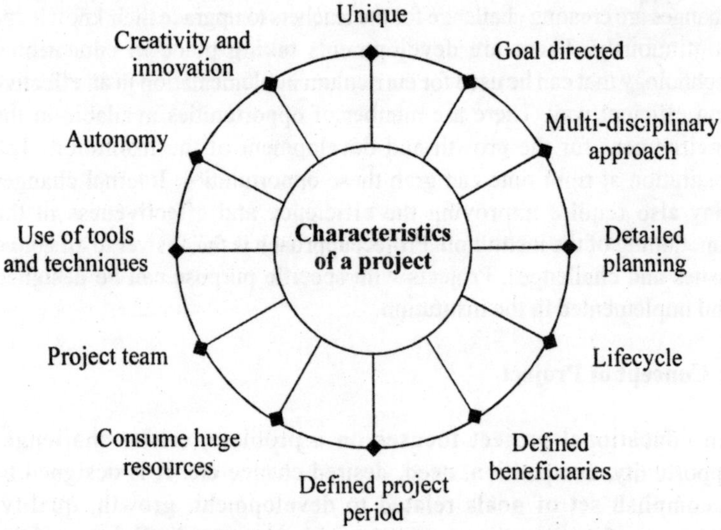

Exhibit No. 26.1: Characteristics of a project

3.1 Unique

Each project is different than other. This difference can be seen from distinctive features of the project. The distinction can be seen on many features like – Project period, objectives, project team, location, external environment, internal environment, inputs, processes, natural conditions, client or beneficiary. All the projects cannot be same on above features. It requires number of logical activities to produce the deliverables to the client or beneficiary. Generally, the activities are different than routine and critical activities require concentration and devotion.

3.2 Goal Directed

Projects are undertaken to achieve specific goals and objectives in a given environment. Project goals and objectives are set to address the real life significant problem or challenge, or competitions. In some situations projects are designed to gap the opportunity. Projects are designed and implemented to achieve those goals and objectives that cannot be achieved in routine way. Project goals and objectives should focus on development and change.

3.3 Multi-Disciplinary Approach

As mentioned earlier projects are undertaken to solve a complex problem or to meet the challenge or to grab the opportunity. In that way it requires the multi-disciplinary and multi-dimensional approach. To perform the activities and tasks of such kind multi-skilled project team is required with relevant expertise and experience. The focus of the project team is to accomplish objectives on time. It requires professional approach. For example, setting up learning resource development centre (LRDC) for Technical Education System. It will require the professional team and team members who have expertise and experience in learning resources identification for various programmes their design, development, editing, formatting, printing, storing, distributing, conducting training programmes for teachers to use learning resources effectively and efficiently, evaluation and continuous improvement etc. This example shows that the availability of experts and their successful working in a team is important.

3.4 Detailed Planning

Projects are non-repetitive and designed for achieving unique goals so detailed planning of the project is carried out to minimize the risk. Detailed planning on tasks, roles and responsibility, resources requirement, finance, training requirements etc. is carried out before project implementation.

3.5 Lifecycle

Each project is designed, approved, implemented, evaluated and terminated or installed for continuous use. So it has got a definite start and finish point. The delay in the project period may spoil the whole purpose of the project. It may not bring desired impact or cost of the project may increase.

3.6 Defined Beneficiaries

Projects are designed to fulfil the requirements of specific beneficiaries. The beneficiaries and their needs are well defined in the project proposal.

The project spells out the change in behaviour of the beneficiaries. It also addresses the ease, time reduction, cost reduction and effort reduction for the benefit of beneficiaries.

3.7 Defined Project Period

Each project has pre-defined and well-defined start and finish point. They are demanding in terms of time. They require round the clock efforts. Projects cannot achieve intended goals in routine way. They need a team of energetic, dynamic and proactive people. The project period is decided using scientific methods such as network analysis, action plan and Gnatt chart.

3.8 Consume Huge Resources

All projects are channelled to bring development or significant improvements. They consume huge resources and variety of resources. Money is one of the important resources. Other resources are machines, material, information, time and manpower. Project team shares all the resources. If we consider the example of learning resources development centre, apart from human resources it would require computers, softwares, printing press, binding machine, projectors, slide projectors, overhead projectors, classrooms, equipment, videography equipment, television, video cassette recorder etc.

3.9 Project Team

All projects are conceived and designed by a dedicated team. This team is formed from the professionals. The project manager uses her/his team building and team working skills to harness the potential of team members. S/he directs the whole business of project management. The constitution of the team depends on the nature of the project but it is observed that experts are drawn and trained from the same organization for project period. If the project design or implementation requires special kind of skills, the experts are hired for a particular task or activity. If the activity is huge and critical also and no institutional member possesses the professional skills consultants are appointed from outside the institution. We have also observed that in some projects experts deployed from outside the organization supported by internal members form a complete team. It all depends on the nature of the project. Both types of teams have got strengths and limitations. The selection of team depends on many factors such as goal requirement, expertise requirement, competence of people, project period etc.

3.10 Use of Tools and Techniques

Projects require variety of tools and techniques right from design to termination stage. Variety of tools and techniques are used to design, implement and evaluate the impact of the project. It should be habit of project team to use project tools and techniques. These tools and techniques are different for different stages of the project. Conceptual, logical and experiential models are used to design the projects. Technology and techniques are used to implement the project. Computer softwares are used to monitor the progress of the project. Field techniques are used to assess the impact of the project.

3.11 Autonomy

Projects cannot be designed and implemented in a bureaucratic way. Project requires team approach. The project team is required to be granted high degree of autonomy to take decisions and implement them. This autonomy percolates down to individual team member with accountability. Project team members are empowered to take any decision to implement the project effectively.

3.12. Creativity and Innovativeness

Projects require immense thinking, creativity and innovativeness at each and every stage of the project lifecycle. The unique idea may save lot of time, effort and resources during the project implementation. It can enhance the quality of product and services. Creatively designed and implemented curriculum may reduce the time of learning and cost of learning. It may reduce the drop-out rate and enhance the quality of learning.

4. Benefits of Project Approach

Project approach has been in use in the past in technical institutions. The focus of the project has been infrastructural development and expansion of the business. It has not been used intensively for improving the quality of learning and quality of services to industry. The project approach has many benefits over routine management. Some of the benefits of project approach are listed in exhibit 26.2.

Exhibit No. 26.2: Benefits of projects

➢ Increase in effectiveness of institutional functioning ➢ Focus on priority thrust areas of working ➢ Permanent solution for serious problems of the institution ➢ Fulfilment of needs of students and industry ➢ Optimum utilization of institutional resources ➢ On the job training of faculty and staff members	➢ Positive attitude of institutional members for innovation and change ➢ Culture to use professional approach ➢ Clarity of purpose and scope of the project ➢ Separate control mechanism for specific purpose ➢ Autonomy and flexibility in functioning ➢ Team culture ➢ Empowerment of institutional members

5. Sources of Project Idea

There are many sources of the project idea. The institution should be vigilant to the external and internal environment in which it is functioning. Project ideas may come from various sources. Some of the sources are listed in exhibit 26.3.

Exhibit No. 26.3: Sources of project idea

➢ National Policy on Technical Education ➢ Programme of action on National Policy ➢ Demand of the industry or society ➢ Idea given by funding agency ➢ Problems being faced by industries or field agencies or passouts ➢ Alumni ➢ Problems being faced by the institution ➢ Change in economical, political, social, technological environment	➢ Change in learning style ➢ Challenge to bring innovation ➢ Competition by other institutions ➢ Opportunities in the environment ➢ Request from other national and international agencies ➢ Programmes of professional bodies ➢ Development in educational technology ➢ Development in education theory

6. Projects in Technical Institutions

The nature of the project would depend on the development level of the institution, nature of competition, challenges, aspirations, problems, nature of reforms envisaged and opportunities. Projects may be for a very short duration say three months to one year. These types of projects are designed to bring one-dimensional improvement in specific area of functioning of the institution. Projects may be of medium duration say one to three years. These projects focus on the major change in the functioning of the institution. They are multi-dimensional requiring inter-disciplinary approach. Projects may be of long duration say three to ten years. These projects focus on innovation, growth and development of the institution. These types of projects require multi-dimensional, multi-skills, and multi-disciplinary approach. Some of the themes for educational projects are listed in exhibit 26.4.

Exhibit No. 26.4: Themes for educational projects

➢ Curriculum development ➢ Curriculum reforms ➢ Classroom instruction ➢ Print and non-print instructional resources development ➢ Examination system ➢ Evaluation of institutional programmes ➢ Institutional development ➢ Service quality improvement ➢ Improvement in support services like accounts, administration, stores, students record keeping, cooperative store etc. ➢ New programmes of higher level in emerging disciplines	➢ Infrastructure development ➢ Community services ➢ Quality of passouts ➢ Quality of instruction material and quality of resources ➢ Quality of training ➢ Reduction of drop-outs ➢ Instruction design for slow learners ➢ Teacher training ➢ Managing linkages with industries and field agencies ➢ Publication of researches ➢ Programmes for physically challenged people

7. Project Cycle

A project goes through number of significant phases from the point of its conception to completion. A number of activities are performed under each phase to assure quality of performance and goal accomplishment. These important phases complete the project cycle. Detailed planning is carried out for each phase of the project. Most of the projects have almost similar phases. Projects in different types of organizations have similar phases with different nomenclature. The names of these phases are used for communicating with internal members of the institution and stakeholders. To complete each phase of the project different types of resources and skills are required. Quality and success of each phase of the project is dependent on the quality of performance of the previous phase. The phases of the project help in monitoring and evaluation of the project. The different phases of educational projects are shown in exhibit 26.5.

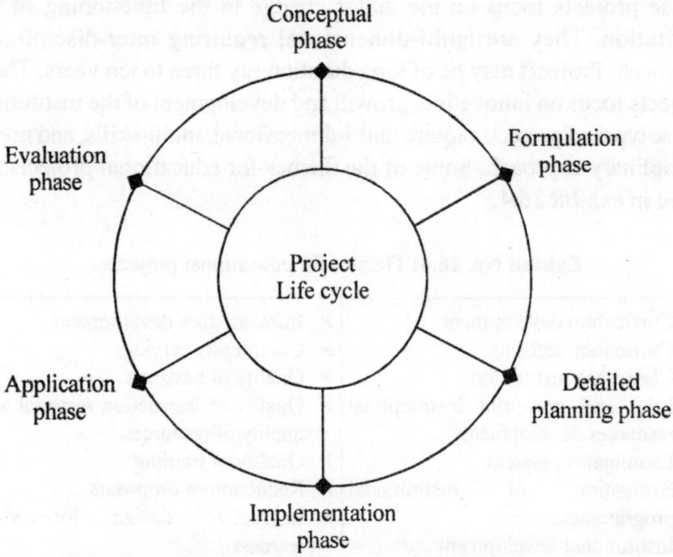

Exhibit No. 26.5: Project lifecycle

7.1 Conceptual Phase

As stated earlier the project ideas come form many sources. These ideas are discussed, deliberated and analyzed among the institutional members. The management of the institution discusses the ideas with the senior members and work out the relevance and feasibility of the idea. In some situation faculty members, staff members and students pressurize the management to provide some facilities or services at the earliest. If the project is conceived on the basis of a significant problem faced by a particular group of students or staff members, they may approach to management to solve the problem. The competition posed by sister institution may compel the institution to design the project to face the competition. There may be opportunities in the environment in which the institution is operating. The institution may design the project to grab the opportunities. The strategic plan of the institution may have challenging, new and different goals. These goals may not be achieved in routine way and may require project approach. On the basis of the stimulus from various sources the project is conceptualized and formulated by a team. In this phase of the project, project team uses techniques such as problem identification, strengths, weaknesses, opportunities and threats analysis and Pareto analysis.

7.2 Formulation Phase

The problem is analyzed using problem tree analysis, or fish bone diagram, or process flow chart. The project is conceived in a holistic manner and the scope of the project is defined. The goals and objectives of the project are formulated. The broad alternative strategies to achieve the goals and objectives are worked out by selected team. The costs of the project, efforts and resources requirements are calculated on approximate basis. The benefit of the project and the beneficiaries are defined. The preliminary plan is submitted to management of the institution for approval. The management of the institution assesses the preliminary project plan and grants permission to prepare detailed plan. If the project is big and requires huge resources the project is assessed by a team of experts and suggestions are offered to workout and clarify certain issues. The appraiser team also grants approval to prepare detailed plan for consideration and implementation.

7.3 Design Phase

On the basis of approval of preliminary plan, a team of experts in the relevant area carries out the detailed design of the project. The goals and objectives of the project are finalized and communicated to concerned internal and external stakeholders for suggestions and comments. The objectives are prioritized and made specific, measurable, attainable, realistic and traceable (SMART) to evolve alternative strategies to achieve them. The goal reach strategies are finalized and action plan is prepared. The network diagram is prepared to finalize the project period. The bar chart is prepared to detail out the significant activities. Resources deployment chart is prepared to commit the resources. The budget is prepared for approval of the project cost. The project team is finalized with team responsibility and individual responsibilities. The monitoring and evaluation mechanism is finalized. The assumptions and risk involved in the project is clarified and risk management contingent plans are prepared. The stakeholders' analysis and their management techniques are finalized. The complete project design takes the shape of detailed project proposal. Apart from these, strategies to ensue project benefit sustenance and continuity are suggested in detailed project report. The management of the institution approves the detailed plan and provide necessary resources and power to project team for project implementation.

7.4 Implementation Phase

In this phase of the project the project team is empowered to implement the project activities. The project manager and project team prepare detailed plan for implantation. The roles and responsibilities of the team members are clearly defined and authority is granted to go ahead. The communication and reporting channels are established. The project progresses with the efforts of the project team. The project team solves the implementation problems. The stakeholders are managed and progress is monitored against monitoring schedule: The deviations are fixed and remedial actions are taken. The project progress and contingent problems are reported to the management of the institution.

7.5 Application Phase

In this phase the project team delivers the goods to the larger group for use. The larger group uses the project deliverables and enjoys the benefits. For initial period the project team assists the user group to ensure right use of the deliverables. For example, learning resources for one subject is prepared by the project team to make the teaching-learning process interesting, joyful, easy, efficient and effective to develop identified competencies in the students. The project team assists the teaching learning process and guides the teachers to use instructional resources in right way and at right time. During the process of instruction feedback is taken by project team to refine the quality of deliverables and its effectiveness.

7.6 Evaluation Phase

In this phase of the project the success of the project is evaluated against predefined indicators and criteria. Project team carries out evaluation of the project to improve performance on future projects. Management of the institution and significant stakeholders also carry out the evaluation of the project. The beneficiaries and stakeholders should declare the project successful.

8. Barriers to Project Management in Educational Institutions

The projects in educational institutions focus on learning of the students. They are related to behaviour modification of the faculty, staff and students. So far hardware aspects are concerned they can be easily constructed or installed using project approach but it is little bit challenging to promote the use of the same for teaching-learning purpose. There are number of barriers that a project manager faces. Some of the significant barriers are listed in exhibit 26.6.

Exhibit No. 26.6: Barriers to project management

➢ Vaguely defined goals, objectives and project strategies	➢ Rigid rules and regulations applicable for innovative projects
➢ Lack of preparation of detailed plans for implementing the activities and deploying the resources	➢ Improper analysis of potential problems, risk and assumptions
	➢ Vested interest in the project may defeat the purpose of the project
➢ Lack of participation of the people during project formulation and design phase	➢ Resources are not committed at right time to complete the activities
➢ Adverse consequences of the project are not estimated before project implementation	➢ Competence of the project team to design and implement the project is not assessed
➢ Tradition bound faculty members, staff members and students not interested to change habits	➢ Lack of valid, reliable and latest information to formulate the project
➢ Lack of strong policy for change and development	➢ Over ambitious project

9. Logical Framework Model for Project Design and Management

Logical framework model is used for designing the big and medium size project to bring desired change. Logical framework model used to assure quality in the design of the project. It is used to incorporate the ultimate goal of the project. This model proposes that the project design should start with participatory analysis of the problem, objective analysis alternative analysis and stakeholders' analysis. The tools and techniques of problem analysis, objective analysis, alternative analysis and stakeholders' analysis are described in chapter on management tools and techniques. Logical framework is used to design, implement and evaluate the project. It is used as a communication tool to convince the project stakeholders to cooperate. It promotes the use of participatory design and implementation of the project. The team approach is commonly used to formulate the project. The design of the project is based on the logic, and cause and effect relationship. The other approaches of project design, implementation and evaluation are also used to overcome the limitations of the logical framework model. Brief description of logical framework terminology is given below.

9.1 Problem Analysis

The problems of the institution are identified and similar problems are clubbed together. The trivial problems are solved using routine problem solving techniques. The projects are designed for significant problems affecting the academic business of the institution. The problem is analysed to find root causes using techniques such as problem tree analysis, fish bone diagram, creativity techniques, Pareto analysis diagram and process flow charts. If the institution is not facing any significant problem but interested to bring innovation or change in the academic business of the institution. This desired change or opportunity is also analysed in same manner.

9.2 Objective Analysis

After analysis of the problem all negative statements on problem tree are converted in positive statements. In fact this indicates the desired change. It may also emanate from the vision or mission statements of the institution. The logic is established in the positive statements and the hierarchy of objectives is reduced to four levels. The four levels are used to club the objectives in the logical framework and named as goal, purpose, outputs and activities. The meaning of these terms in logical framework is different than general meaning.

Goal

The meaning of goal is the long-term effect of the project. It describes the greater and larger justification of the project. Generally goal level objectives are achieved through more than one project. Generally it focuses on the mission of the institution. The goal level objectives emphasize on long-range change in the way of working of the institution. It indicates the enhancement of the image of the institution, or expansion of academic activities, or quality of learning, or placement of students and so on.

Purpose

The meaning of purpose in the logical framework is change in behaviour of the students, faculty and staff members of the institution. The objectives at this level are directly related to enhancement of competence of the students, faculty and staff members. The impact of the project can be seen in the performance of the institution. The purpose level objectives describe the changed behaviour of beneficiaries. These objectives also indicate the contribution of the project in the direction of growth and development of the institution. The achievement of purpose level objectives is beyond the control of the project team. The project team can only help, counsel, guide, support, pursue and train the user group to use the facilities created through project. The purposeful objectives establish the justification of the project.

Outputs

The meaning of the outputs in logical framework model is facilities and results produced by project team for the use of a larger population in the institution. The output level objectives should be necessary and sufficient to produce purpose level objectives. The project team is held responsible to achieve output level objectives. The created facilities and produced goods are called deliverables.

Activities

The meaning of activities in the logical framework is the significant activities required to achieve output level objectives. The vertical logic from goal to activities level is established. The logic is also checked from activities level to goal level objectives. The lower level objectives should be the cause for upper level objectives. If/Then relationship is established among all the levels. The principle of necessary and sufficient condition is followed to check the vertical logic from activities to outputs, outputs to purpose and purpose to goal level objectives. The cause and effect relationship is also checked. The logical framework for a small project in one technical institution is shown in exhibit 26.7.

Exhibit No. 26.7: Logical framework for a small project

Sl. No.	*Level*	*Objective*	*OVIs*	*MOVs*	*Assumptions*
1.	Goal	Corporate image of the institution enhanced	Three times increase in demands of passouts Application for admission increased in three years Consultancy increased four times in three years	Campus selection record All seats filled in first round of counsel-ing Cash book	
2	Purpose	1. Identified competencies developed in students 2. Demand for services increased	After placement no training is required in employers organization Four times increase in companies seeking services in three years	Feedback report Alumni Corresp-ondence	Demand exists in employ-ment market
3.	Out-puts	Competency based curriculum implemented	Certified competencies	Letter	Demand for services
		2.1 Conducted researches	Ten in each discipline every year	Journals	
		2.2 Obtained patents	do	Certificat-ion	
		2.3 Completed prestigious consultancy projects	Fifty lacs revenue every year	Cash book	
		2.4 Community development activities implemented	Ten villages every year	Report	
		2.5 Marketing of services and product completed	Ten new clients every year like schools, industries, field agencies	Marketing strategy Customer survey	

(*Contd.*)

(*Contd.*)

Sl. No.	*Level*	*Objective*	*OVIs*	*MOVs*	*Assumptions*
4.	Activities	1.1.1 Competency based curriculum developed 1.1.2 Competent, trained and willing faculty and staff members 1.1.3 Interactive and practice based learning methods 1.1.4 Opportunity for applying competencies 1.1.4 Facilities to develop competencies 1.1.5 Instructional material developed to develop competencies 2.1.1 Trained faculty to conduct researches 2.1.2 Facilities available to conducted researches 2.1.3 Research topic identified 2.2.1 Facilities for experimentation created 2.2.2 Technology gap identified 2.2.3 Library support created 2.2.4 Incentive policy for obtaining patents 2.3.1 Consultancy projects negotiated and MOU signed 2.3.2 Team appointed 2.3.3 Assignment completed and handed over to client 2.4.1 Nearby villages identified	Approval from the management	Certificate	Demand for technical education

(*Contd.*)

(Contd.)

Sl. No.	*Level*	*Objective*	*OVIs*	*MOVs*	*Assumptions*
		2.4.2 Participatory rural appraisal completed 2.4.3 Needs identified 2.4.4 Development objectives formulated 2.4.5 Interventions implemented 2.5.1 Marketing strategy designed 2.5.2 Marketing strategy implemented			

9.3 Alternative Analysis

There are more than one ways to achieve the objectives of any level. The alternatives are explored and generated to achieve the objectives. The alternatives are generated to the extent that they can be implemented with the available resources of the institution. Alternative tree analysis technique is used to select the most appropriate strategy. The decision is taken on the basis of the competence of the people to implement the decision, time available, acceptance of the decision, resources availability etc. In some situations alternative objectives are explored to bring economy, quality and feasibility in the project.

9.4 Stakeholders' Analysis

Stakeholders play a very important role in the implementation of the project. They may facilitate the progress of the project to any extent. At the same time they may obstruct the progress of the project. There could be three types of stakeholders, i.e. favourable to project, opponent to project and indifferent. The stakeholders' management is very important for the success of the project. The project stakeholders are identified, their stake is estimated and their participation is managed for the success of the project.

9.5 Objectively Verifiable Indicators

The horizontal logic is related to setting objectively verifiable indicators (OVIs) for each level of the objectives. The indicators are established for goal level, purpose level, outcome level and activities level. The logic in the indicators is also checked to ensure the achievement of the upper level objectives in the framework. The objectively verifiable indicators are set in such a manner so that they directly and strongly measure the achievement level of the objective. It is difficult to formulate positive indicators for some activities in such cases negative indicators are formulated. If direct and strong indicators are set they require minimum efforts during the monitoring and evaluation process. The progress of the project is monitored against these indicators. These indicators are set during the design of the project itself. Indicators are helpful in objectively monitor the progress of the project and identify the problem, if any. The solution for the problem can be generated and implemented at the earliest stage. The evaluation of the project is carried out against the indicators at outputs level. The success of the project is carried out against the indicators of purpose level. All the indicators are stated in measurable form that is quantity, quality, and time. Sometimes the place and other necessary parameters are also added. All the indicators should be practical, independent, targeted and objectively verifiable.

9.6 Means of Verification

The next column in the horizontal logic is means of verification (MOVs). Means of verifications are set for each level of indicators to verify the indicators in the actual project situation during implementation. Means of verification s indicate the sources of information to verify the indicators. These may be reports, documents, surveys, interviews, observations etc. The means for verifications for each indicator must be available, affordable, timely and useful.

9.8 Assumptions and Risks

The next column to means of verifications in the logical framework is deciding assumptions. Assumptions are nothing but the external conditions which the project team does not select to control. These conditions may affect the success of the project at any stage of the project. The assumptions are stated from activities level to outputs level, outputs level to purpose level, and purpose level to goal level. These are stated from bottom because the project implementation starts from activities. If the activities are performed and external conditions or assumption do not hold true the project may not progress further. The deviation from assumption becomes the risk for the project. The killer assumptions are stated for each level of the objectives. Killer assumption means the probability of occurrence and level of seriousness of the assumption. It may seriously affect the success of the project. The vertical and horizontal logic for a project is established and checked.

10. Approaches to Project Management

There are two approaches used in project management i.e. blue print approach and process approach. The logical framework and other approaches of project planning are called blue print approaches. In blue print approach the complete project is designed and detailed plan is prepared for implementation. The management approves the plan. The project team implements the plan and minor adjustments are made during the implementation as per needs of the situation. This approach is commonly used in technological projects that are for construction of institute building, establishing the laboratories, setting the library, developing the campus of the institute. The interrelated activities can be identified in such projects and their inter dependencies can be established. Significant body of knowledge is available in managing such types of project. It is very easy to design and manage projects of such kind. The effective and efficient project implementation is possible against planned activities. The objective monitoring and control is possible in such projects. The blue print works as a common language for project team and stakeholders. The resources and time can be easily allocated for such projects. Blue print design approach has got some limitations in the educational project. Educational projects require different approaches. Outcomes in educational projects are not so certain. Behaviour modification components of the staff of the institution and students are required. It is very difficult to define and standardized the behaviour of the people.

Apart from blue print approach process approach is required to be used in educational project management. In process approach continuous efforts are made to design the project to achieve short-term objectives under a big frame. The strategies are designed, implemented and the impact is evaluated. After each stage of progress next level of change is defined and the same cycle is repeated. Major adjustments, experimentation, innovations and analysis are the essential elements of process approach. In this approach the team works openly and with a broad mind to bring desired change. This approach requires high level of patience on the part of the project team and management. Training of the team, team building, organization of resources and planning goes with the progress of the project. The project team may face high level of uncertainty but there is no much risk in it. The only thing is the process may not lead to success in achieving change. On the other hand it would be good participatory learning exercise for the institution. This approach of project management is slow as compared to blue print approach but this is only approach that can bring behaviour related changes. The participation and commitment of project team and other stakeholders can be ensured using this approach.

Process approach is excellent for designing and implementing academic projects like improvement in classroom learning process, self-learning process, learning from projects and field visits, learning life skills, learning coping skills, learning generic skills and so on. In the process of learning students become responsible for learning and teachers act as guide. Students become prime drivers of the learning process. They understand the importance of learning. They struggle for learning. In this process of participatory learning intermediate changes and interventions are possible as per need of the situation. In real sense process approach of project management in technical institution is bottom up approach. It is need driven process in which there is high level of commitment of the students. Project designed through process approach develops self-learning and learning to learn capabilities in the students, staff and faculty members of the institution. The process approach fits in all kinds of institutions whether new or old, traditional or innovative. The process approach assures for better learning for all. The key to success of process approach is strong leadership and teamwork.

11. Project Tools and Techniques

A big range of tools and techniques are available for project management. The tools and techniques that can be used for educational projects are described in chapter on management tools and techniques. There is combination of management, education, scientific methods, psychological theories, educational technology and information technology. Depending upon the need of the institution and project appropriate tools and techniques can be selected. Each tool and technique has got strengths and limitations. One should be aware about the strengths and limitations of these tools and techniques.

12. Proposal Design

The proposal of the project is a document prepared by a team on the basis of analysis of the problem. First the initial proposal is prepared and discussed with internal members of the institution. The proposal is refined on the basis of the comments received from the members of the institution. Then the initial proposal is submitted to the management of the institution for consideration, acceptance and approval. The management of the institution analyzes the proposal and grants green signal for further detailing. It offers suggestions for improvement and investigation. The team further conducts feasibility study to explore the viability of the project. It investigates certain issues and reaches to conclusion. Then the team prepares the proposal and widely shares it with relevant internal and external stakeholders of the institution. It invites the suggestions of the stakeholders on the proposal. The preliminary design of the project is prepared and shared with the management and significant stakeholders. The management examines the project from cost and long-term benefit point of view and approves the proposal for further detailing. The project team details out the project for calculating the project cost, project period, resources required and benefits from the project and associated risk. The proposal of the project is prepared in the format suggested below:

Format of the Project Proposal

Background of the project: The rationale or the brief description is mentioned in this head. The adverse effect of the problem is described in detail. If the project is designed to grab the opportunity the description of the opportunity is mentioned. The benefits of grabbing the opportunities are detailed out.

Project design: The logical framework describing the problem tree analysis, objective tree analysis, alternative tree analysis and stakeholders' analysis is prepared. The logical framework showing the hierarchy of objectives, objectively verifiable indicators, means of verification, and assumption is prepared. The project activity network, work break down structure, action plan, bar diagram, budget, resources deployment chart and responsibility chart is prepared. The target population and type of benefits from the project are described. The cost benefit or rate of return is also described in detail and in concrete terms. The composition of project team and their responsibility are also suggested. The project manager and her/his roles, responsibilities, and authority are suggested in detail.

Implementation schedules: The implementation schedule of activities, use of human resources, machineries, material requirement, cost requirement, consultant requirement is suggested. The alternative means and ways are suggested to solve the contingent problems during project implementation. The plans to meet the risk are also suggested. The stakeholders' management strategies are designed and way to implement them is mentioned. The way of educating or training user group is mentioned. The responsibility chart for specific activity is suggested. The problem solving mechanism is described. Special rules, regulation and norms for the project implementation are suggested. The procedure for procuring the material and appointing consultant should also be described in the proposal.

Project evaluation and success analysis mechanism: In the project design, the project evaluation and success analysis plan is suggested. The evaluators and way of evaluation of the project success is described to avoid the post project conflict and litigations. The stakeholders from their point of view assess the success of the project. The beneficiaries of the project also evaluate the success of the project. The evaluation criteria from all stakeholders' and beneficiaries point of view are described in the project proposal.

13. Project Manager

Every project requires a good project manager and dedicated project team. This holds true for educational projects also. The management of the institution constitutes a project team. After completion of the project team disperses to their respective departments and sections. There may be a core team for large and big projects. This team may get support from different teams at different phases of the project implementation. Depending upon the type and nature of the project, the size of the core team is decided and they work till the completion of the project. The team members are drawn from different departments and centres on the basis of their competence, experience and interest. Team members must be ready to accept the challenges. They should have ability to take risk and push new practices in the institution. They should have passion for innovation and change. They should have strong need for accomplishment with interpersonal skills. There should be clear understanding between head of the department and team members about the roles and responsibilities of team members to avoid potential conflict.

The project manager is a key person in project team. The selection of the project manager is crucial for the success of the project. The success of the project depends on the competence, experience, willingness, creativity, leadership, influencing skills, managerial skills, educational skills and communication skills of the project manager. In the institution one can locate very good people to perform the routine tasks effectively and efficiently but it is hard to find persons who can manage challenging, new, unique and different projects. The role of the educational project manager can be fairly assumed by a person having positive attitude for change and development. S/he should possess latest knowledge of education, education technology, technology, curriculum development, students' psychology, design and development of media, organizing educational events, measurement and assessment of learning, information technology, management tools and techniques and changes taking place in the external environment. S/he should have skills to analyse the big problems differently. S/he should be good in conducting surveys and research studies. S/he should be a good mentor, facilitator, counsellor, decision maker, trainer, encourager and experimenter. S/he should have patience to achieve the objectives of the project. S/he should possess reporting and presentation skills. S/he should have fair knowledge of economics.

14 Methods of Developing Project Managers

The project managers can be developed in the institution to take up the responsibility of design, implement and evaluate the educational projects. The project manager is expected to posses variety of qualities and characteristics to design and implement the project successfully. It is very difficult to acquire these qualities in a due course of time. It requires conscious efforts on the part of the management and persons working in the institution. Following are some methods that can be used to develop good educational project managers:

14.1 Formal Training

Potential project manager in the institution should undergo formal training on educational project management. To start with, they should learn project planning, implementation and evaluation tools and techniques. Number of training programmes are offered by training institutions on project management. Later on, they can attend seminars, conferences, symposiums and meetings on project management. They get very rich learning experiences in the seminars and conferences. They should participate in case analysis work shops, games and competitions on educational project management.

14.2 Self-Learning

Number of innovative projects have been implemented in technical institutions in the past. The case studies and research papers are published in the reputed journals. One can read these experiences and gain insight on educational project management. Number of books are available on general project management that can be a good source for learning new and recent concepts on project management.

14.3 On-the-job Training

Potential project managers should get attached with experienced project manager involved in project management activities. S/he should clarify the concepts of project management with the experienced project managers. Later on s/he should assume specific responsibility in on-going project and learn from experiences. S/he should request the project manager and other colleagues to offer feedback for improvement. Further higher responsibilities should be assumed by her/his that requires higher level of skills. S/he should be conscious for learning while performing a task. During the course of the performance one commits mistake and this is a good source to receive self-feedback for improvement. Next stage in the learning process is undertaking and handling simultaneous activities in the project. On gaining significant experience the potential project manager should independently handle a project right from conceiving the idea to its evaluation phase. This would be an eye opening experience for her/him.

14.4. Writing on the Project Management

One can clarify and learn many skills on project management documenting the experiences. A diary can be maintained to document the learning experiences. These experiences can be shaped in the form of a paper, case study, simulation and published. These written experiences can be shared with larger population in the institution. The experiences can be documented in the print and electronic format.

15. Project Team

As mentioned earlier the project is conceived, designed, implemented and evaluated by a team. The project team is different than other teams. It requires very high level of energy, synergy, creativity, initiatives, coordination, cooperation, effective communication, cohesiveness, commitment, dedication, concern for quality, learning orientation, self-monitoring, introspection and leadership. The team should proactively work on the project. There should be role and goal clarity to all the team members. It should be able to solve all project implementation problems. It should be good in developing relationship with stakeholders to seek their support. It should be fairly good in mobilizing resources for project implementation on its own. It should be flexible to use alternative strategies to approach the problem. It should have capability and capacity to deal with uncertainties. The project team should develop self-propelling culture for project management. The project objectives, team objectives and individual objectives should be properly aligned. The team should establish the process of working in a team and performing the tasks. It should benchmark the performance procedure and performance criteria with best available in the technical institutions. Project team can make or break the project. It should be competent to use modern principles of learning, tools and techniques of project management and use of information technology in teaching learning process. The project team needs to undergo team development and team building process. It should be able to demonstrate example for the rest of the faculty and staff members of the institution.

16. Project Implementation

Once the management of the institution approves the project proposal the project team prepares for implementation. The project team prepares the detailed implementation plan. The cost management, time management, resources management, communication management, reporting management, stakeholders management, project team building, quality management, risk management plans are prepared and discussed in the project team. The roles and responsibilities are made clear to team members. Project team obtains the commitment of the stakeholders. Procurement schedule is prepared for smooth implementation of plans. The project team uses various tools and techniques at this phase of preparation for project implementation. To name some of the techniques are team development exercise, responsibility chart, resources deployment chart, network analysis, work breakdown structure, budget, monitoring schedule, stakeholders management strategy, flow chart, process charting etc.

The project office is established to keep the record of the project. This office takes care about documentation, reports, management of information, correspondence, accounting and audit. The project office works under the guidance of the project manager. Project staff and necessary equipment can support it.

The project manager influences the team members to implement the activities as per schedule and commitment. The project manager coordinates the project implementation activities. S/he guides, supports, helps, and encourages the project team members. S/he communicates, negotiates and influences the stakeholders for cooperation and support. S/he reports the progress of the project to the management of the institution and other related stakeholders.

17. Project Monitoring

Project team implements the project activities and the progress of the project is monitored as per monitoring schedule. Project manager and project team monitor the progress of the project against indicators set in monitoring schedule. The objectively verifiable indicators, time of monitoring and way of monitoring are mentioned in the monitoring schedule. If any deviation is noticed the causes of deviation are identified and problem is solved. Implementation of activities is again set as planned. The process of monitoring the quality of results, effectiveness and efficiency of performance of activities, use of resources, and performance in functioning of the team is also analysed to ascertain the effectiveness and efficiency of the project implementation. The project manager provides extra inputs, support, help, encouragement and training based on the results of the monitoring process.

18. Project Success Analysis

All significant stakeholders evaluate project success. They use their own criteria for evaluating the success. The project team celebrates the achievements of goals if the project is implemented without much of obstructions, barriers, crisis, conflict and controversy. The management of the institution recognizes and rewards the project team if the project is completed on time, within budget achieving the project objectives. The management of the institution considers the project successful if less problems are brought to it for solution. In educational project the students of the institution are very much concerned about the success of the project. They are the main beneficiaries of the project. They analyse the success of the project from learning point of view. They examine that how they are benefited by project. They see how project has made learning process joyful, easy and interesting. They analyse how the project has saved their time, money and efforts. They evaluate the project from the opportunities they received for further, higher and variety of learning. They are least concerned about the project goals. They assess the project success from adverse effect on their point of view. If the students rate the project highly successful it should be considered successful project. Industries, field agencies and employers of the passouts evaluate the success of the project. They evaluate the project from the competence of the students' point of view. They examine the knowledge, skills and attitudes possessed by the students. They see the competence of the students from business point of view. They assess the capability and capacity of the students for the job. They see whether the students are professional in performing the job. They examine the generic skills of the students. If students are excellent on their criteria the employers will rate the project successful. The faculty members and staff members who practice and use the facilities created by the project is another group that evaluate the success of the project. They analyse the success of the project form their easiness, improving effectiveness and efficiency point of view. If the project is increasing workload and creating unnecessary activities in their view they will declare the project unsuccessful. They may create resistance to make project outcomes functional. The government, statutory bodies, professional bodies evaluate the success of the project from legal, professional, social benefit point of view and rate the success of the project.

The project team should undertake the exercise at the time of project design to know the success criteria of each significant stakeholder and incorporate their requirement in the scope, goal, strategies and activities of the project. The success criteria of each stakeholder can be noted in tabular form. The success criteria depends on the type of the project, growth level of the institution, financial condition of the institution, pressure on the institution, education policy prevalent at that time, trend of development of the institution, technology available, interest of the institution members, vision of the institution and preferences of stakeholders. The general stake of significant stakeholders is mentioned in the format for success analysis given in exhibit 26.8.

Exhibit No. 26.8: Project success analysis

Sl. No.	*Stakeholders*	*Stake*	*Success criteria*
1.	Management of the institution	➢ Growth and development of the institution ➢ Corporate reputation of the institution ➢ Cost ➢ Time ➢ Project objectives	➢ Contribution to increase speed of growth and development of the institution ➢ Expansion of business of institution ➢ Quality of teaching learning process ➢ Rate of return ➢ Effective use of budget ➢ Optimum utilization of all types of resources
2.	Students	➢ Learning ➢ Time ➢ Efforts ➢ Career ➢ Money	➢ Fast learning ➢ Easy learning ➢ Development of personality ➢ Optimum use of their time for productive learning ➢ Development of life skills ➢ Joyful learning ➢ Purposeful learning ➢ Friendly treatment ➢ Learning those skills which cannot be learnt on their own
3.	Industries and other major employers	➢ Life long liability for potential employees ➢ Production depends on them ➢ Their investment in the project in terms of cash or kind	➢ Competency ➢ Professional approach ➢ Coping skills ➢ Interpersonal skills ➢ Dealing with uncertainty and crisis situations ➢ Positive thinking, attitude and approach ➢ Self-discipline
4.	Government and statutory bodies	➢ Good education to students ➢ Compliance with rules and regulation	➢ Good citizens to the country ➢ No exploitation of students and their parents

(*Contd.*)

(*Contd.*)

Sl. No.	*Stakeholders*	*Stake*	*Success criteria*
		➢ Discipline ➢ Cooperation in providing information ➢ Institutions pose no problems for government	➢ No litigations
5.	Professional bodies	➢ Adherence to the professional ethics ➢ Updated curriculum ➢ Help in pursuing their objectives ➢ Contribution in terms of technology development, instructional material development and documentation of best practice ➢ Popularization of their activities ➢ At par with international standards	➢ Professional competence of the institution and students ➢ Help in promoting their agenda
6.	Faculty and staff members of the institution	➢ No overload ➢ No exploitation ➢ Proper reward for the achievement ➢ Opportunity for professional development ➢ No frequent changes in curriculum, time table and subjects ➢ No non-academic work load ➢ Participation in decision making	➢ Recognition, appreciation and reward for good work ➢ No allocation of below dignity work
7.	Project team	➢ Resources allocation ➢ Autonomy ➢ No policing ➢ No additional work ➢ No punishment for un-intentional mistakes and mistakes committed during experimentation	➢ Recognition, support, help and rewards ➢ No punishment and misbehaviour ➢ Project goals and objectives

The success analysis during the preliminary design phase helps in incorporating the concerns and ambitions of the stakeholders in the detailed design of the project. It develops confidence in the project team about the success of the project at the same time the quality of design of the project can be enhanced significantly. The project success mapping during the design phase helps to understand the stakeholder's management process. It helps to design strategies to obtain their help during various phases of project management. More importance can be given to very significant stakeholders who can influence the performance of the project. The project team can design and implement the strategies for effective stakeholders' management.

19. Project Management Software

In designing and implementing educational projects computer software can be used. MS Office project management will serve the purpose for educational project. The other softwares that can be useful for designing the learning material are toolkit, INSTA plan, SPSS, power point presentation, photoshop and fox pro. The learning material can be designed and produced for multiple uses. The information system can also be maintained using computer software.

20. Summary

Project approach is essential to solve significant educational problems of the institution. The institution should identify the problems related to teaching-learning. These problems are solved in routine ways if they are trivial. The significant problems are solved using project approach. There are other sources that provide stimulus to identify, define, design and implement projects in the institution. One of the important sources is the vision document of the institution. Numbers of projects can be designed to accomplish missions of the institution. The other sources are opportunities available in the external environment. The institution should be vigilant to competition posed by the sister institution. These sources provide fairly good clue to design and implement the project. The projects are designed to do right work in right way. Project approach improves the effectiveness and efficiency of the functioning of the institution. Projects are conceived, designed and implemented by a professional team. Internal and external stakeholders of the institution to seek their participation and commitment validate project design. There are two approaches commonly used for project design and implementation, namely the blue print approach and process approach. The blue print approach is little bit rigid. The process approach is flexible. In process approach of project management broad framework is defined and various phases of the project are broadly decided. After implementation of each phase evaluation of the achievements is carried out. On the basis of the results of the evaluation next phase of the project is decided and project strategy is designed. The implementation plan is prepared and carried out. Again the results of second phase are analysed and further course of action is decided. The process approach enables the project team to make effective decision without much of damage. The implementation of the complete project is carried out on sound footings. Major change and deviation in the project strategy is possible. The project can be terminated at any phase if it is irrelevant.

Logical framework model focuses on achievement of long-term goals. The project is designed establishing logic from future to present that is objectives are formulated for goal level, purpose level, outputs level and activities level. The vertical logic is checked using if/then relationship or cause and effect relationship. Horizontal logic is established formulating objectively verifiable indicators for each level of the objectives. The indicators are written to measure the achievement of the objectives directly and strongly. Means of verification are identified to verify the achievement of the objectives. These means of verifications should be practical, affordable, timely and useful. The assumptions or external conditions are mentioned from activity level to output level, output level to purpose level and purpose level to goal level. Normally killer assumptions are identified and stated in project design. The contingent plan is prepared to make the assumption real. The project management tools and techniques are used to design and implement the project. The concepts, theory and models of education are used in the design of the educational projects. The detailed plan is prepared in the form of a project proposal and submitted to the management of the institution. The management of the institution duly approves it. The project team implements activities of the project, monitors the progress of the implementation, solves problems of implementation and evaluate the performance of the project. The stakeholders evaluate the success of the project using their own criteria.

21. Activity

You are well aware about the performance of your institution. You know significant problems related to teaching learning and other associated problem. You know the vision, missions, goals and objectives of the institution. You might have read the strategic plan of the institution. Your institution may be having the record of the strengths, weaknesses, opportunities and threats (SWOT) analysis carried out recently. You have a wide range of tools and techniques of project management. You have also studied and appreciated the latest concepts of governance and management of the institution. You have fairly good experience of working in technical institution. You might be having some ambitions and aspirations for improving the teaching learning process and performance of your institution. Using this background design a project that is challenging, unique, innovative, new, focuses on core business and performance of your institution. Gather comments of the stakeholders on the project proposal and refine it. Then get it approved from the management of the institution.

REFERENCES

Harold Kerzner (1994). *Project Management*, Van Nostrand Reinhold, New York.

Harvey Maylor (1998). *Project-Management*, Financial Times, Pitman Publishing, London.

James, P. Lewis (1991). *Project Planning Scheduling and Control*, Probus Publishing Company, Chicago, Illinois.

Paul, C. Dinsmore (1993). *Project Management*, American Management Association, New York.

Ralph Keeling (2000). *Project Management*, MacMillan, Business, London.

Team up-Logical Framework Model.

Index